THOMAS MORTON
of "Merrymount"

*The Life and Renaissance
of an Early American Poet*

by

JACK DEMPSEY
*editor of New English Canaan
by Thomas Morton of "Merrymount"*

COPYRIGHT NOTICE

Thomas Morton of "Merrymount": The Life and Renaissance of an Early American Poet. By Jack Dempsey.

© Jack Dempsey 2000. All Rights Reserved.

contact:
Jack Dempsey
45 Broadway
Stoneham MA 02180/USA
781-438-3042/fax 781-279-0216
jd37@ici.net

and/or
DIGITAL SCANNING, INC.
344 Gannett Road, Scituate MA 02066
888-349-4433/781-545-2100
www.digitalscanning.com

Cover Illustration: Female/Male Tritons in a Bower
from the original front page of *New English Canaan* (1637)

Photo of Merrymount by Jack Dempsey

Illustrations are used as indicated with permission from:
The British Museum, Milwaukee Public Museum, John Hay Library, Massachusetts Historical Society, New York Metropolitan Opera Company, Mashantucket Pequot Museum and Research Center.
All Rights Reserved.

Tradepaper ISBN: 1-58218-209-4
Hardcover ISBN: 1-58218-210-8
eBook ISBN: 1-58218-211-6

"...for dancing is an exercise
not only shows the mover's wit,
but maketh the beholder wise
as he hath power to rise to it...."

---Ben Jonson,
Pleasure Reconciled to Virtue

THOMAS MORTON (1576?-1647?) left behind almost no certain records about himself. Various clues suggest that his family came of middling gentry status in England's West Country (likely Devonshire), where he received excellent Elizabethan educations in both field sports (such as hunting) and in rhetoric and Classics. Like many young gentlemen who had to work for a living, Morton apparently spent time at and/or received a law degree at Clifford's Inn, one of London's Inns of Court, and there took some interest in the intense literary and cultural life that (c. 1590) included Thomas Lodge, young Shakespeare and Ben Jonson. For about the next 20 years Morton may have worked as a West Country lawyer and (like many Devon men) become interested in various American commercial ventures then being financed by courtiers such as Sir Ferdinando Gorges. By 1623 Morton had wed a Berkshire widow and then become embroiled in a lawsuit against her stepson: he first appears in New England c. June 1624, as part of a Capt. Wollaston's company aboard the *Unity* who came to trade, profit and further develop English colonial ventures. When that company dispersed, Morton and a few indentured servants reorganized and renamed their hilltop "Ma-re Mount" (or Merrymount). There in 1627 they staged a MayDay Revel to celebrate and promote their trade (probably including guns) and other relations with Native American peoples and nonPuritan planters; and this, according to Morton, marked the beginning of his long conflict with "Pilgrims" of Plimoth Plantation.

By late 1628 Plimoth had arrested and deported Morton, but no legal action kept him from returning to New England affairs. Meanwhile, more Puritan planters founded Salem and Boston (1628-30), and together they banished him. After a perilous winter voyage home he began to seek redress through Gorges and The Council for New England. By the time the attorney had prevailed in court against Mass. Bay's Puritans (c. 1637) the beleaguered English government could do little to enforce decisions about America. Morton bided his time and composed *New English Canaan* (Amsterdam 1637), a subtle and spirited 3-part prose-and-poetry portrait of Native New England cultures, of the landscape and its "commodities," and of the various planters in the region, each with their different ways of "complying" (or not) with the New World. But the book's secularism and satire were reviled by its few Puritan readers; *Canaan* was also mistakenly confiscated by Royalist censors. As the English Civil War commenced, Morton found his own way back to New England by 1645, to end his days in "the land which he loveth," as his will stated. He was immediately arrested and imprisoned through the winter in Boston, where (for lack of legal charges) he was released "to go out of the jurisdiction" next spring. Apparently Morton journeyed to Agamenticus (York), Maine, where he joined West Country English settlers; and there (John Winthrop claimed) he lived perhaps another "two years."

about the writer

Jack Dempsey grew up in Stoneham, Massachusetts, on the North Shore of Boston. After his B.A. in English at University of Massachusetts at Amherst in 1979, he began writing professionally in New York City, and for many publishing houses there he researched, wrote and edited numerous books in Composition and Grammar, Literature and Social Studies. From New York he took his fiction-writing to Crete and the Greek Islands, where he lived for 2 years till publication of his *Ariadne's Brother: A Novel on the Fall of Bronze Age Crete* (Athens: Kalendis & Co. 1996: Greek translation by Vicky Chatzopoulou 2000), and he has lectured and published on related subjects in both countries.

Dempsey took his Ph.D. in Early and Native American Studies from Brown University in 1998, and he has taught at Wheaton College, Massachusetts. He has also produced two video documentaries on Native and Colonial subjects: *Thomas Morton & the Maypole of Merrymount* (2hrs, 1992), and *NANI: A Native New England Story* (1hr, 1998). The latter is distributed by Shenandoah Films (Arcata CA) and by V-Tape (Toronto).

Most recently, Dempsey has completed a feature-length screenplay called *Merrymount: a different early America*; and in 2001 will publish a new edition of Plimother Edward Winslow's early writing, *Good News from New England: The Killings at Weymouth Colony*. He is also creating (at Phillips Academy, Andover MA) an archive of audio and videotapes that preserve the work of Native historian Nanepashemet/Anthony Pollard.

THOMAS MORTON
of "Merrymount":
*The Life and Renaissance
of an Early American Poet*

by
JACK DEMPSEY

List of Illustrations *(at back)* vii
A Sampler of Remarks on Morton and *Canaan* . . . ix
Contexts & Chronology xvii

CHAPTERS

1: Family, Sensibility, the Times 5
2: Education 29
3: At the Inns of Court 41
4: Exit to America 63

*ANTIMASQUE: AMERICA'S FIRST POETRY IN ENGLISH   83

5: New World, New Life 127
6: Failure & Fortune 153
7: Family Values 163
8: Revel, Arrest & Return 191

*MASQUE: THE RIDDLE OF MAY DAY   218

9: Banned in Boston: Second Exile, *Canaan*, and Revenge . 247
10: Land of the New Creed 291

BIBLIOGRAPHIES
1: Works Cited 317
2: 1492-1637: Influences and Contemporaries . . . 355

INDEX 365

MAPS & ILLUSTRATIONS, DOCUMENTS & ARTIFACTS   376

*dedicated
to my darling niece Allison
(next matriarch of the clan),
to her generation and those after her upon the Earth:
May they honor the past:
May it inspire them as they make their new worlds
with love, with the courage to share,
and the Earth's wild joy of being alive!*

---Maps & Illustrations, Documents & Artifacts---

1) Atlantic Sea-Routes between Europe, West Indies and Native America
2) England and the Borders of its Counties
3) Photo of (goat's head) Seal-impression, and Signature, of Thomas Morton
4) "The Wrong" Thomas Morton portrait in *The Dictionary of Literary Biography*
5) Renaissance world-map showing "the Golden Mean" or Temperate Zones, with Zodiac
6) 1580 "mythology-handbook" engraving, "De Glauco" (Glaucus and Scilla)
7) Scene from Lescarbot's *The Theatre of Neptune* in New France (1606)
8) Map of London c. 1593
9) The Inns of Court: Clifford's Inn
10) Garden behind Clifford's Inn
11) Middle Temple Hall
12) Sketch of Sir Ferdinando Gorges' home
13) Native American "New England" at the beginning of European contact
14) Massachusetts Bay c. 1620-1630
15) Map showing Massachusetts Bay Colony's 1629 chartered lands
16) Colonial New England by the 1640s
17) 1635 Dutch map of New England showing "Lake of the Erocoise"
18) 1800s view "Seaward from Mount Wollaston"
19) 1840s sketch of "Mount Wollaston" (site of Ma-re Mount)
20) A Native New England village c. 1600s
21) Squa Rock, in Squantum, Mass
22) Hopewell carving of mother & child; and a New England Native sculpture
23) Native American "planting calendar" site in Connecticutt
24) "Festivities at Merry Mount"
25) "Myles Standish Breaks Up...Effort to Fraternize"
26) Archaeological artifacts from Ma-re Mount
27) Head of trade-ax, whetstone etc. from "Quincy Patriot Ledger" 1955
28) An original first page of *New English Canaan* (1637)---and five selected original folios
29) Facsimile of the only "1632" front page of *Canaan* (British Library)
30) Front page of *Canaan* from Force's 1832 reprint edition
31) Facsimile of Thomas Morton's Last Will and Testament
32) Facsimile of Thomas Morton's 1645 "Petition to the Honourable Court at Boston"
33, 34, 35, 36) Libretto front page from New York Metropolitan Opera's 1933 *Merry Mount*; and photos of staging for Acts 1, 2 and 3

Thomas Morton in American Letters: A Sampler of Remarks

America's first rascal.

> Harrison T. Meserole, 1985,
> *American Poetry of the Seventeenth Century*

* * *

[There] came over one Captaine Wolastone, (a man of pretie parts,) and with him 3 or 4 more of some eminencie, who brought with them a great many servants...for to begine a plantation....Amongst whom was one Mr. Morton, who, it should seeme, had some small adventure (of his owne or other mens) amongst them; but had litle respecte amongst them, and was sleghted by the meanest servants....And Morton became lord of misrule, and maintained (as it were) a school of Athisme....likewise (to shew his poetrie) composed sundry rimes and verses, some tending to lasciviousnes, and others to the detraction and scandal of some persons, which he affixed to [his] idle or idoll May-polle. They chainged allso the name of their place, and in stead of calling it Mounte Wollaston, they call it Merie mounte, as if this jollity would have lasted ever....

...Morton, thinking himself lawless, and hearing what gain the French and fishermen made by trading of pieces, powder and shot to the Indians, he as the head of this consortship began the practice of the same in these parts. And first he taught them how to use them, to charge and discharge....And these things have been done in the same times when some of their neighbors and friends are daily killed by the Indians, or are in danger thereof and live but at the Indians' mercy....O, the horribleness of this villainy!

> Governor Wm. Bradford [on 1624-7] *Of Plimoth Plantation*

It is ordered by this present Court, that Thomas Morton, of Mount Wolliston, shalll presently be sett into the bilbowes, & after sent prisoner into England, by the shipp called the Gifte, nowe returneing thith[er]; that all his goods shalbe seazed upon to defray the charge of his transportacon, pay[ment] of his debts, & to giue satisfaccon to the Indians for a cannoe hee uniustly tooke away from them; & that his howse, after the goods are taken out, shalbe burnt downe to the ground in the sight of the Indians, for their satisfaccon, for many wrongs hee hath done them from tyme to tyme.

> Judgment against the first defendant before the Massachusetts Bay Court of Assistants, September 7, 1630 (*Records of the Governor and Colony of the Mass. Bay in New England*)

Tho:morton adiudged to be imprisoned till he were sent into England, and his house burnt down, for his many iniuries offered to the Indians, and other misdemeanors. Capt. Brooke master of the *Gifte* refused to carrye him.

> Governor John Winthrop, *Journal* 1630

...a proud insolent man....
>
> Gov. Thomas Dudley, 1631 letter

...keept in the Comon Gaole a whole winter [1646], nothing laid to his Charge but the writeing of a Booke entituled New Canaan, which indeed was the truest discription of New England as then it was that euer I saw.
>
> Samuel Maverick, planter, *A Brief Description of New England* c.1660

...inveterate resentment against the New-England plantations and their leaders. His book...is very rarely to be met with. We know of but one copy in this country...That part of the book which relates to the Plimoth planters, is full of invective and misrepresentation, calculated to gain a degree of indulgence, however, with some readers, from the air of pleasantry which he adopts. He abounds in the vulgar wit of nick names; [Capt. Myles] Standish he calls Capt. Shrimp, [Capt. John] Endicot is styled Capt. Littleworth, Mr. Fuller is Dr. Noddy. It is not known, nor will it be thought worth while to inquire, who are intended by the appellations of Innocence Faircloth, Matthias Charterparty, and Master Bubble....
>
> Nathaniel Morton, *New England's Memorial*, 1669

The character of the Miscreant...is not wholly contemptible. It marks the Complextion of the Age in which he lived. How many such characters could You and I enumerate, who in our times have had a similar influence on Society!
>
> John Adams, letter to Thomas Jefferson, Jan. 26, 1813

...the thoughtless and dissipated Morton...who had rather dance round the Maypole... than be hearing the wholesome and lion-like truths of the gospel.
>
> Lydia Maria Child, 1824, *Hobomok*

Jollity and gloom were contending for an empire.
>
> Nathaniel Hawthorne c. 1837, "The Maypole of Merrymount"

...eloquent, adroit, bold, good-humored, and luxurious and loose in his habits and principles.
>
> John Lothrop Motley, 1849, *Merry Mount: A Romance of the Massachusetts Colony*

The work of Morton is a singular performance. That part of it relating to the customs of the Indians, and the natural history of the country, is interesting and valuable; but the rest abounds in low wit, and that species of lampoonery better befitting a denizen of Billingsgate than a champion of the "honor and dignity of the Episcopal Church." His "seasoning" may be relished by some for its coarseness, but it lacks the true Attic flavor, and is but a miserable attempt to imitate the most execrable and disgusting of the Classic authors, with whose scurrility, buffoonery and mendacity, he fully sympathized. Were the whole work like a few of its chapters, it would add much to its character, and to the fame of its author; as a more favorable estimate of his moral qualities would be warranted, were not the lack of these qualities so striking and palpable even by his own showing.
>
> John Stetson Barry, *The History of Massachusetts* 1855: I, 145

...one of the most picturesque yet least understood characters in early New England history. It has been considered well-nigh a proof of loyalty to treat his memory with scorn.
B.F. DeCosta, 1882, "Morton of Merry Mount"

...absolutely nothing to be said in his favor....a lawless, reckless, amoral adventurer.... a born Bohemian and reckless libertine, without either morals or religion....saturated with revelry and scoffing...[an] amusing old debauchee and tippler....That his moral character was decidedly loose is apparent from his own statements....yet, withal, he was a close observer.... The man had, in fact, an innate love of nature, and an Englishman's passion for field sports. What, except love of adventure, ever originally brought him to New England, is not likely to be known; but, once he got there, he was never able to take himself off, nor could others drive him away.
Charles Francis Adams Jr., editor of the 1882 *New English Canaan*, and author of *Three Episodes of Massachusetts History*, 1892

...the principle aim of the work seems to be a ridicule of the Puritan creed and customs ....Although apparently a happy-tempered, jovial person, who simply lived according to the manners of his time, [Morton's] infatuation for New England, in spite of his unhappy life there, is quite remarkable.
The National Cyclopaedia of American Biography, 1897

....a Royalist rake...a thorn in the flesh of the sober colonists of Plymouth.
Encyclopaedia Britannica, 1911, XI, 882

...a gay gentleman with an eye for trade, author of the most entertaining book on early Massachusetts...very naturally played in with the enemies of the Massachusetts Colony, [and] posed before Bishop Laud's Committee of the Privy Council as an Anglican martyr to puritan spite....One would wish that the authorities had not struck an enemy when he was down; but that was the way things were done in the 17th century....We are heavily in debt to Morton for the jolliest contemporary account of early New England. If he did not love our people, he at least loved our land....Those of us who spend our summers in the less frequented portions of the New England coast have probably met more spiritual descendants of Thomas Morton than of John Winthrop.
Samuel Eliot Morison, 1930, *Builders of the Bay Colony*

...He was undoubtedly broken in health as a result of his confinement and in marked contrast physically with the Tom Morton of 162[7] who had tried to revive the old English custom of celebrating dances....He was the one emigrant to our shores who added something to the joy of life in the drab communities that surrounded him and it is not symbolic of the square deal to accept the prejudiced views of the Puritan journalists....He was a foeman worthy of their steel, and that he held them up to deserved ridicule in his book, the most readable volume on the time he was here, proved to be the cause of his arrest in 1643...He is his own best advocate....He lies unhonored but not unsung among the town's distinguished dead.
Charles Edward Banks, *History of York* [Maine] 1931

...It is not so much good history to present Morton with sly amusement in mortal and unmannerly combat with his betters, as it would be to relieve him from that imposition of his time and seriously to show up that lightness, his essential character, which discloses the Puritans themselves as maimed, to their advantage, for survival, the converse of which---in a crooked way, perhaps, but in a way---Morton presented.
William Carlos Williams, 1933,
In the American Grain

His manner of life...distinctly licentious and convivial....He was himself a worthless rake, in spite of efforts which have been made to rehabilitate his character as a persecuted churchman.
James Truslow Adams, 1934,
Dictionary of American Biography

...a bohemian, a humorist, a scoffer, and a libertine, with no moral standards of thought or conduct.
Charles M. Andrews, *The Colonial Period of American History*, 1934

It was the tongue in your cheek that they hated most,
The last flare of Old England, the reckless mirth.
Steven Vincent Benet, 1943, *Western Star*

...*New England* [sic] *Canaan*, one of the liveliest, wittiest, and most informative books of the day. Though it is not to be taken too literally, for it is obviously a satire, most solemn historians are simply stupid in dismissing the book as worthless.
George F. Willison, 1945, *Saints and Strangers*

"I know he was bad morally....But he was also a very intelligent fellow. If the Puritans at Boston had taken Morton's advice literally about there being [deposits of] lime at Weymouth [Mass.: Bk. II 84], they would have saved thousands of dollars [sic] on their fort at Castle Island, which fell down more than once because it had been built with mud, not lime. Morton's observations on nature were very good for those times...."
G. Stinson Lord, New England geologist/historian
qtd. in "Quincy May Obtain Relics From Morton Trading Post": *Quincy Patriot Ledger*, 1955

Colonizing was supposed to be a serious business!
The American Heritage Encyclopedia, 1963, II, 96

(Morton wears a shabby coffee-colored suit, part cloth and part deerskin. He is overweight and his manner with the minister is complacent, oily and conciliatory.)
Robert Lowell, stage direction for
Endicott & the Red Cross 1964

Thomas Morton xiii

The essence of *Endicott and the Red Cross* seems to me to be its complex spiritual irony, and this can be easily swamped by the spectacle of the mid-summer fete [Morton's Revel within Robert Lowell's play]. In the first production we never entirely got over this problem and after a lot of rehearsal, cutting and re-writing, we had to drop the play before the first night[,] which seriously damaged the grand design.
                                        Jonathan Miller, "Director's Note" to
                                        Robert Lowell's play in *The Old Glory*

I'd be damned if I could understand his nonsense, try as I would. It sounded brave but it made no sense.
                                        L.S. Davidson Jr., 1964 novel *The Disturber*

...a lawyer of dubious scruples and most un-Puritan morals....There is no doubt that the social behavior of the Morton colonists offended the Pilgrim Fathers. But the documentary record reveals that the Merrymount episode belongs not in the realm of moral quibbling, but of interracial diplomacy....The Morton episode was strictly in keeping with Plimoth's policy of decisive action in support of the general welfare.
                                        Alden T. Vaughan, 1965, *New England Frontier*

Like many prose passages in his book, "The Poem" [written for Morton's 1627 Revel] is a maze of Classical and Biblical allusions representing, allegorically, some contemporary occurrence.
                                        Donald F. Connors, *Thomas Morton* 1969

<u>GOV. JOHN WINTHROP</u> [*to Morton in his 1645 Boston jail-cell*]:
    The future! You will be known as a prodigal and licentious gunrunner, who introduced the savages to firearms, erected a Maypole to the Devil, and spread mutiny and drunkenness throughout the countryside. That will be your role in history....
<u>MORTON</u>: ...Then your history is a myth of ironclad, black and white alternatives, full of the limitations and fictions of your own minds. When men regain a true sense of themselves, they'll cease to believe in the bloody alternatives of your history. A new consciousness will arise from man's experience on this continent. It's there in the forest and the Indian village; and it can't be hidden. Freedom is man's natural state!....
<u>WINTHROP</u>: I shall see if I can arrange for your release and banishment from the Colony. You are old and mad....
<u>MORTON</u>: My madness feeds on the atmosphere of this cell, which you call Massachusetts....
                                    from Lance Carden's unpublished
                                      Thomas Morton in the Promised Land:
                                      An Historical Play for an Unhistorical Generation, 1971

...Morton regarded his own colony of Merrymount...as the fountainhead of that erotic energy to which all the new and old worlds might have recourse....[The] Englishman must withhold nothing of himself from the wilderness and the Indian but merge thoroughly with them and refresh himself at the sources of human passion and affection....
                                      Richard Slotkin, 1973, *Regeneration Through*
                                      Violence: Mythology of the American Frontier 1600-1860

...according to one contemporary theologian, Harvey Cox, for whom the rituals of release and clarification are not simply useful terms to describe the effects of festive comedy but fundamental psychic necessities [...], Protestantism, with its emphasis upon man as an historical creature and upon life as a serious business, is especially culpable of divorcing modern man from his festive, historical self and of the psychic dislocation consequent upon that separation ....[Thus] the Puritan invasion of Merry Mount may mark a far more important turning point in American cultural attitudes than nearly anybody (Hawthorne is the possible exception) seems to have suspected to date....Moreover, Morton's deepest message, which I read in terms of release and clarification---that is, a heightened awareness of man's festive identity and his relationship to nature---is inherent in [his book's] form no less than in the overt attacks upon the Puritans....[He] seems a legendary embodiment of the fresh, green beast of the New World, and he continues to speak eloquently to us of a remote time in our infancy when things seemed to have a chance to go another way.

> Robert D. Arner, "Pastoral Celebration and
> Satire in Thomas Morton's *New English
> Canaan*," 1974

Suffice it to say that the pleasure-dome established by Morton, based on peaceful trade and pleasurable intercourse with the Indians of the area, caused Governor Bradford to dispatch Miles Standish to wipe out the settlement.

> Wilcomb E. Washburn, 1976, "The Clash of
> Morality in the American Forest"

Though many writers agree that this "gay gentleman" wrote the most lively and entertaining account of early New England, his lack of value as a source on its history is assumed.... Perhaps it is time to change all this.

> Karen Ordhal Kupperman,
> "Thomas Morton, Historian" 1977

For this unspoiled moment, continent and man fused, the power of the one to arouse awe embraced by the nearly commensurate imagination of the other. Morton's lyrical summary of his findings [Book 2 Ch. 1] should be known by every student of America's past.

> Richard Drinnon, 1980, *Facing West:
> The Metaphysics of Indian-Hating and Empire-Building*

What Locke failed to notice was that the Indians did not recognize themselves as poor ....Thomas Morton was almost alone among his contemporaries in realizing that the New England Indians had chosen [a different] path....Morton has been underrated as a colonial source for too long.

> William Cronon, 1983, *Changes in the Land:
> Indians, Colonists, and the Ecology of New England*

Ultimately, the most abominable quality of worship of the fertility gods was the absence of moral purpose.

> Thomas Pribek, 1985, "The Conquest of Canaan:
> Suppression of Merry Mount"

Morton was an eager observer and cataloguer of the animals of the woods, skies, and sea....although never mentioned, so far as I know, by a historical fraternity which otherwise endeavors to find America's earliest psychological observer. The date for such honor has been moving steadily backward, but it would appear to be difficult to find an earlier visitor to American shores who saw so much and described what he saw with such cogent wit....

As often happens, once the name of a person out of tune with the sentiment of the times is blackened, the historians, rather than doing their own investigating, merely repeat canards ....That historical analysis may be shaped by the scholar's ethnic and genealogical centrality or isolation is a truth which scientists may recognize long before historians do.

        Philip Howard Gray, "Thomas Morton as
        America's First Behavioral Observer," 1987

...The depth of Morton's commitment to church and king has always been suspect, but rightly considered that allegiance in Morton is profound. For without their authority, the texts for which he believes he requires their sanction are null and void. Morton professes an intention to teach the Indians the language of The Book of Common Prayer for the same reason that he asserts that their lexicon is part Greek and Latin and that they pay homage to Pan in their place names. It is the Renaissance, not the Reformation, that is alive in Morton, and during the period of exile in which he wrote the *New English Canaan* the renaissance in which he most fervently believed, the metamorphosis he most earnestly sought to make textual, was his own.

       Daniel B. Shea, 1988, "'Our Professed Old
       Adversary': Thomas Morton and the Naming of New England"

Morton had introduced his chapter on Indian origins with the apparently redundant observation that he had found in New England "two sortes of people, the one Christians, the other Infidels." But now he was subtly implying that, genealogically speaking, there was actually only one sort....To portray the meeting of Indians and Englishmen as a long-delayed family-reunion was meant to be quite a joke on a people who were (as Morton had noted) so desperately intent upon distancing themselves from the supposedly vicious, treacherous, alien barbarians.

       John Canup, *Out of the Wilderness: The Emergence*
       of An American Identity in Colonial New England 1990

Q: How did Morton Street receive its name?
  A: Morton Street, which runs from the Arborway to River Street in Dorchester Lower Mills, was named in 1832 for Thomas Morton, according to "A Concise Guide to the Streets of Jamaica Plain," a publication of the Jamaica Plain Historical Society....He named the place Mare Mount and began to dispense good cheer. The Puritans, scandalized by his revels and endangered [sic] by his arms traffic with the Indians, deported him....

       "Ask The Globe," *The Boston Globe*, 3/1/97: E12

Dear Mr. Dempsey,
    First of all, my apologies for having held onto this for so long, and thank you for having sent it. The "Caanan" [sic] is a fascinating work, and of undeniable historical interest. I also agree that to present it appropriately would require substantial critical annotations and appendices. Unfortunately, it's also this aspect of the book that makes it a difficult project for us. In any case, I do wish you all success. It very much deserves to be made available.

typical response
Editorial Director(s)
American & British Publishers, Inc.
Boston/New York/London

    Along the way, some interesting points....The evidence of Morton's awareness of the "plague's" effects upon Native Americans is significant, but I'm not sure about the rest. In his offer of help, supposedly, Morton turns out to be more than the mere Cavalier pleasure-seeker we think he was. Or does he? Of the myriad poetic allusions, one is curiously missing: an allusion to Marlowe. Morton and crew may be little more than a lot of passionate shepherds, who 'dance and sing/for thy delight each May morning.' Perhaps 'The Poem' is Morton's answer to Ralegh's answer to Marlowe.
    But even without resorting to Marlowe, we can find a contradiction...

"Reader's Report" from "professional" journal
American Literature, 1996

    ...suggests that the editor's sentimental favorite Thomas Morton is to wear the laurel crown of 'First American Poet in English'---The criterion is, however, that he/she must have been 'an English-speaking-and-writing individual who had physical contact with the North American land-mass, and who wrote something in verse that focuses on the experience.' But this rather pedestrian requirement doesn't jive [sic] well with the elaborate modern debates about poesy in general....

"Reader's Report" (1999) from
Publications of the Modern Language Association

CONTEXTS & CHRONOLOGY

1497-1498	John & Sebastian Cabot voyages to "New-found-land"
1500-1501	Corte-Real explores Northeastern American coasts; Basque & other whalers/fishermen begin annual visits
1524	Verrazanno meets Narragansett, Abenaki Native peoples: their varied "Eastern Woodland" cultures derive from "Paleo" & "Archaic" periods totaling at least 13,000 years in "New England" (est. pop. 100,000). Earliest N.E. evidences contemporary with Europe's "Late Paleolithic"
1534-1541	Cartier explores the future "New France"
1562	French attempts to plant in Florida (Brazil 1575)
1569	Mercator's map of the world
1570s	English and Spanish conflicts in the Caribbean
1576	M. Frobisher's first North Atlantic voyage; **THOMAS MORTON** born in Devonshire, West Country England (approx.), "son of a Souldier"
1584	Ralegh, Barlow in "Virginia": first Roanoke colony; Sir H. Gilbert, would-be poet Steph. Parmenius lost at sea off Newfoundland
1585-1587	Davis' voyages continue search for Northwest Passage
1585-1586	Drake's raids in the "Spanish" Caribbean
1588	England defeats the Spanish Armada
1594-1603?	**MORTON** studies law at Clifford's Inn (Inns of Court), London: he likely attends Gray's Inn's *Gesta Grayorum*, major public entertainments for Queen Elizabeth incl. "The Masque of Proteus," which he emulates with 1627 Revels
1598	Sable Island (Newfoundland) camp fails
1602	Gosnold names "Cape Cod"; camps at Cuttyhunk Island
1603	Pring and others follow Gosnold for sassafrass etc.
	Dutch found "New Amsterdam"
	Queen Elizabeth dies, James I crowned
1605	Waymouth voyage to "Maine" waters

1606	voyages of Challons, Pring (2nd): Msr. de Poutrincourt's French at Port Royal, New France: Lescarbot's *Theatre of Neptune*
1607	Popham attempt to plant Sagadahoc, "Maine" (fails 1 yr.)
1608	Champlain and Lescarbot at Quebec and "New France"
1609	voyage of Henry Hudson: Virginia Company founded
1610	Adriaen Block (Dutch) explores Narragansett Bay etc. John Guy of Bristol and others in Newfoundland English plantations in Ulster, Ireland; Bermudas (1611)
1614	Captain John Smith explores and names "New England": his colleague Capt. Hunt abducts 27 Natives for slavetrade
1615-1616	John Mason governs Newfoundland
1616-1618	"Plague" and other European diseases decimate New England Native American populations
1617	Ralegh's 2nd "El Dorado"; **MORTON** "makes acquaintance" of widow Alice Miller of Swallowfield (Berkshire): her stepson dislikes him
1618	Capt. Dermer's New England voyage; Ralegh executed
1619	**MORTON** in minor legal dispute in Axbridge (county Somerset)
1620	Wm. Bradford and English Puritans arrive at Patuxet/"New Plimoth"; **MORTON**, "Capt. Wollaston" *et als* poss. granted small land-patent
1621	Dutch West Indies Co. founded; **MORTON** and Alice marry (Nov. 6) Native peoples of Virginia rise against English plantations
1622-1623	English plantation Weymouth begun and dissolved, leaves Maverick, Blackstone, Jeffreys, other "lone planters" round Mass. Bay.
	King James I issues Proclamation (not statute) vs. gun-trade with "Indians": it is already "spoiling" profits of beads/knives etc. for furs
	Chancery Court rules vs. **MORTON** and wife (June): he "disappears"
	Sir Wm. Vaughan, others in "Cambriol" (Newfoundland) try America: he works at *The Golden Fleece* (London 1627)
1624	**Thomas Morton arrives (June) in New England**: by Fall, he and others prepare to winter at Passonagessit/"Mt. Wollaston"
1625	James I dies: Charles I crowned King of England (March)

1626	George Sandys translates Ovid's *Metamorphoses* into English in Virginia Colony (London 1627)
1625-1627	Mt. Wollaston fails: Morton *et als* rename it Ma-re Mount and make headway into New England trade. Visit of "The Barren Doe of Virginia" (Book 3), a shipwrecked/runaway English woman
1627	May Day Revels incl. "all commers": trade likely includes firearms
1628	Plimoth arrests Morton (June) and maroon him on Isles of Shoals (NH) till September: Morton freed in England.
	John Endicott and others arrive to plant at Salem (Sept.): Endicott cuts down Maypole, demands "better walking."
	Robt. Hayman (of Vaughan's Newfoundland) publishes *Quodlibets*, incl. two poems on America
1629	Morton returns to Ma-re Mount (now "Mt. Dagon"): Endicott's Salem and lone planters at odds: winter famine at Salem, and (acc. to Morton) Ma-re Mount supplies taken. Visits of "Master Bubble" (Book 3)
	Gun-trader Edw. Ashley's career (1629-30) at Penobscot
1630	Puritan "Great Migration" begins (June) as 900 planters arrive with Gov. John Winthrop at "Boston." September: Morton arrested/ banished, Ma-re Mount burned. Servant Edw. Gibbons begins Puritan career: "Great Wat" Walter Bagnall moves to Richmond Island (Maine). Morton survives winter exile voyage, reaches England early 1631, poss. "repairs to Axbridge" and begins lawsuit vs. Mass. Bay. His petitions etc. become drafts of *Canaan*
1631	Sir Christopher Gardiner and Philip Ratcliffe each conflict with Mass. Bay: by 1632 they join Morton's suit at court
	Thirty Years War sack of Magdeburg
	Roger Williams begins American career
	Capt. John Smith's poem "The Sea Marke"
1632	Dec. 19: attorney Morton with witnesses before the Privy Council; but by Jan. 1633, Council "preliminary" decision against him and Sir F. Gorges' Council for New England
	Dutch and various English factions compete for Pequot trade on the Connecticutt River (see 1637)
	Anne Bradstreet (arr. Mass. Bay 1630) begins (acc. to some scholars) to write poetry
1633	Gorges' efforts continue: by Sept. King Charles appoints Wm. Laud new Archbishop of Canterbury: he and Gorges arrange new "Commission for Foreign Plantations."

	November 18: Morton registers *Canaan* (probably then a long legal brief) with Stationers Register (royal licensers)
	Lancashire "witch trials": Galileo faces the Inquisition. A new epidemic (smallpox) devastates Native New England as Plimoth and Mass. Bay planters take over more lands
	Dutch, Native and English killings in Connecticutt
1634	May 1: Morton writes to old planter Wm. Jeffreys in New England to announce the voiding of Mass. Bay's charter, and that he will return with a new Governor (most likely Sir F. Gorges). Boston Puritan public meetings resolve to resist by force of arms
	Wm. Wood's *New England's Prospect*, incl. verse-couplets
1635	Morton (via Attorney General) prosecutes a writ of *quo warranto* (May 6) to finalize decisions against Mass. Bay
	c. 1630s Morton's New England "Pilgrim" rival Wm. Bradford begins his *History of Plimoth Plantation*
1637	Morton's various phases of composition culminate in *New English Canaan*. By year's end the government confiscates most copies, poss. mistaking them for foreign-printed "outlaw" tracts. No evidence of their recovery
	Also, in July, Sir F. Gorges named Governor of New England: he courts Puritan New England and "cashiers" Morton in letter to Winthrop, but Gorges continues to employ Morton as before
	The "Pequot War" in New England: Harvard founded: Mass. Bay's first slave-ship (*Desire*) launched
1638-41	Scottish Presbyterian rebellions intensify vs. Englsh religious impositions by King Charles/Archbishop Laud: Crown's "thorough" policies and forced loans via Earl of Strafford bring Royalists and Parliamentarians near war
1638	Puritan Thos. Tillam writes poem "Upon the First Sight of New England..."
1640	Ma-re Mount is part of "Braintree" and private property, eventually of "Henry Adams" and his 8 sons
	Archbishop Laud a prisoner in London's Tower for "high treason"
1637-1641	Gorges and Morton continue legal efforts to obtain Mass. Bay charter and/or enforce court judgments; but Crown financial woes and rising Puritan Parliament forces prevent any action. April 10 (1641): Morton serves as witness to Agamenticus (York, Maine) charter (in Banks)
	Approx. 20,000 Puritans in New England: the "Great Migration" ends in economic depression on the eve of war. Mass. Bay's *Body of Liberties* includes formal recognition of slavery, and the "Triangular Trade" opens: rum to Africa, slaves to the Caribbean, molasses/cotton/tobacco

	and slaves to New England and America
1642-1643	The English Civil War (April): Gorges rides with Royalist forces as Morton apparently pursues a way back to New England as "agent" of Alexander Rigby *et als*.
	May 23: Morton legal witness to grant of Casco Neck (Maine) by Rigby to Geo. Cleeve. August 23 (1643): Morton seals his will, soon departs for America to end his days. The "old serpent" (Winslow) is "suffered" to winter at Plimoth and (now near 70) can still hunt fowl at "Duxburrow" near the retired Myles Standish's homestead
1644	Spring: Morton rumored a "Royalist agitator" from Maine to Rhode Island. By September he is prisoner at Boston. Court delays "trial so that evidence can be sought against him: Morton jailed through the winter "to the decaying of his limbs." No evidence of any crime can be produced.
	Dissident Samuel Gorton arranges Narragansett Native appeal to King Charles for equal status as royal English subjects: by 1645, with Charles' defeat, the colonies declare war on them
1645	Spring: Morton petitions for release. Since he "ha[s] nothing" (Winthrop) and is "a charge to the country," he is released and ordered "to go out of the jurisdiction." Poss. telling planter Sam. Maverick that he had "received his bane" by imprisonment, Morton journeys to Agamenticus/York (Maine) to join as possible with West Country planters there. Maverick: he died "soon after"
1646	Puritan Roger Williams' *A Key Into The Language of America* incl. poetry questioning Puritan-colonial assumptions
1647	Jerome Bellamie's *The Simple Cobbler of Agawam*
1647?	Acc. to problematic Winthrop *Journal* entry, Thomas Morton lives "another two years" at Agamenticus after release: burial in Clark's Lane Burial Ground (no longer in existence).

1: *Family, Sensibility, The Times*

OF Thomas Morton---English gentleman and sportsman, attorney at law and man of court, American colonizer, poet, and exile---there are remarkably few records. How could a person of his obvious vitality, a man so merrily literate, traveled, and connected to the powerful of his day, leave behind almost nothing in Early Modern archives? When we have considered all that can be known of Morton, and all that has been registered (for better or worse) of how he lived, we may well agree with Nathaniel Hawthorne's summary insight---that the life of "Mine Host" was something more like "spontaneous allegory" than history.

Thomas Morton's likely birth-year, 1576, derives from an estimate of his wife's age, made possible by a series of English legal proceedings recorded in 1622-23. No known document tells more than that, in November 1621, Thomas married a widowed mother, one Alice Miller of Swallowfield County Berkshire; and Banks' estimate that Alice was about 40 at the time (working back from the births of her children) led him to suppose Morton then about 5 years her senior; a common age-difference in marriages of the day.[1]

Morton's family and regional origins are matters of equal inference. A 1631 letter remarks that he practiced law in the West Country before coming to America (Dudley 11), which is consistent with research into the Morton family tree, its heraldry and signet-seals. In England in the 1920s, Banks located seven

---

[1] Banks' deductions (165n12) are consistent with marriage patterns studied by Wrightson (66-120) and Stone (*Crisis* 271-83).

Morton families using a seal with the same goat's head device as Morton's of New England (Banks 160: Illustration); and four of those families hailed from or resided in West Country counties. Later, Banks discovered another court-record placing Morton for a time in Axbridge (County Somerset; qtd. in Andrews 332); and it was to Axbridge that Morton "repaired" much later, to physically recover from the voyage of his second American exile (1630: citations Ch. 9).

A further clue, that his 1627 Maypole stood an unusual "80 foot" tall (*Canaan* 134) also evokes West Country culture (Langstaff interview), as does Morton's use of the words *creeple* "as the name is in Devonshire" for a rattlesnake (77), and *loblolly pot* (of food or broth, 196), a term with Devon origins (OED). As will appear, Morton's chosen law-school residence in London was Clifford's Inn: students tended to stay with fellows from their home-counties at all the Inns, and Clifford's was definitely the choice of Devonshire men who came to study there (admissions-by-county table in Prest 33). Given all this, and the lack of any clues in the direction of other English counties, Devon seems the promising ground for further searches.[2]

Of Thomas' personal appearance we can only suppose that he wore his hair long in the later-named "Cavalier" fashion, for he pokes fun at short "pudding-bowl" or "roundhead" haircuts in *Canaan* (144). But as will emerge from other clues, this must have been a vigorous, hale and fairly-imposing fellow from youth to old age. Of his own early life on the West Country landscape, with its small cottages, cloth-weaving towns and grain-growing countryside dotted

---

[2] This writer has followed up numerous minor leads, including a family of outer Cape Cod who kindly shared promising ancestral records dating back to medieval English villages, but whose family could not have been Thomas'. See also Illustration of the British Museum's painting of "Thomas Morton" that has been published in *The Dictionary of Literary Biography* as Morton of "Merrymount." The British Museum assures us that no further information on the painting's source or commissioners etc. is available; and it is all but sure that New England's Morton did not invent the "lurdan" or "improved specimen-bottle" shown there.

with forest and deer parks, Morton leaves three hints: that he was "the Son of a souldier" (*Canaan* 145), that he had "been bred in so genious a way" that he had "the common use" of hawks and falcons in his hunting (66); and that he was a "gent" or member of at least a "middling" class of gentlemen, for he signed the first page of his book and his will that way, and opinion is unanimous that a known attorney would have been ill-advised merely to claim the social rank.

However, since Morton nowhere claimed that his father had come of the gentry before soldiering, the man (and perhaps this whole branch of the Morton clan) had likely earned the rank for himself and his sons in the way many others did, through military service of the Crown. Morton's future New World employer Sir Ferdinando Gorges raised himself thus, and knew many a "gentleman...[who] had raised himself from a soldier to the quality he had, from a corporal to a sergeant, and so upward...." (*Narration* 48).[3]

If Thomas was born in 1576, his father might have served not only with English detachments sent to the Low Countries by Queen Elizabeth I. The future American explorer Sir Humphrey Gilbert was first a colonizer of Ireland, and from 1567-69 he was raising companies of Devonshire men for operations in Munster (Levermore 1:10: consistent with Morton's remark that Native Americans had "Irish" resemblances, *Canaan* 21, 25). The "Souldier" Morton Senior who fathered Thomas and helped him to gentleman status might also have risen socially just by his marriage to a woman of large dowry. William

---

[3] The years just before and after Morton's birth were demanding military ones (see Tuchman 38, 635). The 1560s saw the "Munster Rebellion" in Ireland, in 1573 came Essex's expeditions, and English raids on the Spanish Caribbean began to increase. Calais and the Netherlands received thousands of English reinforcements through "The Spanish Fury" at Antwerp (1576) to the 1590s, when at least 8000 more were sent (including Gorges who fought with Essex at Rouen in 1591, at Paris and Amiens). The late 1580s, of course, brought the Armada confrontation, and there was another "scare" of Spanish invasion in England's 1590s: this may at least suggest that Morton had a certain social standing to help keep him out (as far as we know) of so much warfare. More below on this aspect of his generation.

Camden called gentlemen "the common sort of nobility" who were either of "worshipfull parentage...vertue or wealth" (qtd. in Riggs 25; also Singman 18). But somehow the family had enough status (it seems) to enjoy a few pursuits of the genteel, sports such as flying the noble birds of the hunt. All this is compatible with William Bradford's estimate of Morton, as one of "some eminencie" (FBH2:46) whose rank was yet within range of "sleights" from a servant or two.

The family does appear wealthy enough to have thoroughly educated Thomas and sent him to "law school" in London. Inns of Court living ran up costs of at least a "very sizeable" £40 per year (Wrightson 186-7), and made it a place where "those of an inferior rank not...able to bear the expenses of maintaining and educating their children" as "sons to persons of quality" were rarely admitted. It was said that there was "scarce to be found, throughout the kingdom, an eminent lawyer who is not a gentleman by birth and fortune" (Sir John Fortescue qtd. in Finkelpearl 5).[4] And yet, Thomas' being sent to the Inns as the "third University" of England (after Oxford and Cambridge) suggests that his family intended him to *work* somehow for his living. In Devon itself, "successful merchants and lawyers continued to found landed families" through this period (Hoskins *Devon* 85). Erasmus had named common law as the easiest route to social advancement; but as Kelso cautions, in these days "law only in its more dignified and important aspects" was recommended as a gentleman's "proper pursuit," and only when circumstances demanded that one take up labor at all (54).

Thomas' chief circumstance was likely an older sibling: his will left his estate to one "neece Sara Bruce" (rpt. in Banks 163). He was probably one of the

---

[4] Besides Dudley (11), Bradford offers a primary-source clue that Morton really was connected with *one* of the Inns by linking him with "Furneffells" or Furnival's (FBH 2:47).

numerous sons of the gentry less-provided-for, at this time when primogeniture dominated inheritance law. Such young men were (by common complaint) all too many in England (and France too), especially round London and the Inns of Court, dispossessed and unemployed youths whose above-average educations fitted them for hard-to-get court positions and bureaucratic posts. "[M]ost of the property went to the eldest son, the younger brothers being despatched into the world with little more than a modest annuity or life interest in a small estate to keep them afloat" (Stone 271).[5]

And yet, despite limited means, Thomas was to move himself into some eminent circles amid the courtly councils governing American colonization and its charters from Kings James and Charles I. Since at least the time of Henry VIII's various courtly revolutions in religious and political mores, a man's rising star had become less the result of "orderly progression" through ranks than of "personal matters...what made power work" (Foley 18-19). Such instabilities allowed both the careerist and the talented but "lowly-born" to make their way: just ahead of Morton on the self-driven path to distinction was poet and master-to-be of the "courtly revel" Ben Jonson, whose career was to span working class hardship, good grammar school, military service and the building of brick walls at the Inns (Loftie 54), as he studied his Classics and maneuvered himself in social terms. There was room for a "common" man to make his English way.

We know nothing at all of Thomas' mother. According to Ann Rosalind Jones' influential study, while there had always been a place in Renaissance

---

[5] Morton's 1622 opponent in court George Miller refers to him as a "person of noe certaine aboade" (qtd. in Banks 171), a condition not necessarily that of Morton's family. For the reader's information, according to the English concept of class or social hierarchy in Morton's day, a gentleman stood roughly equal with a clergyman, merchant, or university graduate (lawyer, doctor etc.); below these stood deacons, yeomen, craftsmen and tradesmen, farmers, trade-appprentices, and then servants and laborers, with vagrants at the bottom. Above a gentleman stood knights, barons, viscounts, earls, marqueses, dukes, and the king above the queen.

courts and "urban coteries" for women in very carefully schooled (and controlled) public roles, including courtesan, hostess and "lady" of the cultural *salon,* "the most widely disseminated feminine ideal" of this period leading up to Thomas' birth was, increasingly, "the confinement of the bourgeois daughter and wife to private domesticity[,] in the households of city merchants, professional men and, in England, Protestant fathers and husbands" ("Nets and Bridles" 41). On the other hand, scholars such as Natalie Zemon Davis find in the records and relationships of many Renaissance women that, where boundaries "around the conceptual self and the bodily self" were "not always firm and closed, men and women...could work out strategies for self-expression and autonomy" ("Boundaries" 53).

The greatest "obstacle to self-definition," Davis finds, was not "embeddedness" or "repression" by the web of one's closest social and community relations, but "powerlessness and poverty." Since it does not in any way appear that Thomas' family was poor, we should look for the presence of Thomas' mother at least where she, as a more or less "traditional" mother of her time and place, would have been encouraged to exert power, in the teaching and shaping of her children in their respective roles, and in their time spent together in private and community life.

Where the medieval worlds of kinship and feudalism had (as in the rest of Europe) guaranteed certain measures of women's social power outside the home (Kelly-Gadol 159), Morton's Early Modern times were moving most women into positions of greater dependence and domesticity. A wife's and mother's duties at this family's "upper-middling" rank included supervision of servants, curing sickness/healing injuries, administering many forms of social "charity" to relations and neighbors (all visible skills possessed by *Canaan*'s author); plus, of course, prime responsibility for the children. In *Canaan* Morton says his "family" used the Anglican *Book of Common Prayer*: nothing there, nor from their Queen (very much involved in Church matters), directly forbade a mother to teach her children thus; and Morton remarks without rhetoric upon a "Deaconess" at later Plimoth (181).

Did Thomas' mother use literacy as many did, to overcome her confinements and other limitations? Given that literature, folkways and proverbs are so much the fabric of *Canaan*'s author, from Aesop's "The Ant and the Bee" to the feats of The Bible's Samson, there must have been a relatively high level of culture about the boy's home. In general the system of public grammar schools was growing, but there was still no place for women there. Yet several historians conclude that *some* women just about everywhere, like some of the less-socially-entitled classes of men, did learn letters. Besides its pleasures and its "gracing" the upwardly-mobile family, the skills proved worth the acquiring for the practices of religion, at markets, in writing letters/making bonds, and recordings of births, weddings and, not least, wills (see Wrightson 190-196). The trials of Job in tandem with the jests of Scoggin, Court Fool of legendary wit, must have lit up the boy's mind in a time when the secular monument of national language was not yet Shakespeare, but still the play *Everyman* (Rae 18).

Even if she could not read, Morton's mother and "hers" lived in a region remarked upon for its greater-in-general "sense of individual identity" (Underdown 103). "Women appear to have been aware of the tensions and contradictions between subordination and their work," writes Susan Dwyer Amussen. "How was a woman supposed to be effective in ordering her servants around or bargaining at the market one moment, and a meek, obedient woman the next?" Amussen finds that "as a result, women limited subordination as much as possible" (53); and this maneuvering *within* the existing society rather than reforming it---except with his own wry suggestions---was Thomas' habitual way in life. "...I will go the surest way to work, at first...[and] see how others are answered in the like kind" (*Canaan* 189).

Given their social station and the "outdoor" nature of Devonshire and West Country culture (more below), we may imagine Mrs. Morton a full rusticating member of the "rovings" and perambulations made round the countryside by entire social circles; feasting on the "venison pastie" she had processed with other women from their hunters' kills, and "spectating" various field sports exclusive to men (Longrigg and others cited below). However much even "old England" and "new" demanded that she be above all "a visible model of submission" to patriarchal authorities of home, church and state (Belsey 159), this was a world filled with women who pushed expressive boundaries. For the whole period of Morton's lifetime from the 1560s to the 1640s was, in terms of gender, one of intense concern about so-called "unruly" women.

If Morton servants were visible with their "sleights," would Lady Morton and her circle conceal their remarks upon the pretensions of their men? Especially in accounts by "reformers" who object to it (such as the voluminous *Anatomie of Abuses* by Philip Stubbes during Thomas' boyhood, qtd. below), women appear to have been very much felt and heard. Of course these records are mostly in the hands of men. But across the age-groups women's presences fill records *pro* and *con* with their parts in every community activity, as readers will notice in the firsthand sources that speak below. Not least, the shared labors of processing food one year of harvest into the next, and women's daily and practical lessons for growing children (including their shares of public ceremony from church to Maypole), were the very ground and beginning of social life for the majority of English males. Then as now, the primary messages bestowed mother-to-child either helped or hindered all later human and other relationships. Holding hands in the Rogation-Day parades around the boundaries of their crop-fields, people shouted and sang, across the anarchic off-beats of a boy's drum, the refrain

> Unite, and unite, now let us unite
> for Summer is a-comin', today
> And whither we are going, we all will unite
> In the merry morning of May....
> (from "The Padstow Mayers' Song")

But, where the 1540s and 1550s had often cheered "the speaking female," such as Anne Askew and others who shared the Protestant struggle to break free of Rome, now the great body of pressures from church, state, and "popular press" (in so-called "conduct books" for "proper" English women) advised that woman be as silent and obedient as possible. She was "respected but not equal" (Amussen). "Women were placed at the margins of the social body, while at the same time, in the new model of marriage they were uneasily, silently at the heart of the private realm which was its microcosm and its centre" (Belsey 150). Perhaps it should not surprise that Thomas' mother speaks "personally" nowhere in the smallest of clues around him, except in his small patience with what he calls the "effeminate" person, who might be uneasy "surrounded" by Native Americans (12). In Thomas' use of the word, he implies that a person is enfeebled by confined domesticity (see *Canaan* Note 46). As he grew up, this was more and more the approved expectation of women, as one of many attempts to close what historian David Starkey called the "Pandora's Box" opened up by the Reformation (15).

There is remarkable consistency in the way Morton notices and responds to women in plight. If Thomas was "the son of a Souldier," how much happy domesticity can we expect his parents to have known? His father may well have died young, especially if he saw action "worthy" the family's advancement by royal gratitude. Even in safe "demobilization" on a bit of land, perhaps he left

Mrs. Morton a widow; for Thomas and *Canaan* are certainly taken with widows, and other grieving women who have pasts antecedent to his own. Somewhere in the mysteries of Thomas Morton's childhood was a family of women that enabled in him a good deal of warmth, wit, learning and human sympathy.[6]

These traits complemented Thomas' confidence in his skills as an outdoorsman. The subtleties of fowling, the stamina needed for the deer-chase, the aristocratic delicacies of falconry must have come early in his life, they are in play throughout *New English Canaan*; and this correlates with a typical gentry-boyhood amid the relative wilds of the West Country, including Cornwall, Somerset, Devon and Hampshire. In Morton's day this was still a forested region in places, the land sloping up and down a gentle hill-country of stream-cut valleys and wood-pasture, where partridge, deer and rabbit led the chase. Mysterious Neolithic and Celtic barrows, hill-forts, caves, "kerms" of standing stone were as much a part of these rolling moorlands as the natural granite outcrops irrupting from the ground. Fortified manor houses, then-abandoned monasteries, market-sites connected by roads (or "tracks") bespoke the English ages of a land already thoroughly "inscribed" with human legend and history. Not least of these were the worn pillars of stone whose Latin marked the paths of Roman Emperor Vespasian's 2nd Roman Legion, and his West Country conquests of 50 A.D. (Whitlock 106; Fox Chs. 1, 2, 7). Persons interested in or

---

[6] If we can trust at all the legal testimony treated in Ch. 4, the group of kinswomen around Morton's wife-to-be, the widow Alice Miller, invited him after some time as her attorney to "come and take a wife" and "live amongst them." (Note Amussen 53 that in this period widows were increasingly careful about marrying a second time, once widowhood had endowed them with more financial and other freedom.)

While typical West Country communities clearly practiced the *charivari*, skimmington (public humiliation "parades" etc.) and even revived the ducking-stool for unruly sexual behaviors (mostly women's), compare Morton's treatment of the grieving "goodly creature of incontinency" or "Doe of Virginia" in Canaan Book 3. His compassion and approach to "Scilla/Niobe" in his 1627 "Poem" as she grieves for her (Native American) children and/or spouse is also within this pattern---as is his giving voice to the "spirit" of Sachem Chikatawbak's mother, in her anger against English "wild" people in Book 1.

educated to the land around them could come of age rather comfortable with the idea of authentic civilizations different from, and older than, their own.

The land-tenants' homes tended to cluster about the greater manor houses, these well-separated from neighbors and church, forming very small communities surrounded by barley and corn, by heath-pastures known for good cream and for the beef they supplied to sailor-crews. "Wet moors," heather and bog, marshes full of birds ran along the region's river-mouths and up into deep wooded valleys. This was a countryside of "outdoor people" as long-evinced by their shire's Celtic name ("Devon" means "people of the land"; Hoskin *Devon* 9). Though the gentry with their tenants stood strongly Royalist in the 1640s Civil War (Oppenheim 64), male self-sufficiency was prized. Morton's generation paid homage to ancestors and contemporaries who resisted outside plunderers, from the Saxons and Danes of the early Middle Ages to the Algerian corsairs still raiding Devon seacoasts in 1617. Conservative Catholics had held their own awhile against the violent imposition of Anglican (early English Protestant) religious changes: for two years in fact (1547-9), the farmers, laborers and some gentry of Cornwall and the region had mounted "The Western Rebellion" against the new English Prayer Book and the removal of their sacred images, old rituals and Latin mass (Hoskins 233). Although since then, many a Protestant innovation had been welcomed, satirical folktales and rhymes kept alive some disdain for all outside authorities (Whitlock 76, 176).

A strong social value of "neighborliness" held families and communities together (below), but adventuring took thousands of these Devon men into maritime, Irish and American "wilderness" posts by the 1620s. The "West Country Adventurers" beginning to colonize Ireland in the decade before Thomas' birth were reading Peter Martyr's translated *De Orbe Novo* and hoping to profit by Spanish mistakes in "policy" (Canny 593). Spirited historian Banks boasted that Devon men were exploring when the "weavers of the East" counties were still "arguing supplies" (*York* 68-9). Until one came of age, however, there were local adventures born of each season on the land, in the markets, on the "greens" or commons of the towns. "Barley-Break" partners with linked arms charged and chased their opponents through the surrounding fields and, as they got older, into the woods. There was "concern" in the 1580s over "masterless" serving-girls, who found one position or another in the homes of more than one family at a time (Underdown 37). And Stubbes (97): "Every boy huggles his pretty pussy, and runs-up a cottage...." Whether 1594 found teenage-Thomas a "groundling" at the theatre watching amorous London stage-play between Jupiter and Ganymede in Marlowe's *Dido of Carthage* (or whether he read it), the drama's open sexuality impressed him so that, years later, he found "the like" nothing harmful among his fellow-planters in New England (*Canaan* 137).

Most importantly to a boy here, "[H]e was a poor gentleman in fact who could not discourse learnedly of...the hunt" (Kelso 157). Morton casually shares some of his lifelong pleasures at it: sitting quietly at sunrise in his "blind" or "stand" while his well-fed dogs chase the deer to him (72); blasting away at sanderlings and shorebirds in seasons of what were called "blood sports" (63-4); inexplicably "admiring" certain creatures, as he later would American crows, "what should be the cause" (66); extending individuality itself, at times, to animals (he describes his colonial "household" with the remarkable phrase "nine persons, besides dogs" (86).[7]

---

[7] Devon people were respected for their knowledge and breeding of various dogs, for ex. the Talbot for hunting deer, the smaller Gascon for rabbits, and the "bracket" (like an Irish Beagle) whose small size helped it "smeuse" small game in the undergrowth (Longrigg 8-11, 27-9, 49). The "mastiffs" eventually used in America were bred for hunting boar and as guard-dogs.
See Peterson 4-45 for photos etc. of various matchlock, snap-hance, new "dog-lock" and other firearms eventually to play their part in Morton's American story.

As noted, the social spirit of the region called for expansive display when whole retinues of family and servants with their Devon stag-hounds roved the wild lands, hunting here, encamping and feasting there in the outdoors: both the "gentle bloods" and land-tenants relished the wild Red Deer always troubling their crops (in hard weather they stayed home and fed upon stocks of Fallow Deer kept in "parks"). Longrigg and Cummins paint lively portraits of these outings including troops of ladies in full feasting-regalia, their headdresses quite askew by journey's end. "Venison pastie" was the usual main feast, one's hosts managed some good French wines if they could, and the "socially ambitious" were eager to be heard shouting the latest "bastard French" to their hawks and hounds (Longrigg 46; Cummins Ch. 1-4).

Dozens of popular "practical guides" were available to supplement field experience *and* begin a boy's pleasures with reading, such as works on everything from farming to fowling by the prolific Gervase Markham, including *Hunger's Prevention* (full list of his works in Bennett 155-7). This poet and outdoorsman who by 1613 even wrote himself into authority on "proper English roles" for "husbandman and housewife," wove together the skills of the landsman and the learned:

> [A] skilfull Angler ought to bee a generall Scholler, and seen in all the liberall sciences, as a Gramarian, to know how...to Write out discourse of his Art in true tearmes, eyther without affection or rudeness. He should have sweetnesse of speech, to perswade....He should have strength of arguments, to defend, and maintaine his profession against envy or slander. He should have knowledge in the Sunne, Moone, and Starres....He would not be unskilfull in Musique, that whensoever eyther melancholy, heavinesse of thought, or the perturbations of his own fancie stirreth up sadnesse in him, he may remoove the same....He must be full of love, both to his pleasure, and to his neighbour....Then must he be liberall, and not working only for his own belly, as if it could never be satisfied: he must with much cheerfulnesse bestow the fruits of his skill amongst his honest neighbours, who being partners of his gaine, will doubly renowne his tryumph...
> (*The Pleasures of Princes; or, Good*

Mens Recreations, 15-17)

Kelso shares from Sir Thomas Cockaine's *Short Treatise of Hunting* (1591) to explain why sports were more than games to "chase away the dumps and refresh the body":

> Hunters by their continuall travaile, painfull labour, often watching, and enduring of hunger, of heate and of cold, are much enabled above others to the service of their Prince and country in the warres, having their bodies for the most part by reason of their continual exercise in much better health than other men have, and their minds also by this honest re-creation the more fit and the better disposed to all other good exercises....

Thomas was trained up for the English gentleman's highest social duty, to be strongly prepared for any "exercise" in the service of Crown and country. English educator Roger Ascham devoted a treatise to the virtues of handling the bow; and many other humanist writers on the ideals of education, with influence that reached into West Country grammar schools and tutorships (Dowling Ch. 6), concurred with Continental views like Michel de Montaigne's:

> It is not sufficient to make his minde strong, his muskles also must be strengthened: the minde is overborne if it be not seconded....All sports and exercises shall be a part of his study: running, wrestling, musicke, dancing, hunting, and managing of armes, and horses....[For] it is not a mind, it is not a body that we erect, but it is a man, and we must not make two parts of him. (159, 175: 1580: John Florio trans., London 1603)

The rigors required of body, mind and spirit required to learn the natures of landscape and animals, their rhythms and habits, rooted Morton's sensibility in a rugged self-confidence and independence. To comprehend the individual who acted as he did in America and created *New English Canaan*, we must not over-separate his "philosophy" as derived from literature and what he calls his "disposition." He tells us (with fiction added of course) that his "undaunted spirit [had been] nursed with meat/Such as the Centaurs gave their babes to eat" (152), most likely meaning that *he* believed that his early training(s) from subtle and skilled teachers of the hunt stood him in good stead; that he was proud, but as was proper and expected of his social place, in Aristotle's sense of "the mean." (The scholars' best example was pride itself, which "ideally" stood between vanity, an excess of character, and false or needless humility, a defect of it).

Latin was still in such use that a boy might have noticed in his first tastes of Cicero these echoes between his experiences of nature and the social values schooled into him: ancient ideas of "civilization" were rooted in understandings of "man" as an animal, "fitted by nature to come together" in groups, communities and states (*Good and Evil* 65, Wright trans.).

Hawking and falconry, seldom begun before the 10th birthday, were high challenges in patience with a "pet" whose will remained its own (Longrigg 34). This hardened but versatile maturity could help a man render his "Prince" (as Queen Elizabeth was known) the full measure of duty, and they underwrite many values and criteria of judgment in Morton's book. He admires "perfection" in "the use of the senses," "impatience confuted by example" (119), concern for servants and hunting-animals (63, 77), the use of "waters" and herbs (Book 2), and the ability to improvise for survival (87, 168). Not only is some of his sharpest satire reserved for men both inept and sanctimonious amid the natural world (124, 125-7, 148, 166): his voice is in part that of a hunter taught that food is not a weapon of political ideology, that the role of provider means responsibility for other lives. He repeatedly pays attention to whether or not the people around him are well-fed: he is indignant when later New England rivals fail to let "unsanctified" or "carnal" men like himself bring in "a little fresh victuals" to sickly new arrivals who are not witnessed members of church congregations: he resents his lifetime's trend of insults to traditions of "neighborly" reciprocity, not only from Puritans who have "made use of his [own house] in the like case" (181), but as well from quite secular Englishmen of Weymouth who cheat each other at every opportunity (*Canaan* Book 3).

"Mine Host, that loved good hospitality" he styled himself---This was to signal his readers that Morton hailed from a variety of English culture long-rooted in neighborly traditions, customary rules of reciprocity that (as in many less urban parts of the world) worked to ease and refine life, amid the demands of gaining sustenance from a sparse landscape. At least as old (in Europe) as ancient Greece, this kind of social code was "said to be the darling of Religion" (180): "Charity" became "indeed the mark of a good Christian" and the bond of a generation of people who came of age under Elizabeth, such as the anonymous "old Souldier of the Queen's as the Proverb is" who kept Morton from bodily harm at a crucial moment (146). According to a number of historians, this code helped to reconcile the folk-traditional and the Christian aspects of the world shaping young Morton in the 1580s. The labors and rewards of cooperation were obvious enough in the cyclical labors of a farming village, while "communal feasting" (Fowler 8) was "no mere fabricated link with Golden Age feasts of the gods, but Christian practice, related to the Eucharist," and in obedience to Old Testament strictures that "the stranger shall eat and be satisfied" (*Deuteronomy* 14:29, 26:12).[8] Devon historian and antiquary John Hooker commended another

---

[8] As in Morton's case, community values as primary as food-sharing are often associated with women and/or expressed in feminine imagery: "Charity" is derived from practices represented in innumerable images of "three women"---the Fates, the "Carites" etc.---found in all the archaeology, folklore and literature of the West. In Morton's day they appeared (for ex.) as "Three sisters, the daughters of Jupiter, whose names are Aglaia, Thalia, Euphrosyne... Whom the Poets feigned to be the Goddesses of all bounty and comeliness,....to wit, that men first ought to be gracious and bountiful to others freely, then to receive benefits at other men's hands courteously, and thirdly to requite them thankfully..." (gloss to Spenser's *The Shepherd's Calendar*, Maclean ed. 441).

Devon man, Sir Walter Ralegh, for his public-spirited uses of wealth and service too (Strathmannn 24).[9]

By Thomas' adolescence in the late 1580s, however, the massive economic and social shifts that marked the 17th century were beginning to dissolve the order of "Old England" which had emerged from the medieval manor system and now characterized the majority of English towns, guilds and parishes in Morton's day (Hutton 261). The voice of Sir Thomas More's *Utopia*, published over 60 years before, could still speak for young Thomas' times:

> Your sheep...that used to be so gentle and eat so little. Now they are becoming so greedy and so fierce that they devour the men themselves, so to speak. For...the nobility and gentlemen...are not content with the old rents which their lands yielded....They leave no land for cultivation, they enclose all the land for pastures.... As though forests and game preserves were not already taking up too much land....The tenants are turned out, and by trickery or main force....And if they beg, they are thrown into prison as idle vagabonds....[*Book I*]

Furthermore, this "society in which ritual and festival were utilized for many different purposes at many different levels" (Hutton) began to encounter "a direct ideological challenge from early Protestantism," on issues often related to "festive culture" or "sports": these ranged from games of "bowls" on the village green (Elizabeth shared in annual May-games till 1602), to fundraising "church ales" and the high public pageants of the cities' Lord Mayors' shows, with their preChristian allegorical figures tricked out for performing "street-theater." Many such activities became linked in the more ardent Christian mind with threats to the social order and/or power structure. Willison cites a representative example in "Sabbatarian" complaints that "Whitsun-ales" were degrading Christian

---

[9] Cicero *On Duties* 549: " It is exceedingly adventageous...for those who desire to exercise power justly and honorably, to build up their popularity and influence among other peoples by entertaining their representatives."

properties, and ideals, by carrying inebriated festivity into sacred precincts, people "in bright scarves and ribbons, their legs gartered with bells, riding hobbyhorses and dragons...into church and up the aisle piping and playing," with onlookers standing up on pews "to cheer and laugh" (462: see also Fletcher 89's list of other typical behaviors in church, which included card-games, spouse-beating, and births of puppies).

As Thomas grew up, England's population almost doubled between 1550 and 1650, and not a few years of serious crop-failure aggravated social and economic problems. England's need for trade and its lack of high-value resources turned investors toward even more enclosure of public or common lands for the wool industry's grazing of sheep, and the highways and country became notoriously full of "masterless" people displaced from all stations of life as the consequences mounted. Conflicts intensified toward political struggle as class-lines reformed themselves: at the higher end, aristocratic elites began to manifest various forms of "retreat," "down endless corridors of secrecy toward...illusory repositories of privacy" (seen most clearly, as cultural historian Patricia Fumerton shows, in elaborate "privatizing" trends in country-house styles, in ever-more-costly court functions that squandered government wealth, in "power" displays of conspicuous consumption by increasingly exclusive and bankrupt social circles). In one sense, this culminated in the emergence of something Morton (as well as Fumerton) remarked, the post-Elizabethan emergence of a more "selfish" form of selfhood whose outward expression was the cannibalistic profit-motive of nascent capitalism (see Chs. 7 and 9; Note 158). Such were the "inner conditions" of England, turning to "explore" America.

Morton's middling gentry were finding the new mercantilism useful toward their own advancement: there was "social and intellectual withdrawal" from the "lower orders" here too (Fletcher/Stevenson 12). Servants and the laboring members of communities were increasingly "banished" from traditional places in the feasting hall and other stations, and public hospitality was mourned in verse that once had celebrated magnanimous relation.[10] The root cause of all this, and whether complaints were mostly wishful thinking about an "organic" England that had never been, is debated in detail in studies by Marcus, Ingram, Petegorsky, Hill, Girouard, and Raymond Williams; but Hutton's insistence on a convergence between fears of "popular disorder" and "novel economic patterns" seems reasonable (261). Morton's share of this withdrawal appeared in later remarks about "the illiterate multitude" and in his scolding of "our English beggars" (48); but he also offered thoughts on why such people were "not able to transport themselves" from "stuffed" jails to better conditions. He never quite became a "gentleman Ranter" (like many a contemporary studied by Friedman 192-216), but Morton told his readers what he knew of the workings of power (multiple examples in *Canaan* 155-169).

The cultural air around him began to fill with strident voices of reform, resistance and nostalgia. There were as many "schools" then as now trying to locate the issue of the period in economics, religion, politics etc.; but there can be no doubt that the very way in which people saw themselves and lived their daily lives was being critiqued and "re-formed," in conflicts whose terms set the stage for Morton's conflicts with Puritan New England. As people defended their traditional values, Wrightson says,

> It was not so much that the people stood outside the world of orthodox religion....They thought of themselves as Christians and valued some of the services of the church greatly ....[But] they were content to take their standards of behavior not

---

[10] Even Longrigg's sources on the social fabric of "the hunt" suggest that the "socially ambitious" would "no longer dine with their uncouth retainers[,] but at table by the fire" (32-3). Religious and social practices were often near-indistinguishable: as Guibbory (*Ceremony and Community* Ch. 1) puts it, "[C]onflict over religious worship involved two competing ideas of order---one based on unity, wholeness, and hierarchical integration, the other on division, opposition, and difference."

> from the law of God contained in Scripture, but from the more familiar canons of good neighborliness. (204-5)

As Ingram remarks on the day's close relation between "devotion and disturbance" (117), neighbors might use church communion-service to help settle a quarrel, or avoid the service altogether to preserve at least the "quietness" that seemed like "communal harmony." (Morton's gloss to his text on the "need" for one race to dominate "the other" in America tried to "justify" this with the ideal of "quietness," 113). But according to Hill (*World* 59) and Fletcher/Stevenson (131, 233), Morton's West Country was perhaps the most energetic region holding onto folk-practices and staging near-riotous protests against "reform." These "wood pasture regions contained communities in which people had a stronger sense of individual identity" that was generally noted elsewhere (Underdown "Taming" 128-31): they also preferred to handle offenses against the community in a social-ritual rather than legal or religious way, including the wild symbolic procession called the skimmington, in which (for ex.) a wife who cuckolded or beat her husband was paraded, ridiculed by citizens and perhaps "washed" via the ducking-stool. Morton's Book 3 chapters on a woman dubbed "the Barren Doe" both reflect and depart from such practices.

Where, then, did neighborliness and some reformers' values part company in young Morton's world?

> ...The young men and maids, old men and wives, run gadding overnight to the woods, groves, hills, and mountains, where they spend all night in pleasant pastimes...and lord over their pastimes and sports [is] namely, Satan, prince of Hell. But the chiefest jewel they bring from thence is their May-pole, which they bring home with great veneration....This stinking idol, rather, which is covered all over with flowers and herbs...[is borne into villages] with two or three hundred men, women and children, following it with great devotion. And this being reared up...they...set up summer halls, bowers and arbors hard by it; and then they fall to dance about it, like as the heathen people did....
> (Philip Stubbes' 1583 *Anatomie of Abuses* [modernized] 149)

Against such a reformer's depiction and accusations (which especially accused females of abandoning Christian sexual mores in the "woods"), came voices such as this young woman's of 1623 Wiltshire, who complained that whenever her village's new Puritan-affiliated minister

> takes his green book in hand we shall have such a Deal of bibble babble that I am weary to hear it and I can then sit down in my seat and take a good nap...for he speaks against us for our dancing....We had a good parson here before but now we have a puritan....(qtd. in Johnson 295)

Certainly the "hard" economic and social dislocations were driven by equally empirical dynamics; but more often than not, the social conflicts round young Morton found expression in moralistic terms:

> It is all one, as if they had said, bawdry, heathenrie, paganry ...is equal with the word of God; or that the Devil is equipolent with the Lord...For do they not nourish idleness?....Do they not draw the people from...godly lectures and sermons?....When the church of God shall be bare and empty; and those that will never come at sermons, will flow thither apace....This showeth they are not of God, who refuse to hear his word....(Stubbes 144)

Out of this would come *Canaan*'s many satires against evangelical presumptions, as well as Morton's "unheroic" but canny responses to their social effects. In one chapter's secular anticlimax, he foils a plot to maroon him in New England by pouring out among "good protestants"[11] his "Claret sparkling neat,"

---

[11] *Canaan* contains many unique reversals of terms which others use so literally in these conflicts. Andrews (332n6) cites a personal letter received from C.E. Banks after the latter's search in England for records of Morton's past, and relates that Banks had "acquired further documents" about Morton (the Chancery suits explored below), one of which noted that Morton wore a "pectoral cross" "as souvenir of a friend." (A pectoral cross is "an ornamented plate, cloth or other decoration worn on the breast" {OED}: sometimes a piece of armor or a "coarse linen next the skin," they were worn by Catholic bishops and abbots beginning in the 16th century.) "Morton was perhaps a Catholic," Banks remarked.

Amid other statements of Morton's such as that he found "Christians" (not merely "Separatists") lacking in charitable virtues, that "Hell is in Westminster" etc., perhaps he was most of all a "re-interpreter" of the cultural forms passed down to him (as his education exhorted---next chapter). Since the West Country had mounted its full-scale Rebellion, Morton's home-region likely bestowed his most basic "scepticism" toward cultural forms enforced by outside and distant would-be authorities. His ally the "scholar and traveler" Sir Christopher Gardiner, later found "without" Puritan morality, also wore a scapula bearing a "Papal order" of knighthood (FBH2: 137n1). The wearing of Catholic symbols by ostensible Church of England Protestants may and sharing with them the tasty, nourishing virtues of shellfish roasted fresh on a Cape Anne beach (117). In the lyrics surrounding Morton's youth we hear the "Song" to come in New England:

> Let charming beauty's health go round, in whom celestial joys are found,
> and may confusion still pursue the senseless woman-hating crew;
> and they that woman's health deny, down among the dead men
>   let them lie...
> In smiling Bacchus' joys I'll roll, deny no pleasure to my soul;
> Let Bacchus' health round quickly move, for Bacchus is a friend to love....

Below in Wrightson's efficient summary (205) are Christian divines' own complaints circa 1600, when Morton was about 26, or 37 years before *Canaan*. Based on the words of Puritan preacher William Perkins, who so influenced later New England churches,

> 'So long as they live in ignorance,' wrote Perkins, the people lived 'either of custome, or example, or necessitie, as beasts doe, and not of faith'....It allowed people to believe 'that...God hath provided [an earthly] salve for every sore'...that fornication was 'but the trick of youth'; that 'a man may do with his owne what he will and make as much of it as he can'; that working, sporting, or revelling on Sundays was not offensive to God; that drunkenness and alehouse haunting were 'good fellowship'; that the upholding of popular festivities of manifestly pagan origin was a thing indifferent; that sober godliness was 'affected preciseness.'

The language ("a salve for every sore," "a thing indifferent") foreshadows many of the terms of Morton's collision with New England Puritans. But the West Country was not what many Parliamentarians and ministers' documents claimed, "a dark corner of the land" lost in "ignorance." The attempt to uphold "hospitality" for "all comers" as a value across lines of class, economics and ideology was an attempt---like Scepticism in philosophy---to trim extremes in behavior, to avoid radical ruptures of the social fabric (Popkin finds that sceptics and "atheists" were simply "more anti-Protestant than anti-religious," 96). This

---

represent a holding-on to tradition in the face of radical changes. Morton and *Canaan* mention many a saint but they are all safely within the Anglican liturgical year.

meshed with other approaches to the crises confronting England, such as the Anglican Church attempt to stabilize "the body" on a theological level by way of Adiaphorism; a doctrine deeming the liturgical forms of Christian worship "indifferent" or "alterable according to circumstance," as long as the fundamentals of the creed were met (Hall 151; Blunt 11). In other words, "indifference" was not a synonym for either "atheism" or even anti-Christianity, but a common or mainstream antidote to extremism in the country, the court and the court of law.[12]

More than a decade after Christopher Hill's scholarly explorations of voices from "the lower fifty percent" of England's largely disenfranchised population, studies continue to find that in general the "rural populace" "took from the church and its rituals what they wanted. The place of Christianity as such in their lives "was only tenuous, but their reinterpretations of the church's holidays, its rites and the role of its clergy boosted the forms and structure of popular culture" (Fletcher/Stevenson 9; Marsh 189; Ingram 113; Harris 21). Perhaps, for all the independent individuality desired in the young West Country gentleman, that greater value of "quietness" meant even more. On his first page of *Canaan* Morton frames the entire work within an argument for "moderation, and discretion" in English and American behavior---and by Book 3 these are exactly the two values transgressed, to comic-catastrophic result, by the

---

[12] Greenblatt *Renaissance Self-Fashioning* 248-9: Those who sought a "legitimate release from dogma and constraint" in the "pleasurable satisfaction of desire, even within marriage," were condemned under "tenacious" Augustinian tradition as "mortal sinners who exclude God." No wonder that later Morton's would-be plantation so easily appealed to people, where already "wanton speeches" and "foolish dalliance" with one's own lawful spouse were conceived by Puritans as "play[ing] the adulterer...by inordinate affection" towards anything other than God (George Haskins, *Law and Authority in Early Massachusetts* 141-151).

ardent minister-cum-frontiersman "Master Bubble." "In haste and single-handed" (124), he lunges for control of everything that crosses his "mazed" path.[13]

By the 1630s England's extreme (Civil War) polarities meant either Royalist traditionalism or Puritan cultural revolution. Some people, though, before the crisis, did attempt "reinterpretations," such as poet and pamphleteer Nicholas Breton with his 1626 *Fantastickes*, in whose prose-poems of daily life, Christian aspiration and the folk-mythologies of nature could both contribute to religious, social and personal well-being. Other people, like New England's wry mild-mannered Samuel Maverick, a West Country "Church of England man" and "old comer" since 1623, simply tried to live out the older code despite losing odds. Maverick, a "gentleman of good estate" whose values included trying to induce his African "servants" to "breed," was by 1638 nonetheless dubbed "the only hospitable man in all the country, giving entertainment to all comers *gratis*" (Josselyn TV12). He was also nearly the only man of the eventual "new neighborhood" with a good word to say about "Mine Host of Ma-re Mount."

But there were other sides indeed to Thomas Morton: the gentleman outdoorsman also received tutoring and/or schooling such that his "familiarity with classic authors" was at his fingertips throughout his life and the pages of his book (AC345n1). We turn to see how his body, following Montaigne's phrase above, was seconded by his mind.

---

[13] Compare another Devon man bound for America, Sir Walter Ralegh, with his own "discontent hovering between faith and skepticism" (Greenblatt *Ralegh* 101). When faced with a minister's inability to define "what is that sperituall & immortall substance breathed into man," Ralegh was told that "demonstracion...was against the nature of a man's soul[,] beinge a spirit" ---at which Ralegh, just like Morton trying to eat his dinner with "Master Bubble" (*Canaan* 124), replied that he "wished that grace might be sayed; for that quoth he is better than this disputaction" (*Ralegh* 100-101).

2: *Education*

> The most evident token and apparent sign of true wisdom
> is a constant and unconstrained rejoicing, whose estate is like unto
> all things above the Moon, that is, ever clear, always bright....Is
> it not [Philosophy] that cleareth all storms of the mind? And
> teacheth misery, famine and sickness to laugh? Not by reason of
> some imaginary epicycles, but by natural and palpable reasons....
> She loveth life; she delights in beauty, in glory, and in health.
> But her proper and particular office is first to know how to use
> such goods temperately....
> --Montaigne, "On the Institution and
> Education of Children" (1580/1585; 3: 70-72)

In the 1500s scholarly learning ("the smell of the lamp") was still generally despised, as the impractical opposite of a knight's or gentleman-soldier's crucial importance to the community.[14] But the century of Morton's birth saw gradual change in this. As war to some degree "ceased to be the gentleman's chief profession [and] he was challenged to help solve the complicated problems of an increasingly complicated world" (Kelso 116), Europe's and England's nobility began to look to the achievers of "civil honors" to guide and maintain their traditional powers over public affairs and matters of state. (20 years of war with Spain had also ended in 1605: see Grafton/Jardine xiv, Dowling 179, Stone *Past and Present* on these gradual changes in attitude, helped by the exemplary support of Henry VIII and the English throne after him.)

Humanist scholars and educators---from the Spanish Juan Luis Vives' lectures at Oxford, to the writings of Sir Thomas Elyot (*The Governour* 1531), of

---

[14] See "America's First Poetry in English" here for much more detail on conceptions of literature, poetry, and poets around young Morton and to which he responded.

Erasmus, Colet, Linacre and Sir Thomas More (to name a very few)---these teachers, laboring through the decades-long expansion of the system of Universities and Inns of Court, virtually transformed the century's idea of the basis of human civilization, the place of learning, and its potential.

At the heart of the *studium humanitatis* was the Roman philosopher Cicero's concept that "eloquence," the persuasive command of language, knowledge and ideas, had alone sufficed to "gather scattered mankind together in one place, to transplant human beings from a barbarous life in the wilderness to a civilized social system...to equip them with laws and judicial safeguards and civic rights" (*De Oratore* 1: 9, 151).[15] And while the higher nobility and courtiers began to adopt the various skills necessary to this fashionable "self-fashioning" for courtly advancement, whose principles were laid out in Baldasar Castiglione's *The Courtier* (English trans. 1561) and Robert Peterson's *Il Galateo* (1576), "middling" gentlemen too were exhorted by "conduct books" to "own" their learning:

> Alas, you will be but ungentle Gentlemen, if you be no Scholars: you will do your Prince but simple service, you will stande your country but in slender stead, you will bring yourselves but to small preferment, if you be no Scholars....Therefore...confess it, profess it, embrace it, honor it; for it is it which honoureth you, it is only it which maketh you men, it is only it which maketh you Gentlemen. (Preface to Sir Stefano Guazzo, *The Civile Conversation*, G. Pettie, trans. 1581)

Learning was now "justified" at least as it bettered one's service to the Prince; but the student's boldness and independence were prized by the most respected of these educators, his (and sometimes her) becoming, as Ascham's *Schoolmaster* 16 said it, "never afraid to ask" questions, the more to match the

---

[15] Grafton's *New Worlds, Ancient Texts* (90) and Greene's *The Light in Troy* (171) describe the birth of humanism as a function of the new European "dialogue with antiquity" at the heart of the Renaissance. But ancient Europe's definition of eloquence bore within it a concept of "civilization" with catastrophic implications for Native North and South America.

"vassaile" to his increasingly complex duties. Just as "the highest value in all serious writing" lay in its *inventio* or *use* of its wealth of skills, so the pupil with potential to become the "agent" of the Crown was to be allowed the "freedom to recombine spontaneously the elements gleaned and internalized" from books and training, to the end that "we will not merely follow our masters...we will be able to surpass them" (Greene *Troy* 173: on humanist education in England see also Halpern 37; Schoeck; Kohl).[16] Guazzo (81) admired the "great discretion" he saw in some parents and educators who, "in their children's infancye, [would] begin to embolden them before their betters, and to make them talk with them: whereby they [came] to have a good audacitie, and to be resolute in their behavior."

Ascham too struggled to transform medieval models based in "butcherly fear" (14). His recommended methods---"of good understanding the matter...cheerful admonishing, and heedful amending of faults, never leaving behind just praise for well-doing" (16)---seem to have echo in the poise of *Canaan*'s prose, whose author had only "genious" or genial things to say about his early years. *Canaan*'s many astute examples of people creating their own difficulties, trapped in violent farce by their own assumptions---these resemble an Ascham-like habit of mind, a high awareness or caution with the chain of human cause and effect.

Human beings were conceived as fundamentally imitators. Hence the master's "humanity" was crucial: better to encourage boldness and pride in ability, for a student with "overmuch fearing" might be driven to "some

---

[16] This attitude, some critics claim, was only for the already-elite: Grafton/Jardine caution that "In the Renaissance...the price of collaboration in the renewal of art and literature was collaboration in the constriction of society and polity" (xiv). Queen Elizabeth re-issued *The Homilies* or *Certain Sermons...* to be ritually repeated every week at compulsory church services "for the simple people," as the cover put it (Alfred J. Hart, ed.); which went much to remind the public that even an "evil" Prince was better than rebellion or no government at all.

misorderly shift...to beguile you much and himself more" (16). "Therefore," Ascham warned, "to love or to hate...to good or to bad, ye shall have as ye use a child in his youth" (35).

So the forces began to gather round young Thomas that would harden him further and make a serviceable man of the boy still learning the cycles of nature and agricultural time, the ways of neighborly "quietness" and revel:

> --*Strike it up, tabor, and pipe us a favor*
> *Thou shalt be well-paid for thy labor...*
> *I mean to spend my shoe-soles to dance about the Maypole*
> *I shall be blithe and brisk, leap-and-skip, hop-and-trip*
> *Turn about, in a rout, until very weary weary joints*
> *can scarce frisk...*
> (syncopated madrigal "Strike It Up, Tabor")

The Anglican Church was another world of annual cycles, one revolving round the fixed date of Jesus Christ's birth on December 25, and the other chief one (His Resurrection) determined yearly by the moon at springtime's Easter. The Church calendar and *The Book of Common Prayer* (1549) invested every day and practice with The Bible's Old and New Testament symbolisms, with sanctified ceremonies for feast days of martyrs and significant events of Christ's ministry. Morton's remarking the return of New England's cranes on Saint David's Day (March 1: 64) tells something of his mind becoming poised between natural and philosophical worlds.

Surely the habits of mind promoted by humanistic study and literacy added to Thomas' enjoyment of the elegant order, the shared enthusiasm of Anglican Church membership. (*Canaan*'s droll critique of Puritan "Separatist" oratory tells much of his appreciation for public speakers and for Church service as a place of high culture as well as religion.) In the season of Lent in anticipation of Christ's Passion, and on crop-protecting Rogation Days (*B. C. Prayer* Guilbert ed. 148), "The Great Litany" was recited by whole communities in "call and response" as they made their processions under the sky:

> O God the Father, Creator of heaven and earth,
> *Have mercy upon us---*
> O God the Son, Redeemer of the world,
> *Have mercy upon us---*
> ...From all blindness of heart; from pride, vainglory, and hypocrisy; from envy, hatred, and malice; and from all want of charity,
> *Good Lord, deliver us---*
> ...From lightning and tempest; from earthquake, fire, and flood; from plague, pestilence, and famine,
> *Good Lord, deliver us---*
> ...From all oppression, conspiracy, and rebellion; from violence, battle, and murder; and from dying...unprepared,
> *Good Lord, deliver us---*

As the confinements of book-learning bore down on the boy, there were yet further worlds of meaning to escape into and absorb, not least the traveling troupes of mummers' shows featuring dramatic last-moment calls upon ancient "Aesculapius," the miracle-working healer of dying heroes; the mighty deeds of the Nine Worthies (seen in wall-hangings and paintings old as the Middle Ages) performed in "street threater"; or if one was fortunate, a home-bound Devon sailor's own half-boasting account of that far-off Newfoundland (now being lectured about at Oxford, no less, by the colony-promoter Richard Hakluyt). Those seas where the codfish swamped the boats had only just swallowed Sir Humphrey Gilbert himself (1584, as Thomas turned 7). With his ship, overladen with weaponry, had sunk the "new" continent's first would-be poet in English, the promising Stephen Parmenius.

Indeed the lives of the "man's man" Adventurer *and* of the scholar of high humanistic letters seemed convergent just ahead of Thomas Morton. Sir Philip Sidney's brief bright life met its end (1586) as Thomas turned 10. England grieved and the process lit new pride in Sidney's achievements in the English language. Perhaps Thomas was young yet to understand the need for a *Defense of Poetry* like Sidney's (qtd. here in "America's First Poetry" section), but he was certainly caught up in the rising "Renaissance" of his country's language:

> Ye goatherd gods, that love the grassy mountains,
> Ye nymphs that haunt the springs in pleasant valleys,
> Ye satyrs joyd with free and quiet forests,
> Vouchsafe your silent ears to plaining music...
>
> ...For she whose parts maintained a perfect music,
> Whose beauty shined more than the blushing morning,
> Who much did pass in state the stately mountains,
> In straightness passed the cedars of the forests,
> Hath cast me, wretched, into eternal evening
> By taking her two suns from these dark valleys...
>
> (from *The Old Arcadia*, 1580)

Whether tutored in the family home or in a West Country grammar school, Thomas grew up relatively well-prepared for his complicated world and the two major shocks it faced: the increasingly visible achievements of the "pagan" or "Classical" Western past in Greece and Italy, and the existence of "Newfoundland" or America with its myriad civilizations. Popular and pedagogical interest in both increased through Morton's youth, after a long epoch of build-up on the Continent. According to Weiss (205-7), "the new archaeology had developed (beginning in 14th-century Italy) as an effort both to master ancient building-techniques and to rescue (or at least record) the fast-disappearing ancient world and its learning." By the 1520s the "discovery" of America had created a body of published literature, and he could find the ancient world and the New in the pages of his Latin and English readings.

Did Thomas, confined now away from his friends and hunting dogs, open his homework's ponderous tome to discover his first conceptions of American "Indians"? A schoolboy's translations included Roman historian Tacitus, who spoke of Rome's "savage and far-away" tribes:

> The Germans themselves I should regard as aboriginal, and not mixed at all with other races through immigration....And,

> beside the perils of rough and unknown seas, who would leave Asia, or Africa, or Italy, for Germany, with its wild country [?]....They [do not] confine the gods within walls....They consecrate woods and groves....The king or chief...is heard, more because he has influence to persuade than because he has power to command....[T]hey do not even tolerate closely contiguous dwellings. They live scattered and apart, just as a spring, a meadow or a wood has attracted them....No nation indulges more profusely in entertainments and hospitality. To exclude any human being from their roof is thought impious....Of lending money...they know nothing---a more effectual safeguard than if it were prohibited....[They are] squalidly poor....Yet they count this greater happiness than groaning over field-labor, toiling at building, and poising the fortunes of themselves and others between hope and fear. Heedless of men, heedless of gods, they have attained that hardest of results, the not needing so much as a wish....   (*On the Origin, Geography, Institutions and Tribes of the Germans*, 709-732)[17]

Educators labored to inculcate the knowledge and virtues of the Greek and Roman worlds, stressing also the differences between those epochs, and a consciousness of "the contrast between antiquity and the present" (Trinkhaus 4). The result was an emerging new sense of culture itself; of differences caused less by God's involvement or wrath than by secular factors of time and space. "Difference" took on, more often, new shine. Once a "degenerate" result of a single Creation "gone wrong" (*Canaan* Bk. 1 Ch. 2), the repeated "discoveries" of different cultures now became repeated hints or subtexts recalling Europe's own "pagan" past, including indeed its own version of the Original Sin-less natural world and human body. Here and there, "difference" even began to be celebrated and learned from. As medieval Europeans awoke to their predecessors, "respect

---

[17] What some call the utopian descriptions of "primitive and unspoiled" German tribes in Tacitus' works were calculated, it is said, to help chasten and reform Rome's decadent imperialism. A practicing schoolboy learned more than grammar in translating Tacitus' famous remark, *Solitudinem faciunt, pacem appellant*, or "They make a desert and call that tranquility": "They exterminate peoples and call it peace."

Others find "too many unlovely traits" in Tacitus' tribes for them to serve as a conscience or utopia, and assign his work "history's highest function," the "moral improvement" of *all* readers (Church and Brodribb, translators above, *xii*). As we historicize Morton's definite shares of ethnocentrism, we note that in either reading of the above, "tribes" remain at the "primitive" end of the "improvement" message ostensibly meant for "all."

for antiquity" began to undermine "ethnocentric self-assurance," and thus "prepared some of them to be both more observant and more tolerant" (Rowe 7).

The first 20 years of Old-New World contact had been catastrophes for Native peoples of the Caribbean. But the shock-waves traveled back from Columbus' voyages too, "shattering the Biblical mold of human cosmography and...geography" (Slavin 141). Before long it seemed reasonable to some, such as influential northern humanist LeFevre d'Etaples, that if any "virtue" had existed in "pagan" peoples of early Europe, then it might also exist in "Indians" (qtd. in Levi 22). Johannes Boemus' *Omnium Gentum Mores* (1520) was widely studied and lent momentum to such views, and by the 1550s Sir Thomas More had located his Utopia across the Atlantic. According to Hodgen's study of early "ethnographic" writings (132), it was soon no longer sufficient just to see and gather facts on foreigners' ways: the "critical distance" this bestowed upon one's view of *home* also facilitated critique of home's order; and, ideally (to some), led to more creative choice about what "orders and institutions" were to be "ordayned" and practiced.

Direct allusions in *Canaan* reveal that Morton's early studies followed paths laid out for a boy up to age 14 by masters such as Sir Thomas Elyot: he read, after applying himself to the prescribed Lily's Latin grammar (Bennett 1965: 169), the fables of Aesop, the enchanted pastorals of Virgil and Ovid, perhaps echoes of the Greek epics of Homer, the myths and verse-admonitions of Hesiod. In later teens, as Morton acquired the skills of fencing and archery, wrestling and horsemanship and perhaps early firearms, studies at once more serious and practical took up his time: the letters, logic and rhetoric of Cicero, meant to equip him with precise thought and potent argument, often followed with moral philosophers from Aristotle's *Ethica* to Erasmus' *Institution of a Christian Prince*.

As Dowling (Ch. 9) and others lay out these guidelines, it appears that as Morton neared his decisive twenties (in the 1590s), the generally-required number of Latin and Greek authors was extended to include such salty sensibilities as Lucan, Terence and Juvenal, Euripides, Aristophanes and Pindar. These perhaps aroused Morton's taste for theater and social satire. The medieval *trivium* of Grammar, Logic and Rhetoric, built upon by the proto-universities' *quadrivium* of geometry, astronomy, arithmetic and music, now opened its intellectual doors to "newer" subjects as well; ranging from economics and politics to astrology, cosmography, "physic" or medicine, modern languages such as Italian and French, and common (vs. civil) law.

Of course, The Bible was the indispensable counterpart to the "pagan" half of what was called "religious humanism," which sought to preserve the "best" of the past within the "true" religion. But again reflecting its author's education, each reach within *Canaan* for convincing example or metaphor is as likely to come from Ovid as from the Gospels. Morton's direct reference to Latin (Roman) authors only (no Greek or Hebrew) suggests the "middling" level of his schooling and family resources for it. George Chapman's landmark translations of Homer were yet to come (1611/1615), but most Western myth taught and built in plain sight upon *The Iliad* and *Odyssey*.

Ascham's "revolution" against "masterly beating" of students (as a self-defeating approach) likely bestowed the "double trans" method on Thomas. This was not unlike the medieval student's learning his Latin by colloquies, "disputations" and dialogues (Wilson 50), as Morton and teachers translated admirable passages of classic works back and forth, discussed and improved them together. (See Prest Ch. 7 for a best bibliography of young men's readings, further including Catullus, Livy, Plutarch, Seneca: Mercator's *Atlas*, the only one in Europe till 1635: the learned local histories of Camden, Holinshed's *Chronicles*, Spenser's *Faerie Queene*, and again, Sidney.)

As the student gained skills he moved on to the *topos*, a short inventive dissertation upon a given idea (for ex., the soldier's vs. the scholar's life or importance, what it was like in the Garden of Eden, etc.): *Canaan*'s rhapsody on New England landscape (53-4) may be based partly in this tradition. The "character book" was in vogue now as developed by Overbury and Fuller, and its "witty compendium of human types" gave something to the form of *Canaan*. He would have been expected to creatively apply more recent readings (for ex. Juvenal's *Satires*) to his observations of his generation's contentious social maneuvering ("Come forth, ye great Dardanians!" Juvenal had mocked at fellow Romans trying to "write" themselves noble-Trojan lineage---Gifford ed., I:V, l.162).

As for the more quotidian humanity about, he found that his "Classics" spoke a wealth of witty ways to express the humor of wild young boys. While Lucan took the "gods" out of narrative, and showed his Caesar a "bloodthirsty ogre" (Duff ed. xii), Martial's *Epigrams* could give packs of these youths a secret dog-Latin code for enjoying themselves---at the expense of overpoweringly noisome elders (people seldom bathed), at the revolting table-manners of certain cousins (Ker ed., LXXIV), at leeching house-guests (LVII), and, of course, puns of all carbuncular description (XLIX).

As Morton advanced, more demanding stages transformed all this into his oratory, the ability to construct and deliver convincing declamations, including the skill of improvisation with what was at hand (Aristotle's "available means") and one's inner store of cultural abundance, or *copia*. The "modern" difference was very much in method; which in general now rested upon the master's "suspension of sovereignty," in order to promote *creative* intelligence. Ideally the student became new master of what Plato had called "the universal art of enchanting the mind by arguments" (qtd. in Halpern 50).

Morton's career embraced both action and learning: he built a prosperous New England life and won his legal case defending it in England's high courts. Having taken his education seriously and respected its traditions, he seems to have kept abreast also of the printed accounts and Bristol sailing-crews' stories of the New World. West Country mariners had been part of the English expeditions since their much-vaunted "forefathers" Sebastian and John Cabot's journeys, the first "known" Englishmen to follow Columbus (McGrath 81-91). Sir Humphrey Gilbert, and Captains Frobisher and Davis led famous searches for a Northwest Passage to the East during Morton's youth (1576-87): Sirs Walter Ralegh and Francis Drake received high honors as explorers and harriers of Spanish America, and by 1602 (with Thomas in his mid-20s), Bartholomew Gosnold (briefly a student at the Inns) had attempted the Northeast's first plantation-style settlement on Cuttyhunk Island, Cape Cod. Pamphlets describing, promoting and debating the colonization of "Virginia" (then the entire east coast of America) began to serve as "escape literature" in more than one sense by way of the hawkers' carts of the 1580s and '90s. Before long, "trading companies" or "corporations" of "adventurers" in the fishing and fur trades (including the earliest ones energized by Sir Ferdinando Gorges) were making better-organized searches for the right men to sail their ships and develop plantations (Levermore 1:19; Slafter 30, 196). West Country men offered long experience with the Newfoundland, in return for high wages (if the fishing and/or trade was good), for exemption from the wars, for adventure.

"To be strong from nature, to be excited by the powers of the mind; and to be inspired, as it were, by a divine spirit": this was the integrated being that to Cicero meant "genius." Morton paid attention to the philosophers shared with him, and not surprisingly looked more than once to the original Greek "Cynic" Diogenes; whose irascible motto "Live like an animal" meant that independence ---if one truly desired it and consented to pay the price---was possible; and very much a function of "seeing through" every last pretension of "civilization," including all other people's conceptions of "duty" itself. (See *Canaan* Note 568).

Still---though men like Gorges preferred to hire the "gentleman of a good family, industrious, and of faire condition" (*Narration* 18, 49)---Thomas Morton betook himself to London's Inns to study for the bar. Groomed as a gentleman, strong and skilled in body, and proud of who he was in the midst of "the illiterate multitude" (116), he had a full 25 years' English living to do before he took ship for America.

3: *At the Inns of Court*

While Morton's family, with at least two sons, possessed means enough to lodge and school the younger Thomas in the capital city, their share of gentle status was apparently not much older than that of the father's "Souldiering." If we ask why Thomas apparently saw no military service himself, the answer must have to do more with temperament than ability. And there must have been somewhere a helping hand within the system allowing him the luxury of such a choice, a decision running contrary to the sense of duty espoused in his book. The fact is that such able young men without major means were cannon fodder. The England of Morton's grandfathers had emerged from its bloody Wars of the Roses to a relative stability in Henry VIII, and Elizabeth had been Queen for 18 years at Thomas' birth in 1576. But external relations were otherwise. Elizabeth's long wars against Spain on the seas, in America, in France and the Low Countries were sending waves of Englishmen 4000-strong at a time into the navies and across the Channel. From 1589-92 over 12,000 men fought in France alone: another 6000 assisted the Netherlands and, by the time of the Irish Revolt under Tyrone (1598), the Crown had spent heavily to muster and equip 100,000 soldiers and seamen from the counties and boroughs.[18]

---

[18] The ranks of these men included Ben Jonson, said to have killed and "stripped" in Homeric fashion a foe in single combat; the future captain Myles Standish of Plimoth Colony, who was still in Holland after troop-withdrawals in 1605 when he met "the Pilgrims"; Sir Humphrey Gilbert, in The Netherlands in 1571; John Smith, there in 1596 after schooling and apprenticeships (Barbour 1:lvii); and earlier, the translator of Acosta and Las Casas, Edward Grimston, who served in Calais. Many American "adventurers" had a first taste of foreign parts and training in the "martialist" techniques of "subjection" in these wars. "The Thirty Years War" raged on, meaning

Ironically, the strength England had devoted to helping the Dutch establish their frontiers (by 1595) allowed Philip of Spain to rebuild the Armada defeated when Morton was about 12 years old: the whole decade of his time at the Inns saw England's taxation tripled, its foreign markets closed in the countries caught up in the wars, and at least two major alarms of new Spanish attempts to land in England. There was also now such unemployment that the "Poor Laws" first issued in 1576 were expanded in 1598 and 1601, including "relief work" programs in which the "masterless" and "vagrants" were set to work processing the raw materials produced by a given parish (hemp, flax or stocks of wool, for ex.). The more "sturdy beggars," rogues and vagabonds were to be transported to Virginia at the cost of the counties "afflicted" with them, but these ideas of the Privy Council's (urged by men like Hakluyt) were not yet any large program or practice (Quinn *England* 333). Across Europe, official Acts like 1597's "For the Punishment of Rogues, Vagabonds, and Sturdy Beggars," began to demand public whippings of "vagrants," and their forced placement in "labour as a true subject ought" (qtd. in Cameron).

Poorly funded and staffed, these Acts largely failed, and as peace approached (1605), waves of demobilized soldiers added to the tents on public commons and the country's burgeoning crises. With ranks of displaced people increasing through the 1590s, then, and because the Inns were "considerably more exclusive than the universities" (Prest 27), we see that Morton's class and means, however slight in relative terms, must have made for crucial differences in his life as he neared manhood. Inns of Court men did answer the calls to military service: so Thomas was somehow able to decline the experience of war,

---

(most of the time) France and Sweden's Protestant Alliance vs. Austria and Spain. It ravaged Western Europe till 1648 and killed an unprecedented 8 million civilians: the dawn of modern "total war" (Dyer).

and able by character to continue with his own plans while others accepted it. *Canaan's* contempt for "quondam [sometime] drummers" and other satirical remarks on "martialists" in general may reflect some rancor left over from his first days in London, against peers and colleagues at the Inns who questioned *his* mettle for having declined war-service. The poet in Thomas would meet these types again. He prided himself on service and duty---but he always wrangled to render it on the most pleasurable terms he could wrest from his circumstances.

The Inns of Court were the four law schools of London---less a school than a place of internship---and more. Besides housing the lawyers, officials and clerks who served and did business there, they were also a mixture of gentlemen's club, college, trade union, finishing school and cultural matrix in which the realm's elite mingled with the aspiring, and vice-versa, each making valuable contacts and taking part in different aspects of a rich literary and performance-loving environment. Morton, moving to this vibrant and crowded city of over 100,000 people, skirted the bad bubonic plague year of 1592 and entered Clifford's Inn probably in 1593 at the average age of about 17: Clifford's was part of the so-called Inner Temple (which included Clement's and Lyon's Inns), whose three counterparts were the Middle Temple, Lincoln's Inn, and Gray's the largest of them all.

As noted, Morton with a host of Devonshire men was now part of a student population of over 1000 men (Finkelpearl 5: a sample admissions-process in Bald's *John Donne* 55). Like them, he was surrounded by a much larger body of would-be courtiers and theater-figures, ambitious wastrels and cozeners and indigent silk-clad sons of the upper classes, these roosting at all the Inns "to see the world" of London and beyond, to scout a good marriage if not clinch connections for personal advancement, or just to use the Inns as housing while "finishing" oneself, with a smattering of law and, in the city's "studios," the social graces from fencing to dance and music.

Together the Inns were under the direction of a "Master," Crown-appointed and with "religious authority" only: for example, the eminent divine Thomas Hooker, later a leader in the colonization of New World Connecticutt, had been Master for seven years just before Morton's arrival and had led the Inns as a model of "passionate moderation" (Loftie 14), making sure that "both Canterbury and Geneva" were heard from in the pulpits of the students' chapels.[19] Below the Master were the Benchers, senior members of the bar who ruled each Inn in a kind of self-perpetuating oligarchy; and the two main divisions below them were the Utter (or Outer) Barristers, the professional body of practicing attorneys who pled and argued cases before the Benchers, and the student or Inner Barristers, who learned by almost every method except direct lecture, since there were no "professors" devoted to teaching.

A student judged ready was "called to the bar" to deliver a Reading (a well-supported interpretation) of a statute and be formally admitted an Utter Barrister: the time needed to reach that point was (within Benchers' discretion) indefinite---students typically had 7 or 8 years' "continuance" but a 3-year "program" was not unheard of. Within three years of admission one had to begin participation in "moots": these were mock-disputations conducted in "homely Law-French" on some legal matter before three Benchers and two Utter Barristers (Finkelpearl 9), and were held along with Readings during the "vacations," those weeks between the regular sittings of the courts. (Like theater-productions, moots could be delayed by outbreaks of plague, which was the case between June 1592 and June 1594; so Morton's time there was lucky in a second way).

---

[19] Hooker's successor was Nicholas Balguy (Master 1591-1601), a man who "never showed any tendency toward Puritanism" (Prest 197).

"Bolting" was a less formal version of these exercises in extemporaneous argumentation, held among students after midday meals and suppers: they studied at least as much by watching and listening at the Court of Common Pleas and in Star Chamber proceedings as they did by reading the King' Statutes, Acts of Parliament and the precedents of common law.[20] When students had proven themselves in a Grand or Inn of Chancery moot, by a number of years of service to Utter Barristers in "paralegal" kinds of duties, and by composing their Reading for the bar, they usually got their chance to matriculate. With a minimum 12

---

[20] The infamous Star Chamber was "not established by a statute of 1487, as was once believed" (Hurstfield/Smith 156), but was "part of the King's Council (with the addition of certain judges) sitting as a law court; nor was it restricted by common law procedures." The Star Chamber became a "valuable prerogative court for bringing swift punishment" to those "who exploited the difficulties of enforcing the common law," who bribed judges or intimidated juries. Since the country's basic system of justice rested on common law (i.e., a body of precedents and Parliamentary statutes applied with the assistance of juries), the Star Chamber appeared increasingly tyrannical as the powers of Parliament gained in the 17th century: it was an apparatus belonging more to Roman law (still in force on the Continent), in which judges presided without a jury, and royal edict could constitute law (see Chambers *et als* 529).

Two issues pertinent to Morton emerge. First, since common lawyers by-and-large resented the growth and powers of the Star Chamber as an increasing sign of royal disregard for the people's will and the rule of law--and since the lawyers' representatives in the House of Commons increasingly criticized the Crown for its pressurings of judges and other offenses---perhaps something of Morton's own manner and degree of Royalist partisanship can be better gauged through comparison with his professional colleagues. He did, after all, return the favor of legal accusations and encourage Star Chamber-like proceedings against Plimoth's Edward Winslow before the Council for New England in 1634: see AC322n1, and Ch. 9 below.

Second, the controversy as to whether James I's 1623 "proclamation" against the sale of guns to Native Americans had the force of law receives a bit more light. Precisely the differences at issue in criticism of the Star Chamber's autocratic ways, stood between belief in Continental/Roman law's support for the statutory power of "royal edict," and in the English common law's departures from Continental practices. When Sir Edward Coke (a Clifford's Inn man) was Chief Justice, he ruled in 1610 that a King's word was not statute (document in FBH2:55n1): later Sir Nicholas Hyde (of the Protestant-stronghold Middle Temple) took up similar critique of royal prerogative (see AC26, 35; Loftie 78; Prest 37). Therefore, until better evidence arises, Morton seems correct in his judgment that English law could not be used to enforce a King's proclamation. His efficient reply when the Plimothers made an unusual invocation of James' authority in ethical matters was that "The King is dead, and his displeasure with him." Citations in Chs. 6-8 treating the Plimoth/Ma-re Mount conflict.

years' practice one might (with wit, luck and the right friends) become a Bencher.[21]

London's skyline both sides of the Thames with its magesterial and daunting towers, its theater-flags flying across the water in Surrey; the elaborate warren of tenements, offices, greater halls, closed-off courtyards and "walks" that made up the Inns system, all of it hallowed with the traditions and decked with the relics of its great alumnae, must have inundated even a well-read youth from the counties as he took up the student's routines of work and recreation. For most of each term wearing a traditional sleeveless black gown with a flap collar, and a round black cloth cap (sumptuary laws forbade long hair and swords), Morton and his fellows were served meals at carefully-ranked tables in hall, in company with the barristers and Benchers (holding forth from dais places in their knee-length gowns tufted with velvet and silk). There were prayer services morning and evening with either the Master or one of the permanent "preachers" assigned to the Inns in the 1580s to combat Catholic infiltrations (more below). And since Clifford's Inn was "by St. Dunstan's Church in Fleete Street" (WPF3:111), Morton may have begun his days there, or in the nearby Church of St. Mary's shared by the Inner and Middle Temples. Its prayerbooks bore on opposite covers the Paschal Lamb and Pegasus (Loftie 10).

The so-called "Mosque of Omar" too might have drawn the student of Inns history: this was one of several "round churches" within this city ward of Farringdon Without, constructed on sites where the Inns' legendary founders The Knights Templar ("of the Temple") had settled in strength in the early 1300s.

---

[21] Most basically, a student had to demonstrate that he knew the laws, was fit himself to "govern" the Inn of his masters; had to have shown himself a man of "discretion" and enough "means" to pay for his Reading and its customary feasts; and (in one case cited by Prest 62) he could be denied his "degree" unless judged "of a sociable disposition." In Coke's words, "confer-ence with others...is the life of studie" (qtd. 117).

Even if the Inns had more prosaically emerged as "hostels" so that groups of lawyers on business could be "assured of a bed and a reasonable dinner...in an inhospitable urban environment" (law historian Holdsworth qtd. in Prest 417), a youth might take himself round the circle of sculpted busts of those knights in the chapel (noting a few lawyers' portraits mixed in), and consider how the fortunes of those knights of the Crusades had fared. Their own wealth, it was said, had at last made the Templars outcasts, charged as both "Gnostic idolators" and as laggards in the Christian military cause in the Middle East.

The Templars had settled on land close by a spacious open meadow sloping down to the Thames: despite London's growth, fields, fruit trees and woods with rabbits for the hunter lay to the north and west of this area, and students used them for gentlemanly exercises. The social shift toward civil jousting was borne out in the sight of law students at stretch on the knights' former "tilting grounds." Passing from halls to courts to libraries in his studies, Morton's paths grew constricted by high ornate peaked townhouses fronting on tiny lanes and alleyways, ranging from the "unsavory" paths siding Lincoln's Inn and the Temple, to the elegant wrought-iron and stone doorways of King's Bench Walk. Gray's Inn, the largest and most aristocratic, had its own private walks, but Clifford's frontage along Fleet Street's traffic in "dust or mud" also included access to "the calm, quiet, green recesses" of a small garden "among the old houses" behind St. Dunstan's-in-the-West. Loftie's sources described this unusual amenity as "an airy place and neatly kept," adorned with rows of lime trees "set round the grass plots and walks" (81---see Illustrations). From the waterside at River's Steps (one of many ferry-landings), cries of "Westward Ho!" called boatmen to take "charterparties" across to Surrey, with its theaters and bear-baiting pits, its "sixpenny whoredom" of brothels or "stews" where the rules of "puritanical burghers, the Lord Mayors and other authorities" had no legal jurisdiction (Ashley 15).

Sources agree that at this time only about 15% of students actually passed the bar: the lack of university-style formalities of curricula and instruction, the countless doorways into other careers and the extraordinary cultural energies there all helped to bring down that percentage. Yet students were encouraged to explore and make the most of everything London had to teach as the English crossroads between King's court, city, country and Continent, because knowledge of public affairs, from Whitehall scandals to European wars, could be important in later practice. So the hopeful lawyer had to be self-directed or at least determined to improve his lot in order to keep on tack, not only through the massive readings (below) but also in acquiring the skills that meant status and advancement. He kept notes in a "commonplace" book on dynamics of the cases observed in nearby Westminster courts; kept up with Fleet Street gazettes and "corantoes," attended paid sermons or talks by visiting barristers who worked the county circuit-court assizes; learned to maneuver in yet another language, another code to play, in moots with peers and before the Benchers. Now the outdoorsman began to see the uses of so much early discipline with books. Ancient eloquence, carefully salted in, was part of appropriating the powers of tradition, gave strength to fledgling arguments---it could make one more than just another "uncheckable tongue" in a peer group that bred sharp urbanity as a norm (Finkelpearl 67).

Since the 1550s the printing press had been replacing the Inns' "aural" instruction methods (observation and discussion) with textual ones (Prest 132); but by Morton's early 1590s there, only one of the four main Inns (Lincoln's) had a library in anything more than name, so students had to cooperate, share printed texts and circulate old manuscripts while elders guided them through what "stacks" there were. They pored over Statutes and Acts, plowed through Canon Law and Littleton's *Tenures* (on common customs and land-tenure practice as locally construed); through Toffel's first printed edition of *De Laudibus Legum Angliae* (1567), more Latin and "Law-French" studies, plus the emerging "books of method" by which one acquired techniques for comprehending the fundamental principles of law. Most important was to develop one's commonplace book(s) toward a Reading of a chosen Statute; and this meant years of mining the records for precedent and useful opposition, keeping current with "year books" and reports of related cases, digests, abridgments and summaries, new writs and statutes, and collating these with notes from boltings, moots and others' Readings. Despite even the waves of helpful guides and the first systematic law-textbooks appearing now, so "frustrating, inelegant and tedious" a program (most readably detailed by Prest Chs. 6 & 7) must warn us that "mere...admission to an Inn certainly cannot be taken as evidence" that a youth "received there a legal education of any kind" (153). This applies to Morton despite the signature on his book: writer Thomas Lodge also signed his works "of the Inns" but never passed the bar, though he held other degrees. On the other hand, statements on Morton's West Country lawyering are cited above, and he pressed high court suits in the 1630s (Ch. 9). *Canaan* is very much constructed out of all the Inns could teach, and law was a main aspect of both.

Morison (*Builders* 4-5) shows the young Richard Hakluyt discovering his passion for "Cosmographie" at the Middle Temple office of his elder cousin: *Divers Voyages* (1589) both attracted men and investors toward America and won Hakluyt a minor government post, showing that such interests were common and useful at the Inns. Devon man Sir Walter Ralegh, already of Ireland and Virginia, was ensconced at the Middle Temple by now (c. 1594) and keeping reputedly irreligious company with Thomas Hariot and Christopher Marlowe

(Strathmann 43), trying to revive his career after disgraces in "love" at court. In 1595 he sailed to Guiana, and young John Donne of the Inns read what Ralegh wrote of it: in 1596 Ralegh took many Inns men, including Donne, to his great raid on Spanish Cadiz, and Essex recruited more for duty in Ireland three years later.

Meanwhile, Ben Jonson, whose satires and lyrics influenced Morton's *Canaan* poetry, was then just back from war-service and finding his way into Inns-sponsored acting and writing productions. Donne returned from the sea to become known round Lincoln's Inn as a playgoer, ladies' man and proponent of the fashionable "sweetness and strength" school of poetics. He was writing (if not publishing) lines for his erotic *Elegies* that (in XIX below) foreshadowed figures in Morton's "Author's Prologue":

> *License my roving hands, and let them go*
> *Before, behind, between, above, below.*
> *O my America, my new found land...*

For many reasons, such as Donne's decision for a second voyage, it was said that great literary lights (such as Surrey, Spenser and Sidney of earlier generations) were scarce round the 1590s Inns (Riggs 29); but there were numerous smaller talents. A chief one was Thomas Lodge, who became a strong influence on Morton. Lodge, a gentleman almost 20 years Thomas' senior during his own days at the Inns, had earned his letters at the Merchant Taylors' School in London, had an Oxford degree and a voyage to the Canaries and Azores under his belt, and suffered within respectable society for his "leanings toward a literary career and, worse...toward the Roman Catholic faith" (Rae 14). Lodge's "leanings" had already produced his popular *Reply* in defense of entertainments staged at the Inns and on the stages of London's just-beginning public theatres. Like the greater Sidney's *Defense of Poetry*, Lodge was resisting a rising tide of antagonism toward such arts and diversions that had begun back in the 1570s, and reached now from Stephen Gosson's *School of Abuse* to Stubbes' *Anatomie*.

The versatile "Thomas Lodge of Lincolnes Inne, Gentleman," on his way from pamphleteer to poet-playwright and (at last) "Doctor of Physic," had also helped to instigate in the '80s a satirical reaction against current conventions of Petrarchan poetry, with its conceit of the helpless melancholy lover, in favor of an style more like the Roman Ovid's, at once more worldly, ironic and direct. His *Scillaes Metamorphosis* (c. 1588-9) made the "little epic" or epyllion the Inns' fashionable form of the '90s, and the young Morton arriving there soaked up "the delectable discourse" of that work, perhaps in performance as well as on paper. Lodge had turned the "nymph" Scilla's innocent resistance to being seduced, and her "punishment" for resisting, into a multi-leveled edification-story (as he saw it) for this most "cynical" of English audiences: "Contayning the detestable tyrannie of Disdaine, and Comicall triumph of Constancie: verie fit for young Courtiers to peruse, and [for] coy Dames to remember" (*Scillaes* 1589 title-page, *Works* Vol. 1).[22]

"Glaucus would scarce know her, if he met her," Lodge warned his audience of the abuse this nymph Scilla had suffered at the hands of both pirates and "rough writers." "[Y]et my hope is, Gentlemen, that you will not so much imagine what she is, as what she was" (*Dedicatorie*). Lodge was demanding from his audience of carbuncular "penny-knaves" a simultaneous reaching-out to sympathize with Scilla's *own* world and sufferings, and to a critical appraisal of the sea-going "rogue" Glaucus. His unmet desire for Scilla, ridiculously *self-involved* rather than pathetic in Lodge's vamping lines, wrested laughter,

---

[22] We can best understand/appreciate both Lodge's and Morton's related works with the epyllion by looking at them simultaneously; but we do not yet have enough of Morton's New England and other contexts for that task. See "Antimasque," "Masque," and Chapter 8 for very detailed treatments of these complexities and worthwhile literary connections.

"worthy lessons," and (for Lodge himself) London social status from that otherwise-"despised" world of books and ancient legend.

> *The deafe nill heare: both she and Love together*
> *Haue made a match to aggreuate my griefe:*
> *I see my hell, there rests no hope in either:*
> *From proud contempt there springeth no reliefe,*
> > *What rests there then but since I may not gaine her,*
> > *In piteous tearmes and teares for to complaine her.*

Morton learned things from Lodge, from his seaside-seduction scenario to the sympathetic/ironic treatment of it, and applied it in his own 1627 "Poem" written for his New England May Day Revel (Ch. 6; "Masque"). Lodge's ridicule of the self-absorbed Glaucus also seems exactly Morton's approach in his treatment of the "melancholy" young Englishwoman he encountered in New England (details in *Canaan* Book 3). Young Shakespeare himself took similar lessons from Lodge in his first published poetry at this time, *Venus and Adonis* (1592-3: see Keach 45-51). If there seemed a lack of many "great" lights at Morton's Inns, the ones rising just now included England's greatest.

Relief from study, desire for fellowship, social advancement---It would be surprising not to find young Morton seated along the edge of Inns stages with friends in their best ostentatious silks (Finkelpearl 92), especially at the end of his second year (1594), which saw one of the largest and most important "Christmas Revels" ever staged at Gray's Inn. Presented before Queen Elizabeth, *Gesta Grayorum* included multiple components, ranging from lyric poetry by Thomas Campion and speeches by Sir Francis Bacon to (possibly) Shakespeare's first play, *The Comedy of Errors*. There were public processions to which the government contributed great pomp along with contingents of cavalry, a masque including dancing and parts for over 130 participants; and according to historians Green (101) and Welsford (167), *Gesta* marked a turning-point in the masque's development, establishing future norms of the genre under Ben Jonson and his fellows, and crystallized the elements of "pastoral idealism" (as love of nature was called in the city), which had long-informed Elizabethan poetry. Morton was to "re-produce" all this in America.

Essentially, the Inns' men elected a colleague to play a "High and Mighty Prince Henry, Prince of Purpoole" (after a not so elegant district near the Inns), and then surrounded him (and Queen Elizabeth) with word and performance that deftly, without either deep ironic resentments or fawning, created a satiric image of the pomp, rituals and "smoke and mirrors" that underlay power at the real-life court. With great solemn abandon every participant received a mock-office, "Henry" was presented arms and a shield bearing Jupiter's image: royal pardons were issued for every conceivable offense before the fact (with a few inconceivable ones thrown in), there was "dancing till late" and a mock-trial; and as the nights of entertainment reached into January, an "altar" was set up for "sacrifices" and incense to the "Goddess Amity," round which "ladies" danced as "Nymphs and Fairies, with instruments of musick, and...very pleasant melody with viols and voices...hymns and praises to her deity" (*Gesta* 18). An array of proto-Polonius-style "counsellors" delivered ridiculous orations on "learned mysteries" and the secrets of "Trismegistus" (24), and as members of the "court" lambasted each other, the Inns' affection for nicknames took over (Johannes Shagbag, Rawbone Dishwash, Ferdinando Fartwell, Peter Pinchpoole etc.). The revels shifted to waterside, and the spectacle continued using a small fleet of Thames barges filled with singers and blazing torches: then back indoors came a performance mixing action, poetic dialogues and dances to music, which marked the emergence of the new courtly masque before the Crown.

Gesta's wisp of a story concerned the seaside Greek demigod Proteus "and the Adamantine Rock," his magnetically-charged island whose power he used to keep the Prince and "seven knights" captive. An "Esquire" arrived to rescue the men and delivered a speech showing Proteus that the true "attractive Rock of Hearts" was Elizabeth herself (46). Proteus admitted himself outmatched and, with no option except to release the seven, he struck the island-scenery with his staff; and when he and his "attendants" (including one "Amphitrite") reached the rock, the men emerged from within it "in a very stately mask....in couples, and before every couple came two pigmies with torches....[They] danced a new-devised measure...After which, they took unto them ladies; and with them they danced their galliards, courants....And they danced another new measure," disappearing after bows to the Queen. When the "Courtiers" followed the players with a further dance, Elizabeth exclaimed "What! shall we have bread and cheese after a banquet?" (49). Still more performances followed through the days, including establishment of a new legal code ("none may come into his Highness' presence that have eaten any clams or windy meate," 54); and at last an "Antimask of Mountebanks" took place, in which "The greatest master of medicine Aesculapius" appeared with his "fellow artists of severall nations" (60), to perform a healing by means of "musical charms," songs sung with a "Chorus":

> What is't you lacke, what would you buy,
> What is it that you need;
> Come to me, gallants, taste and buy,
> Heer's that will doe the deed...

Ailments addressed included old age, "Lost maidenhead," "greife of the spleene": verses spoke to each ailment with a comic incantation of cure, and the Chorus cautioned at last, "Yet let us not [in] too much lyccor delight" (62), meaning the "powder" mixture distributed by "Aesculapius," that preserved one from "fate" (60). A few last "Familiar Recipes" were thrown in:

> If any lady be sicke of the sullens she knowns not where, let her take a handfull of scimples I know not what, and use them I know not how, applyinge them to the party greeved I know not who, and she shall be well I know not when...

Finally a player named "Parradox" appeared, to mock virtually everything under the sun from the learned circles of ancient Athens and current religious factions ("my father a Jesuite, my mother an Annabaptist" 65), to Biblical-sounding proverbs ("A flatterer deserves to be loved better than a true friend; for oyle cures better than vinegar" 67). So closed *Gesta Grayorum*'s revels, with more short songs in honor of "the Kinge of Love and Pleasure" and the raising of a "May-pole" onstage. Players and guests were to "circle it with your caprians [fertility-related] daunces" in honor of the "Feast of Venus Citherea" (72), "Parradox" in the lead with his "Disciples."

It will fully appear that Thomas Morton did not forget this remarkable invention when, in his late forties on American soil, he needed a way to consolidate his trade-relations with other planters and Native Americans (Book 3 Ch. 14 "Of The Revels"; Ch. 8 here). The production's own advice (*Gesta* 21) that a gentleman should learn its skills, to discourse and "make emblems" of meaning and power, stayed with him. So did *Gesta*'s small measure of jokes at other races' expense (about "Negarian Tartars," "pigmies" and "Nager the Indian" on 38, 48 and 57) reinforce other peer-attitudes, which he absorbed and repeated. Other "tropes" could work in the other less-ethnocentric direction, such as the "court fool lore" that taught Morton ahead of time how foolish it was to lump "one...for another" of a different race (*Canaan* 110).

But America was still 20 years distant: for now, participation in such events, besides the "courtly trivium" of music, dance and fencing in the studios--- was all but demanded of the student. Time and moneys rendered in service to the nobility "obliged" them in turn to reciprocate with patronage. The personal skills needed to motivate other people and raise cold cash for these events also told the Benchers when one was ready (or not) to advance within the hierarchy;

and the graces hopefully gained helped to distance a man from "merely" common lawyer peers (Prest 224).

Constant events---from enormous feasts put on in Middle Temple Hall to the "Grand Days" of All Saints' and Candlemas, from elaborate Readers' dinners to the weeks of winter and spring revels under the elected "Lord of Misrule" or an appointed "Master of the Revels"---this cultural intensity was the life of the Inns until about the midpoint of James I's reign in the early 1600s, when sharpening divisions in society as a whole began to draw men's energies back to theological dispute and politics (observed by all the Inns sources cited here). As Morton's schooling progressed and became in some way his profession, student-participation decreased even as the Inns' population peaked around 1610: invectives against such mainstays as theater and dancing were on the rise in print and pulpit.

Just before Morton's arrival there Elizabeth's government had passed measures refining the religious code that dictated compulsory church-attendance, once-yearly communion (at least) and an oath of allegiance. Preachers assigned to combat Catholic influences on students warned them not to malinger in nearby woods or back-gardens where "Jesuit agents" might lurk. While Lincoln's Inn and the Middle Temple were "hotbeds of Puritanism," the common law establishment in general was said to be "riddled with Papists" (Prest 174), perhaps due to its tenacious and at times heavy-handed devotion to precedent and "old customary" law (Eusden 25).[23]

---

[23] R.C. Bald's *John Donne* (66) describes the general situation of most English Catholics, who "wished to be loyal to the Catholic Church, but the law of England had established the royal supremacy, had penalized all those who refused to subscribe to the Thirty-Nine Articles [the "creed" of the Church of England], or to attend Anglican services, and had branded as traitors all those in Roman orders who entered the kingdom....To the logical mind there were only two courses open: either to accept the Anglican settlement and abandon the old faith, or to accept the full consequences of the papal supremacy and work with Elizabeth's enemies for her downfall. Yet the majority of Elizabethan Catholics refused to do either...." [ctd]

The Inns played full parts in the coming conflicts: as early as 1602 a "new intractability" in students against overbearing authorities was complained of, but during Morton's days there (c. 1593-1600) it was by most accounts still possible to hold a middle course. When Elizabeth died in March 1603, her successor James I --- who mostly despised common lawyers for resistance to his "divine right" over law---took occasional advantage of old prerogatives to "visit" and "correct" both universities and the Inns, and playwrights such as John Marston mocked him immediately for it (Finkelpearl 69). Riots too broke out during many an Inns MayDay Revel as conflicts intensified (Marcus 214): "The Scholar King" bore as he could with witty tongues sharpened by Inns repartee, and Morton would later exercise his share of the same attitudes more than once.

Clearly he was "inscribed" by his years there, by the workload, the feasts and cameraderie, the perilous attractions of brothel and faction. The Inns honed early training in confident self-assertion, added skills by which a man could manage to express "sensitivity to the shortcomings of the monarchy" and other powers (Prest 222). Like his peers there, Morton admired pastoral's feeling for land and nature, and the "vicious realism" inspired by the racier Classics. The Inns practiced a humanistic sense of ritual play or "solemn foolery" based in

---

Quinn (*England* 367) points out that despite Elizabeth's efforts from 1585 to 1603 the government "could not eliminate" Roman Catholicism, and that a de facto recognition of the right to Catholic rites, in private at least, became the rule till 1640. Still, even quasi-Catholics might have reason to consider American options.

Between Morton's remarks of affection for *The Book of Common Prayer* (43, 116), his wearing a "pectoral cross," his clearly ironic plays with the term "good protestant," and his obvious attraction to "pagan" literature, folk-ritual and Classical metaphor, perhaps we can only speak generally of his character in terms of an Inns of Court-style cultural eclecticism (*Gesta*'s brilliantly unified cacaphony of styles, symbols and ideologies is an example of this.) Historian Peter Hulme's senses of the word *polytropic* (a term Nietzsche also celebrated in *The Gay Science*) may be useful in characterizing the man Morton was learning to become: "The word 'polytropic' comes from the epithet applied to Odysseus in the first line of the *Odyssey*. Usually translated as something like 'the man of many ways,' it contains at least three interconnected meanings: one is simply 'much-travelled'; another is something like 'cunningly intelligent' or even 'slippery and deceitful'...and a third is 'much given to troping, to the use of tropes'" ("Polytropic Man" 20).

ancient ideas of fraternity and art, and let go the extremes of Christian conventions, those that seemed tame as they faded on the religious stage (Gardiner Ch. 5), and those of increasing violence in the streets and public forums, including Parliament.

Mainly-oral instruction taught Morton better to match wits, to deflect the personal aspects of conflict (and avoid libel) with fictionalizing tricks (Sir Francis Flatterer, Sir Randall Rackabite); to score his points with witty allegorical stories and "feigned" example. Such shared make-believe as filled so much of Inns life was meaningful because, like the revels and masques put on (in part) for public London, it was engaged with, critiquing and having effect on the conduct of real political power, spreading sophisticated and uncontrollable insights about every illusion that power employed to justify the existing lines of force. To be the butt of Inns satire was not good omen for being taken seriously anyplace else. Much of the Inns' cultural production and many alumnae came to share what was called (by the "school" of Sir Edward Coke) "the common law mind": "that is to say, a deep respect for the common law as guardian of the ancient constitution and arbiter of relations between king, parliament and subject" (Prest 221). New England would be Morton's main stage for practicing these arts and values.[24]

---

[24] What produced a culturally-conservative Morton nonetheless capable of surrounding his every word about would-be English and Christian America with the ironies of his title *Canaan*? Certainly it is Inns-style irony to proclaim oneself a Canaanite/Philistine against increasingly Puritan cultural "reforms" (see *Canaan*'s "Bacchanal Triumph" and notes). Guibbory and others anatomize many kinds of instruction then available on the making of "emblems"--- that is, images of "power" that further the "powers" of their makers (such as Spenser's endless experiments in *The Faerie Queene*).

As will be seen in Ch. 8, the 1627 Revel was such an activity: Morton "studied" the masque under its original master Ben Jonson, for whom "from the very beginning the resolution of discord...was a defining feature of the form" (Orgel ed. of Jonson's *Masques* 13). Indeed, the "traditional grotesquerie" and "chaos" of the form's "Act One" or "Antimasque" (from "antic" or ancient dance), was in English eyes analogous to the "raw" worlds of "pygmies" and Native Americans (hence "Indians" and "Nagers" in this part of the show). Typically at a court performance, antimasque gave way to the image of "ideal order," the more stately masque itself analogous to England's "civilizing" of the Newfoundland. Morton, then, as Jonson's imitator, may likewise have begun to conceive of the antimasque and "raw" America in not dissimilar ways: "not as a simple antithesis" to "the orderly world," but "essentially as another aspect of it, a world

The "atheism" with which he (like the Inns) was later charged was a misnomer for other influences. Thomas' West Country heritage and his Anglican Adiaphorism were compounded by the typical lawyer's secularism and religious "indifference," as well as by the Renaissance revival of Greek and Roman scepticist philosophy. (So did Morton complain when a guest conceived him as "past grace and further learned as many other Scholars are," 125.) Formal scepticism's "goal" was *ataraxia,* or "peace of mind," achieved by the acceptance of "the way the world appears to be," and by "healthy doubt" about the possibilities of "absolute" knowledge (Mates 7, 61, 66). Ideally, it led to moderation of thought and deed. It "cured a man of a swollen imagination," keeping his ever-inventive ego in humane bounds, by stressing the permanent protean *flux* of all things---and, hence, the inevitable "plurality of philosophies" one simply had to expect to find beyond the horizon. (See Tetel 38, 99 on Montaigne's approach to this "Pyrrhonism"---an approach based in "humility," he argues, as against the "crow" of the self often found in Ronsard.) Scepticism (not "atheism") helped to lead Morton down a writer's path not far from John Donne's in his "libertine" phase, a mode shared by Ralegh, Hariot, Marlowe and others seasoned by Inns cultural affiliations.

Finally, by dwelling upon the Inns we begin to see Morton as very much a part of both his cultural mainstream and its more idiosyncratic elements. We learn that Clifford's Inn "always paid its own way and had its own customs, its

---

that can therefore ultimately be accomodated...and even included in the ideals of the main masque" (Orgel 13). "[F]or through the antimasque we comprehend in what way the masque's ideal world is real." These are the same dynamics that inform the anti-ethnocentric themes near the heart of *New English Canaan*.

Also, if Morton was keeping up with reports from the Newfoundland, he was reading accounts that (in the 1590s, and up till 1622) in general granted human and cultural legitimacy to Native Americans (reviewed in Delgado Gomez and Pennington). All this at least disposed him to be able to observe and listen when he actually arrived in "New England," saw the devastation wrought there by epidemics, and the dignified Native reactions to it---including *Europeans* conceived as "wild people" (107).

great days and its peculiar rules"; that it treated its servants well and by tradition passed food to the poor from some of its feasts (Loftie 77), and we see better the man who planted in his own way in New England, without creating any model of progressive idealism. The Master's was a position of authoritative benignity to which one was supposed to aspire, a protective father and guide to his students who felt bound to reciprocate in turn. So did Morton later invoke his "master" Gorges' partner, Captain John Mason, as "a true foster Father and lover of virtue" (96).[25] As we study the Inns' foreign artistic inspirations (Welsford, Lee and Prescott detail French and Italian borrowings), and find that Thomas Lodge and others insisted in the best epyllia-poetry on an "articulated consciousness of the immediate historical context" (Keach 40), we read the New England "Poem" and "Song" in new light: it emerges that the historical and much other context of this very early colonial poetry was to be defined, by Renaissance Morton, as Native American.

And of course, "Jokes at the law and at sex, legal joking about sex, sexual jokes about the law"---these constants of Inns culture inform *Canaan* too: its "basic action" is in part a legal dispute, made entertaining through irrepressible humor for an educated audience: it is a "learned and earthy" presentation for people assumed to be the erudite equals of its author (Finkelpearl 30, 43). The "free and candid speech" of the Inns, which Ben Jonson praised so highly as a function of the conjoined "Humanity and Liberty" he found there, is both plain and cautiously "pied" at times in Morton's book. Instilled with pride of his class and the gay independence of his West Country roots, gifted with bodily vigor and a

---

[25] "When I was of Lincolns Inne, the fashion was (and I think is still) after dinner upon grand and festivall dayes, some young Gentlemen of the house would take the best Guest by the hand, and he the next, and so hand in hand they did solemnly passe about the fire, the whole company, each after other in order; to every staffe a song (which I could never sing) the whole company did with a joyn'd voice sing this burthen: 'Some mirth and solace now let us make,/To cheare our hearts, and sorrows slake....'" Robert Hayman, *Quodlibets* (1628: 44).

worldly education, Morton (an attorney or not) went out to meet that world much like his peers who "finished" at the Inns, a "passionate moderate." The changes coming to their world, however, were going to make the studied style of "indifference" practically impossible.

4: *Exit to America*

If Thomas spent the average seven years at the Inns, he was 24 or 25 when he "graduated" in the year of the birth of his future king Charles (1600). Elizabeth's programs for the distressed were doing what they could, assisted by the 1598 passing of Spain's Philip II, and by the slow end of costly wars, with markets reopening over the next five years. If Morton left London by 1603 for his reputed West Country practice, he escaped yet another plague year (40,000 died in London): he missed the passing of his life-long Queen Elizabeth, and King James I's coronation too. As peace took shape with Spain, James began to conflict with Puritan forces at home in a wrestling-match over royal, religious and Parliamentary powers. (1604 brought on his infamous Hampton Court remark, "I will hound [dissenters] out of the land.") Within the generation it would be civil war. In 1605 came the Gunpowder Plot to blow up Parliament, which made open toleration of Catholics less likely; and economic conditions were little help. The displaced of all social ranks, from farmers thrown out by enclosure to sons of the gentry with small means, began to seek alternative lives:

> [There] was also a general peace concluded between the State and the King of Spain...whereby our men of war by sea and land were left destitute of all hope of employment ....Some there were, not liking to be [mercenary soldiers] to foreign states, thought it better became them to put in practice the reviving resolution of those free spirits, that rather chose to spend themselves in seeking a new world, than servilely to be hired but as slaughterers in the quarrels of strangers....   (Gorges *Brief Narration* 16-17)

Unfortunately little information has surfaced about these prime decades of Morton's life: if he had "all things fitting" the falconer with him when he did go to America (*Canaan* 66), odds are he had access at least to English hunting-lands in his manhood.[26] The only other hint is that he claimed to use the Anglican *Book of Common Prayer* "amongst his family" (142). But he stepped into documented history in 1619 when (now about 43 years old) he became involved in "a suit in the ecclesiastical court (Bishop's Consistory)" connected with "the Diocesan Registry at Wells." He was apparently living in Axbridge in the West county of Somerset (Banks qtd. in Andrews 332). According to Banks, this suit was based "on an allegation of slander or blasphemy"; but whether Morton was plaintiff or defendant (or any other aspect of the case) cannot be learned. The document added only a cryptic remark (presumably Morton's) about "going to church" and his wearing of a "pectoral cross...in memory of a friend."

If Morton really did have Catholic sympathies, this suit illuminates a bit more of his conflicts with Puritans, perhaps how Salem's John Endicott could think him "a Jesuit agent" in New England. At present it does little more than confirm Morton's habitual West Country life and whereabouts. (Note in Ch. 9 that when second-exiled back to Old England, he "repaired" to the same Axbridge: research there might prove worthwhile.)

How, then, did Morton find himself in the vanguard of "New England" less than five years after this? This was a man to admire people "circumspect to do their actions by advice and counsel, and not rashly or inconsiderately" (*Canaan* 29). Since the late 1590s after "law school" Morton must have been

---

[26] The evolution of England's monarchy included the King's claim that much forest and land belonged exclusively to him: he then granted "rights of chase" to supportive nobility, converted "chase" lands to "parks" by enclosure and sold off further rights within it, essentially granting access to food and resources in exchange for power and money. The process made hunting in England an activity much-restricted to the upper classes by 1600 (Longrigg 14: Cummins Chs 4 & 5). The social aspect ("to rusticate") was by this time more important, to those of means, than the food. Poaching was a crime, but English field sports--and legal criteria based on money, not class ---did make hunts accessible to yeomen (Longrigg 27). Castiglione, the Renaissance model of courtly men, deemed hunting a "manly exertion" second only to war as "the true pastime of great lords" (63): most Puritans scorned it for this reason (Axtell *Essays* 48).

journeying on horseback now and then, like most attorneys, between outlying counties and London's courts of legal process (citations below). As he made these trips, he acquired more of England's mainstream cultural vocabulary found in his future book; and from the hawkers' carts and the bookshops round St. Paul's Churchyard, where "American Literature" was born, more of the necessary New World facts came to hand that could cause a reasonably-established man to venture the Newfoundland.

Morton's favorite name for himself, "Mine Host," is a trace of his origins and his activities. For that name's best-known user before him was no less than old colleague Shakespeare's Sir John ("Jack") Falstaff, roguish hero of a generation of demobilizing Elizabethan "souldiers" and their sons, who made up their share of audiences for productions of *Henry IV* and *Henry V* (staged 1595-98), and for The Bard's less-successful revival of "Jack" in 1600's *Merry Wives of Windsor*. If Thomas was in such company at the theater while in London (or at least, if acquaintance Ben Jonson thrust some of *his* admired Shakespeare into his hands), it was easy for a Morton to wish himself a Falstaff, a model of complicated devotion to his Prince as well as a "consummately shrewd realist," "keenly observant of himself and others" (Bowers qtd. in Harbage 335). Later in New England "Mine Host" would operate in like manner, using every form of "indulgence" and "hospitality" to recruit his "ragged regiment" there, and vaunting it all in his book.

Thomas was also a likely reader of French writers (at least in translation) including Ronsard and Montaigne. The latter's late essay "Of Coaches" (1588, translated 1603: *Essais* III) was influential for the "relativistic" way it met the fact that "Our world hath of late discovered another." In his "report" of "certain Spaniardes" who had "fortuned to land in a very fertile, pleasant and well-peopled country" looking for gold mines, Montaigne took up the recorded attempts at "welcome" by Native peoples---who had been "ransacked and razed...for the trafficke of Pearles and Pepper." These "guests" had *claimed* to be "quiet and well-meaning"; "but," Montaigne's "Natives" replied, "their countenance showed them...otherwise. [T]heir King, since he seemed to beg [for gold]... shewed to be poor and needy....[T]he Pope, who had ["given" America to Europe]...expressed himself a man loving dissention, in going about to give unto [others] a thing which was not his owne....

> As for victuals, they should have part of their store. And for gold, they had but little...[it was] meerely unprofitable for the service of their life, whereas all their care was but how to pass it happily and pleasantly.... As touching one only God...they would by no means change their religion ....As concerning [Spanish] menaces, it was a signe of want of judgment, to threaten those whose nature, condition, power, and meanes was to them unknowne. And therefore they should with all speed hasten to [leave] their dominions. (*Essais* III-145, Florio trans.)

By 1606 there was even a French attorney of budding renown publishing poetry about, and producing "theatre" in, the northern reaches of the Newfoundland called New France---Marc Lescarbot, another lettered gentleman whose modest but elegant *The Theatre of Neptune* included Native American "tritons" in their canoes (Illustration from Richardson trans.), as part of a coordinated flotilla of welcome for the aristocrats then supporting the colony at "Port Royal." (More on Lescarbot in later chapters: no doubt those "tritons" were the same Native people hunting up daily food and trading-furs for the ill-prepared Frenchmen---two practices Morton would also follow later on.)

These same convergences of cultural life and the Newfoundland produced as well Shakespeare's last play, *The Tempest*, in Morton's London of 1611. Partly based on the struggling Virginia Company's private accounts of a shipwreck in the Caribbean and the rescue of men presumed dead, the play's source-documents serve here as a barometer of the change coming slowly over Morton's readings about America. For Virginia's Native peoples, antagonized already by

Spanish forces before the first English arrived (Feest), had themselves killed one of those shipwrecked stragglers; but a "lieutenant governor" in command "would not by any means be wrought to a violent proceeding against them...thinking it possible by a more tractable course to win them to a better condition" (qtd. in Langbaum 133).

But the first major English-"Indian" war---the "Conspiracy" of Powhatan peoples in 1622---loomed already. For this document's next sentence already conceded "some measure" of English "revenge" to be due. No doubt it was exacted, leading to the war; and by the time (1625) that Morton could surely have read of this in Samuel Purchas' follow-up to Hakluyt's volumes, *Purchas His Pilgrims*, Purchas himself voiced an angry England no longer interested in proving itself superior to Spain's Black Legend:

> Can a leopard change his spots? Can a savage remaining savage be civil? Were not we ourselves made and not born civil in our progenitors' days? And were not Caesar's Britons as brutish as Virginians? The Roman swords were best teachers of civility to this and other countries near us....(qtd. in Langbaum 133)

Such was the spectrum of voices around Morton's gradually-formulating personal approach to the New World---which was certainly in favor of "civilizing," but by "moderation," and through commodities that created sociocultural change (if not necessarily dependency): things such as salt and, as we'll see, firearms.[27]

Influences are one thing; but for specifics we must look to see who might have benefited most from Thomas Morton's signing aboard. Bristol seaport had long sent explorers to the New World (or, they hoped, *through* it to the East via

---

[27] There was also "the Paradise school" of New World writings, including passages from Verrazzano (1525), Ralegh (1584), Brereton (1602), Smith (1616), Mason (1620) and Alexander (1624)---treated in the next section, and including Morton's apparent "running interest" over the years in poetry about America.

some Northwest Passage). From the 1580s to 1605 the efforts of Davis, Gilbert, Gosnold and others had led fishermen and fur-traders to carry English claims upon the New-found-land's rich natural resources. (Helping them was Spain's present decline, France's early American disasters, and the Dutch chief interest in trade with the *East* Indies.) By 1605 the self-made gentleman Sir Ferdinando Gorges, knighted after long service in the wars and now governor of Plymouth, took up the Crown-approved effort to create something more profitable in America than just seasonal fish-flaking stations. Those already sold their "green cod" to French Catholics for their many meatless days in honor of saints, and the bottom of each barrel to African replacements of Native slaves in the West Indies.

The English Crown wanted permanent settlements, permanent new sources of massive wealth without the heavy political costs of extracting this from domestic subjects. Gorges, excited by reports from mariners and Native Americans abducted or "invited" back to England (*Narration* 17), sent out more ships (Challons, Pring) and, in 1607, a fully-supplied colony to Sagadahoc in "Maine." But this and every other try at "planting" failed, all the way to 1620 (Gorges called Hakluyt's volumes a "painful collection" and had the ambitious man's debts to prove it).

Information was gathering from Native Americans held or hosted in Gorges' Somerset home, including Epenow of Capawac/Martha's Vineyard, who told tales of gold to get himself back where he could jump ship; and Tisquantum/Squanto of Patuxet, future helper of Plimoth Colony. More data came from Captain John Smith's reports c. 1614, such that Gorges remained "assured" that "in time [he] should want no undertakers, though as yet [he] was forced to hire men to stay there the winter quarter at extreme rates" (24). By 1620 his courtly and commercial lobbying brought him the "Great Patent" for

Northeastern lands from Maine to Connecticutt, from King James' new-formed Council for New England. Gorges' legendary energies and ambitions began to cast wide nets for men with the skills to make his visions work:

> ...To descend from those generals to more particulars. What can be more pleasing to a generous nature than to be exercised in doing public good? especially when his labor and industry tends to the private good and reputation of himself and posterity: and what monument so durable, as erecting of houses, villages and towns? and what more pious than advancing of Christian religion amongst people who have not known the excellency thereof? But, seeing works of piety and public good are in this age rather commended by all than acted by any, let us come a little nearer to that which all hearken unto, and that forsooth is profit. Be it so....But art thou of a greater fortune and more gloriously spirited? I have told thee before what thou mayst be assured of, whereby it may appear thou shalt not want means nor opportunity to exercise the excellency of thine own justice, and ingenuity to govern and act the best things, whether it be for thyself or such as live under thee, or have their dependency or hopes of happiness upon thy worth and virtue as their chief....(*Brief Narration* 64)[28]

Gorges' Patent, however, was immediately criticized as a monopoly by stockholders of the larger Virginia Company concerned with the southern plantations (at least operational, meaning turning a profit). These adventurers the new Patent "debarred" from exploiting northern regions, so they incited a Parliament committee against it with the charge that it channeled mere (or too much) "private gain" to individuals such as Gorges.

Efforts to reapportion or reorganize the lands (first claimed *en masse* by virtue of the voyages of Sebastian Cabot, Gilbert and Ralegh) continued into and past 1623; but mostly, as the patent-less Plimoth colonists could testify, confusion and conflict ruled American land-claims. (Struggling Plimothers published their *Mourt's Relation* in 1622 to try to demonstrate occupation and industry, if not "ownership," in the Massachusetts.) As Gorges looked about for an attorney's

---

[28] I cite this source published much later (1658) because with it Gorges himself sums up his own appeals made early in the 1600s. More with Note 74.

counsel, this very confusion became crucial to Morton's departure for New England.

Since about 1617 and through "about...foure yeares" (Morton qtd. in Banks 180), Thomas had been making "acquaintance" with a widow of Swallowfield, Berkshire County (which lies, as he might have said, in "the golden mean" or "middle zone" best for love, directly between London and Devonshire). Alice Miller, a mother of six and pregnant with a seventh child when her husband died in 1616, lived on the properties of a "life jointure" in his sizeable estate "for the Raysinge of childrens portions" (173), and she had "imployed" Morton in "some business that concerned her." In time, claimed Morton in court records (below), he "was solicited by some of her neerest of kinne to take a wief and come live amongst them."

But in 1620, the year before that documented wedding, it is recorded by at least one source that Morton and other individuals were "granted sundry Pattents" by Gorges' Plymouth Council, "to settle" in the Bay of Massachusetts (Gardener 1). Why would a man of limited means, and about to marry a widow with at least a life-estate in land, buy into or enlist himself in the comparatively risky venture of a New England plantation?[29]

---

[29] This necessarily-long footnote examines whether or not Morton actually had a legal documented right to be and to plant in New England.

Adams (AC8: "no evidence"), and Ford (FBH2:46) say that Morton and his American fellow adventurers did not "trouble" to obtain a Patent (that is, a government permit or commission to live on, use and "improve" by enclosing and extracting profit from a bounded tract of land). Holly (8-9) reports that the Council for New England records, generally well-preserved, are "missing" for just these years. But one Henry Gardener (*New England's Vindication*, London 1660) wrote an account not explored in detail by Adams, Ford or Connors.

Gardener was writing with regard to "one Pattent of Boston" to reveal the history of a "Mis-understanding," "To answer such as say [King Charles] has no Title to that vast Empire, from New-Found-Land to Cape-Florida." Gardener declared himself in this same first paragraph no friend to opponents of belief in this royal Title, including "Libertines" who (he said) wished only "to do what is good in their own eyes." Nor did he leave "some Israelites," and "the rest Egyptians," free from his scorn. Bear in mind that Thomas Morton---except as he still "existed" in stray copies of his *book*, that had survived 23 years after their bulk confiscation (see Ch. 9)---was by Gardener's 1660s virtually "long gone," a trivial episode in a dark past that few still thought would amount to much in England's greater history.

The Miller family's wealth was substantial enough to result in the court-case that gave us these records: maybe a far-flung luxury investment could help a working lawyer of "no fixed aboade" to impress, with foreign and court

> In other words, Gardener first-off positioned himself as consciously aligned with *no* side in the dispute between Puritans, Royalists' and Morton's "parties," and "others" for whom he said there was "no king but Christ," as they argued who had or lacked authority to be in Massachusetts at all. This editor reads no particular alignment in his document, but finds equal irony toward each of the self-declared factions.
> Now, Gardener's combing back through the history of Patent-grants, with the sources available to him in 1660, began with mention of the "right by discovery" established in Henry VIII's time via the Cabot, Gilbert, Greenfield [?] and "Rawley" expeditions. Next of those who "procured Pattents" on his list were "my lord Popham and others," whose actual settlement-voyage took place in 1607; their plans faded at "Saquadahock" where (he reported correctly) there remained only ruins and fruit-trees. After three more entries (which mentioned more failures, including the infamous Captain Hunt's abduction of 22 Natives who "would not work," etc.), Gardener's entry for 1619-20 described "King [sic] Letters Pattents to the Council of Plymouth [England], and after confirmed by Pattents of Incorporation to certain Lords, but great troubles arose in Parliament, that it was a monopoly...."
> This correlates with Gorges' *Narration* (34) on the charges *he* tried to answer in Parliament noted above; and Gardener's next entry states: "Then the said Council granted sundry Pattents, as to Capt. Willeston, Mr. Tho. Morton, some of Dorchester and other, to settle in the Bay of the Machechusets [sic]." Directly *after* this entry comes the one for 1621: "There were divers of Robinsons Tenents of Amsterdam and other Merchants of London joyned to settle a Colony nigh Cape Cod"---a description (unmistakably Plimoth Plantation) whose detail, like the others, shows that Gardener sought out the primary accounts (such as Winslow's *Good News*) to be had around him.
> He would have had to work, and supplement what he found perhaps with business documents such as letters and corporate logs: the mainstay Bradford's *History* was not published until the 19th century, and Smith's works were by then good sources on New England's first planters, but not with regard to who possessed legal patents. (Gardener's pages 2 and 3 also relate some wording of the Boston Bay charter granted to John Winthrop's Puritans; and Gardener's record rings almost word-for-word with Morton's---Book 3 [159]---on some of *that* charter's crucial legal stipulations.)
> In all this not-poorly-corroborating detail, we perceive a certain higher likelihood that there really was a Patent granted in *some* form to Morton for a share in a company's attempted plantation. The reasons for and duration of that grant return the reader to the main question of what brought Morton to New England at all.
>   Secondary note: The other chief document supporting a Morton legal-right-to-plant was written by his "old comer" friend Samuel Maverick, present in New England since arriving with the Weymouth company---there, in fact, before Morton. Maverick wrote (*Description of New England* 238-9) that in "1632 or thereabouts" Morton had received "considerable" patent to New England lands: the claim is also in Maverick's "Letter" to the Earl of Clarendon (40). "1632" is possibly a misprint for "1623": or, "1632" may refer to later *different* grants, for Morton was by then in the thick of a circle of men who *could* sign or promise him into some new arrangement; and he claimed large tracts far from Ma-re Mount and Boston Bay in his final New England days. Maverick's is problematic support, not least because this "C of E" West Country man was on such cool terms late in his own life with Puritan Boston Bay that he declared, not unbravely for being in their midst, that Morton's *Canaan* was the most accurate account he had seen on New England and themselves (see Chs. 9/10; and Ranlet offers a good sketch of his life).

connections. It might also signal Alice Miller as a landed widow that her new paramour was not long for English parts.

Since there does appear to be something to the recorded hints that Morton at this time procured some form of share in a colonial venture (previous footnote), the answer may be that Morton, as a lawyer to Gorges, was serving for a fee (not necessarily money) as what land-conveyancers call a "straw." He and other pseudo-grantees on a new Patent document were paid to let their names be used as empty "Cyphers," as Gorges kept trying to dissolve the appearance of a monopoly on "his" New England.[30]

Several people including a well-known ship's captain were named with Morton ("Willeston" for Wollaston, an officer on Morton's eventual ship *Unity*)--- This gave credibility to Gorges' move to placate the committee and appear to open competition for the "undeveloped" wealth in those American patents. A few inside players of inferior class and means, but with that desirable quality of "industriousness," would be allowed a modest appearance of ownership. From the lower social end, it looked like a move beyond the fish-trade's standard pay, the transient's share of profits that depended entirely upon one's own good fishing; as if American land-title, like its wealth, was indeed "trickling down" to any Englishman. The title of one best-selling pamphlet had read: "Nova Britannia. Offering Most [Persons] excellent fruits by planting in Virginia: Exciting all such as be well-affected to further the same."

As publicly stated or implied, aristocratic monopoly on American wealth was the problem that had created the committee. But this was only Gorges' next

---

[30] Gorges and Morton are mostly supposed to have first met via Morton's "Souldier" father, but other means were in place. Investment was one: though failures were the rule in anything beyond fishing ventures, John Smith (Arber ed. 1:259) reported West Country ships making excellent profits by 1620. As early as 1536 maritime connections to "many gentlemen of the Inns of Court" and of West Counties, men with an "interest in Cosmographie," had resulted in the disastrous "Voyage of M. Hore" to the Northeast, where starvation led to cannibalism (Burrage *Voyages* 106).

move with a lawyer to hold off Parliament and the rival investors at their backs, till he could arrange for the revised Patent issued in his son Robert's name for the settlement at Wessagusset/Weymouth in 1622.[31] As will appear, Gorges used Morton however he pleased in their decades of affiliation. And after all, if there was any *use* of this patent within the next four years before Morton sailed, it was only that Wollaston went fishing. Something else had to happen to put Thomas (newly-married, legal stepfather of five young women and a son) on a transatlantic ship.

It began with Alice's son, George Miller, almost as soon as George Senior had died and Morton's acquaintance with Alice commenced. According to Banks' full study of the probate documents, the father's 1616 will had named wife Alice and son George as joint executors; had given Alice "life jointure" (as opposed to title in her own right) in the estate, and each daughter a share of "certain

---

[31] Gorges was only trying to dissolve appearances for awhile, which is why no official records "had" to survive long-term (though this does not change the fact that particularly relevant pages of Council records are "missing" as noted---other such "mysteries" gathered below). Bradford of course disliked Morton but estimated that he had "some small adventure (of his owne or other mens)" in Massachusetts lands (FBH2:46). Rabb's "number-crunching" study of English investment in early colonies reports (26-30) that about 1 in 700 "gentry" became investors between 1575 and 1630: the Weymouth colony was backed early-on by 5 men of no more than gentleman-rank, these small proto-capitalists beginning to outnumber the private fortunes of aristocrat/adventurers, and their self-made imitators such as Gorges.

Investment gave rise, perhaps, to part of Morton's motive when, with his English options few, he tried so hard to reorganize and sustain the American "Mount Wollaston" company in 1625 New England (below). A memory of a "straw" deal also might explain the insistence of his will-and-testament (1643) that he owned and could devolve title to substantial New England tracts (Banks 157, 163). Because he became *the* lawyer who drove the official 1634 erasure of all land-grants, Morton would have realized that he was thereby erasing (probably) his own earliest claim---though there was at least one still lingering afterward, the "Plough Patent" (Ch. 10) that survived strongly enough to wreck Gorges' ambitions. So, perhaps in Morton's last two desperate American years (Ch. 10) he tried to make this early straw-deal appear to have been an actual transfer of title---a not-unknown legal chip. There was no American "Registry of Deeds" except the then-uncompiled history of the Council for New England's acts within royal land-dispensations: by 1635 Gorges himself, the named grantee of several royal land-patents, had to resort to posting-by-filing "deeds" for friends' titles with the "Master in Chancery" (Preston 305). In existing English law, possession of the written deed was all but possession of land; so a common-law barrister leaving (one-way) for America would want to record at least a claim, in *some* available and legally-recognized form, which might later constitute half the battle of ownership for his family.

annuities" drawn from it for their support till marriage. And it left son George (still a teenager) heir-apparent, who "in those days stood *in loco parentis* by custom and law" (Banks 150-1). As the older worldly Morton's and Alice's legal relation developed beyond friendship, George feared---understandably, but without understanding the law---for his inheritance. In fact, his mother's mere "life-jointure" could not affect it, but the youth must have dreaded legal cunning by this stranger.

So George began to try to undermine Morton's character in his mother's eyes, calling him "a very turbulent and troublesome person ...base...and of noe worth" (171); and in the same period, George landed himself in court for several refusals to pay out his sisters' annuities (156). Even so, by early 1621 he convinced his mother to make "triall" of Morton's affection by a stratagem. She was to sign over to George all her interest in the estate for the term of a 50-year lease, and "if at the end of [one] year Morton remained her suitor honorably then the lease was to be void" (152).

Once George had this lease locked up in a trunk (in those days possession of the deed was virtual possession of what it stood for), his conduct toward Alice (now "tenant at will") radically worsened. In Morton's and his mother's court affidavits, he not only wished aloud "for the speedy endinge of her daies" but monopolized or refused her Swallowfield's kitchen facilities and well-water. He sold off her cattle and farm-produce and otherwise "made a show of being Maister" at her expense (175). By autumn 1621, Morton claimed, Alice "did send [for himself] to come to her to proceed in perfecting their marriage," which was cautiously performed out of town but nearby on November 6.

After all of 10 days uncomfortable cohabitation, the family "snatchinge and snarlinge and brawlinge at every meale" (176), Morton and Alice broke into the trunk and "defaced and cancelled" the lease. By June 1622, George (now about 21) filed suit against Alice and Morton for "trespass"; and though "disputes about land inheritance and tenure were the main professional concern of common lawyers" (Prest 121), matters went downhill from here for Thomas Morton.[32]

Charges relate that George accused Morton of being "not only an importunate suitor" but also "especially" intending "to sho[w] his owne cuninge and unlawful ends and to gaine the whole estate to himself" (171). Morton countered that George had paid almost nothing "since his intermarriage" with Alice "for and towards the maintenance of her children" (175), besides the arrogant and "unnaturall" treatment of their mother. Amid the court's traditionally bombastic exchanges of word and accusation in order (Banks says, 149) to obscure clarity where necessary, the two men's charges agree that they flashed weapons and even came to blows. George's may or may not have struck Alice (as Morton charges, 184), but at her age and with the possible gamut of emotions beneath all this, it would not be surprising if true that, as Morton adds,

---

[32] Adams' and Ford's argument (distributed throughout the 1883 *Canaan*, Adams' *Three Episodes*, and Bradford's *History*) that Morton arrived in New England in 1622 with the first Weymouth settlers is undone by these court documents, as well as by others discovered by Holly (treated below), unavailable to them. Morton himself does write twice (see *Canaan* Note 150) that he arrived in 1622, either confusedly or to maximize his apparent "experiment of the country." But at times his memory was better. Minor Wallace Major's groundbreaking 1957 *Dissertation* on Morton (much-cited but unpublished) brings forth another Morton-document cited nowhere else: a "petition" of Morton's to King Charles I's Court of Requests ("Bundle XXXVII, 1636, rpt. in *MHSP* LIX [1926], 92"), dated June 21, 1636---just as Morton was putting last touches on *Canaan* (Ch. 9). In the petition Morton tries to date events with the phrase "in or about the year of our Lord God 1624," and adds that "your said subject [was] then minded to travaile and to make a Voyage into New England aforesaid, which he shortly after performed" (qtd. in Major 9). Further language there reinforces the 1624 arrival-date as Morton adds that "your said subject about twelve yeares since departed out of the Realme of England, and travelled into New England in the parts beyond the seas").
    Banks must also be right that no lawyer thus invested in a suit against George Miller would likely choose to be out of the country when a verdict was imminent. Nor (as Banks says) would those alert scribes of Plimoth have been likely to leave the presence of a man like Morton unremarked on *their* side of the Atlantic, had he been there so early, claiming with his "typical methods" (treated below) a share of their fur-trade business when even Plimoth's first admitted rivals had yet to land in New England, namely the Weymouth planters.

the older Alice was then (Feb. 1622) "with Child," and "did shortly after...miscarry." The child cannot have been her first husband's.

On June 8, 1623 the Chancery Court, "upon full and longe hearinge of both parties" (187), decided that plaintiff George should "enjoye" not his mother's Swallowfield but a subsidiary farm "called Wivalls," and render Alice and daughters their annuities. Alice was to "enjoye" another place called Stanford, and time found Swallowfield in the hands of daughter "Susan Miller...spinster" (189). Now, since the court's finding matched the legal fact from the start, that Morton had "nothing in the premisses but in right of his wief," and that "if he should live asunder hee should suffer her to enjoy her own estate" (188)---why did Morton suddenly "disappear," until history found him a year later in New England?

His later detractors made much of the report that he "sould all [Alice's] goode even to her wearing apparell," and dropped out of sight of the court, which had essentially found against Alice and himself. But, in the court's later words, as it apparently sought some kind of monies (court fees? damages?) from Morton, it only "appeareth by affidavit" to have been the fact. As Ranlet points out (10), the clothes-selling charge flew both ways (183 in Banks' gathered documents), and was thus likely a mutual court-fiction. Alice received an award under judgment: she was still living. After seven years' association, and such detail of caring for her in the document-language, this "theft" of her clothes seems generally as simple as the rest of George's and others' charges, and we cannot know who attested the affidavit. (Again, Banks adds that getting *some* form of language on paper against the foe was half the game, 150.)

Further, this affidavit, recorded with the June judgment, claimed that Morton had not been "heard of since February." Did he abscond before judgment was rendered? He was under no arrest-warrant: he had been issued instead a notice on February 1 that year of a "Peremptory order to the defendant to show cause why decree should not be made final." By that November, there was only George's claim that he was "endeavouring to find out holes whereby to elude performance," and "declyninge all obedience" (188).[33]

"Performance" of what? The judgment had provided for Alice: George was "willing to abide" it. Why was Morton apparently unwilling, since all payments "to and by" his wife passed neither to nor from him, but circulated within the estate's economy? Banks' scrutiny showed no punishable deed or even unsavory motive to be "reasonably charged" to Morton concerning Alice's wealth (152; and recall Amussen's study in Ch. 1 here, that widows in general were in no rush to remarry). So it seems strange that Morton should consider himself so "worsted" (159) by this verdict that he utterly dropped out of the social web; and to the degree that his 1620 involvement with American land-patents began to seem a better option for his latter (late forties) days, than either making do with Alice, or otherwise toughing out his career on the rural court circuits. Adventure was one thing: this was a man who probably enjoyed the long dashing horseback-ride he made to get back from London to Alice with the marriage-license, before she changed her mind from listening to the young knave. Transatlantic America---that was a different proposition.

At least till further searches in English records, then, it seems fairer to call this a mystery than to let stand the shallow slanders of Morton's Puritan and later enemies, who also tried to connect his obscure Massachusetts arrival with

---

[33] Alice died sometime after 1623's judgments and before her daughter Margaret's "portion" came due from the estate (Banks 189).

On George Miller, see Banks' appended brief record of another suit, which record tells of his 1620 involvement in a very colorful incident concerning possession of a certain pew in church (155). As George fought for his interests in court with regard to his sisters' annuities he characterized his father as mentally incapable of having made a valid will, disclosing (Banks 156) "the extremities to which he could go in slander to defend himself."

their own completely unsupported statements that Morton had to be shipped back to England because of a "foul suspition of murther" (Thos. Wiggin 1632, qtd. in Ford's edition of Bradford's *History* 2:76n1). Plimoth's Bradford and Edward Winslow ("Petition" in Mass. Hist. Soc. *Procs.* V:133), with Boston Bay's John Winthrop and Thos. Dudley (Chs. 9-10, Sampler), all with intense common cause against Morton, claimed that he had been "vehemently suspected for the murder of a man [in England] that had adventured moneys with him, when he came first into New England" (Dudley's words).

Nearly four years after the court-suit against George---in November 1627 ---a "writ" of some kind *appears* to have "coincidentally" brought this rumor or charge across the desk of then bureaucrat John Winthrop's desk. Fully cited in Ch. 8 below, its *apparent* date places it just after Morton's May Revels, and before his first arrest by Plimoth; but it claims to tell of Morton's personal affairs going back to this earliest "exit to America." We must venture just ahead of the story to clear this source of later smoke.

Suffice it for now that there are serious problems with "The Winthrop Papers," both in "John's" and his editors' handling of this "writ" (problems treated in full in Chs. 7-10). And there are more in Bradford's equally-vague words, that "a warrente" had been sent from "the Lord Cheefe Justice [then Sir Nicholas Hyde in England]" to Winthrop's Boston court in 1630, that Thomas Morton might be punished "capitally for fouler misdemeanors there perpetrated" (Dudley Letter).

But by no one's account was this "warrant" ever shown to or seen by anybody. Neither Morton nor the court's own recorders were told the charge written upon it at his first American "trial" ("they have a warrant now, a chief one too" he mocks in Book 3). But Winslow and Wiggin, not then knowing the full story themselves, naively revealed that the originator of this charge---which supposedly drove Morton's English disappearance, and his bumptious American arrival---had been none other than Morton's "wife's sonne," George Miller (who in his later days became a Puritan adherent). Still, the critics were undeterred. Ford (for one) in his notes to Bradford's *History* perpetuated the charge as "nothing improbable"; and yet he demonstrated in the same textual breath both the biases of these writers, and their utter lack of documentary substance. Banks demolished the charge on several grounds.[34]

We have seen good reasons to assume that Morton's family was not without means to help him in a spot; and that he had some kind of practice supporting him during the years between the Inns and Alice Miller. He was not a desperate man. Legally he had "nothing...but in right of his wief" in her Berkshire properties, as a lawyer he knew it; and since the feud with George resulted, after all, in Alice's own "reduction" to a smaller estate, Morton (the admirer of *Don Quixote*, 1605) may well have decided to "live asunder" and spare her more. It is the most parsimonious explanation.

"And what hazard will not an industrious mind and courageous spirit undergo," Thomas asks in Book 1 (10), then drawing upon his Horace: "Ardent

---

[34] Considering the age of this cloud on Morton's character, which even his greatest scholarly antagonist (Adams) had to admit was nothing *but* vapor, it seems fair to quote Banks (157):

"The extensive search which I made [in the 1920s] throughout all the indictments and warrants issued on the authority of Chief Justice Hyde during his term of office 1627-32 fails to reveal any record of such a proceeding against Morton, nor do the Sessions Records of Devon covering gaol deliveries for the same period afford us any entry of his name as a prisoner at Exeter [as Winthrop's court insisted, in order to "return" Morton to England, that is, put him in second exile from Massachusetts]. While this evidence is negative, a still surer corroborative testimony is Morton's own silence on the subject. Had he been acquitted after trial of such a charge, or released from arrest on suspicion raised by his Puritan enemies for lack of evidence to prosecute, we should have had a full exposition of their contemptible slanders as proof of their relentless antagonism. He never missed an opportunity in his book to relate their petty persecutions of him and it is a sound conclusion that nothing of the kind ever took place because of his failure to mention it in defence of his position. We may attribute this 'foul suspition of murther' to the vicious mind of his stepson." Nor does Banks mention that to his life's end Morton never showed a qualm about return *per se* to England. Though as late as 1633 Winslow still brought it out before Court and Council (Ch. 9), no record reveals any other remark or action upon it, and no such charges were ever raised by anyone outside Puritan circles.

trader that he is, he rushes to the furthest Indies, fleeing poverty through sea, through riches, through flame." Morton moved out, and quit trying to fight for a piece of English land: there was too much competition these days. If he was still so angry years later that he unfavorably compared England's "irregular young people" with Native American youth, he certainly may have refused now to pay one shilling of any judgment. There was promise of little "quietness" between men of Morton's and George's neighborly codes.

He moved out, but no divorce-proceeding has come to light. Perhaps Alice and Thomas planned his return if and when the boy matured; but Alice passed away before they met again. Like his ancient Brutus cast out of Troy and early Rome besides, Morton would voyage to avoid an "unquiet life" (17). Seeing (as above) that by now England had been two years at war with "southern Virginia" Native peoples, this relatively informed and "circumspect" move to New England converged neatly with the needs of Sir Ferdinando. Gorges' biographer Preston notes that just now in the evolution of his plans and policies, Gorges was looking less for experienced mariners and more toward the lucrative fur-trade returns brought in by the landsman.

If Thomas showed Alice this migratory deference, perhaps she reciprocated with personal goods, articles he could sell for better "quarter." Consider: she had to change abode in compliance with the court: people often dispose of such goods at such times; and, on Morton's side, he could see 5000-6000 Devon men trying their American fortunes in 250-300 ships per year (Oppenheim 34-5). George might have grudged Morton even this sort of help in buying the gear an outdoorsman would want for such a voyage. It was Thomas' pride to cultivate complete independence of external circumstances, to find happiness within himself by reverencing the voice of reason in the soul (so counseled his Epictetus, called upon later in further dire straits, *Canaan* 172).

Letters should leap no longer to deny him a valid emotional basis for his "flight." He may have seen his first child miscarried, his attempt to make a home for himself ended in bitter wrangling over money.[35]

Prest noticed that "interest in maritime exploration [was] particularly fitting for a West Country man" and member of the Inns (162). Another slightly earlier Elizabethan gentleman, Thomas Whythorne (who in 1571 published the earliest-known collection of English madrigals) came to much the same decision after disappointment in a love affair (Osborn ed., 60):

> I determined to spend a time in foreign and strange countries, the better to digest all the changes that, hitherto, I had felt and tasted. And when I came beyond the seas, I endeavoured myself as well to know the customs and manners of the people where I came, as also to learn their speech and languages.[36]

---

[35] His 1627 "Song" devotes verses to "the heart opprest with grief" within "the Melancholy man" (137), recommending dance and erotic contact as "cure." As he writes of his indentured youths with a comparison to "Gammedes" perhaps by now he carried if not called himself bisexual.

Morton's biographical story continues in Chapter 5. Near the end of the typical promotional tract *Description...of New Albion* (1648: rpt. in Force 2-VII, 34) is an appeal to sweeten Morton's move somewhat, to "the kinde Gentleman that in England doth not live without...law-suits and troubles, [who] may settle here...and live in plenty, and variety of all sports, hunting Deere, hawking Fowl, fishing, and...dainty fruits...." *New Albion* also promised that, "together against a few naked salvages," Englishmen "may...with sword, and the word [of The Bible] civilize, and convert them...and by trading with them for furs, get his ten shillings a day...."

[36] Did Morton come alone to America or did means afford at least one personal servant? *Canaan* ("nine persons besides dogs," "seven-headed Hydra") mostly confuses. But (speaking as textual editor) *Canaan* is replete with clues that it was at least partly dictated aloud. And, as Morton in his last American sojourn began to go about his affairs, Winslow noticed somebody at his side, "a very atheist and fit companion for him" (Ch. 10).

"Make room, make room...!"

ANTIMASQUE:
AMERICA'S FIRST POETRY IN ENGLISH

> [W]hen any one of these pantomimic gentlemen, who are so clever that they can imitate anything, comes to us, and makes a proposal to exhibit himself and his poetry, we will fall down and worship him as a sweet and holy and wonderful being; but we must also inform him that in our State such as he are not permitted to exist: the law will not allow them. And so when we have anointed him with myrrh, and set a garland of wool upon his head, we shall send him away to another city. For we mean to employ for our souls' health the rougher and severer poet or story-teller, who will imitate the style of the virtuous only, and will follow those models which we prescribed at first when we began the education of our soldiers.
> ---Plato, *The Republic*, c. 390 B.C.: 99-100

Who is North America's first poet in English? What is America's first English poem, and can we decide these things with any certainty? As we close the millennium that made English the dominant language on this continent, does anybody care? What will the answers to these questions tell about the earliest colonization of what became The United States? What will they tell about America after 500 years of that story?

It may be that research will place before us no single indisputable name or poem's title for these unclaimed American distinctions. We may also wonder why America should care at all, when Western civilization in general has not missed much---or has it?---being scarcely aware of its own first identifiable poet and her works. (It was a woman, a priestess named Enheduanna, daughter of Sargon of Ur; who composed erotic lyrics as part of her culture's high worship of its Deities---see Qualls-Corbett.) Perhaps Americans would learn worthwhile things in Greece, where the merest informal recitation of lines from Homer will draw a crowd of all ages and put them in a trance; or in Italy, where a clear majority know at least that old Virgil sang the Gods-given, Roman right to rule for the house of Augustus.

Maybe America lost track of its "first English poet" because the colonies, especially in Puritan and Revolutionary times, so deliberately and thoroughly broke with Old World traditions, and poets find it hard to "amount to much" without tradition. But again, *did* America really make the cultural breaks it thinks it made in this regard? Doesn't its indifference (and sometimes, exile) for poets replicate precisely the contemptuous views of the Old World's Plato, quoted above? As Kurt Vonnegut, Jr. remarked at a tiny grief-gathering in New York City years ago, upon the corporate end of a literary press---Here concern for poetry is "like caring about lacrosse."

But we will find that, as we do explore this in detail, the identity of the person *most* deserving of the title "first American poet in English" will also bring it home to us why most Americans (even teachers of English) have scarce a good clue about these questions.[37]

Literate Western cultures since the honey-tongued "Athenian Bee" have described poesy and its practitioners with a language of mixed fear and contempt. For the author of the toweringly influential *The Republic*, a work at the very fountainhead of scholarly tradition, the intolerable creations and influences of poets were too likely to have bad effect upon "our guardians" (meaning the combined manpower of the state and senior male property-owning authorities). Too much poetry or too much credence in it would make them "too excitable and

---

[37] An informal, long-running poll by this researcher has usually received three responses: 1) "Huh? Maybe later!" 2) The Pilgrims, but no idea of what "American poems" were written by them; 3) Anne Bradstreet, same "no idea" about the poems/dates etc. Bradstreet in fact comes *ninth* chronologically among possible first American poets in English. Plato ("Broad," in demotic Greek, or more loosely, "Fatso") salutes his own Manifest American Destiny.

effeminate" (84; qtd. further below). Cicero, as Rome's most influential inheritor of Western literary cultural tradition, largely followed his Greek forerunners. For Cicero the poet's definitive endowment was "ardour of imagination," "something similar to frenzy" (*De Oratore* 275). The poet was supposedly given more than others to "believing" in "fictions" (a term treated below), and even worse, was likely to lead *others* to believe that there was "substance" to what he/she had to say. Amid the demands of the "real" world as defined by emperors, popes, patriarchs and property, poets and poetry "savor[ed] of madness" when listeners were so overpowered that they lost their true sense of things "important" in the world. No sunshine was to be wasted upon what authorities deemed "empty and ridiculous" language, mere "volubility of words" (*De Oratore* 147); as opposed to their own well-reasoned, long-enduring plans for propagandizing and/or forcing populations into profitable empires. In the "real" world, "culture" meant a male elite ruling over obedient warriors, women and laborers.[38]

Societies across historical time and cultural difference have tried to explain this uniquely "overwhelming" power ascribed to poetic language, as a function of everything from meter to "proper morality." The constant has been the anxiety that, as William Webbe (for example) put it in his *Discourse of English Poetry* (1586), "an apt composition of wordes or clauses, draw[s] *as it were by force* the hearers' eares even *whither soever it listeth*...Plato affirmeth [this] to be...an enchantment, as it were to persuade them anything *whether they would or no*" (spelling modernized, emphasis added: rpt. in Arber ed.).[39]

---

[38] Not that poetry alone could carry dangerous content---"Such then is our theology," as Plato put it. "Some tales are to be told, and others are not" (*Republic* 82).

[39] In Sir Philip Sidney's influential words in Thomas Morton's day (explored further below), even if the poet "never lieth," it is only because he supposedly "nothing affirmeth" (*Defence* 136). Across the English Channel at that time was largely the same situation, France's *la Pleiade* of poets including Ronsard standing up to "pressure on poetry to be something less than its full self," a "game or a sermon" only (Castor 24). Apparently, poets can too easily imply that *all* "agendas" are

But how should we proceed to search for America's first English poet and poetry? How should we define the crucial terms?[40]

"First" here will mean the earliest chronological year in which a given writer composed---not necessarily published---the verse in question.

"American" is of course more difficult to define, and here is no claim to have reached an "objective" standard. But the attempt is necessary. So, here, the term (like "poetry" below) is meant to function *as inclusively as possible* in our search. "American" will here mean poetry written by an individual who had physical contact with the North American land-mass---who was *here*, even if only for a day. Thus, "American" poetry will be, in the highest priority of its communication, *concerned with North America*---It qualifies as "American" because the clear majority of the referents for its words/signifiers are *here* on this continent; and because, for its (broadly-conceived) intended audience of people who speak, read and write English, most of its linguistic meanings, emotional impact(s), and other "reasons and rewards for reading it," if any, derive from and "depend" upon North American land, peoples, and/or history. The "American" poet knows and is consciously dealing with the fact that he/she is "addressing"

---

fictions, human constructions; and this is no help in keeping subject-populations disciplined and mobilized for services that enrich a society's elite.

William Webbe's was "the most extensive treatise on the subject that had as yet been published" in England (Atkins 151) until Sidney's *Defence* (1580-82, not printed till 1595). Roger Ascham, another educator concerned with the examples being set for young people, felt that "that rapt inclination" toward "the poetic" was "too ranging of itself, though it [cannot be] helped forward where it is, and would not in any case be forced where it is not" (qtd. in Halpern 54).

A less anxious theory of poetry's power came a bit later from Sir William Temple in 1689. He wrote that poetry seems so much more powerful than other forms of language because of its synesthetic effects: it "assemble[s] all the powers of Eloquence, of Music and of Picture, which are all allowed to make so strong impressions upon human minds" ("Of Poetry," rpt. in Witherspoon/Warnke 547).

[40] Let us first dispose of one important possible confusion about these questions. This is definitely *not* to ask what was the first poetry composed in America, or who composed it. That can only be answered with reference to Native American people(s).

America, as a subject of poetry and, perhaps most desirably, for the people(s) on that land.[41]

But why stipulate that "American" poetry can only have come from somebody who was here? Couldn't a Wampanoag write "Italian" poetry if

---

[41] It may interest some to know that editors of *Publications of The Modern Language Association*, publishers of (as they say) "the best of its kind, whatever its kind," have found this concept of "American" to be "rather pedestrian." Be that as it may, these questions remain to be asked. Why? The first and oldest reason has been "moral." That is, all the American poetry written before that first minstrel of Puritan values, Anne Bradstreet (who, again, comes in fact no less than *ninth*), was ignored by critics because it had all been found (as we'll see) even more "morally wanting" than artistically bad. If it offered reader, teacher and classroom little evangelical use, it was unfit for consumption among the first Puritan congregations and, later, when "the minister" himself usually taught "Literature" courses (if they were offered at all) at America's first great schools big and small. Thus education stood poised to ignore or condemn a Whitman's *Leaves of Grass*.

Some students grew up to be publishers. And soon, who in the American corporate world could imagine school administrations purchasing textbooks---from those first *McGuffey Readers*, to the 1990s' waxy chapters on "Spirit," designed in Marketing and written by wage-serfs ---if those books enshrined on page 1, say, not Bradstreet's Christian *angst*, but a quasi-pagan seance or a bawdy frontier lyric as First American Poetry? It was deemed more ethical to ignore the question entirely. If somebody's poem had commemorated the first mass baptism of benighted American "red men," Americans would know it from childhood to the Halls of Montezuma.

Such a "seance and song" *are* the poetic fact, as we shall see. But Christian ministers, along with lawyers, editors and deeply-"interested" cultural patriarchs, produced and policed the news-journal reviews that for generations pumped perennially-flagging Biblical ideals (for the laboring classes) into America's mainstream criteria of "Literature" (see Baym 84-85: Guillory 263; Graff *Professing*; and Charvat's anatomy of these critical values as early as the 1830s).

More recently, as moral reasons give way to would-be scientific ones, current academic discourse would hold that "American" can have little to do with a poet's having been here, seen and experienced the continent. For *language* is now conceived as the all-distorting or at least always-intervening "dark filter" imposed by one's tongue and therefore culture: language is such an obstruction, trapped (and us with it) in its own circular self-referentiality and dead-end, mirror-like effects upon perception and meaning, that nobody "saw" America, or "wrote about" it. "Discourses" in Europe had "written" ("inscribed") its people in every sense, and "wrote" what they said from cradle to America and the grave. "Being there" is irrelevant. In poststructuralist assumptions, even "the idea that the earth goes around the sun is not an *improvement* of the idea that the sun goes around the earth. It is a shift in perspective," and not a perception about the "actual" universe (critic Barbara Johnson qtd. in Scholes 99).

But, in Scholes' exceptional critique, "All talk about human perception has got to reckon with the actual mechanisms of that perception or it is metaphysical in the worst sense of that word" (94): "If we are totally cut off from things, language must be one of the things" (105). Indeed, after more than two decades' institutional dominance, devotees remain unable to show (for ex.) when and where "language" emerged from other forms of (equally determinative?) communication; or began to have such incapacitating or ideological effects upon hominids or humans; or how these critics seem to be exempt from their own core-postulates.

Familiar reading(s) can gain new interest in the light of evolution and nonWestern European concepts of "human being" (for exs. Bermudez, Carroll): text as something produced by bands of primates. I hope readers will factor in these issues and grant that we can still proceed.

he/she adhered as strictly as anybody else to Italian poetic conventions and subject-matter? In most-inclusive terms---Probably. But few European people would become insistent that a Wampanoag who had never been to Europe had actually made the true full grade of authenticity. Unless we really are as utterly circumscribed by language as some critics claim (previous footnote), it seems to defy "sense" that a Wampanoag could equal or surpass an Italian person at "the most authentic possible" Italian poetry.

Perhaps we lay hold of something if we similarly grant that no poetry could be *more* "authentically American" than that composed by Native Americans, in their own languages. This is most obvious because, even with all arguments about the obstructions of language factored in, "Native people" *means* that they were *here* the longest. "Authentic American" must have something to do with being here. Even if all Native peoples crossing the Bering Straits were blinded more by preexisting language than by snow, we know that their languages evolved, like everything else over time, on this land. Those languages grew (the land and its life demanded new sounds/signifiers), and changed (an existing idea/word had to be modified in the light of unfamiliar experience with "reality").

Their languages, then, took on "American authenticity" as they became more able to describe, particularize, or embody the "facts and flavors" of *this* continent, of this place and no other. In fact, both Native languages and English will more or less forever be in this process. "American" language began when any tongue began to tell about *this* place, about these peoples and creatures and land, to the degree of particularity that they could not be "blurred into" or "mistaken" for any other. "American" means there were/are actual *referents*, there, in that place, *corresponding* to the words/symbols (whatever they may be) in a poem's communication. "American" language denotes and communicates, through the imperfect lens of language, America and American entities *as such*. An "American poetry in English" is known to the degree that it performs the same function as every other "American language."[42]

As for "poem" and/or "poetry"---In order to keep our considerations as open as we can, we should employ as little as possible "expert" theory or definition. For now let us think not-too-rigidly of "poetry" or "the poetic" as a *quality* in or achieved by language; and of a "poem" as an at least-apparently "finished" or completed "unit" of communication or expression. The court of consideration can remain wider if, as we survey the contending verses, we absorb from *them* the differences in conception, and so in results, of "American poetry." We must not exclude the kinds of verse written for "practical" reasons (for example, to "advertise" America, to aid the memory, etc.) nor valorize verses born out of more clearly intellectual, moral, or (as they say) "purely artistic" intent. The admired defender of "ancient learning" in England's "battle of the books," Sir William Temple, cautioned that "After all, the utmost that can be achieved or, I think, pretended by any rules in this art is but to hinder some men from being very ill poets, but not to make any man a very good one" (*Of Poetry*, 550). The reader must decide when and where both poetry and poem emerge.

But it may not predetermine too much if we do ask for a certain level of "artistic preconception" from contenders. If we know something of how these authors conceived their *own* actions in taking up the poet's pen, we may the

---

[42] Partly for the same reasons, Latin, the West's previous imperial language, evolved into French, into Spanish, etc. Also, as Rowe explains origins of *anthropology* and *ethnography*: the latter had its 15th/16th-century origins in Hebrew *goy* and Greek *ethne*, meaning all "the nations" said to be "outside" the self-appointed human "cultural center of the world" (as Israel's "Chosen" concept and Greece's *barbaroi* term for "strangers" implied). In a sense like ethnographic writing "confirmed accurate," a poem will be "American" as it delivers something about place and/or peoples *there*, *"outside"* in that "nation that is not us"---even and especially *after* we have looked, in Richard Price's words, "*at*, as well as through" the language crafted into writing about that given nation (*Ethnographic History* 3).

better explain where each of us first sees those forever-arguable entities, the true poem and truly poetic.

At least within the most anciently-known and widely-accepted Western European definitions, a "poet" has been conceived as a "maker," and a "poem" a product of language "made or created" (*Oxford English Dictionary*). Poetry is some kind of "effect of language" that a person consciously sets out to produce, rather than an apparently-accidental "indefinable quality." Ben Jonson, like his whole generation influenced by Sir Philip Sidney (below), reflected that a poem was not only made---it "feigneth and formeth a fable." "The fable and fiction" were for him "the form and soul" of the art ("What Is A Poet?" in *Timber*, 1641). Many a contemporary essayist (here, Owen Felltham) agreed that "the words being rather the drossy part, [the] conceit I take to be the principal" (*Resolves*, 1628: "Of Poets and Poetry"). We can gain useful tools with a brief further look at conceptions of poetry during these English decades between "Discovery" and the 1620s-40s, when English texts about America began to burgeon.

The question was approached from a number of directions, such as whether "true poetry" should have a "Classical" form, should have a particular meter if one at all, should be "moral" or, necessarily, no more than whimsy. Certainly most often, poetry was recognized as something "above" or at least *different* from "the level of ordinary prose" (*OED*): poetry stands distinct from ordinary language and writing because it communicates "something more" than the literal sense or sum of words. It is something not always "in" the meaning *and/or* the form; yet it may require interplay between both to be known at all. Perhaps the above demands for "a well-crafted conceit" near the heart of "true poetry" emerged from this necessity to say more than just literal "reference" can say on its own.

Cicero's *De Oratore*, a most influential text in Europe's Renaissance, came to this problem in exploring the orator's and the poet's need, as potent communicators, to "illustrate and adorn" their speech with words having "metaphorical" qualities. This became necessary when literal language was found inadequate for experience, "when that which can scarcely be signified by its proper word" had to be somehow communicated, "that *the whole nature* of any action or design...be more significantly expressed" (376-77, emphasis added).

An English approach to this came from Arthur Golding's 1567 translation of Ovid's *Metamorphoses* (a "mythological handbook" for would-be poets including "a short survey...of the nature and value of true poesy"). For Golding, poetry is language so arranged that the reader must "seek a further meaning than the letter gives to see," in order to claim that she/he has fully understood or plumbed the intended message(s) of the words ("Epistle" XV, 1. 542; text in Kermode 521). Poetry for Golding is what the reader *experiences* through this process of seeking.

Sir Philip Sidney's watershed *Apology* or *Defence of Poetry* (printed 1595), terms poetry "an imitation," "a speaking picture" (110); an "image" as distinct from "the philosopher's word" (116). For Sidney, as for Greek Aristotle and Roman Horace, poetry was usually both teacher and entertainer, working by imitation (*mimesis*) and "fiction" (*mythos*---Howell 158-160; Goldman 68). Sidney's purpose is defense rather than theory, and he does not pursue what *radically* distinguishes "poetic language" from other forms of it. But he does contrast what he conceives as poetry, with its origins in "divine delightfulness," and a "school art" that he says "philosophers" later made (141). Sidney gently elevates (or perhaps restores) poetic language to the status of religious experience, suggesting that despite the many kinds of hostility to it described in his essay, poetry merits mention in the same breath with the Bible and its Psalms. The Psalms are poetry (106), "nothing but Songs":

> For what else is the awaking [of King David's] musical instruments, the often and free changing of persons, his notable *prosopopeias* [personifications], when he maketh you, as it were, see God coming in his majesty, his telling of the beasts' joyfulness, and hills' leaping, but a heavenly poesy, wherein he showeth himself almost a lover of that unspeakable and everlasting beauty to be seen by the eyes of the mind, only cleared by faith?

The "definition" is itself an imitation: "poetry" is something that *feels like* hearing David's instruments animistically "awaken," it is *like* what one may feel in imagining "God," or "the beasts' joyfulness, and hills' leaping." It was these pictures, crafted into a *conceit*, that Sidney selected in order to make "art": an invention that would make others know and feel *as he had* ("poetry") in the presence of his "object."

As we seek more conceptions of "poetry" by the earliest English generations whose offspring colonized America---a period which J. W. H. Atkins' detailed survey found "vague and confused" (138), full of "confusion and poverty of ideas concerning poetry" (156)---we find that many speak in "imitative" terms like the above, reproduce what they strive to describe. Others, for example George Gascoigne's 1575 *Notes on English Verse*, take a technical approach to recognizing "true poetry" and debate the need for and effects of various techniques of rhetoric in achieving it; usually specifying (in Gascoigne's words) the "most necessarie poynt...to ground [a 'delectable poem'] upon some fine invention" (31). The demand for deliberate craft and a conceit seems to be consistent. But Gascoigne's adjectives (delectable, fine) promise more than anything else to take us into wholly subjective realms.

Another trend sought to identify poetry (or rather, to debate its right to exist) according to moral and/or social agendas. Spanish Catholic Father Jose de

Acosta's magisterial *Natural and Moral History of the Indies* (1588-9) herded together "vain philosophers," "Greeks and Romans," Native Americans and "poets" *en masse* and proclaimed them "heathens" all, because of the idolatrous confusion they supposedly shared regarding Creator and created thing, born of an "inordinate" love of beauty. On not dissimilar grounds, humanist educators generally regarded poetry as "unwholesome for young boys" and suffered anxiety over "the problem of poetic content" in the Classical authors' texts they so admired (Halpern 47). Poets, like "fire, wind, swift air...stars...[and] the beauty of these things," were dangerously likely to lure the young from duty to God and Empire.

Puritans too, according to Robert Daly (*God's Altar* 55), strove to define and enjoy poetry as "descriptions of God's world, not creations of the poet's fancy." They had something in common with Anglican readers of *The Book of Common Prayer*, which (like the Bible's *Luke* I: 46-55) celebrates the "scattering" of "the proud in the imagination of their hearts." The "growth of Puritan feeling...challenged anew the status and value of poetry" (Atkins 102), and its selfstyled "new creatures" reborn in Biblical literalism became explicitly anxious that, without incessant pounding upon the public psyche, people might resort to imaginative thoughts of their own.[43] Either that, or "frothy bumbasted words" themselves would break their constant attention to "God" (Higginson's *New England's Plantation* in Force 1:12).

---

[43] Greenblatt 113: "[The] extreme violence on both [Catholic and Protestant] sides exists precisely so as to deny the contaminating presence of the imagination---of human making---in one's own beliefs. Only by destroying the other will one assure the absolute reality and necessity of the order to which one has submitted oneself and hence fully justify [to oneself as well as others including political "masters"] this submission." An interesting anatomy of reason, order and authority to place beside the transhistorical accusation that poets and poetry will be the ones trying to "make" people believe things "whether they will or no."

The Ramist revolution in rhetoric of that day, furthermore, had "moved" poetry to a relatively humble place within a scholar's or speaker's *inventio*. If all went well in the next few Protestant-political decades, poetry in a Puritan world would be considered less the "prideful" ability to "make" or "create," and more the ability (from Jehovah alone) merely "to come upon," "discover" or "lay open to view" His Works and their power to evangelize.

Poetry for this "school" was to be one flank of transnational Puritan "cultural reform" in favor of Biblical values. As Perry Miller sums it up, a Puritan usually "expected that the example set by the Classical poets might guide him to achieve a higher virtue in life...[Poetry should be] a speculum or compendium of the profoundest spiritual mysteries drawn from the most diverse learnings. " And yet, for all that, Miller concludes that "most of them probably gave it little consideration as an art...and remained curiously indifferent to the quintissential breath and finer spirit of the poetic idiom" (*Puritans* II: 546). We may agree with Bercovitch (2) that Miller "drastically underrated" the Puritan "aesthetic dimension"; but "indifferent" still seems a strange term for people who, if they could have (as A. L. Rowse remarked), would have shut down Shakespeare (*A Biography* 71). Even the great Renaissance expositor of the "idols of the tribe" Sir Francis Bacon, though he granted that poetry was more than "wine of devils" (*Essays*, rpt. in Witherspoon/Warnke 40), demanded that its matrix "imagination" be held a subservient handmaid to his definition of "reason"; and "not to oppress it" (qtd. in Howell 157).

Our findings then? "Poetry" as the effect of a "conceit" crafted out of language, that powerfully communicates (that is, replicates in the reader) the effects of coming to perceive, understand, even feel his/her chosen experience, subject, etc. Not forgetting "poetry" as language simply made "delectable," technically sophisticated, socially useful---These were the most agreed-upon concepts at the time of the English birth of American letters.

We should add two of the broadest: George Puttenham's 1589 *Arte of English Poesie*---although it shared some of the fears seen above and was cited at times by Puritans against the liberal arts (Hammond 9)---described poetry as simply "any witty or delicate conceit" (qtd. in Atkins 160). Edmund Spenser, like a number of "masters," combined all these definitions. For him poetry was "no art, but a divine gift and heavenly instinct," "adorned" with but not "gotten" by "labour and learning," a language touched with "a certain *enthousiasmos* and celestial inspiration." Spenser's multiple aims hopefully led, he wrote, toward the "fashioning [of] a gentleman," and instilled in him approved moral and social "doctrine by example" (his unpublished *English Poet*: see Maclean, ed., *Faerie Queene* 427).

And so we turn to contending examples from primary sources.

It should be mentioned that the learned young scholar Stephen Parmenius, born in Hungary c.1560 and eventually a member of Sir Humphrey Gilbert's 1583 expedition to North America, might have seized the title of "America's first English poet" with relative ease. His American visit came earlier than any (known) poetic contender, and he was, as Quinn and others conclude, without question a "maker" quite likely capable of the "epic of the exploration of eastern North America by the English" (Quinn 3), which he fully intended to write upon seeing the place (and that is why he took ship with Gilbert).

Unfortunately, Parmenius drowned when his ship ran aground off Sable Island (Gilbert's ship, overloaded with weaponry, disappeared on the same voyage home). Secondly, though some of Parmenius' appreciable compositions survived him, these were all pre-American, and written in Latin. Early English-American letters would not have suffered for gaining Parmenius' verse, woven with spiritual as well as geographical explorations, the former including Hermeticist theories of "the dual nature of the function of the human soul" (Quinn 35) that were much debated during the Renaissance. Parmenius imagined himself a Virgil's role in the budding Empire, and filled early pieces with "subjected foreign peoples" and storm-tossed ships:

> Now having launched our Ship we plough across
> The Ocean; now may you provide fair winds,
> Fair goddess. Be both poop and prow to us,
> Be our ship's anchor and direct the sails
> Of this our craft in all her voyaging....
> [1575 poem to Queen Elizabeth,
> trans. from Latin by and in Quinn, 10]

For all this, however, when Parmenius actually came to write (still on ship off the coast of the Newfoundland), he tried to warm up with several letters home. The expedition (focused on mineral wealth) had so far seen "only the barren shoreland" and failed to penetrate the "thick interior forest": "the wild, impenetrable woods, the high, bare headlands, the dubious minerals, the plentiful fish, the absence of native inhabitants---all these added up to very little" for Parmenius (Quinn 55-6: The "absent" Native people were Beothuk, already despised for refusing European trade and most other contact). Parmenius wrote: "Now I ought to tell you about the customs, territories, and inhabitants; and yet what am I to say, my dear Hakluyt, when I see nothing but desolation?"

Heck of a try. Poetry lost that day perhaps but, as will appear in relevant relation to this story, a major theme of Euro-American art was born.

The elder Richard Hakluyt's editorial efforts to improve (and make more convincing to investors) the writings about America---which, by 1600, had produced "an extensive library of the sea"---can suggest how American poetry slowly emerged from "exploration prose":

> The first, immediate impression had, in his eyes, much
> more interest---usually more value---than the considered

> and generalized impression of men who had gone over a particular course many times [and took] much indeed for granted....[Haklyut's writers] should not be allowed to spend too much time on the day to day progress of the ship....[but] describe the people of the strange country in as much detail as possible and make comments on the fitness of the place for trade or settlement....He did not expect assessments of scenery, though he appreciated... the impression it made....
>
> (Quinn *England* 220-221)

Certainly "the poetic" returned in passages of the first mariners' descriptions of scenery and of Native peoples. In English these included the promisingly-named "Dionyse Settle," who accompanied Frobisher; Captain Davis' accounts (1585-87); Ralegh's Virginia of the 1580s, which, like Guiana, brought no "American verse" from that accomplished author; and the voyages of Gosnold, Pring, Brereton and Waymouth between 1602 and 1605. These were almost a "Paradise school" of Northeastern writers whose dominant notes John Smith, Levett, and Morton (with others) took up in the following decades. (Best full editions are Burrage, and Quinn's *English New England Voyages* and *North America from Earliest Discovery*.) But only "New France" planter Marc Lescarbot wrote or published any deliberately American poetry through this period (*The Theatre of Neptune* 1606, and *Les Muses de la Nouvelle France*, published with his *History*'s third edition in 1618). There was grace to some of it, though laced with imperialism's ventriloquoy, as when a colonist-welcoming man in "Indian" costume (one of the players of *Neptune*) sang

> Now, I am about to try
> My luck upon this rocky coast.
> Perchance upon the shore will lie
> Something for your cook to roast.
> And now, monseigneur, if you see
> Within the locker of your sloop
> Some caraconas,* give to me   *bread
> And I will share it with my troop.
>   [Richardson trans., 26]

The English struggled on. Captain John Smith's first book, *A True Relation of...Virginia,* appeared in 1608, and he more than others before him liked to punctuate his prose with couplets and quatrains. But none of it (according to editor Philip L. Barbour) was Smith's own: it came from Martin Fotherbey's *Atheomastix*, a sententious translation of Ovid (for exs. see Barbour ed., *Works* II: 125 and III:326). Most of Smith's books were festooned with commendatory poetry, and there may well be a contender among those compositions. We should trouble to find out, if only because we have located scarcely one poet for the first 125 years of England's relationship with North America, from Cabot's 1490s to the 16-tens.

The poem below, first seen in the front of Smith's 1616 *A Description of New England*, appears to be the work of a trio, Michael and William Phettiplace, and Richard Wiffing, "three "Gentlemen and Souldiers under Captaine Smiths Command: In his deserved honor for his Worke and worth." It recounts one of their and Smith's adventures among the Powhatan and Pamunkey peoples of Virginia; and Smith's capture of the leading *werowance* Opechancanough, in a skirmish that is also pictured on Smith's maps (text below slightly modernized from Barbour I: 317).

> Why may not we in this work have our mite,
> That had our share in each black day and night,
> When thou [Smith] Virginia foiled, yet kept unstained;
> And held the King of Paspeheh enchained.
> Thou all alone this savage stern did take.
> Pamunkey's king we saw thee captive make.
> Among seven hundred of his stoutest men
> To murder thee and us resolved; when
> Fast by the hand thou led this savage grim,
> Thy pistol at his breast to govern him,
> Which did infuse such awe in all the rest
> (Since their dread Sovereign thou had so distressed)
> That thou and we (poor sixteen) safe retired
> Unto our helpless ships. Thou (thus admired)
> Did make proud Powhatan, his subjects send
> To James his town, thy censure to attend;
> And all Virginia's lords and petty kings,

> Awed by thy virtue, crouch, and presents bring
> To gain thy grace, so dreaded thou hast been;
> And yet a heart more mild is seldom seen;
> So, making Valour Vertue, really;
> Who has nought in thee counterfeit, or slie;
> If in the sleight be not the truest art,
> That makes men famoused for fair desert.
>   Who saith of thee, this savors of vainglory
> Mistakes both thee and us, and this true story.
> If it be ill in Thee, so well to do,
> Then is it ill in Us, to praise Thee too.
> But, if the first be well done, it is well
> To say it doth (if so it doth) excel!
> Praise is the guerdon of each dear desert,
> Making the praised act the praised part
> With more alacrity: Honour's Spur is Praise;
> Without which, it (regardless) soon decays.
>   And for this paines of thine we praise thee rather,
> That future times may know who was the father
> Of this rare Work (New England) which may bring
> Praise to thy God, and profit to thy King.

We have three useful terms and points to work with. First, is there above at least enough of *any* of our three main criteria to make us decide, right-off, that this could be *First*---the earliest English we can find that seems to be both poetry and, in some definite way, about America?

On promised grounds of inclusiveness, let us assume that there is. So, secondly---In what way(s) is the poem *American*?

To find out, we gather up and look at its elements: "seven hundred stout men," it says, live in Virginia under the "proud" "savage grim" and "dread Sovereign" called "Powhatan," "King of Paspeheh" and "of Pamunkey"; where now, "all Virginia's lords and petty kings" bring "presents" to gain English "grace." What we find of substantial reference is: two accurately-rendered Native American tribal names, one personal name, and a fairly-agreed-upon English-colonial term for Native American political hierarchies ("lords and petty kings"). Their "dread" of Powhatan we cannot confirm. Their dread of the English we can; for the poem commemorates the model of virtue found in Captain John Smith's (and the authors' own) forcible subjection of those tribes, led on by Smith's capture of Opechancanough in battle. *Smith's* actions and qualities, hence his credibility about America, are the reason for the poem (they will inspire you to believe what he says in this next book about New England). And thirdly, if there is a "fable and fiction" crafted into the verse's "form and soul," it is just that about Smith; supported by some authenticity-bestowing Native language and (English) testimony of "murderous intent." Conclusion goes to the readers.

Hopefully they will find it relevant here, since we have seen Sidney's defense of poetry, to look further at Plato's original attack on it:

> The best of us, as I conceive, when we listen to a passage of Homer, or one of the tragedians...the best of us, you know, delight in giving way to sympathy, and are in raptures at the excellence of the poet who stirs our feelings most....But when any sorrow of our own happens to us, then you may observe that we pride ourselves on the opposite quality---we would fain be quiet and patient; this is the manly part, and the other which delighted us in the recitation is now deemed to be the part of a woman....And the same may be said of...all the other affections, of desire and pain and pleasure, which are held to be inseparable from every action---In all of them poetry feeds and waters the passions instead of drying them up; she lets them rule, although they ought to be controlled, if mankind are ever to increase in happiness and virtue....[W]e are ready to acknowledge that Homer is the greatest of poets...but we must remain firm in our conviction that hymns to the gods and praises of famous men are the only poetry which ought to be admitted into our State. For if you go beyond this and allow the honeyed muse to enter, either in epic or lyric verse, not law and the reason of mankind...but pleasure and pain will be the rulers in our State.

Captain Smith, one of those Thomas Morton might have called a "Martialist" (*Canaan* 156), continued to publish through the 1620s; and a contending (1631) poem of Smith's own appears below. Meanwhile, however, after the above 1616 publication, the next contender does not appear until 1625: the Anglican Reverend William Morrell, of whom little is known except that he spent a year (1623-24) among the small company of would-be planters at Wessagusset/Weymouth on Massachusetts Bay.

The site's first colonists (under merchant Thomas Weston in 1622) had failed, and a second group under Robert Gorges arrived there with Morrell and fellow-minister William Blackstone along for their spiritual maintenance. Yet within a year most of Robert's people departed, Morrell with them, "having scarcely saluted the country" according to Plimoth's William Bradford (*History* II: 336).

Morrell, "a good classical scholar...man of observing mind and gentle tastes," busied himself at Weymouth composing "a Latin poem" (Adams *Three Episodes* 157), which by the time of publication (London 1625) he had also put into English. In *Nova Anglia*, or *New-England....A Briefe Enarration of the Ayre, Earth, Water, Fish and Fowles of that Country*, Morrell began by proclaiming his subjects and purposes in a way that, briefly and in parts, fulfilled Ben Jonson's dictum that a "fiction" constitute true poetry. (Morrell's own English translation presents problems this editor cannot ease: slightly modernized below from *Mass. Hist. Soc. Colls.* I [1792], 125-139.)

> Fear not poor Muse, 'cause first to sing her fame
> That's yet scarce known, unless by map or name:
> A Grand-child to earth's Paradise is born,
> Well-limb'd, well-nerv'd, fair, rich, sweet, yet forlorn.
> Thou blest Director, so direct my verse
> That it may win her people, friends commerce;
> Whilst her sweet air, rich soil, blest, seizes my pen
> Shall blaze, and tell the natures of her men.
> New-England, happy in her new true style [name],
> Weary of her cause she's to sad exile
> Expos'd by her's unworth of her Land,
> Entreats with tears Great Britain to command
> Her empire, and to make her know the trine [Trinity]
> Whose act and knowledge only makes divine.
> A royal work well worthy England's king
> These natives to true truth and grace to bring....

Interestingly, Morrell seems aware that (unless somebody counts that 1616 poem in Smith's book) he may well be "first" at least chronologically. He sets out with promising energy to weave together what it feels like to be there ("sweet air, rich soil, blest") with indeed a conceit, that this land is "like" a "sweet, yet forlorn" woman imploring the evangelical and other "command" of "Great Britain." But the fictive female figure of America slips through the minister's fingers, and suddenly above he furnishes flatly literal lists of natural conditions and commodities. A stock touch of merry May respirates a failing fiction:

> Blest is this air with what the air can bless,
> Yet frequent gusts do much this place distress....
> Whose looming greenness joys the seaman's sense,
> Invites him to a land if he can see
> Worthy the Thrones of stately sovereignty.
> The fruitful and well watered earth doth glad
> All hearts, when Flora's with her spangles clad....

Is it contradiction or confirmation of Plato that, throughout *Nova Anglia*, its few arguably-authentic American *and* poetic breaths fill Morrell's lines mostly in association with women?

> Besides, their women, which for the most part are
> Of comely forms, not black, nor very fair:
> Whose beauty is a beauteous black laid on
> Their paler cheek, which they most dote upon.
> for they by Nature are both fair and white,
> Enriched with graceful presence, and delight;
> Deriding laughter, and all prattling, and
> Of sober aspect, graced with grave command:
> Of man-like courage, stature tall and straight,
> Well-nerv'd, with hands and fingers small and right,
> Their slender fingers on a grassy twine
> Make well-form'd baskets wrought with art and line...
> Rare stories, Princes, people, Kingdoms, Towers
> In curious finger-work or parchment flowers.....

This recalls Morrell's first imagery; but he can sustain no more-than-literal discourse, no unity beyond that of a catalogue. Morrell has felt the vigor of New England's air, enjoyed its light and climate, glanced over its "aborigines" (as

Adams dubbed Native peoples in amplifying Morrell's "disgust" with them, *Three Episodes* 158). But perhaps he has not in some deeper sense *been there*, except in an America where, "hopefully," Native American extinction will make his people heirs to clearly-rich land.

> If Heavens grant...to see here built I trust
> An English Kingdom from this Indian dust.

Is Morell's *New-England* more American than the poem by Smith's colleagues? It certainly tells more about the place and people; but whether *as poetry* it should supplant the "conceit" of Smith's colleagues is left to you.

The next contender dispenses with evangelism altogether---He is the "fantastical"-tempered Welshman William Vaughan, an Oxford-trained and thoroughly-traveled gentleman who, with a circle of Elizabethan colleagues, for six years financed an attempted plantation at "Trepassy" (*a/k/a* Cambriol) on the southern tip of the Newfoundland peninsula. Vaughan voyaged there and bestowed the latter name himself in 1622, hoping that his personal presence might turn the tide of profit his and the new King Charles I's way. Despite his two-year stay, it did not (Rowse details the reports of "idle fellows'" lack of industry there, *Elizabethans* 172). But after two years more Vaughan found a use for the verses he had apparently written in the New World, turning them into *The Golden Fleece* (London: Francis Williams 1626), a poetic potpourri gathered to celebrate King Charles' 1626 marriage to Queen Henrietta.

Fleece was "Divided into three Parts, under which are discovered the Errours of Religion, the Vices and Decayes of the Kingdome, and lastly the wayes to get wealth, and to restore Trading so much complayned of" (title page). And, Vaughan promised, this "compound of truth and fiction, quaint prose, and still quainter verse" had been "Transported from Cambrioll Colchos...commonly called the New Found Land, by Orpheus Junior, for the generall and perpetuall Good of Great Britaine." The Dedication told his King,

> This no Eutopia is, nor Commonwealth
> Which Plato faign'd. We bring Your Kingdom's health
> By true Receipts, which You will rellish well.

But for all the "quaint" literary qualities of *The Golden Fleece* (including Don Quixote and "Marsilius Ficinus" in the allusive backgrounds, 4), that was all Vaughan had to say about America in verse, passing chapter after chapter instead upon religious factions, on "proving the Pope AntiChrist," explaining "how to restrain lawyers" and the uses of tobacco. Vaughan had fictionalized his authorship as "Orpheus Junior" and then (Pt. 3 Ch. 1) been "required by Apollo to discover where the Golden Fleece lyes," that is, to tell readers what was the substance behind the book's many conceits and ironic poses. In a main sense, it was America's legendary wealth, "reduce[d] into one mayne Trade, to the Plantation and Fishing in the Newfoundland"; and this, he adds, was "the generall cause which [had] moved Orpheus to regard this Golden Fleece" (Part 3 *Table of Contents*).

> This is our Colchos, where the Golden Fleece flourisheth
> on the backs of Neptune's sheep [beaver etc.], continually
> to be shorn. This is Great Britain's Indies, never to be ex-
> hausted dry. This precious Treasure surmounts the Duke
> of Burgundy's Golden Fleece, which he called...by reason
> of his large customs...received from our English Wools....(10)

An "advertisement poem" in the front of Vaughan's book called this quasi-inspiration "the Golden Fleece moralized." Vaughan, this poet ("Stephen Berrier") meant to say, had transformed a Greek-mythical or "pagan" symbol into what Renaissance authorities of many stripes would deem respectable. These planters, including John Mason and John Guy, had no problem making light of the mercenary motive they shared in hoping to "fleece" America of its wealth. But

Berrier emphasized one thing about the Newfoundland as it was symbolically made a wedding-gift to King Charles: it was real, in all "poetic" as well as other senses:

> Orpheus but late[ly] our woods did make to ring,
> And to his Harp great Charles his Carols sing[s]...
> Orpheus now forsaking Easterne Greece
> From Westerne Colchos brings the Golden Fleece;
> Which no Eutopia is, nor fairy-land,
> Yet Colchos in Elisian Fields doth stand....

"American poetry" perhaps, but fragments only, struck off an anvil whose hammer has other purposes. This came more of what Rowse called "exaltation of temperament" (174) than from America. Vaughan and his colleagues, mostly libertine lovers of raucous rhetoric, would have cheered themselves up with poetry and/or fictions wherever they'd planted. Vaughan cast slender ones over what they all wanted from American land and peoples, and both "in their own right" he mentioned no more than you have seen.

Colonizer Thomas Morton did not care for Vaughan's *The Golden Fleece*, and in disparaging its conception of America, chose the word "respect" as that work's antithesis (see his poetic "Epilog" to *Canaan*'s Book 2).

Speak of the devil(s), it does appear chronologically that Morton and his fellow-planters at "Ma-re Mount" in 1627 were the collaborative authors of the next-contending English-American poetry: *New English Canaan* claims that "The Poem" and "The Song" at the center of their company's May Day Revels that year (as well as other later verses) were "performed" and sung "with a Chorus" at the "Boston Bay" settlement, whose brief success so troubled the planters of Plimoth. In 1636 Morton told a court that American "writeings" had been taken from him (Biography Ch. 9): perhaps he somehow mentally held onto the parchments once "fixed to the Maypole" (Bradford's *History* agrees they did exist); or like the later Roger Williams, once exiled by the Puritans he may have "dr[awn] the Materialls in a rude lumpe at Sea, as a private helpe to my owne memory, that I might not...lightly lose what I had so dearely bought in some few yeares hardship" (1643 *Key*, 83).

Ma-re Mount's "Poem" and "Song" are two parts or phases of a program of calculated entertainments. Like many another early English colonizer (from Davis to Gilbert and generations of fishermen), Morton and his "servants" were would-be competitors in the fur trade. To help themselves attract both European and Native American traders to their hilltop outpost, they adapted some of the most convenient and enjoyable comforts of home to their cause (including the Maypole itself, country-dance and song, even strains of Neoplatonist theory most likely from Morton, the Inns-trained man of letters). "The Poem," with its "Spenserian mix of history and fiction, Hebrew and Classical mythology" (Bush "Spenser's Treatment" 592), offers an American-centered fictional narrative within its imagery---This concerns the need to console a "discovered" and grief-stricken woman, "Scilla," who symbolizes Native American culture in the throes of catastrophic "plague" at the time; and to induce her to share a hence-yearly rite of renewal or "hollyday," which will promote English and Native American connection on many levels of life.[44]

---

[44] This reading of "The Poem" is fully substantiated in "Masque: The Riddle of May Day" later in this volume. Below is a hopefully-helpful "revision" of Morton's poem, with a very few of its figures either slightly simplified or replaced with more literal language, in order to reveal something of the richly meaningful coherence and clarity that this scholar finds in the work.

> Rise, Oedipus, and if you can, unfold
> What means death's whirlpool underneath the mould,
> When woman, solitary on the ground
> Sitting and weeping her children was found---
> Till the Goddess of human lovers did acquaint
> Grim Neptune, James, with the tenor of her plaint,
> And made him send forth heralds, to the sound
> Of trumpet loud---at which the sea was found
> So full of Protean forms that this bold shore
> Presented woman a new paramour,
> As strong as Samson, and as patient
> As Job himself---directed thus, by Fate

"The Song" then brings all kinds of Classical and Renaissance poetic tropes to serve the same ends on another "easier" level, one surer to be acted upon by people(s) of that frontier: it is the lyric to which the young men and Native "lasses in beaver coats" were to dance and find their way to "marry" each other, human harmonies and demands of trade coalescing in the Song's final images. "Nectar"---the "drink of the gods" in a beloved woman's eyes, which Ben Jonson's "Drink to Me Only" "would not trade," even for immortality---this was the substance, at once spiritual and erotic, behind Morton's metaphor.[45]

> To comfort her and country so unfortunate.
> I do profess, by our Great and beauteous Mother,
> That here's a wise fool's choice, for her, none other;
> Even though she's sick, because no sign,
> Till now, can bring her race to health with mine.
> Oh healer of healers, Asklepios, come! I know right well
> Man's labor is lost, if we should hear her knell,
> That call of our Great Mother none ever withstand---
> But She is Love, and She points to land
> With proclamation that the first of May
> At Ma-re Mount shall be kept holy day.

[45] Terence C. Cave's study of French *Pleiade* poet Pierre de Ronsard and his *Les Bacchanales* (c. 1552-1560) provides a good comparative source for excavating the deeper levels of Morton's poetry. As "The Song" carries on the hopeful agenda begun in "The Poem," and invites men and women to find their spiritual solace and physical "delights" in each other here and now, so in Ronsard's "bacchanals." Cave: Ronsard had in mind a "medium through which the unified divine force of inspiration is bodied forth in the spectrum of human passions"---"[T]he true poet," Cave continues, "although dealing with images which might be condemned as fictions, uses these...as a cloak in which to convey to man the hidden truth....Ronsard clearly perceived the enduring value of myth as a means of embodying profound insights" (264). On a would-be English poet's study of Ronsard's forms and themes, see Prescott 76-115, Lee 210-216, Merrill 56.

Morton's "Song" shows his lighter touches as we compare it with other published music of the time. See for example 1597's *The First Booke of Songes*, 1610's *The Muses Garden for Delights*, or 1617's *The Third Book of Ayres* (all these sources extensively reprinted in works edited by Auden, Ledger and Whiting; see Kermode 2345 for further primary music-sources).

The standard madrigal "Now Is The Month Of Maying" trills a blithe, almost cruel note of mocking banishment for all forms of "winter" and sadness, culminating in a call to "dainty nymphs" to "speak" and "play barley-break," a meadow-game "designed" to partner men and women. Morton's "Song" takes a gentler approach to "the melancholy man" while trying to rouse high spirits; and it is worth noting too that in the matter of possible "erasure" of Native American men through "Scilla's" courting, that "The Song" promises to "revive" the "bloud" of the man, his race as well as his spirits.

As we consider some of Morton's obvious allusions to much-employed symbols and figures ("Nectar," "Hymen," etc.), his reading in humanistic works on the human passions, spirituality, and morals seems apparent, and he is relatively well-informed and able to gracefully

With these two poems alone we suddenly find ourselves in conversation with "climents of a higher nature than are to be found within the habitation of the Mole" (*Canaan* 141). They are complete, coherent, deftly and thoroughly handled "fictions" in verse that carry on sophisticated multi-leveled play with a substantial number and range of English and Continental cultural traditions; and the same is true of Morton's "Bacchanall Triumph, " which in couplets sometimes awful, sometimes witty, turns many a cultural form and expectation upside-down, as it weaves perceptive fictions round New England's peoples, events and landscape-settings, and mocks Plimoth's "pitiful perplexity" over Ma-re Mount, chief rival to its trade. (See *Canaan* for much further detail; but "Triumph" was composed later than the "Poem" and "Song," either in 1629 New England or in 1635-7 England.)

If Morton's 1627 poetry alone was such rich verse focused upon American subjects, why was it so long absent from "the American canon" to the point where virtually no one ever heard of it? Given the kinds of verse assembled by the hugely influential Moses Coit Tyler (like Morrell, a Protestant minister) in his foundational 1880 *History of American Literature* anthology, it must appear that

---

express an intelligent position, something notable amid American frontier contingencies. Cave: Ronsard's Bacchus "rises above conventional moral judgments, harmonizes vice with virtue, and converts potentially destructive qualities into a source of strength" (256). In his Bacchus we have "not...a god of drunkenness but...a god who utilizes the forces of the human personality, even those which a stricter code would condemn as potentially sinful, [toward] the liberation of the mind and of passionate impulse from conventional limitations."

One meaning of the Renaissance was the rebirth of a different cultural environment for the body with its "willful" ways, and Morton lived it (and so wrote it) in New England. Leading early humanist Marsilio Ficino's influential commentary on the republished Plato's *Symposium* (1484) was both admired and notorious for its effort to rehabilitate the human passions (*furores*). Ficino's work was considered "the original *trattato d'amore*" and "the first treatise on love to formally reconcile a love both morally enriching and based in instinct and sexuality" (Levi, "Neoplatonist Calculus" 237). For tracking this one strand of Morton's poetry we realize that the Renaissance itself, familiarly conceived as a rebirth of a sometimes-sacred unity between spirit and flesh, was expressed in *Canaan* as nowhere else in any Euro-American text. One can scarcely surmise from *any* of his Northeastern-colonial colleagues that there *was* a Renaissance going on around them. "The erotic" in America c.2000 AD ensues as small surprise.

Morton's poetry did not suit Tyler's personal tastes (or those of many others after him). There was certainly no objective or aesthetic reason that Tyler believed in enough to defend in open debate. He simply led his readers to assume that Morton and *Canaan* (along with most other contenders in these pages) had never existed, and so forced himself to make the best of Puritan writers; who possessed "little skill in and little regard for" literature "as a fine art...as the voice and the ministress of aesthetic delight" (*History* 1:8).

It would have been this public-lecturing, university-teaching Christian editor's nightmare to allow the public to experience, *before* those sober hardworking American-Pilgrim role-models, a rollicking English Renaissance man who laid open the Puritans' deepest vanities and mocked their anxieties as self-induced delusions; and who proved his charges with his own bodily and literary élan in America, coupled with a repeated call for colonizers to use "moderation, and discretion" (*Canaan* 9) in coming to inevitable terms with Native American humanity.

The former Congregational Reverend Tyler was less than interested in Native American peoples. He wished *his* Americans to understand them as "anthropoid animals" living in "mental childhood" (1:156, 178); as "fierce dull biped[s] standing in our way," "nude patriots and Stoics" who "deserve no history" (1:10, 2:213-215). And so Tyler could not possibly comprehend *Canaan's* verses, or see them as anything but outrages against the critical code built upon Plato by ardent Christians; which (see Charvat, Elson for ex.) was *itself* aimed at "teaching" most "good Americans" *themselves* to remain intellectual children. For Tyler, the one ray of American poetic light until Anne Bradstreet had come "on the banks of the James River" in Virginia (1: 53), from George Sandys' attempted translation of Ovid's *Metamorphoses*.

Tyler was truly hungry for *belles-lettres*, but he was also prosaically hungry for a meal every day; and how many American educators could depart the straight narrow critical path *and* keep getting paid good university-trustees' money? (See Vanderbilt on Tyler's career-transition from minister to public speaker to professor: he very much felt "the eyes of propriety" upon him.) So Tyler indulged as he could with seven pages on Sandys' effort to become "the morning-star at once of poetry and of scholarship in the new world" (1: 55); an effort made especially admirable, Tyler wrote, by its defiance of the "rough desert" all around Sandys, by America's "oppressive tasks of...official position" and by the "frightful Indian massacre[s]" of the 1620s (prompted by an unmentioned English invasion of Virginia). Tyler crowned Sandys' Ovid (London 1626) as "the very first expression of elaborate poetry...the first utterance of the conscious literary spirit articulated in America" (1: 54).

Sandys at least helps us see what was already on paper as (for example) Morton composed his poem "The Author's Prologue" (*Canaan* 7), which combined (deliberately or not) the conceits of Morrell's American "woman" and Sandys' first-page "Argument" from Ovid:

> Fire, Aire, Earth, Water, all the Opposites
> That strove in Chaos, powerful LOVE unites
> And from this Discord drew this Harmonie
> Which smiles in Nature....

All this was "in" America. But not "of" it. Sandys informed "Prince Charles" that this work was "a double Stranger: Sprung from the Stocke of the ancient Romanes, but bred in the New-World, of the rudenesse thereof it cannot but participate; especially having Warres and Tumults to bring it to light instead of the Muses." *For Sandys*, America was the opposite of inspiration (reason for writing). America may have added "rude tumult"---wild energy?---to his lines about Hercules. But his Niobe weeps for nothing American. America is in no way part of this Ovid's intended meanings, impacts, and/or rewards for reading. Sandys' "morning star" heralds The Parmenius Problem, the colonizers' ongoing needless escape from a mirage of "desolation."[46]

Contemporary critic Frank Kermode followed Tyler in calling Sandys' translation America's "first literary poetry (balladry aside)" (523). Literary, and poetry, perhaps: America's, not likely. Sandys was a speaker of English in North America translating Latin writing about Greek myth. If a Japanese-speaking-and-

---

[46] Contrast with Tyler's own contemporary, scholar Charles Godfrey Leland, whose international and eclectic practice of letters included open-minded studies not only of American culture but also of (for ex.) European "witchcraft" traditions, of Etruscan civilization (a likely descendant of Philistine/Canaanite ones), and American "Slang, Jargon and Cant." After publishing his 1884 *Algonquin Legends*---based in the pioneering practice of actually talking to Native New England people and taking them seriously as capable custodians of their own 13,000-year civilization---Leland wrote (1902):

"Very few persons are aware that there has perished, or is rapidly perishing, among the Red Indians of North America, far more poetry than was ever written by all the white inhabitants, and that this native verse is often of a very high order....[T]he most inspired poet can never feel that he is really "heart-intimate" with scenery, if it has for him no ties of tradition or folklore. When I was young, I felt this lack, and bore in patience the very common reproach of Europeans that we had a land without ancient legends or song. But now that I am older grown, I have learned that this want is all in our own ignorance and neglect of what we had only to put forth our hand to reach. We bewailed our wretched poverty when we had in our lap a casket full of treasure which we would not take the pains to open. Few indeed and far between are those who ever suspected till of late years that every hill and dale in New England had its romantic legend, its beautiful poem, or its marvellous myth---the latter equal in conception and form to those of the [Norse] Edda---or that a vast collection of these traditions still survives in perfect preservation among the few remaining Indians of New England and the Northeast Coast, or the *Wabano*....And I venture to say from the deepest conviction that it will be no small occasion of astonishment and chagrin, a hundred years hence...that so few among our literary or cultured folk cared enough to collect this connected aboriginal literature. Unto which I may truly add that, when such collection was made, there were far more critics to find fault with the way in which it was done, than persons to do it....

"The traditions and, to some extent, the languages and histories of the aboriginal tribes are quite as worthy of being taught at our universities to all who propose to become American scholars as many other branches [of knowledge]....But the true value of work like this is, that the country will be, if those who love it so desire, once more repeopled....I venture to express the hope that all who love nature in New England will turn to the study of its folklore and thereby secure the final flash of gold on the mountain tops....and see in all Nature new charms" ("Preface" to *Kuloskap the Master and Other Algonkin Poems*).

Thomas C. Parkhill's 1997 *Weaving Ourselves Into the Land: Charles Godfrey Leland, "Indians," and the Study of Native American Religions* (Albany: State U. of New York Press) provides one perspective on the no-doubt "naive" Leland.

writing scholar is ordered to inhabit a Berlin library, and there translates Egyptian songs of Babylon into couplets, the result is not likely "German poetry."

We return to the final phases of our survey. The next possible "first American poetry" came from that same William Vaughan's small company of gentlemen who briefly affiliated themselves with Northeastern plantations. This was *Quodlibets* (London 1628) by one Robert Hayman, like Morton a Devonshire gentleman and 1590s Inns of Court graduate, who somehow after 1621 succeeded Captain John Mason as "governor-general" of the Newfoundland's "swarming fishermen." Like his colleagues, Hayman styled himself "Lately Come Over from New Britaniola, Old New Found Land" with "Epigrams and other small parcels, both Moral and Divine," which he had "composed and done at Harbor Grace." His Latin title means "What You Will"---or, as Sir Philip Sidney explained the word in other context, "Whatever I shall try to say shall become verse" (*Defence* 147: recall Puttenham's idea of poetry as simply "any witty or delicate conceit".) Hayman's work included four "books" of original work and a pair of translated "epistles" from "that excellently wittie doctor Francis Rabelais"; and behind some of his briefer "Whatevers" were some of Morton's social values. Hayman advised a "good friend" and fellow-planter,

> Sterne, cruell usage may bad servants fetter;
> Wise gentle usage, keepes good servants better. (30)

Hayman and Thomas Morton might have shared beverages if they had met:

> Though Puritanes the Litany deride
> Yet out of it they best may be descried;
> They are blind-hearted, Proud, Vaine-glorious,
> Deepe Hypocrites, Hateful and Envious,
> Malicious, in a full high excesse,
> And full of all Uncharitablenesse. (5)

And "To One of the Elders of the Sanctified Parlor of Amsterdam" he wrote,

> Though thou maist call my merriments, my folly
> They are my Pills to purge my melancholly,

> They would purge thine too, wert not thou Foole-holy.

But these things did not bring Hayman to the same poetic pitch as they did Morton. Hayman found the air "salubrious, constant, cleere" and worked three prosaic couplets on it into his page 53. Near the end of *Quodlibets*' first "book" he then attempted a whole "Skeltonicall continued rhyme, in praise of my New Found Land" (first below from his page 19); and he made one further attempt to address the New World (below, from 34). Such was "the American-English tradition" when Morton came to it:

> Although in cloaths, company, buildings faire,
> With England, New Found Land cannot compare:
> Did some know what contentment I found there,
> Alwayes enough, most times somewhat to spare,
> With little paines, lesse toyle, and lesser care,
> Exempt from taxings, ill newes, Lawing, feare,
> If cleane, and warme, no matter what you weare,
> Healthy, and wealthy, if men carefull are,
> With much much more, then I will now declare,
> (I say) if some wise men knew what this were,
> (I do beleeve) they'd live no other where.

Witty? Delicate? And yet, Hayman tried again.

> 'Tis said, wise Socrates look't like an Asse;
> Yet he with wondrous sapience filled was;
> So though our New Found Land look wild, salvage,
> She hath much wealth penn'd in her rustie Cage.
> So have I seene a leane-cheekes, bare, and ragged,
> Who of his private thousands could have bragged.
> Indeed she now looks rude, untowardly;
> She must be decked with neat husbandry.
> So have I seen a plaine swarth, sluttish Joan
> Looke pretty pert, and neat with good cloathes on.

Them was his sentiments. For others who noticed how much was lacking, Hayman provided "A Napkin[,] to wipe his mouth that waters at these deserved Commendations":

> Thus for this hopefull Countrie at this Time,
> As it growes better, Ile have better Ryme.

But it was hardly America's growing "better" that might improve English poetry about it.

By 1631, the publication-year of the next remotely-possible poetic contender, Captain John Smith's careers as colonist and author were over: his *True Travels* had appeared the year before, and his last work, 1631's brief *Advertisements for the Unexperienced Planters of New England, or Anywhere*, included his only known original poem, "The Sea Marke" (in Barbour, ed., III: 265). The poem appears to dramatize the act of passing by a shipwreck, and offers clear meanings beyond the literal about the American voyager John Smith's difficult final years:

> Aloofe, aloofe, and come no neare,
> the dangers doe appeare;
> Which if my ruine had not beene
> you had not seene:
> I onely lie upon this shelfe
> to be a marke to all
> which on the same might fall,
> Than none may perish but my selfe....

Every word and beyond-literal meaning in the poem has its referent not in America but, again, in John Smith, old explorer of New World lands and waters. That is the extent of its three-stanza description of, connection or reference to, America: the "sea-mark" is a shipwreck awash off any coast. Only the reader can nominate/disqualify it, but likelier candidates seem apparent.

We have now considered seven contenders before reaching the full-publication year of *Canaan*'s array of American poetry; which included, besides the "Poem" and "Song" of 1627, "Bacchanall Triumph" possibly of 1629, and the 1630s "Author's Prologue"; which we shall not examine, in order to make room for others. Such as? We should include the rhymes within William Wood's 1634 prose survey, *New England's Prospect*: Wood broke up his pages with four versified lists of New England trees, animals, birds and fish (39, 41, 49, 54), and, true to his promise to avoid "voluptuous discourse" (19), he let none come closer to sensuality than this:

> Kinds of All Shellfish.
> The luscious lobster, with the crabfish raw,
> The brinish oyster, mussle, periwig,
> And tortoise sought by the Indian's squaw,
> Which to the flats dance many a winter jig,
> To dive for cockles, and to dig for clams,
> Whereby her lazy husband's guts she crams. (54)

It was a mark worth shooting at. Few wasted their bullets in that direction. We begin to understand the *Eli, Eli, lama sabbechthani?* of American critics for "something more"; though they were not so nailed to their crosses that they could not have brought themselves, in Morton's late phrase, to "crawl out of this condition," and admit (to the peril of tenure) that *Canaan* had been written.

Anne Bradstreet, according to critics cited below, began her poetic "apprenticeship" at this time (the early 1630s), having survived a "lingering sickness" and settled at Ipswich and Andover, Massachusetts. She cannot be left out, but we should treat other shorter contenders first. One is William Bradford of Plimoth Plantation, who arrived in 1620 and began his prose *History* circa 1630: Westbrook's review of documents (111-12) shows that Bradford wrote little or no verse before perhaps 1647, and then (into the 1650s) a small "Verse History" among other "poetic dialogues" on religious issues. Before this, Bradford apparently had composed "six quatrains" on the death of his beloved pastor John Robinson in 1626. But, as above, we may question whether there is sufficient indispensable connection to anything American in the basic "conceit" of that work, the death of a beloved friend one "missed"---because of residence not in America, but simply "far away."

But because we cannot be certain when he wrote stanzas such as the following, they should be included here. These lines appear to concern events of the early 1620s, when control of New England seemed especially undecided because Native Americans were beginning to demand and acquire firearms for their trade and services. "The gain hereof to make they know so well," poet Bradford rued,

> The fowl to kill, and us the feathers sell.
> For us to seek for deer it doth not boot,
> Since now with guns themselves at them can shoot.
> That garbage, of which we no use did make,
> They have been glad to gather up and take;
> But now they can themselves fully supply,
> And the English of them are glad to buy....

And that is the entire field of English-American poetic contenders up through the 1637 publication of Morton's *New English Canaan*. Given the sheer volume of undeniable poetry in that book, it must be obvious that, if we have not been able by this *chronological* point to proclaim "America's first poet and/or poem in English," we can only construct those things upon wholly ideological grounds, rather than on historical sequence and record.

To challenge this, let us extend this search at least to include the little-known Puritan Thomas Tillam, whose "Upon the first sight of New-England June 29, 1638" expresses, according to critic and editor Harrison T. Meserole, "dedication mixed with wonder as he viewed the land that was to be shaped into the modern Canaan." And, Meserole adds, "none other recorded his response in lines so unmistakably inspired and genuinely lyrical" (397).

> Hail holy land wherein our holy lord
> Hath planted his most true and holy word:
> Hail, happy people who have dispossest
> Yourselves of friends, and means, to find some rest
> For your poor wearied soules, opprest of late
> For Jesus' sake...

Poetry alright. But Tillam's ship could be anchored off Sidon or Tyre. He sees Palestine, not America: he sees a representation, a hopeful mirage or overlay, produced by his ideological commitment to Puritanism---in fact, a mirror, that can protect his fragile (easily "tempted" or threatened) sense of identity and purpose from the overwhelming actualities that teem with life upon the continent before him ("untamed" Nature, plus unknown multitudes of human beings both different from and indifferent to himself). Few Native Americans would argue with Bercovitch about the Puritans' "breathtaking" gifts for "sweeping assertion": Tillam's poem demonstrates how they "created America in their own image" (9).

This is something quite different from Thomas Morton's use of European mythological language(s) to describe, articulate and address American subjects. The "Poem" and "Song" *reach out*: Tillam's immersion in a Biblical worldview, the very fabric of his poem, inscribes his fellow community-members ("among you"), as well as the new land, as the habitations of "Satan's wily baits." Whatever their respective "individualities," they and this are to be feared and distrusted (as much as the "self") in all relations. "Ideally" here, nothing *but* Christianity will "reach" Tillam.

Does any of this disqualify Tillam's work and/or all Puritan poetry here? Certainly not. But, beyond this, "America" in Tillam's poem and Puritan poetry is mostly blank, there "to be shaped" to what Roger Williams was beginning to call a "delusion" (with reference to England's utterly-invented "rights" to Native American soil: see his *Key* 167).[47]

---

[47] Bercovitch, *Puritan Origins of the American Self* (138): Almost every Puritan poet repeats this pattern exactly because of his/her commitment to such ideology: they write of "America," Bercovitch explains, "either exegetically, as a figure of heaven, or metaphorically, to denote a haven from civilized [sic] corruption, or literalistically, to suggest topological (rather than typological] comparisons"---for example, finding cause to wonder at America because it partly shares the same latitude and "fertility" as familiar Old World "gardens." So did Morton; but it

We might predictably assume here that changes in historical perspective have merely changed "the" idea of literary quality; but the discriminations attempted in these pages have little to do with setting up any new model of "great" poetry. That is forever best left to the reader. What needs to be recognized is that Tillam's "inspiration" is not *America*, but a Puritan Parmenius Problem he expresses in couplets: his reason for "singing" is to cry in the "waste," like those before who "scarcely saluted" the land.

To reach much further would only repeatedly illustrate the problem. (Welcome to American cultural history---and "The past is prologue"?) Williams' 1646 *Key Into the Language of America*, written by a man who, in his own words, feared to see too much about American ways (192), was filled with verses, and scarce a line spared the shoehorn as he forced the land and Native people to serve as semi-bestial allegories for Christian self-castigation. Jerome Bellamie's *The Simple Cobbler of Agawam* (London 1647: rpt. in Force 3:VIII) at times gave its prose "a little use of my stirrup" with couplets mixed into its New England portrait:

> The world is full of care, much like unto a bubble,
> Women and care, and care and Women,
> and Women and care and trouble.

The true heights would be scaled soon enough with Reverend Michael Wigglesworth's 1662 *The Day of Doom*---"a supreme realization of the Puritan theory of poetry and, incidentally, one of the most popular, as well as one of the aesthetically and morally most revolting, poems ever written in America" (Westbrook 105-6). It was the new dawn of simultaneous achievement in "popular" and "revolting": we wuz on our way.

---

lacks both forbidden tree and serpent; rather, as soon as one walks it one meets some human individual.

Only through Anne Bradstreet---whose heart "rose" within her at first sight of New England---was America allowed once again to speak its powers, described so fearfully above. She could not stop feeling and speaking them. It made her a luminous spotted beast in her own mind.

> Then higher on the glistering Sun I gaz'd,
> Whose beams was shaded by the leavie Tree,
> The more I look'd, the more I grew amaz'd,
> And softly said, what glory's like to thee?
> Soul of this world, this Universes Eye,
> No wonder, some made thee a Deity:
> Had I not better known, (alas) the same had I.
> ("Contemplations" 4: from
> *The Tenth Muse*, 1650)

Could a poet's and reader's salvation (in every sense) depend more upon the "correct" position of a comma (in relation to "alas")? This untamed multiple possibility of message is just the kind of instability that confirmed, and confirms, those curiously consistent idolators of nature, namely poets, as dangerous. Bradstreet is "naturally" joyously alive, and though she does "belong to this world" as much as anyone might, she is relentlessly haunted by the fact that her culture forbids her exactly that (on pain of violence; and so Plato was either dishonest or naive, for "pleasure and pain" ruled his Acropolis as well as America's cities on a hill).

And as Bradstreet submits, as any individual submits, the world fades, and dims. In the true Puritan sense of the term, the world and self are *reduced*, from the overpowering "glory" of the Direct Encounter above, to a "clue," about a "God" whose reputed Eternal Elsewhereness she must endlessly, silently suffer and forgive. From this, like every laborer within a Christian Capitalist Patriarchy,[48] Anne Bradstreet can squeeze sustenance, but she cannot live it as

---

[48] Though this term (fully historicized in Ch. 7) may at first seem too "monolithic and political," who will present a substantial example of European colonists who themselves would have rejected any of those terms for their religion, economics, or dominant social structure? Though the terms set off defensive acrimony, they do describe the intertwined Western European religious,

something in harmony with "the welfare of her whole eternal soul" ("Dear Children" 243). She knows that it is not *necessary* ("natural" or needful), this cross she loves and respects in all troubled innocence as her culture, her church, her community. Her people's leading "ethnic trait" is their belief *that* beliefs, in their minds, can and must make them "separate," in every sense. The lines above show a woman in electrifying contact with the very life-blood of living, what all religion and Sir Philip Sidney too call the Divine; but Bradstreet, as woman and poet, must fight and pay eternally for this---her experience makes her, literally, the life of poetry. It is not allowed.[49]

---

economic and social systems that arrived in North America after 1492; and that here in America, more often than not, encountered an "Earth-centered" (religious), Communal (economic), Quasi-Matriarchy (social structure). New England Native ways in these categories had been practiced via recognizable cultural forms far longer than anything in *hegemonic* practice in Europe during these colonial times.

"Matriarchy" is still all but academic-career suicide, ridiculous to researchers who dutifully restrict themselves to books and libraries, and ridiculed at "conferences"; but it is close to the way very many Native people (not to mention others round the world past and present) describe their own cultures' most potent centers of traditional, moral and other authority.

Not surprisingly, academics largely dismiss *this* as a figment of oral-historical revisioning by "marginalized" peoples---based, one supposes, in a familiar "need of cultureless Natives" to imitate (aware of it or not) whatever drops from the "center," the table of Euro-American Romantic, liberal-progressive, or "New Age" discourses. Academics, like relatively dogmatic feminists, deny complicity with such a revolting perpetuation of ethnocentrism; but they have little ground to stand upon until they can bear to confront overwhelming evidence that many respectable civilizations have honored (and still honor) women and gender-equality without being compelled to it by "liberators."

This, in turn, would put the still-oppressive edifice called "history" (a mere 4000 years of culture centered in male power and literacy) in new perspective; one that education for democracy, rather than training for Christian Capitalism, *should* be revealing---namely, the contexts of much older, widespread and sophisticated so-called "women's civilizations" that now stand, thanks to archaeology and "confessed" or not, all around "the story of Western Civilization." High-tech, gender-egalitarian, world-exploring trading cultures were the long-extant, non-racist matrix of "history." And yet, like Thomas Morton for most of "our" history, "we" know nothing about them. *Cui bono?* Old Zeus, like the Demi-urge of Christian Gnosticism, continues to insist that He created his origins. No "education" is ignoring these frontiers, these crucial *perspectives*.

[49] And look at the damage thus wrought upon her extraordinary potential. Even at the high point of Bradstreet's poetic stock amongst critics, here is what they say of her work as "American poetry." Piercy: it would be "a neat trick" to demonstrate any correspondence between Bradstreet's life and work during her 1630s "apprenticeship" (43-44). Hensley, 1967 editor of her *Works*: "She seems to have written by way of escaping from the conditions of her experience, not as expression of what she felt and knew"; "New England never enters her book: the landscape, the emotional weather of the New World are totally absent." She adds of the early "Four Seasons" that

Understandably in her cultural environment, Bradstreet turns away all she can of her seemingly-divided self back to "the Word"; a *representation* that, submitted to, entitles her to food and shelter from her kinsmen. That is why her poetic achievements would not have been brought down or up if she had spent her life colonizing Africa instead of Massachusetts. She manifests American poetry, but dares not conceive it.

For "danger" lives on outside of canonical plantation life, in the form of something more divine, beautiful and dangerous than Christianity's Satan.

It is old Proteus himself, *the* Renaissance figure of change and "Mutabilitie." When Bradstreet looks beyond her share of the collective's fearful sureties, she sees the people of her world transformed, from Saints to mere "sectaries" (245); pretenders-all, that is, to "the truth" (and this goes as well, she painfully admits, even for her people's most devoutly-honored "elect"). For Bradstreet's serious spirituality, the troubling bond of humanity "out there" is only an equal share of being as "deceived" as everybody else. This knowledge, reached for with great effort in a late and turbulent letter to her children, is her last hope for refuge from the honesty of perception and expression which is her gift (or hereabouts, curse).

Straining with all her mind and might for peace with "God," Bradstreet flings herself at last into the relativistic cosmic predicament of all people living in the poststructural universe. She will not "die" there as she was warned; only find herself anticlimactically "unchosen" (that is, like everybody else); forever responsible for her own life, as a function of what values she chooses to live, of what prices she chooses not to pay. (She does, after all, repeatedly manifest the

---

it "woodenly reproduces England, like snow-scenes on Australian Christmas cards" (xiv). Nor do more recent *Complete Works* editors McElrath and Robb report any reason to disagree about this 1630s "apprenticeship" that came to first-publication in 1650.

complaint that "something is missing" from the world of obedience, etc.) On the one hand, the "empty" or "free" universe is intolerably random, and she will not brave it; and on the other, it is pure opportunity---she tastes, and suffers that she dare not reach for too much more ambrosia. Bradstreet's culture has not dared teach her that "Self-fashioning" *is* "The Renaissance" eternal---that *living* is (or should be) the ultimate deliberate work of poetry. "Out there" in the supposed wilderness, nobody really dies: like demi-god Proteus, "with the help of Priapus," they only forever dance the changes, round and round "The Great One Turning" of the "universe."[50]

"He that played Proteus best" was the individual who prospered by embracing New World demands for change in thought and deed. We are not comparing persons but ways of being alive in America and thus of writing poetry about it. "Proteus Morton" is not so much a figure of excess (as Erasmus would have it), but another Proteus the humanists knew: that of Pico della Mirandola's "Oration: On the Dignity of Man" (1486), in which this "pagan demigod" is humanity itself. And his gift, direct from Deity, is no less than what

---

[50] Survival and maximum enjoyment of living may not seem at first to compare with "errands into the wilderness," but the peace of mind or *ataraxia* that ideally comes to those who "go by the appearances of things" (or as said above, those who "affirm nothing") is worth consideration. Mates 67: "Instead of trying to conduct his life on the basis of supposed 'facts' about the external world," such a "philosopher" "goes by the appearances." Sextus Empiricus (for many the true spokesman of Scepticism) was "indifferent" to others' claim that this was not practicable: "To the contrary, he considers that in getting free of beliefs about a supposed 'reality,' [one] not only avoids various unnecessary evils but also is less drastically affected by the necessary ones."

Contrast Bercovitch *Puritan Origins* 23: The New England Puritan theocracy's "massive effort at control" "insisted" "with unusual vigor" that each person entertain constant "anxiety about election...[This was] "not only normal but mandatory, [and] hysteria, breakdowns, and suicide were not uncommon. Nonetheless [they] continued with increased energy to regiment selfhood," even resorting, he adds, to Saint Augustine's *Confessions* as a more rigorous model of literate (if not literary) self-examination. Where was Bradstreet to find any *life* for herself? She could not even "surrender" hers to her husband's life: "foolish dalliance" or "inordinate affection" to one's spouse was "to play the adulterer" with God as cuckold of the soul (Haskins, *Law and Authority in Early Massachusetts* 141-151: see also Greenblatt's early-Christian citations in *Renaissance* 304n56).

Cicero called the "full right to range wherever he pleases" ("Oration" rpt. in Davies 67):

> Neither a determined dwelling-place, nor a unique shape, nor a role that is peculiarly your own have we given you [says God to Adam], so that you may have and possess what habitation, shape and roles you yourself may wish for according to your desire.... [You], restrained by no limitations, of your own free will in whose hand I have placed you, shall appoint your own nature....We have made you neither celestial nor earthly...you may form yourself in what pattern you choose. You will be able to degenerate into the lowest ranks...[or] be reborn into the highest ranks, those of the divine.

We have seen the humanists' own fear of poets. But for many, such as Giovanni Battista Gelli, "human nature" if definable at all was a Protean "charging up and down the Chain of Being at will"; or as Juan Luis Vives' 1518 *Fable About Man* envisioned, an acting/miming ability that at last induced The Gods to pronounce human beings divine (in Cassirer 390).[51]

---

[51] By way of contrast, those who may doubt the reference below to Poe's "philosophy" might consider this 20th-century example of culture, scripted for America by the Morton's-day victory of (Biblical) Puritan values---the New York Metropolitan Opera Company's 1933 *Merry Mount* (Libretto by Richard L. Stokes; this and stage-photographs courtesy of Archives' Mr. John Pennino).

In Act 1 of 3, protagonist William Bradford confesses to his Elders that he is tormented by dreams of "Astoreth, pagan goddess of the moon"; and before long he meets one "Lady Marigold," a colonial "newcomer" who seems to fit the bill. But, Marigold agrees to marry a "Cavalier," who has a very attractive Maypole at his "neighboring hill." Bradford "insists in a jealous rage that the Puritans at once attack the intruders' camp." In Act 2, Marigold's Cavalier is killed by jealous Bradford---who then suffers a dream confirming that, in exchange for his lusted-after goddess, he will "sign the Devil's book" and "curse New England with flame and bloodshed." This, somehow, brings Act 3 to open with a graceful "murderous attack upon the settlement" by "Indians," in which Marigold suffers so that she cries aloud her Cavalier's name again. Bradford explodes that he "will go beside her to hell," and "proclaims his repudiation of God." He and she are about to be executed "for witchcraft" when Bradford reveals his "mark" from "Satan," "conjures up a bower of flames," and "strides" into it "with the swooning Marigold in his arms. The Puritans, in horror, chant passages from the Lord's Prayer." *The End.*

Morton: "And how much these things are different from the actions of mazed men, I leave to any indifferent man to judge. And if I should say, They are all much alike, they that have seen and heard what I have...will not condemn me altogether" (182-3).

Such talk. Small wonder that for so long there was little room for poets in Euro-American schools. "What then are we to make of the undoubted zeal for education displayed in the Massachusetts of the seventeenth century? In short," Hugh Kearney's study concludes, "the educational barriers erected by the early Puritans against social and intellectual *change* proved to be almost too successful in creating a conservative-minded Bible Belt" (300: emphasis added). Two hundred years later this was still much the case, according to comprehensive study by Ruth Miller Elson (*Guardians of Tradition: American Schoolbooks in the Nineteenth Century*---see for example 230).

But American letters must not sing along with Christian Capitalist Patriarchy as it digs in its heels for a bold backwards turn toward the inevitably multicultural 21st century, by way of a "return to the fundamentals" that have *already* spearheaded much more than five hundred years of human and ecological catastrophe. There can be no denying Morton's and *Canaan's* complicity in the (continuing) commodification of every living thing in North America. But at the same time, both can help us, to prevent another age of Tyler-like, needless cultural regret, like that of this century's *Wasteland* poet, Christian ideologue T. S. Eliot; who confessed himself sorry that he had ever read and perceived the luminous "pagan" wholeness of life, by way of James Joyce's *Ulysses* (published that same "wasteland" year). We must return to "the beginning" in almost every sense if we truly desire an honest morality or literature on this brutalized and re-brutalized continent (this was the view of the great poet William Carlos Williams---*In the American Grain*). Reconceive everything, toward a renaissance of living on a living Earth. It must be clear that this is not separate from "literary matters."

Morton and *Canaan* truly sang "America" first in English. It cannot hurt anybody more than it will empower them to welcome back both of these, as long-abused but honorable endurers of the same demonizations that followed after their own; of American land, of Native Americans, of women of every race. By the 19th century, Edgar Allan Poe had offered up what had to follow from the other path: "the death of a beautiful woman" as "the most poetical topic in the world" ("Philosophy of Composition" 1850: 279). Unfortunately, the death of "Woman" is still at the heart of "the mainstream," an everyday and multiform "cultural event" from fiction to factoid news.

The more do Americans need to know that about this same land, these same people, Thomas Morton of "Merrymount" and *New English Canaan* began and continue to speak---with the poetry of nothing less than love.[52]

---

[52] "Pygmalion in love with his own handiwork is to be compared with those who, too much in love with their own good works, trust in themselves, wherein no life is to be found, until they emerge from themselves, and turn toward the true Venus, which is to be explained as true love of God and of one's neighbour, through which the virtues become alive and fruitful." Carel van Mander, *Painter's Manual* (1604: qtd. in Kermode 523).

Morton's "first American poet in English" stock has been rising. If Leon Edel's 1959 *American Literature* anthology still opened with nothing before Edward Taylor, and 1973's *Makers and the Making* editors Cleanth Brooks, Robert Penn Warren and others omitted Morton completely, a 1974 Macmillan anthology edited by George McMichael positioned Morton after the prose of John Smith and William Bradford. Nina Baym's and others' 1979-85 *Norton Anthology* placed Smith (prose) first, Morton second; and the 1990 *Heath Anthology* (Paul Lauter *et als* editors) also featured Morton thus, as second writer and, manifestly at least, the first with "American poetry."

5: *New World, New Life*

With his one known chance to marry and find himself a home of "quietness" in shambles, Morton cast about for just the right voyage---preferably, one that would carry him where even a shadow of a title to some land might become something to build upon. Sir Ferdinando Gorges, still trying after 20 years to "plant" the lands once called Northern Virginia, saw in this lawyer-acquaintance a man with the requisite skills for his next effort. Not long before, Gorges' West Country circle of impatient investors had outfitted John Smith himself with support that Smith no longer received from his original Virginia Company (Arbour 1: lx). Smith's 1614 voyage and the map he then laid before Prince Charles had resulted (Smith claimed) in the northern land's new name, "New England."

But beyond the naming, all had failed. By 1618 Gorges' Captain Dermer had found "Hollanders" coasting northward from "New Amsterdam" (est. 1603) "for trade with the natives...in the right of our Patent." "Their answer was, they understood no such thing, nor found any of our nation there" (*Narration* 40). So Gorges and associates had felt "forced" to cast about quickly for new and determined planters, and tried "means...to draw into those enterprises some of those families that had retired themselves into Holland for scruple of conscience," namely the "Pilgrim" congregation then in Leyden and Amsterdam exile. From these ardent Christians, investors reasonably expected more orderly and so more profitable operations.

But Plimoth had managed to launch itself without obligation to Gorges for financial help; and besides, since their first winter in America (1620-1) had cost half their company's lives, they were still recovering, and other aspects of trade had gone wrong there too (Ch. 6). As Morton's court suit (above) had concluded, investors with inside information knew that Plimoth was still shipping scant profit home. So Gorges had not waited for Plimoth to develop, but tried in 1623 to revive merchant Andrew Weston's Weymouth post nearby them, with about 50 people under his son Robert. And still, within a year they had quit as well, "having scarcely saluted the country." The much-debated demise of Weymouth continued this history of New English disarray, while the Dutch explored the Hudson and the French the St. Lawrence, making headway up major rivers of Native American trade.[53]

So as Spring 1624 approached, Gorges made arrangements to send Morton and 30 indentured youths aboard his Captain Wollaston's vessel *Unity*. Gorges had recently stood before Parliament defending himself from charges of monopoly (treated in the previous chapter), and painting a portrait of the American Northeast:

> [The] enlargement of the King's dominions, with the advancement of religion in those desert parts, are matters of highest consequence, and far exceeding a simple and disorderly course of fishing...for that so goodly a coast could not be long left unpeopled [sic] by the French, Spanish or Dutch....[The] mischief already sustained by those disorderly persons, are inhumane and intolerable; for first, in their manners and behavior they are worse than the very savages, impudently and openly lying with their women, teaching their men to drink drunk, to swear and blaspheme the name of God, and in their drunken humor to fall together by the ears [argue], thereby giving them occasion to seek revenge. Besides, they cozen and abuse the savages in trading and trafficking, selling them salt covered with butter instead of so much butter, and the like....[and] they sell unto the savages muskets, fowling-pieces, powder, shot, swords, arrow-heads, and other arms, wherewith the savages slew many of those

---

[53] Much more detail on this plantation's failures in Ch. 7. As Morton made ready, its scattering original or "old comer" planters took up their Morton-period places in New England, such as William Blackstone who moved alone to Shawmut/Trimountain/Boston; Samuel Maverick (noted above) who moved to Winnisimmet/Charlestown; and William Jeffreys, an important shaper of Morton's final fate.

>   fishermen, and are grown so able and so apt, as they become dangerous to the planters....(*Narration* 38)

Gorges spoke for "cleaning up the territory." But he knew the ethics of expediency already the rule, already feeding profit to many including himself in the chamber. His appeal was now to Parliament's increasingly Puritan "moral" interests, but the underlying facts of behavior in the Northeast were both as he said, and something more.

Sir Ferdinando's own generation of self-made gentlemen-speculators had come to their wealth by cooperating with and building upon those Newfoundland practices, "humors" as Morton would call them. Cohabitation with Native American women, the trade of contraband items between the races and cultures, and "revelry" (*Canaan*'s repeated word for English folk customs and different Native gatherings) had been normal components of life in the America now being shared by such radically different peoples. In Native American societies, as Morton's men would soon find, intertribal socializing, marriage and kinship were already the indispensable *contexts* of trade and material exchange. (Cave's *Pequot War* is a recent survey full of examples.) Fishermen and fur-traders had followed suit for 100 years, "complying with [these] humors" in Morton's phrase for the ways of the peoples who controlled the land. Such a makeshift "social fabric" or quasi-familial relationship between civilizations had evolved in order to smooth over the inevitable negotiations of American wealth and power. Soon, thanks to England's newfound "moral" concerns born of Puritan times, all this would swiftly change: Morton's very career was to consummate one period of transatlantic contact, and begin another.[54]

---

[54] Eccles' *France in America* (24), Calloway (19) detail early acknowledgments that related northern Native peoples controlled most aspects of interrelations, in "New France" at times even restricting Europeans' travel to maintain control of trade with them. Duncan (123) offers many obscure sources on the earliest fishing-settlements of the Maine coasts; and Gorges himself, who had long sent ships to trade as they could in the region of the Kennebec's "Merry-meeting Bay," was

Unity would sail in March. The attorney gave George Miller's Chancery Court officials "a slip instead of a tester" (*Canaan* 143) and kept out of sight, likely studying up on previous voyagers' reports at Gorges' Somerset estate, then a colonial "headquarters" and matrix of maps and men in the business. "...I will go the surest way to work at first, [and] see how others are answered in the like kind" (189).

> The [Eskimo] people of the country, having espied us, made a lamentable noise, as we thought, with great outcries and screeching: we hearing them thought it had been the howling of wolves....We brought our musicians, purposing by force to rescue us, if need should so require, or with courtesy to allure the people. When they came unto us, we caused our musicians to play, ourselves dancing and making many signs of friendship....[We] were in so great credit with them upon this single acquaintance that we could have anything they had. We bought five canoes...the clothes from their backs.... They took great care of one another....They are very tractable people, void of craft or double-dealing, and easy to be brought to any civility and good order....(Capt. John Davis, 1585 *First Voyage*: rpt. in David ed. Hakluyt 336-8)

In two months Morton would be face to face with peoples as "strange" to him as Germans to old Tacitus:

> We had a youth in our company that could play upon a Gitterne, in whose homely Music [New England Natives] tooke great delight, and would give him many things, as Tobacco, Tobacco-pipes, Snakes skinnes of sixe foot long, which they use for Girdles, Fawnes skinnes, and such like, and danced twentie in a Ring, and the Gitterne in the middest of them, using many Savage gestures, singing Io, la, Io, la, la, Io: him that first brake the ring, the rest would knocke and cry out upon....(Martin Pring, 1603: rpt. in Quinn ENEV 220)

---

referring to the above "immoral" practices when he called Native peoples "tractable [as long as] discreet courses be taken with them" (qtd. in Rowse 99). Those "courses" were still in action when Weston's 1622 ship arrived at Damaris Cove and found that people had "newly set up a may pole and were very mery" (Pratt's *Narrative* qtd. in FBH1:256). At the other extreme of the Northeast near "New Netherland," Capt. deVries recalled too that Algonkian Canarsee people had "given... stranded men our daughters" in establishing relations (*Portrait* in Raesly ed. 174). More detail follows. McBride's "Legacy" and Grumet's *Northeastern Indian Lives* reveal further the political importance of social bonds.

But these were peoples whom even the old soldier Sir Humphrey Gilbert had found it wiser to approach in other than martial ways:

> ...for solace of our people and allurement of the savages, we were provided of music in good variety, not omitting the least toys as Morris-dancers, hobby-horse, and May-like conceits, to delight the savage people, whome we intended to win by all fair means possible....(Edward Hayes on Gilbert, 1583: rpt. in Quinn *Voyages* 2:385)

"The Natives are very impatient, when for English commodities they pay so much more of their money, and not understanding the cause of it; and many say the English cheat and deceive them," Roger Williams wrote (*Key* 211, 218). We know, of course, the cozening and abuses, the degradations, the polite thievery and conquest within this "fair means" approach to Native America.[55] But as we look for the particular roots of the methods that Thomas Morton's company employed, it begins to emerge that, except for the unwritten codes of pleasure and short-term profit, there was virtually no "ideological" commitment of any kind in the majority of the earliest colonial population that Morton was about to encounter.

Since at least the mid-1500s, red and white peoples had lived together in no more "natural antagonism" than that between the different peoples of Europe ---trading, stealing, fighting, intermarrying, and salting their intercourse with condescension for the ways of "foreigners." The vast majority of "New Englanders" till at least the 1620-30 Puritan "migrations" cared very little for the mission-centered kind of colony in most senses of the term; and the copious

---

[55] The excellent collection of studies in Wm. W. Fitzhugh, ed.'s *Cultures in Contact* (1985: for ex. 35) recognizes multiple examples of early "trouble" caused by both transatlantic sides: "As ...in Frobisher's case...wrestling matches, games, and friendly trading [during Capt. Davis' voyages] gave way to increasingly serious pilfering, culminating in a bold attempt to steal the ship's anchor and boats by severing the ship's mooring." Cooperation and cozenage; or as J. F. Fausz' *Contact* study of the same dynamics along the Mid-Atlantic (Virginia) Coast calls this, "Patterns of Anglo-Indian Aggression and Accomodation" (225).

complaints about this, from ardent Christian newcomers at Plimoth, Salem and Boston, corroborate what James Axtell has called "the tip of a moral iceberg" about the early Northeast (*Essays* 157).[56]

Hence further reasons for the relatively tolerant, playfully poised spirit of *Canaan*, though it is first a colonizer's text speaking out in favor of colonies. Transatlantic crossings by this time were not some "miraculous thing" (*Canaan* 169) to these people of the coasts and river-trades; and in multiple ways Thomas Morton was prepared for the rigors of the life. *Canaan*'s relative ease in the face of the overwhelming "unknown" continent, its peoples and customs, emerges very much from this habitude, from the support Morton received from America's "old comers" and their Native networks. Of course his company shared each their degrees of Europe's late-medieval psychological heritage toward "wild" lands and peoples in "those desert parts," the "wilderness"; but Morton mocked such terms for New England (54, 116). He and the experienced crewmen knew that America was more or less like "the forest" at home, a place that was "far from being unexploited or devoid of men." Neither wholly wild nor isolated, it was only a place "on the extreme fringes of [their] society, where men could venture and meet other men, some of them so wild that they were mistaken at first for beasts"---a place (to them) almost without rules or ruler, both unnerving and exhilarating, a place of sometimes-pleasant "cognitive dislocations" "between

---

[56] While all these operations were founded upon the extraction of American wealth, some period writers, from Hakluyt ("Purposes and Policies to Be Observed in Colonization" (1578, in Wright 16) to Ralegh (in a manuscript "prepared for private circulation and for the eyes of Elizabeth" circa 1596, qtd. in Pennington 186) stressed that American Natives should be both "employed" as "factors" in trade, given firearms to assist in the pursuit of riches, including the conquest or "removal" of uncooperative fellow-tribes. The nearby French even before Champlain followed the same policy (see his *Voyages* in Levermore 1:163, and "Antimasque" herein). Champlain added the revelrous "Order of Good Times" and Lescarbot's 1606 "Theatre of Neptune" performance to their colonial methods. While the Dutch had a death-penalty in place for any trader of firearms (Fiske I, 154-5), they almost always winked when a Mohawk or other Native along the Hudson River Valley showed up with a good stock of inland furs to be had, or when it served to further access to the best (Iroquois) peltries.

savagery and culture." Tolerance and stereotype, "fair means" and condescending colonialism inscribe *Canaan* as they inscribed the men who, with Morton, made its story happen.⁵⁷

Unity sailed from London "with provision of all sorts fit for a plantation" (53) on March 23, 1624 (Holly examines ship's records in detail). A bad leak in the hull was repaired some days out, but water damaged food-supplies and tightened everyone's rations (Ford, "Wollaston" 221). They sighted land on June 25 (then New Year's Day), and the ship coasted Cape Ann peninsula, unloaded barrels of salt for use at the struggling fishing-station there, spent some weeks fishing in local waters and taking on stores of processed whale or "train" oil. From there, *Unity* readied to proceed to Virginia on other common business. Morton, not in "command" but certainly a "landsman" to heed, must have been scouting the while for what was either a Weston-like "plantation" effort, or a mere plan to stay through a winter or two, for development of existing Gorges enterprises. By summer's end the ship's company began to split up to make the most of opportunities.

Since *Unity*'s basic mission was to supply and develop existing ventures on the land, the marketing of indentured men's contracts was discretionary with the ship's controlling officers and agents. One Humphrey Rastall, a "merchant" of London and Bristol who had also seen the Mediterranean as an agent in

---

⁵⁷ Quotations are from Jacques LeGoff's "The Wilderness in the Medieval West" in his *The Medieval Imagination* 53, as he also paraphrases historian Marc Bloch. Hayden White's essay "The Noble Savage Theme as Fetish" (in Chiappelli, ed., *First Images*) points out (129) that where a culture's (or a colony's) structuring, most fundamental metaphors for making sense of the world allowed for what he calls *continuity*---that is, the sense that space-and-time produced "differences" among peoples did not affect their fundamental, shared humanity ---such metaphors typically resulted in relative toleration of difference. Not surprisingly, those who understood "the forest" at home fared better in America than their urbanized counterparts. But groups with "metaphors" characterized by what White called *contiguity*---by conceptions of difference between groups as generic, categorical and irreconcileable---those tended to produce relative intolerance of difference in the communities they established.

"dealings of very questionable legality" (Holly 24), had brought aboard his recent business managing such servants: he and Captain Wollaston were responsible for their keep and whatever labor they performed. (Examples of their contracts, plus the average servant's expectations and rights regarding conditions of life and labor, appear in both Ford's "Wollaston" and in Mass. Hist. Soc. *Procs.* XIV [1875-6], 359-381.)

Improvising (as was common) to make the most of the voyage, Rastall chartered a smaller craft and took several servants to Virginia, with *Unity* ordered to remain at work off New England. But Rastall did not return after the promised eight weeks: instead, a letter from him told Wollaston to bring *Unity* to Jamestown. But by now, Wollaston lacked sufficient "vittles" for that voyage, and had to seek them from Monhegan Island fishermen to the north. After doing so, they never made it to Jamestown, but fought autumn's "contrary winds" a whole month before they gave up and turned for London, arriving back in Feb. 1625.

At some point between that Monhegan trip and *Unity*'s departure for Virginia (early October), Morton and his "consociates" disembarked, and were set up at "Mount Wollaston" on the southerly rim of Massachusetts Bay.

There they found (as Wood described the place, 57) "very fertile" soil and "great store of plain ground without trees" that was "very convenient for farmers' houses": this was much-tended "Indian" land like the nearby "Massachusetts Fields," an area densely populated by Native groups since at least the Paleolithic (c. 9000 years ago). For trade the harbor tides here ran too shallow for vessels bigger than shallops, but this could have virtue in defense against a possible French raiding-vessel (there were English ones too). Morton and however many men first with him agreed to try this "Little Neck of Land" (*Passonagessit* or Trumbull's *Pasco-naig-es-it*, "near the little point": FBH2:49n2), with its "dainty fine round rising hilluck" (54) and ever-changing view of the wooded, white-sandy islands (Brereton had called it "a white sandy and very bold shore"). At first they survived on shellfish---Morton grew "cloyed" with plentiful lobster "the first day I went ashore" (87); but he learned to bait his hooks with the meat and catch bass. It began to seem that, pending Native objection, he and his dogs might hunt up deer.

It was late summer: the oft-reported scents of a "garden" were on the air, and the great bay's thousands of birds from herons to sanderlings. The mainland's edge here was mostly green saltmarsh, behind them away from the coast rose the forests of the Blue Hills, and the navigable, fresh-water mouths of the Monatoquit ("many villages") and the Neponset rivers emptied into the bay just north and south of the men. This was Smith's (and Levett's, and others') "Paradise of all those parts" (Arbour ed. 2:719): Native peoples had watched "first light" flood the sky above the sea for generations, and described it as The Creator's first thought of the day. No record tells directly of Morton's first contact with Massachusetts people: no doubt wariness, as with Plimoth, made them wait. But there had been a common scenario for decades:

> ...the next day, we determined to fortifie ourselves in a little plot of ground....[B]ut the second day after our comming from the maine, we espied 9 canowes or boats, with fiftie Indians in them, comming toward us...and being loth they should discover our fortification, we went out on the sea side to meet them; and comming somewhat neere them, they all sate downe upon the stones, calling aloud to us (as we rightly guessed) to doe the like, a little distance from them; having sate awhile in this order, Captaine Gosnold willed me to go unto them...but as soon as I came up unto them, one of them... knew me (whom I also very well remembered) and smiling upon me, spake somewhat unto their lord or captaine, which sat in the midst of them, who presently rose up and tooke a large Beaver skin...and gave it unto me, which I requited.... While we were thus mery...the rest of the day we spent in trading....(Brereton, *Relation* 1602: rpt. in Levermore 37)

Shuffleton's study of intercultural America would call this "ethnic semiosis": different peoples *sat down near each other* first, and deliberately exchanged signs before anything else, signals that calmed the tensions of mistrust. Any number of messages (weapons shown or concealed, posture, faces) expressed aspects of intent, character, degree of aggressiveness, before the least verbal pretense came into play, and careful management of these protocols was proving crucial in the fortunes of voyage and village alike.[58] By and large this first century's men had kept their wits about them till things grew "merry" and profitable---minds "seconded by the body."

Morton's first contact, with a woman in the Native role, seems to be hinted at in the "Poem" he wrote for his later Revels (134): this woman was "sitting on the ground" at first sight, but "solitary" and "sick with grief." Most writers record the Native practice of visiting the burial-places of loved ones (43) and it was not unusual for colonists to meet Native women here (Mourt 77-9, Winthrop's *Journal* WJH2:68). They, after all, were the farmers of Massachusetts Fields, the harvesters of hills' and seashores' bounty.

Unfortunately, grave-visitation was more likely than ever before. Where John Smith had seen between 20 and 40 "habitations" along the waterways (*Description* 1614: Arbour ed. 192, 706-718), where "coasters" from Verrazanno (1524: Wroth 139) to Champlain (*Works* 1:325-7) to the Pilgrims (*Mourt* 63) had seen or estimated "Thousands" of New England Natives---all this thriving civilization had been reduced, by "plague" in the space of perhaps five years (1614-18), to what Morton had to call a "Golgotha" or place of skulls (20).[59]

---

[58] The "circumspect" Morton preparing for New England might have noticed in Rosier's 1605 account the reaction of Pemaquid tribespeople who, when refused these quasi-ceremonial "niceties" before trade, responded with "discourtesy," such as actions ensuring that English guns would not fire, and behaving in a "devious" semi-hostile manner, "though doing them no harm" (in Quinn ENEV108, 412n1). The later *family*-groups of Puritan planters were not prepared for these very traditional, usually harmless Native forms of "brinksmanship" (Ch. 7).

[59] Champlain's 1605 map of "Malle Barre" (Nauset, Cape Cod), reprinted in *Works* 1 and Trigger *Handbook* 165, offers multiple visual evidences of high population, showing at least a dozen settlements centered on large structures like those described in Mourt (77-9): fish-weirs, cornfields and large sea-going boats on the map also suggest large collective efforts to gather and

The peoples he met were the survivors, perhaps no more than a *tenth*, of a population then recently numbering between 90-135,000 persons, from Maine to southern Connecticutt regions. The collective names by which these peoples are known---Abenaki, Pennacook, Massachusetts, Nipmuc, Wampanoag, Narragansett, Pequot and others---usually told something of the place which a group of "the people" called home-territory. *Massa-chuseuck* denoted the people of "the big rock region" or "of the great hill," and *Narra-gansett* those peoples "of the little bay" (Caduto/Bruchac 148). But these collective names subsumed many smaller bands of interrelated families: the *Wampanu* or "people of the East" (for ex.) included the Pokanoket, the Aquinnah or later "Gay Head" of Capawac/Martha's Vineyard, and others, each of these names denoting unique features of location, identity and culture.

Similarities of Eastern Algonquian languages and Northeastern Woodland life-ways and legend had given these peoples much in common through the centuries before epidemic devastations. Natives early-on in Gorges' custody "at first hardly understood one the other's speech" but soon found their differences "no more than that as ours is between the Northern and Southern people" (*Narration* 26), while Winslow found of the surviving populations that "in a hundred miles distance of place, both in language and manners...they very well understand each other" (591). The specific adaptations demanded by New

---

produce food; as do the 2-acre "Boylston Street Fish weirs" of c. 2500 B.C.E. As noted, *Monatoquit* means "river of many villages" (Horner 2); and archaeologists have found signs of high Native population-densities and resource-use (extensive quarry-pits, etc.) through this whole region, from Boston Bay to Weymouth to the Blue Hills, Morton's "backyard."

For full citations on these epidemics see *Canaan* Bk. 1 Ch. 2. Secondary sources for this introduction to New England Native American history and culture(s) include but are not limited to: Trigger *Handbook* Vol. 15, Marten, Tuck, Salisbury, Krech, Simmons, Cronon, Bragdon, Axtell, Russell, Wallace, Wilbur, Peters, Speck, Hauptmann and Wherry, Grumet, Etienne and Leacock, Leland; conversations/interviews and/or work with Nanepashemet, Slow Turtle, Tall Oak, Thomas Doughton, Ann McMullen; and with scholars associated with various regional institutions such as the Haffenreffer, Peabody Essex, and Robbins Museums in Middleboro (headquarters of the Massachusetts Archaeological Society).

England's various landscapes connected these peoples across time, too, with the earliest inhabitants. The families and individuals before Thomas Morton's eyes had been in the midst of change in their own right, with their recent more settled ways around maize-farming (about 600 years old here at the time). But even decimated by Old World diseases, they remained the heirs of a life in continuance at least since the glaciers had scoured the land of their first tracks; and their ways had also learned from the far-reaching traders of the Midwest and North.

The first known "Paleo-Indians" had entered New England about 13,000 years before, roaming forests of spruce, pine and tundra vegetation that also supported caribou and mastodon: these began to disappear as the climate warmed between 10-8000 years ago, and a new diversity of plants and animals made human life a bit easier to sustain. Interestingly, these first peoples lived less along New England's milder southern coasts than in norther locations "more clustered and spectacular" (Hauptmann/Wherry 20); and this was also one of the great periods of Northern culture, sometimes called the "Maritime Archaic" (c. 9-6000 years ago).

While the continuities are still under investigation between contact-period New England and this ancient seagoing culture of "primitive high technology" and rich storytelling, aspects in common with Native peoples of the European period are clear in the records, such as the ceremonial use of red ochre, and the skills needed to build and pilot large sea-canoes. Ancient stories (explored by Leland, and Simmons *Spirit*), collective practices such as "drives" of game animals into hunters' ambushes (Tuck "Tradition") and careful burials were quite similar across the earliest human Northeast.[60]

---

[60] Rosier's 1605 *Relation* details Native New England deep-sea whaling (Burrage 392); Winthrop (WJH1:108, 1633) marvels at Long Island "canoes" that carry 80 persons. By the 1630s northern "Tarratines" were still sailing south, "100 men in 3 canoes" to raid Agawam and other places

The long Archaic period (Early, Middle and Late ran roughly from 9 to 6 to 4000 years ago) saw certain changes and breaks from the first peoples. To the north, "Paleo-Eskimos" began to displace the Maritime Archaic peoples, languages and cultures of northern Labrador. By 3000 years ago only only a few southern areas (Belle Isle, Maine etc.) still reflected the early practices, but the new peoples held on to the raising of ceremonial mounds and the uses of red ochre into the contact period (Tuck "Regional" 42-3; Reynolds 103, 106). To the south, groups of hunter-gatherers began to move about less frequently: between 8-4000 years ago camps something like the later unfortified villages began to appear near the sites of early fish-weirs, tools became more specialized, and population increases called for increased social and ritual activities, to maintain cooperative relations within the ecosystem.

As climate and food-gathering both eased somewhat, human needs and culture-creativity encouraged each other. Tribes and bands depending on the same fish-migrations each spring developed them into causes for intertribal "revels" (*Canaan* 22, 29, 33 etc.) and traditional gatherings, at which all kinds of relationships (of politics, power and kinship) were fostered and expressed in story and music, custom and sports, and in objects from practical trade-goods to works of art and craft. Morton's thinking on this world led him to guess that it was as old as the "frozen Sea" (16).

(WJH1: 66; and Josselyn, 23, 102). Dickason (100) recounts the French first reports of "red Indians" and red ochre-use etc. Tuck and the early chapters of Trigger *Handbook* 15 detail its use in the colonial period, and its continuance is related via oral tradition (source: Mr. Paul Levasseur and other New Bedford, "Iron River" area Native people: the "Iron River" flows through Dartmouth, is named for its red color and deposits of bog-iron).

According to historian Ann McMullen of Milwaukee Public Museum (1997 conversations) as well as living Native Northeastern historians, Cahokia and Midwestern connections possibly gave rise to oral traditions about the arrival of corn (and other things) from the south and/ or west, the corn in the ear of a crow.

About 3000 years ago the Archaic ways shaded into "Woodland" (divided also into Early, Middle and Late). This period saw trade contacts with and possibly some immigrants from the then-Adena Midwest: what Jennings (*Founders* 170) called micro- and macro- trade networks began to permeate and connect New England with other regions more than ever, carrying local perishables and long-distance "luxury" goods, ceramics and copper. Imported too were some aspects of the Adena's more hierarchic social structure, home-building styles, artistic and ceremonial practices. By the Late Woodland (c. 1000 years ago) maize cultivation and other more settled varieties of horticulture arrived in southern parts, probably more Midwestern influence from "Hopewell" cultures there, whose networks of trade (centered on Cahokia in "Illinois") spanned much of the central and eastern continent (Fitting 45).

All the chief characteristics of Native New England, then, remarked in early accounts---skilled use of the sea and soil, relatively egalitarian social forms based in the necessities (and ease) of food-getting, eclectic trade and cultural networks---these were the results of exploration, experiment, borrowing and invention not so different from Europeans'. Although in time, contact with these latest strangers brought more change than any other, the land had been by no means static before the English dropped first anchor.

In the north, where Morton reached as far as the Kennebec drainage, peoples lived on a soil that discouraged agricultural life-ways: in general they held to the Archaic's rhythms of coastal gathering and winter inland hunts of moose and deer (fur-trade demands did more than agriculture to "settle" the Abenaki and others: Russell 179, Snow 138-42). But by 900 A.D. or so, maize, beans, squash ("the three sisters"), tobacco, herb-cultivation etc. had taken some hold in southern locales as far north as the Merrimack River. After the labors of spring planting, summer weeds, and autumn gathering came the winter benefits of stored corn, to ease the year-end month or two of slender diet. It is thought that agriculture developed mostly as response to a problem, the growing insufficiency of resources round the older "estuarine" camps and settlements. Native New England population had still been increasing at contact (Bragdon *People* 86).

If people now began to organize more of their year around the needs of cultivated lands, how did this affect men's and women's accustomed roles in providing for life, and the distributions of power in the community? Salisbury asserts that the previous six centuries of changes had "scarcely even modified" what he believed were the long Archaic period's general assignment of "political" roles to male hunters and "domestic" ones to women (*Manitou* 40-1): a more recent study finds that each of the region's peoples, groups and persons "participated differentially" in traditional roles and practices of power (Bragdon *People* 182). Major factors influencing behavior included the particular location's demands for obtaining food (how much "independence" a place could support), and how location affected a people's place in trade, both before European contact and after the arrival of valued transatlantic commodities.

Discussions of "power" are hazardous. We must keep separated, from our concept of Native American life here, all of that sense of "hunter-dominance/domestic submission" that emerged from European "prehistory," and was so endemic to the European-colonial cultures of Morton's time. In Native New England, as in other historical places (including Europe!), "domestic" was (and still is) conceived as a place of power, powers inseparable from "public" or, in European terms, "political" powers. The hunter---to put it bluntly, the man with the power to "dominate," however briefly and imperfectly, through his threat of violence---was all but completely "controlled" (if we must put it that way in "scholarship") by his awareness of his own dependence upon his community; "controlled" by the rich rewards and more complex forms of power and pleasure found *in being part of* the main social group. "Life" for this typical male was not usually conceived as a constant demonstration (at others' expense) of an illusion of "independence" from the complex of human activities and relationships that make up life "around the home" (domesticity). The most "powerful" Sachems of the "historic" period were always described as limited in their powers for the same kinship-based reasons.

Academic (that is, European-based) models and proponents of hierarchical "dominance and submission" have *never* demonstrated the New England existence of anything approaching a consistent "system" that could have compelled or enforced behaviors against individual will. The proof lies with what happened when Native "loose confederacy" in "King Philip's War" (c.1675) met "highly disciplined" English soldiers drawn from a "highly disciplined" English population. For Native peoples, New England's natural and "intertribal" environments simply allowed for too many *options*: Europeans had devoted far more time to building systems for forcibly limiting people's choices.

There are Levett's and a few others' mentions of wife- or (more accurately) spouse-beating, but even at the heart of the "domestic scene" the woman's powers were at every point the hunter's match. The most efficient example is a short witty Penobscot tale about the "supreme" hero-hunter Gluskap (of Abenaki and other reportedly "patriarchal" northern peoples). In a match to see who has real power (if any) to "compel" behavior from others, "master" Gluskap is "shamefully defeated" by a baby (as a woman somewhat gleefully watches and explains: in Leland 120). The "dominant hunter" is "overpowered" by his own respect and feelings for them: in European terms, he has been passively "inscribed" with a social code "repressing," one supposes, less "civilized" urges. But the tale is what Europeans would call a comedy---"Life wins" because the contest of powers resolves in "marriage." As we come nearer the peoples Thomas Morton actually dealt with, we note that while the creation-legends of relatively patrilineal northern peoples appear to begin with a female giving birth (Leland 15), southern records usually speak first of "Kiehtan" or Cautontowitt (Simmons *Spirit* 39), a male-identified deity in most written accounts. And yet, the observers spoke often of the powers of a "Squa Sachem" as leader, of prominent women as go-betweens (Winslow 283; Morrell *New England*), and as keepers of vital knowledge such as patterns of stars and planets that guided agriculture (Verrazanno 139; van Wassenaer in Jameson *New Netherland*; Williams 156, Caduto 70). Whether or not a matrilineal system of inheritance and "public" or "political" power was "adopted" in the south as "recognition" of women's importance (Salisbury 41), Morton was in the Ma-re Mount area most likely to encounter women of relatively public and powerful roles.

Besides their long common heritage, then, the peoples here also shared other traits. For all of them, the natural world was alive with spirit and/or Manit, generally defined as the living power or mystery of the Creator that infuses all things. Kinship---bonds of blood intermarriage, "tribal" alliance" and spiritual meaning---connected these peoples laterally and in some senses hierarchically to all other creatures.[61]

---

[61] "To our way of thinking, the Creator set the pattern for all things. Everything was given its original instructions about how to be, about its function in the world. So all things have an inherent power, which we call *manit*. Each variety of stone has its own *manit*; some make good blades and pipes, some can be carved, while others can make fire. You can't expect everything from every stone, because each has its own *manit*. The same is true of trees, animals, people, everything. A person can achieve access to *manit*, and use it for his own advantage or the group's advantage. It can be used for evil, too. The manipulation of that power is a ceremony, and the way to communicate that is in an altered state, a dream or a trance perhaps. So a medicine man, a *powwow*, is someone who does this....Different people had different strengths and skills, different *manit*. And so different people would be called upon depending on the problem." Nanepashemet, qtd. in Rolbein, "The Thanksgiving Myth"

As Morton's company took up this new life, then, they were surrounded by a human world of ancient continuity, only recently reduced to a "place of skulls." Nanepashemet (late Director of Plimoth Plantation's Wampanoag Indian Programs: in Dempsey, *Morton* interview) likened the impact of these epidemics to the sudden and persistingly destructive impact of a nuclear weapon: Bragdon saw Massachusetts peoples "coping effectively" ("World View" 28) within "a framework that provided them with limited options: they could evacuate their lands, they could consolidate and fight, or they could attempt to accomodate themselves to the newcomers."

It appears that people of the Neponset Massachusetts accomodated the men left by Captain Wollaston's *Unity* late in 1624. Despite the region's recent history of kidnappings and violent encounters with French, English and others (*Canaan* 103), their Sachem Obtakiest, *a.k.a.* Chikatawbak, saw a use for his guests not unlike the one that his contemporary, "Massasoit" Ousamequin of the Wampanoags, had found for Plimoth's planters three years before. The Massachusetts' needs became the Morton company's opportunity.

Like most other aspects of Native life in the 1620s, what are now called "intertribal" relations were much disturbed by drastic losses of people. The Massachusetts were now suffering the worst incursions of "Tarratine" or Micmac raiding-parties from the north, who c.1614 had managed to kill the previous "Massasoit" or High Sachem, Nanepashemet of Mystic (Medford). The Massachusetts were seeing further challenges in their North Shore inland back-country (roughly between the Charles and Merrimack Rivers) from the Narragansetts, a people relatively better-off amid the epidemics; and they lacked effective, traditional Wampanoag help from peoples to the south close to Plimoth, decimated by disease.

What was happening here? The demand for guns in Native southern New England had sharpened with the early 1600s. Once the "first contact" peoples, from Eskimo to Beothuk to Micmac, had realized even the limited advantages of guns in their intertribal rivalries (see Bock 116 and Wade 21), the Micmac roundabout Champlain at Port Royal began to demand that "the French suppl[y] their Indian friends with muskets [circa 1603] and steel-tipped arrows"---which enabled their Sachem Mabretou/Membertou "to undertake a successful war against the fierce Massachusetts Indians." In Champlain's account (1907:108-113), Mabretou's war parties returned victorious from "Almouchiquois" or Abenaki territories (on the Saco River); all of which suggests a number of different New England targets for warriors with the advantages bestowed by guns. (The unreliable firearms of this time were less any real advantage in American combat than they were an *unknown* terror, a thunderous sign to one's rivals, of alliance with new powers of uncertain but frightening potential.)

These events had repercussions in The Massachusetts that were felt just before the Plimothers' and Morton's arrivals (1620/1624 respectively). *Mourt's Relation* (78) recounted the death of Massachusetts High Sachem Nanepashemet due to Micmac warriors, in the decade just after Champlain's trade-activities. One result of that killing, besides that of making the familiar "Massasoit"/Ousamequin the region's new major power near the Plimothers, was the movement---for fear of further raids---of Native peoples round Boston Bay, particularly Neponset Sachem Chikatawbak's plague-surviving people from "Mount Wollaston" at Quincy, where Morton encamped. Chikatawbak's people were "the people of the land" there, and so the prime trading-partners of Morton's company for whatever he had to offer. And, meanwhile at this time, according to history in Williams' *Key* (235) and other southern New England-focused sources, such as the anonymous *Journal of New Netherland* (Jameson

Narratives 273), Dutch and French traders on "Frenchman's [Narragansett] Bay" were trading guns for the "extraordinary gain" to be had for both sides. Native people, the *Journal* adds, "endeavored no less to procure guns" than Europeans worked to get pelts.

We can build upon these clues with three others to show that Morton's trade was indeed the Massachusetts Bay Natives' early moment of opportunity to acquire guns. We have the remark by another New English visitor, Captain Thomas Dermer (qtd. in FBH1:207), that Native peoples near "Charlton" or the Charles River on "Boston" Bay were, early in the decade, "less to be feared" than others of the region. Second, the well-known 1622 Royal Proclamation against "irregular" trade (in guns too of course) stated that firearms had *already* "spoiled" a trade that had once exchanged cheap English goods for furs (document rpt. in FBH2:107). And third, in the anti-Morton letters of 1627-28 that Bradford wrote to the Council for New England, he claimed (with his share of exaggeration) intelligence of twenty-odd pieces sold by Morton, and fifty to sixty already in Wampanoag and Narragansett hands (Letters 62-63). Those guns had probably become a *component* of those numerous tribes' "dominance" over more northerly Massachusett peoples such as those around Morton, Chikatawbak's Neponsets and others.

The Neponsets, likely arranging English trade and firearms to help their problems, reciprocated by leaving their vulnerable land-base at Passonagessit, with its "champion" fields cleared for crops, for nearby Moswetusett, a hummock of wooded higher ground along Squantum peninsula with great strewn boulders forming small "chapels" along the southerly beach toward "Boston Bay" (as they stand there today). Perhaps the people felt more secure there with its natural half-"moat" growing deeper with the tides (Horner 3; Salwen 170). Further out, Squantum is a place of wooded steep seaside trails, fortress outcrops of eroded gray puddingstone overlooking the islands: from Squantum heights the Neponsets had already driven away some English under a Capt. Myles Standish, back in 1621. (*Mourt* 71; *Canaan* 103; see "Masque" on what Morton found quite significant there.)

They gave living-space and furs in exchange for tactical advantages: it seemed the thing to do. French and Dutch guns, their protections and their destructive consequences, had been reconfiguring similar relations across the Northeast despite their actually rather limited usefulness as a weapon in America.[62] Also (as noted), just before 1624, another of Gorges' agents Captain Dermer had reported that, while the Pokanokets (Wampanoags just south) "hated" the English, those near the "Charles" River were "less to be feared." One year later Captain Levett observed "2 fowling pieces, one pistoll and some half-pikes" in Native possession (in Levermore 2:628). Guns had begun to arrive.

Higginson slightly later (and with reasons, of course) described the area as one where Native people "profess[ed] to like well of our comming and planting here," because of the "reliefe and defence from their enemies" gained, "wherewith (I say) before this Plantation begun, they were often indangered" (1629-30: in Force 1:12:13). Levett before him had observed the interpersonal aspects of trade that either helped or hindered a newcomer. Perceiving Native people's reserve, he told them that "If they did not truck it was no matter, I would be good friends with them, at which they smiled and talked one to the other, saying that I had the right fashion of the Abenaki Sagamores" (2: 623).

---

[62] Major (*Dissertation* 22-3) cites Louis Morton's "The End of Formalized Warfare" (*American Heritage* VI, August 1955) and other sources to give a sense of the "realities" of guns there and then. Because they were heavy, slow to load, useless in damp weather, of poor mechanical quality, and of short range (deadly accurate at best within 50 yards), guns (in Wood's phrase) did one "more credit than service," added fearsomeness to reputation. But it was *body armor* that made the literal combat-difference in New England's earliest colonial wars, which were fought all but hand to hand. See the letters of May to September 1637, from the Connecticutt "front lines" of "The Pequot War," in Winthrop's *Papers*.

It can hardly have been otherwise, then, that Thomas Morton's new life at age 48 began with Native America's conditional consent concerning *Nittauke*---"my land," (Williams *Key* 167). The same passage of *Canaan* that blusters about whose "humors" or cultural ways are followed in New England admits that this company of outsiders is "as few as might be" (113); and the same book forewarns on multiple levels that only the man who can "comply with her humor" will be the one to "carry" her (140).

We have seen multiple reasons to imagine that Morton's first or most important Native encounter at this time was with a woman. Whatever began his life at future "Quincy," he no doubt took up his autumn "survey of the country" with his dogs, at increasing ease. Morton's utter comfort with his social class is clear when he says he "endeavored" his rambles and records "whiles our houses were building" (53)---a tidy omission of the grammatical and human "subjects" carrying him, indentured men sweating in the sawpits. He wandered inland up the tidal flats, walked oyster banks "a mile in length," followed freshwater streams into the Blue Hills, negotiated the tops of beaver-dams, pried, made notes on the astonishing density of animals, game and food-sources. This was an aspect of "paradise" created by the epidemics, which both appalled him with the sight of multiple Native villages turned into heaps of human bones, and reassured him as a colonizer that this "act of God" had made the land "the more fit" for Englishmen.

He recorded the names of only the highest-ranking Native males he met. Yet Morton saw, and so acted in, and so wrote about the "new" land in ways as unique as his particular past had made him. The paradigms and metaphors given him in youth for understanding the worlds of nature and peoples, his English sports, common law and Classical "pagan" readings were the building-blocks of his response to America. They functioned not as a "palisade of language" (Slotkin) round his sensibility, but as what we might call a more permeable "frame" for seeing. Morton's seeing, actions, and writings are not to be compared only with Puritans' of his time.

We learn about him also in contrast to his predecessor Sir Walter Ralegh. Ralegh wrote that at first he had never seen "a more beautiful country, nor more lively prospects...the deer crossing in every path, the birds towards the evening singing on every tree with a thousand several tunes"---and Greenblatt's *Ralegh* remarks that "It is unlikely that Ralegh was ever conscious of the tension between his primitivism [sic] and his plans for the exploitation" of America (112). Colonizer and critic share an ethnocentric European conception that wherever "earth herself, without compulsion, untouched by hoe or plowshare, of herself [gives] all things needful," what we suddenly have before us is "the landscape of wish-fulfillment, the unspoiled world of man's imagination" (112).

Next we know, this "place" is written of by Ralegh and Greenblatt between them as "primitivistic": America, in their assumptions, is not being enjoyed properly or portrayed "realistically" until it has been "sackt, turned, [and] wrought." In Ralegh's terms, this means robbed of "maydenhead," and in Greenblatt's, it means the only "realistic" human behavior that might have been expected eventually to "prevail" (one supposes). Together, colonizer and critic construct a pre-decided dualism between "unspoiled world" and "the ethic of empire and aggressive capitalism" (112). In this scheme of the world and the psyche, a "glimpse for a moment [of] the serene beauty of the land" embodies a kind of "virgin moment of the mind," that "invites" its own quasi-erotic "contradiction." But these are the dynamics of only one *kind* of "cultural mind"---whose phases of invasion, and layers of writing, together construct both "virgin" and "hostile" nature (111).

Ralegh's Folly is not to realize the source of "hostility" within himself, and in the nature of his "adventuring." His desires are those of a courtly proto-capitalist: his "wishes" include the conscious intent to commit acts of violation in other human worlds for his own benefit. Much because of the uncriticized ethnocentrism within his "education," Ralegh monologically "fashions himself" on this suddenly "hostile" Nature and "hostile Natives." Why are they hostile? Because both, notwithstanding the wishes of colonizer and critic, know of nothing "pre-decided" about their "new future" within capitalist "development." How can this false destiny seem "pre-decided" to a 20th-century criticism? Because colonial-American "education" continues (by increments known as careers) to imagine and present its history as History, its (professed) Faith the one synonym for Religion, its nature Human Nature. (See below on roots of this at Plimoth and Boston Bay.)[63]

Comparing Morton, we see *his* own conscious commodification of America; but, as *Canaan*'s Books 1 and 3 lay out the unmistakable "Native contexts" for the entire English approach, we find there no "unmotivated" hostilities, no people practicing "unconscious" violence. We do find repeated in word and example the call for "moderation, and discretion" on *both* sides in this new and inevitable transatlantic relationship. Morton forgot neither the "plague" nor the people(s) he met, but converted them (as he converts all his English and American economic, moral and other experience) into a multisided *human* evaluation of the Native/European frontier. Even his supposedly stock-pastoral

---

[63] Halpern's study of "primitive accumulation" in the English Renaissance describes the "Late medieval culture" that tried to comfort itself by "master[ing] the disturbing alterities" of Classical texts. These also presented schoolteachers with "the problem [sic] of poetic content," something they had been forbidden for centuries (Halpern 47). While Ralegh perceived his own guilt and futility as a "hostility" outside himself, scholars today continue to present as universal the colonizers' "nomenclatorial pressure" (Kathleen J. Myers on Oviedo in Williams/Lewis' *Early Images*), their urgent psychic need to impose names upon things.

passages are more complicated; for if "pastoral" implied that one had "exposed only the best side of a shepherd's life and...conceal[ed] its miseries" (as Pope summed it up), this was hardly the case in *Canaan*, where the reader/colonist was assumed to possess a Morton's confidence in the outdoors. The "miserable" were either learning or dying needlessly, and so were satirized because they refused to listen or be helped.

The Inns' mercilessness toward stupidity built upon Morton's sportsman's joys to make him a "pastoral realist." Born and bred under the worldly generation of "Prince Elizabeth," already sanguine with the idea that "Hell" was to be found "in Westminster under the Exchequer Office" (171), Thomas did not need to find either hostile wilderness or Utopia in the "paradise" before his eyes.

There was spring's white snow of the dogwood's fallen blossom, the north country mountain covered in white birch forest; and signs of Native people all about, massive shell-heaps by the seashores where clans without number had feasted "many days together." These "wilds" even had an English-landscaped look, from generations of burnings of the underbrush "at the spring and fall of the leaf." The rainbow sheen of the hummingbird and its bill "like a Spanish needle" fascinated him: he could not discover what it fed upon, nor the mysterious *Muskewashe*. "Boll Armoniack" or red ochre oozed from the ground. He tasted the local grapes, the beach plum and cherries "yet as wild as the Indians" as Wood said (41). Like Devon, the land was full of stories too, as he'd soon discover nearby at Squantum's Squa Rock. Native people would speak their dreams, of "Great Manitous" Kiehtan and Chepi at the southwest and northeast of their world; of giants Maushop and Granny Squant; of black wolf and other beings of the deepest forest; of crow, who brought corn to the land in her ear; of Morton's "admired" raven (66) who, properly rewarded, guided hunters toward the game.

He came back from these rambles to the "building" hilltop, saw the dogs fed, opened his day-book, and started to write things. The pages became his 300-plus years of infamy. Perhaps another life can come of those ashes.

> ...The more I looked, the more I liked it. And when I had more seriously considered of the beauty of the place, with all her fair endowments, I did not think that in all the known world it could be parallelled.... In mine eye, 'twas Nature's Masterpiece....(53-4)

6: *Failure and Fortune*

As English presence increased in the 1620s beyond the seasonal fishermen, traders, and recent kidnappers, badly-weakened Native peoples were forced from merely "not knowing what they were" (*Canaan* 103) to the effort of finding out "whether they would be friends or foes" at the first plantations building houses for families in their midst (Plimoth 1620, Weymouth 1622, Naumkeag/Salem 1623 and much more by 1629). What first brought peaceful contact and help to planters were the benefits to Natives of "quiet trading" (104), such as Native men with experience of Europe, Samoset and Tisquantum for example, assured the Sachems they would gain from the effort. In historian Nanepashemet's view, Natives' reaching-out (and the appropriate responses from Englishmen) *made* the difference: in all previous attempts, with New England Natives either indifferent or antagonized, would-be colonies collapsed (qtd. in *500 Nations* out-take in Dempsey, *Nani*).

The alternative approach was overwhelming force of arms. We have seen that this only became a near-unanimous English approach well after Hakluyt called for war-seasoned soldiers to "square and prepare" Natives for "preachers" ---after, that is, 1622's main war in Virginia (see Purchas qtd. in Hulme). But while early Plimoth and Salem underwrote their most basic sense of being secure, permanent plantations with martial discipline (Vaughan 96; and Ch. 7), Morton's present "Mount Wollaston" (1624) lacked the ideology and the manpower for that, and practiced the methods of Bristol-based adventurers seen above.

Nevertheless Mount Wollaston, like its predecessors, simply failed---until Morton reorganized it round Native hunters provided with guns. Thus he purchased a nucleus of partners who were likely to become dependent on powder and supplies, if not "bound in loyalty" (Quinn Renaissance Influences" 79); and who reciprocated with access to the local inland rivers' headwaters, prime country for beaver and fur-animals. The stranger in *Canaan*'s "Master Bubble" chapters (Book 3) was thus guided as far inland as Nipnet/Nipmuc country: certainly Morton's more capable youths (see below) took the journey, with Native men's similar permission and guidance. (For it is just the lack of attention to Native words and ways that causes all of Bubble's problems and results in most of the threat against Native "wifes and children"). By 1627, Morton's compliance brought the settlement to a new phase; and these Englishmen, using home's May-time folk practices as a stage in every sense, reached out for wider connections by inviting "all comers" in the region to socialize and, of course, invest themselves in further ventures. How did this remarkable evolution come about?

A 2-shilling garden-hoe or iron trade-ax bought in London could buy, in New England, 16 shillings' worth of beaver (a stout 1-lb. pelt): Bradford never knew the price less than 14 (Adams *Three Episodes* 196). The most basic expectations were, then, something like 800% profit, and still the relatively experienced company of Wollaston's and Rasdall's made little apparent effort at land-based trade. The only visible difference between the early trade attempted there and Morton's was that---publicly, at least---"truck" was at first only in beads and cloth, farm tools and axes ("bells and fells"). Morton, to keep the place going, had to offer something more; because that trade-environment had been considered "spoiled"---by French, Dutch and English trade in guns---since at least 1622. James I's proclamation of that year officially confirmed Plimoth's William Bradford (FBH2:44) that, a good 2-3 years before Morton's operations, the "promiscuous" trade in guns had already "overthrowne the trade and commerce that before was had, to the great profit of the planters" (proclamation in FBH2:313).

We have seen why Massachusetts people likely demanded guns from Morton's company. To Englishmen of methods different from his, guns not only required more venture-capital and cut deeply into profits: each one armed and took a good deal of fear out of its Native owner (Wood 79), and created a potential hindrance to the future increase of wealth to be extracted. These were the explicit reasons for James' proclamation; and yet, though investors and Parliament too condemned such trading, no statutory action resulted. Just when *Unity*'s company was beginning to break up, James died (March 1625)---and Morton, moving to the fore, held the common law view that James' indignation died with him.[64]

Company agent Humphrey Rasdall's move to begin converting the 30-odd indentured servants into cash by transporting them to Virginia and selling them off "at good rates, selling their time to other men" in the labor-intensive tobacco-fields there, proved problematic. His own character, short ship's rations and other treatment (carefully reviewed by Holly) must have lessened the young men's confidence in him. Virginia, they knew---just as Plimoth had been locally broadcasting to its discontented servants since 1622 (Winslow 565)---was now surrounded by "hostile" remains of the Powhatan "Confederacy," a war of

---

[64] "But insolently he [Morton] persisted [in gun-trade], and said the king was dead and his displeasure with him, and many the like things" (FBH2:55, purportedly quoting Morton between May 1627 and his 1628 "arrest"). Also in *Letter Book* 62. As to whether royal proclamation had statutory force see Note 20.

attrition going on since the sudden massacres and answering English slaughters of the first summer.

Thomas must have encouraged them with precedents from the kind of indenture-law that covered other ventures when men "broke up" on the land, and were "given liberty to shift for themselves" until they could re-coordinate with London or Bristol managers. (They did so at Salem in their first hard year 1629: Hutchinson 1:20, *Canaan* Bk. 3 Ch. 22). Besides, if these young men quit, what would become of Morton himself now, perhaps about to lose "his own or other men's" moneys; a man who had come a long way, and had left not very much of material substance behind him?

> ...[T]his Morton...having more craft than honesty...in the others' absence [in Virginia], watches an opportunity, and commons being but hard amongst them...got some strong drink and other junkats, and made them a feast; and after they were merry, he began to tell them, he would give them good counsel. You see, saith he,[65] that many of your fellows are carried to Virginia; and if you stay until this Rasdall return, you will also be carried away and sold for slaves with the rest. Therefore I would advise you to thrust out this Lieutenant Fitcher [a ship's officer]; and I, having a part in the plantation, will receive you as my partners and consociates; so you may be free from service, and we will converse, trade, plant, and live together as equals, and support and protect one another....(FBH 2:47-48, modernized)

There was no lack of rumor or published documents about the conditions awaiting Virginia's indentureds: Jennings (*Invasion* 79) cites sources printed in 1622 that *defended* those plantations by reporting that 1 in 3 of the 6000 people so far shipped there were still alive. In 1613, Spanish visitor Don Diego de Molina reported "slavery" and "miserable" rations there, and "not a year when half do not die" (Letter in Tyler ed., *Narratives of Early Virginia* 220). Biased as Don Diego

---

[65] "Saith he"---Possibly, Morton's actual speech was related to Bradford by Edward Gibbons, one of the original servants at Mount Wollaston who was later "converted" in a religious sense and became prominent in the Massachusetts colonies (his full story in Chs. 8-10).

might have been, Woolverton finds a virtual "penal colony" there by the same year (56-7).

Back in Devonshire, men "penniless, naked and starving" were roaming West Country towns for work (or hiding from service in Charles I's new war against Spain and other ventures: Oppenheim 60). Thus were Morton's Falstaffian counsels "easily received": Fitcher was thrust out and managed among various neighbors till a ship returned him to England. Morton seemed to have an answer for everything: with a detailed idea of his past we can now see him simply calling upon his various skills, easing the "hard" fare as a hunter could with meat, adding the liquid "junkats" that a few extra shillings could buy; making a "feast" of it in Old English and the Inns' "merry" style, not sparing his alma mater's "company of equals" sociality while dispensing advice in his "clients'" and his own interests. He was expected to improvise: Gorges encouraged the success of men "their own stewards" (*Narration* 58), and bound his ships' companies to "expect the miscarriage of their voyage to be laid unto their charge" (18).[66]

Keeping the venture alive also followed John Smith's advice that a person become "seasoned" to the country before judging its prospects (qtd. in

---

[66] Neither Banks' nor DeCosta's searches in English court records produced any trace of legal objections over Morton's maneuver in "refinancing" these young men's indenture-contracts. There *was* prosecution by merchant-investors of a suit in the Court of Common Pleas concerning Humphrey Rasdall, for *his* later mismanagement of indenture-related and similar business: the fact that those comparable records survived (see Holly 11) may give a bit more credibility to the "negative evidence" concerning the legality of Morton's initiative, since investors (when they knew whom to prosecute) had means to try to make up their losses. Any records of illegalities by Morton would have been bronzed 300 years ago by the traditions of "objective" scholarship illustrated in the "Sampler of Remarks."

Early in New England, runaway servants or "lazy boys" (Wood 90) were being fetched back from the forests; but Morton's company continued on their own through his first exile in 1628-9, and after (Mayo 17, Bradford FBH 2:50, 54). They were at last "dispersed" by Captain Endicott. There is no record (Hawthorne's short story notwithstanding) that any were arrested, flogged or returned as delinquents to "masters," though Winthrop records such practices against others still considered under obligation of contract (WJH1:158).

Kupperman "'Brasse'" 135): Smith's own interventions were legend, and early capitalist broadsides such as *Nova Britannia* (1609: Force 1:12) had warned against the "golden dreame" in favor of sheer persistence. At work here also was the voice of Cicero from the gentleman's books, exhorting the "scholar" out into the sunlight and dust of service, and granting plantation-life a modicum of genteel status (Baron 293). In that pitch to the boys was even a hint of Epicurus' "garden": in Europe such "ideal community" concepts were based in "voluntary, free work carried out at will" (Heller 119); and in Native New England the company had seen what resembled the successful practice of that already, as Roger Williams did in the shared labor of clearing and planting fields (*Key* 170).

Given these factors, this must have seemed *the opportunity to create* one's life in at least some ways. (Servants Gibbons and Bagnall did just that, in opposite directions: Chs. 8-10.) If Virginia meant 2 in 3 chances of being worked or clubbed to death, it is even possible that Morton wanted to help these young men, in the best traditions of Inns Masters' paternal concerns for their charges (Lowie 18).

Where Gosnold (1602) had quit Cape Cod when down to 12 fellows (Burrage 340), Morton kept going with seven. This was just when Salem's Devon-man Roger Conant was doing *his* all to keep that fledgling station alive too. However Morton turned these "stout knaves" (116) into successful up-country fur-traders, they did not take long before they wished to "have wifes," but found themselves "unwilling" to "labor to make a voyage to fetch any over" from what had been "home."

Along with the benefits of trade increased by kinship-relation, such an idea, or "harmless mirth" (if that was all it was), became the center of 1627's MayDay revels; and this the poet Morton summed up in his later phrase that "He that played Proteus (with the help of Priapus)" accomplished these things (140).

Recalling the masque of "Proteus" acted out before Elizabeth at Gray's Inn more than 30 years before (1594), he consciously fancied himself the youths' liberator from the "adamantine rock" (the "attractive escape that became a prison"), their indentures: early capitalist advertisings for American volunteers had made the New World a mirage of escape from myriad problems, and Morton now turned to his own American ends the young men's energetic desires for this world, for life and wife (many other examples of this "frontier" fraternization in Canny "Permissive").

In the process of learning from Native people how to prosper here, these men came to see the best hope of attaining their "expectations" by intermarriage, or something like it: an option marked "by continuity, rather than change" (Bradley 41), one widespread enough to result in Puritan laws against it, and already part of French experience just to the north. As fellow-lawyer Marc Lescarbot sketched this in 1610, such relations were a genuine mixture of mutual liking and cool manipulation: in a sense either side might have viewed the other this way:

> Anxious about their old [French] friends, [Natives] asked how they were all getting along, calling each individual by his name, and asking why such and such a one had not come back. This shows the great amiability of these people....And consequently by a certain gentleness and courtesy, which are as well known to them as to us, it is easy to make them pliant to all our wishes. ("Conversion" 69)

Trade and visiting-habits---*Canaan* mentions both being and having house-guests---grew sufficient to make a stockade-fence or palisade "needless" (119). Up-country trips with Native guides, a norm of these men's practice (127, 142, 144) built up the interracial confidence which only life shared "outside the pale" could promote.[67] Learning Native languages, the ways of American animals, how to paddle a canoe (and how not to)---these small cooperations, mixed with sexual attractions and other motives, were balanced by equal shares of ethnocentrism, the surrounded Morton boasting that English ways were the "rule" (113), and Native people actively demonstrating their "better content with their own" (50) while becoming increasingly enmeshed in European manufactured conveniences.

Upon these bases, Morton grew bold enough (if we can believe Bradford) to give Native people what they demanded in exchange for their wealth: the sense of power and security, of *options* in this daily new intercultural (colonial) process, which the English also derived from guns. Morton was not unaware of "some dangerous persons" about, but he knew the difference between them and the racial-*cum*-racist generalizations being broadcast by his English rivals (113: see Ch. 7). Armed Natives were no more "potential enemies" than other beings in the world, when a host of daily encompassing social practices convinced them that they were respected *partners* (Morton's word to the young men) in this relationship.

---

[67] Jennings (*Founders* 347-52) provides an overview of intermarriage as a substantial part of early and later Native-European trade (though least practiced among the English)---In his view, so-called *metis* communities directly descended from these practices suggest the very real and different possible outcome(s) of an "alternative" colonial method or policy. To Nicholas Canny ("Ideology"), English lack of experience outside the pales in Ireland helped colonists to "believe" racist stereotypes in favor of imperialism; and even so, many "went [Irish] native" by intermarriage (or less formal arrangements) until the application of military discipline there. This was also the case in early Spanish Florida, where colonizers married into Calusa and Arawak matrilinies and made more cultural "adaptations" thereby than Native people did (Deagan 305). On the "need" for such discipline in New England see Notes below; but Essex's organized starvation of Irish "rebels" occurred to Bradford in New England, too: see Ch. 7.

As for Morton's comment that the Plimoth "watch-house" was "needless" see the next chapter: though the comment is often dismissed, men without their families along do not value their own lives less than planters with them. Book 3's Chs. 10 and 12, on the Puritan "Master Bubble," generate their comedy precisely from the disparity between the man's interpretations of Native "signs," and the behavior of persons *within* these old "norms" of trade who cannot imagine why "Bubble" is so afraid.

To Morton, the difference was worth remarking. For by 1626, "by means of this help" he and his "consociates" saw their "prosperity, and hope" expanding all the way from "Sowams and Narragansett" (Bradford Letters 62-3) to Maine's Kennebec River, a key access to the choice north country where winter's thick pelts swung heavy in the trader's scales.

From 1626 to 1627 they were near their peak: this year Morton's shallop "gleaned away all" that year's best beaver from Maine, to the reputed value of 1000 English pounds. They had managed to "sail inside" thick competition for those furs, bypassing fishermen, the planters of Piscataqua (who were "threatening" to pursue a land-patent, FBH1:449); and their most substantial and serious neighbor, Plimoth Plantation. But the men of soon-to-be Ma-re Mount had come near the life-blood of Plimoth. Just as "all planters in the land" were beginning "to taste the sweetness of the country" (Bradford Letters 36), Plimoth reached the Kennebec as well in the person of Edward Winslow, who followed fishermen there and traded Plimoth's first surplus of corn with Abenakis to "good success." With a long struggle behind them in Europe and New England, the now-encouraged Plimothers could by no means allow a rival to interfere with their sole profitable enterprise (Willison 229). Morton's actions---gun-trade, his calculated Revels to come---"bred a kind of heart-burning" in his neighbors (155), and they were bound to act.

7: *Family Values*

We have seen the stories of Thomas Morton (as a "Bristol school" colonizer) and of Native American New England come together, historically, as one of dissimilar peoples trading and interacting in "cautious coexistence" (Calloway 20; Fitzhugh), within long-standing customary practices that had evolved from the needs and ways of both civilizations. It has rarely been recognized that, in the full contexts of 100 years of transatlantic contact, Plimoth and later Puritan plantations represented deliberate radical departures from customary ways of inhabiting the region. But this is what most explains the explosive conflicts between Morton's and Plimoth's histories, for both these English parties took trouble to portray the other as (to say the least) misguided in their methods of colonization.

How, then, did Morton and the leading Plimothers (William Bradford, Edward Winslow, Myles Standish) find themselves head-to-head by 1627? In that year Plimoth's men had become their plantation's financial "undertakers," responsible for its failure or success. How they had come to New England together illuminates their methods of planting and their motives against Morton's Ma-re Mount.

William Bradford, born 14 years after Morton in 1590, had grown up an orphan under the care of grandparents and uncles, yeomen in the eastern-England Yorkshire county farming villages of Austerfield and Scrooby. By his teens, young Bradford---under the care of Puritan congregations who where agitating for religious and social "reforms," including the printer and "elder"

William Brewster---saw his early poor health improve, and he formed deep lifelong bonds with his religious fellows. The bonds carried them all through a brutal period of public executions and harrassments by officials of church and state, that beset Puritan movement(s) anew as King James thundered his famous 1604 warning from Hampton Court's conference on "reform." As Puritans unsatisfied with slow change evolved into "Separatists" who would depart altogether from the "corrupt" Anglican Church, Bradford elected to flee with one early group, who migrated to Holland by 1606-1608.

Living in poverty amid the overwhelming cosmopolitan atmosphere of The Netherlands, Bradford worked in the silk trade, and at last settled in Leyden with his admired pastor John Robinson's people in 1609. Among them, Bradford met the future Plimoth "business agent" Isaac Allerton (of whom nothing previous is known); and Edward Winslow, a printer's apprentice six years his junior, a Worcestershire son of a salt-victualler and King's School graduate on Continental tour, who was taking up various Puritan points of view (Morison's ed. Bradford 86n2).

These people nearest William Bradford (plus his first wife, wed in 1613) shared for years the privations, persecutions and communal bonds of basically "Brownist" religious dissent from the Church (and hence the state) of England. Since the 1580s, "Separation" had implied, as ideologue Robert Browne had put it, that "true Christians" were compelled to deny a state church that failed to exclude those persons deemed irreligious; and secondly, that no civil magistrate had any church authority, that this rested solely with the Bible-interpretations of congregation-members (Harris *Saga* 10). In fine, these Separatists proposed to create their own social and political realities out of their interpretations: their church-authority was to become a civil one, as they (in Browne's words) "united by a public covenant." The issue of where, on what landscape they could make this happen, was the reason they had left their English villages for Holland and America.

Certainly for the core-authorities of these eventual colonists, the never-"official" but revered leader Brewster, and Bradford too, there was already a strong public reason never to recant their creed, in the fact that Browne himself had already done so, settling for a comfortable "C of E" post (1584) after a taste of exile and poverty like their own. For their dedication these Separatist families had suffered all but the worst that James' government officers could inflict on them, and they took their deepest solace from the teachings of their pastor John Robinson. But this itself brought them further torment of spirit, for once separated from Robinson by government spite, by their voyage and his death, they could never find themselves a satisfactory replacement (Willison Ch. 17).

By the time they inhabited New England, then, Plimoth's "core of believers" shared a deep sense of religious and cultural mission, one that had been denied full expression in almost every sense. Personal bonds, their regard for each other, their pride in their shared ideals had grown stronger as they endured together years of fear for their families, poverty, punishment and ridicule. The influential divine William Perkins (qtd. above Ch. 1, and influential on later John Winthrop too, Ch. 9) had helped to steel them against hearing anything more than ridicule in the majority's views of their ways: "*In England at this day, the man or woman that begins to profess* [their idea of] *Religion, and to serve God* [as they prescribed], *must resolve with himself to sustain mocks and injuries even as though he lived amonst the enemies of Religion*" (1618: qtd. in FBH1:14, italics Perkins').

The soon-to-be Plimothers had benefited from, but not approved, the toleration of The Netherlands that had sheltered them; and they separated themselves from that culture also, in fear that their children might assimilate to a less (by their standards) religious culture there. As they began to encounter similar "problems" in America, Morton and *his* worlds stood all around them in the same way, the two groups on New England soil like a more intense embodiment of the same voices contending over religion and culture since their childhoods. The cultural terms of Bradford's objections to Morton---his educated "Atheism," his pleasure with "Old English" folk practices, "pagan" and Anglican traditions, his practice of law---these echo the struggles in England just as Morton's mockery echoes the ridicule of these Puritans and Separatists by their original communities.

Besides such hardening cultural differences, another long-suffered aggravation at Plimoth made Morton's "gleaning away" the fur-trade more intolerable. This was Plimoth's "merchant adventurer" financial backing, in essence a "company store" relationship that generated mountains of debt in Plimoth's first 10 years, and was a direct function of their vulnerability---poor and poorly connected, isolated and all but desperate---in the early capitalist environment. This vulnerability had been demonstrated to Bradford's people in 1618, when a mixture of ineptitude, exploitation and betrayal caused the drowning of most of the "Blackwell group" of Puritan radicals on an exile-voyage of their own. Even as future-Plimothers had begun to meet a better range of backers such as Andrew Weston and Robert Cushman, in the attempt to arrange ship's passage to "Virginia" they were constantly pressured to sign contracts that stipulated intolerable terms for the labor in America. Work was to be regimented wholly for the sponsoring corporation's profit, not in the least for themselves or as partners. These terms and pressures to sign them are explicit in the records, and the Plimothers' refusals caused their bad (but not final) break with Weston, on the dock of their departure for New England.

By then, so many Separatists had decided against the already-contentious enterprise that the financiers in London secretly filled the waiting *Mayflower* with "Strangers," more traditional (Church of England and/or secular-minded) planters whom they hoped would better-ensure immediate profit. The cost, of guaranteed internal strain amongst the planters and therefore against success itself, was ignored for as long as possible.

Both "Saints" (as they styled themselves) and Strangers suffered nagging insecurity over the fact that a clear government charter for plantation-land was lacking. The intolerable labor-contracts were meant to somehow ensure the merchants a profit before the consequences of this problem too might strike; and dockside negotiation of these points was what delayed *Mayflower*'s departure till September, and virtually ensured a winter disaster. When that had occurred, when half their company was dead along "Burial Hill" above the frozen shores of Patuxet, the "adventurers'" first supply-ship (Nov. 1621) furnished Plimothers with additional hungry mouths, and a letter; which scolded them for having sent *Mayflower* back without profitable commodities.

If this truly characterized the kind of support Plimothers endured---an almost crushing burden of responsibility for every failed or pirated fishing-trip, every vessel lost at sea---so much less could they tolerate competition from "outsiders" in America. By 1627 Bradford, Winslow, Allerton, and Captain Myles Standish, the last to join them after his war-years in Holland---were taking internal steps against their prison of debt by becoming Plimoth's "undertakers," in exchange for their control of its trade. This "public covenant" in America would require external economic actions too.

Besides their long-baffled social mission and economic burdens, a third kind of hard experience affected Plimoth's responses to Morton and Ma-re Mount. The "Pilgrims'" first two encounters with Native Americans had epitomized the first century of contact: first, Cape Cod Nausets had nearly driven them back into the sea, in anger over many early kidnappings (as well as conflict with men like Champlain); and then, two Natives who had survived such abductions, Samoset and Tisquantum, brought crucial help with survival in the spring of 1621 (FBH1:199; note that *Canaan* 104 remarks Plimoth's wonder over English-speaking Natives). As Plimothers found their way in the new land, after sources in Europe had prepared them to find "brutish men...cruell, barbarous and most trecherous" (FBH1:56), they began to experience Native civility and humanity.

But, just as Morton's arrival had made him part of a pre-existing political order on the land, so had Plimoth's. Before their first year had passed, the Sachem Corbitant of the Nemasket Wampanoags was trying to destabilize the months-old formal alliance between Ousamequin/Massasoit's dominant Pokanokets, and the Plimoth English, by which both had gained some confidence about the other (FBH 1:225; Winslow 548). Corbitant was then known as the "most likely to succeed" to Ousamequin's "High Sachem" status (Winslow 548), and was feared among the Wampanoags as "too conversant" with their traditional Narragansett enemies (*Mourt* 73). Apparently Corbitant tried to fracture the powers Ousamequin appeared to have gained through English alliance, by threatening the life of their chief go-between Tisquantum, at Nemasket. By the time the Plimothers under Standish had finished zealously answering their treaty-obligations of mutual protection, the party with its firearms had "much terrified all the inhabitants there," wounded several women and children (*Mourt* 74), and filled the air with their threat to hunt down and "revenge" Corbitant---"to the overthrow of him and his."

In a "wilderness," a relatively small incident; but these events echoed through networks of a human landscape, and Corbitant, overpowered and publicly embarrassed, doubtless grew more "conversant" with the Narragansetts.[68] For just after this year's first small harvest at Plimoth, the infamous "bundle of arrows" arrived at their door, supposedly from the *formerly-friendly* Narragansetts (FBH1:242; Winslow 517). Putting together Plimoth's two accounts of this "message," we see that Bradford and company may have suddenly feared that they had allied themselves too soon in the unknown land, with the less powerful but more local people. For where Bradford now read Narragansett "ambition" to take over regional dominance after the epidemic-deaths of so many Wampanoags, Winslow added (on his first page) Plimoth's emergent, anxious awareness of the Narragansetts as "a great people...reported to be many thousands strong" (517).

For all Plimoth knew, a major power-shift was about to take place in the land, whose depths they had sensed but had scarcely probed. They knew that such a shift had happened only recently, with the death of Sachem Nanepashemet c. 1616. Perhaps they assumed that another could bring attack upon their families, or cripple hopes of trade to sustain their "mission."

Brinksmanship, the aspect of diplomacy that most exploits fear of violence, was part of Native peoples' interrelations (Morton's Sachem Chikatawbak displays it against Narragansetts, including threats to "cut off" Englishmen as well, in *Canaan* 38-9). But, even though Native warfare here *had* included full battles involving numbers of warriors and killings, the social bonds that were the *contexts* of these "traditional feuds" underwrote the basic long-

---

[68] That this "news" traveled far and wide is seen in the fact that by Sept. 1621 the Pilgrims had secured their first wide-reaching treaty (in FBH 1-227) including almost all local Sachems, who *initiated* efforts to each become "King James his man." Since Plimoth had already sealed agreements with this region's High Sachem (which meant that the "lesser" Sachems were bound by those terms too), this redundancy suggests Plimoth's further efforts to reassure themselves in familiar terms: paper, ink and "oaths before God and King."

standing assurance that families, women and children and enfeebled elders, would not be harmed.[69]

Plimoth's families had not been prepared in any way for this game of nerves, and they were without any of the Native groups' palpable reassurances about its actual rules. Without inside allies or experience, the details of Plimoth's response---sending the snakeskin bundle "back with bullets in it" (FBH1:241) and immediately beginning a stockade-fence around themselves---had to come less of the "Bristol school" of diplomacy and trade as remedy, and instead reciprocated "no small terror" among the Narragansetts. A direction in method had been taken. By Spring 1621, the Plimoth houses were more than half-enclosed, the palisade "very cheerfully" built (FBH1:242, 244).[70]

---

[69] This is not to say or suggest that Native Americans never committed such acts against other Native peoples; only that no evidence of anything of the kind has ever been found or recorded in/about New England.

[70] It seems unusual that the powerful Narragansetts should be so shocked and terrified by the militant answer to a threat or warning they had supposedly issued. Williams (236) and Bragdon ("Great Action") relate many details of the social forms and place(s) of such "threats and insults." Ford and other editors of Bradford share Winslow's apparent assumption that Narragansett numbers alone made them "warlike" (qtd. in FBH1-240n2). This was certainly related to the reading the Pilgrims did before leaving Holland: in which they "learned" that it was a Native American delight "to tormente men in the most bloodie manner that may be.... [The] very hearing of these things, could not but move the very bowels of men to grate within them, and make the weake to quake, and tremble" (FBH1-56). Wood wrote of the Narragansetts, however (1636: Vaughan ed. 81): "I never heard they were desirous to take in hand any martial enterprise or expose themselves to the uncertain events of war, wherefore the Pequots call them women-like men." Culturally Wood was closer to a Puritan than to a Morton.

It is very important also to bear in mind, as this tragic series of apparent misunderstandings unfolds, the high levels of mutual fear and mutual lack of knowledge shared by all these parties. The confusion is most apparent as one compares Bradford and Winslow with the shorter "Narrative of Phineas Pratt" (one of the Weymouth men: MHSC 4, IV, 476-77, and quoted in FBH 1-241). From him we learn that, early-on in Plimoth/Narragansett relations, the first messenger sent to the colonists (summer 1621) had come to sue for peace-and-alliance; that is, for a treaty like the rival Wampanoags were securing. But (Pratt's story claimed, through the words of the second Native informant at Plimoth, Tokamahamon), *that* original Narragansett messenger had himself either changed his Sachem Canonicus' mind after meeting with Plimoth, or this messenger held back Plimoth's diplomatic "presents" and angered his Sachem toward Plimoth---resulting in the bundle-of-arrows above. The point was, as Tokamahamon reported, that the Narragansetts had intended and still wanted peace, alliance and trade, as Plimoth did.

Confusingly, this hardening of relations was both *despite, and because of*, the Natives' ensuing response of angry silence and fear: this will shortly be clarified. But we can see the early confusions already in play that meant that a certain kind of relations, a certain direction, had been decided. The differences between Plimoth and Morton made neither English party "right." They were the results of different backgrounds and beliefs, different methods of the same business, the extraction of American wealth for European ends.

It is, however, accurate to say that, since Plimoth "family values" forbade close contact let alone intermarriage, their approaches could not produce results harmonious with long-standing ways. At Plimoth, cultural, economic and Native-political factors now began to drive them toward a second more consequential experience of the events with Corbitant.

Although their first summer (1621) had brought returning strength, and "no wante" (FBH1:230), the rumbles of Native anger and the planters' digging in *to stay* hardened and reinforced each other. The collective feeling needed to drive ("cheerfull") such a massive 10-month project as this full palisade around Plimoth must have seemed like the old emotionally-bonding unity of purpose, coming back after first-winter's darkness, deaths and dissensions. But 1621's harvest was also small; and as the cold of their second New England winter settled round them, unity met frustration again.

November brought *Fortune*, the first ship from home. It bore almost no supplies, but furnished Plimoth with the aforementioned letter from Weston for the backers, expressing their "worthy distaste" over the unprofitable *Mayflower*'s voyage. Upbraiding these survivors for their supposed laziness and hairsplitting, the letter (FBH1:233) made it utterly credible that the plantation's "life" depended now upon lading *Fortune* with commodities: if not, "*all the other adventurers should*" quit their support (Weston's italics). Further, the ship dropped some 35 new mouths to feed without a "bisket-cake" of their own, "lusty young men, and many of them wild enough" (231). These hands were set to getting "the towne impayled round."

The "cheer" of this November was not elaborated on, but Bradford's next and final entry for the year (1:244) concerned some of this "new-company" who declined his call "to worke, (as was used)" on that Christmas Day. Lightly mocking their hosts' Separatism, the men "said it went against their consciences to work on that day." Bradford abided, but returned to find them, significantly, at "sports," "gameing or revelling in the streets" very much in old Elizabethan tradition (245). Now Bradford returned the ironic use of "conscience": it troubled his "that they should play and the others worke," and the Governor bade them "keep [in] their houses." After that, "nothing...that way" was attempted within the Plimoth pale---"at least openly," Bradford mused.

The next prominent activity was a no-exceptions first general muster of arms or "training day" (1:244), led by Standish in Spring 1622. Of the Natives it is recorded only that Plimoth's "allies" the Pokanokets "seemed to frown on us, and neither came or sent to us as formerly" (275). By April, news arrived that French pirates had stolen every bit of the Plimoth effort to please their backers with *Fortune*. With that news came worse: in March, surprise attacks by Powhatan "Confederacy" peoples against Virginia plantations had killed 347 English in scarcely two days' coordinated strikes. Plimoth moved to fortify even more (into March 1623; Winslow 565). And yet, now there were "frowns" not only from backers and Native people. "Diverse" other Englishmen "amongst us," as Winslow put it---perhaps those "revellers"---

> seeing the work prove tedious, would have dissuaded [others] from proceeding; flattering themselves with peace and security, and accounting it rather a work of superfluity and vain glory than of simple necessity. But

> GOD...having determined to preserve us from these intended treacheries, undoubtedly ordained this as a special means to advantage us, and discourage our enemies; and therefore so stirred up the hearts of the Governors and other forward Instruments, as the work was just made serviceable against this needful and dangerous time....(565)

Virginia's news had been terrifying. Yet, to keep most men working here in New England, Winslow had to refer them to "the Enemy of Mankind": he told them that "Satan" was "blinding the judgement" and "causing reasonable men to reason against their own safety." But onward into that winter, with the arrival of yet more "wild young men" at Weymouth (August-September), another of Plimoth's "forward Instruments," Standish, was still encountering the same behaviors and "lack" of beliefs outside Plimoth's palisade. Weymouth's men as the latest newcomers had encountered what Morton's "school" called normal relations: they "feared not the Indians; but lived [with them], and suffered them to lodge with them; not having Sword, or gun, or needing the same" (Winslow 566). By Plimoth's accounts, they were the only ones surrounded by mutual and uneasy silence.

With these things laid out in simple chronological order, it grows easier to understand the emotional dynamics and long-baffling mixture of friendly and fearful contacts that brought Plimoth's early years to that turning-point known as the Weymouth affair.[71] With their second harvest small as the first, Bradford, Winslow and Standish all made half-desperate sea-voyages round the territory seeking out Native corn for their starving people. Amid this "dangerous time"--- at Monomoy (Chatham), at Cummaquid (Barnstable), at Nauset, Nemasket and

---

[71] As mentioned in the Preface to *Canaan*, American scholarship owes a huge debt to editors Ford, Adams, Charles Deane and others. At the same time, they appear to have discouraged simple chronological analysis in their *presentation* of the documents laid out in the Mass. Historical Society's 2-volume edition of Bradford's *History*.

Manomet---they received food and counsel, found themselves "much impressed" with the "personable, gentle, courteous and fair" Sachems and peoples they met (FBH1: 282-87; Winslow 536-43); and they did not miss the people's widespread fear of themselves. ("So many times, upon conceived occasions [of attack by these visitors], they would be all gone, bag and baggage"; 536).

Winslow was aware of the need "to settle their affections toward us" (548); and, rushing to make new treaty with Corbitant when misinformed that Ousamequin/Massasoit had died, Winslow was reminded bluntly that Native people "liked not" having Plimoth guns aimed at them, even in professed "salutations" (556). But, when the revived and grateful Ousamequin (or, Plimoth's friend Hobbamock, with reasons of *his* own) tried to pay the doctor's bill with "helpful" rumors---of a supposedly widespread "conspiracy," *amongst the very peoples feeding them*---everything "courteous and fair" lost credibility. Willison (224) noticed correctly in the narratives that, for some reason or lack of one, Winslow used no special haste getting back to warn Plimoth of the "plot."

There, other reports from Weymouth (via colonist Phineas Pratt, qtd. in FBH1:292) were pouring in, of *their* increasing disorder due to hunger (that is, ineptitude amid plenty). The Weymouth English themselves began a plot to take Native corn-supplies by force. Standish---already like the others "thin, distraught, and irritable" (Willison 214), as his contentious voyages for corn demonstrated---was despatched with armed men, to strike first at the supposed Native roots of all this trouble. At Weymouth he led the killing of three Native men they had found "insolent" and threatening before (FBH1:295; *Canaan* 111): at least three others were killed elsewhere; and three of Weymouth's English stragglers, so "base" as to have done menial labor for Native people (Winslow 288), were killed in retaliation by Chikatawbak's Massachusetts. The men had been building boats in barter for food.

According to Bradford, the results were that trade in furs and corn virtually halted for almost three years to come ("ther wher we had most skins the Indians are rune away...and sett no corne"; letter in FBH1:296). The Plimoth families, "all togeether unprovided for trade" (235), managed after that to "now and then" bring in a deer via "one or two of the fittest appointed to range the woods" (305). But, as none "amongst them...ever [had seen] a beaver skin till they...were informed by Squanto" (235), they simply could not compete with freewheeling fishermen and others; who did business not in the "toys" of company-truck (345) but in commodities Native people wanted, and (paternally enough) were "trusted with." Further, nearly all of the Sachems promisingly contacted during those food-voyages were now dead, either of "fear" or of diseases contracted while hiding "in swamps"; and "very many" other Native people died with them (FBH1:296). Tisquantum had died of a "fever" on Cape Cod more than a year before.

Bradford's only mention of Native people after this (beyond descriptions of failed trade-ventures) was in the scolding words of their Pastor Robinson against what were called Standish's tactics (1:368); and then nothing, until Winslow's 1625 journey up the Kennebec with Plimoth's first surplus-crop of corn (1:439). Even then---into July 1626---Bradford's Plimothers "raw and weak" appealed for support (Letters 46): they were borrowing from home again, through Allerton, to make up for wealth now apparently inaccessible outside the palisade.

By Spring 1627 they were eagerly reaching for better business through the Dutch, in order to pay "those great sums which they stood charged with" (2:17). But New Amsterdam's advice to Plimoth was to buy into the growing wampum-trade, and to peddle what they purchased northwards---away from Dutch interests to the south. This becomes our best measure of Plimoth's next period of trade, for it took them two years to trade away all the wampum purchased from Dutchman de Rasieres (2:43).[72]

As a result, though, Weymouth had been dissolved as any kind of rival. A year after the killings, Gorges' son Robert's company tried to revive the place, but as usual, with neither "local contacts" nor adequate outside supply, they failed. Somehow, Bradford's "undertakers" struggled their way into the increasing wampum-trade, and used it to "cutt off...trade quite from the fishermen, and in great part from other of the straggling planters" (2:43). We note that Bradford relates this in a pilgrim's-progress sort of way, as if readers have pre-approved Plimoth's struggle for sole entitlement; and it will appear that such self-entitlement, this ethnocentrism, was a direct function of Puritan programs for "control" of local trade. Trade was the life of their religious, cultural and social missions; and this was where Morton's developments began to "threaten." Ma-re Mount stood between Plimoth and the north.

Morton's removal would make up half their immediate plans. However, of great importance to later "American culture," since there was also a near-total lack of Native assistance, control of English individuals as laborers *within* the colony---those who gathered and processed American wealth---became crucial. Where Plimoth "discipline" could not "reform" its less zealous workers, Bradford

---

[72] "Actually, the Pilgrims were not good Indian traders" (M.W. Major, *Dissertation* 25). "Love thinkes no evill, nor is susspitious," Bradford wrote (FBH2:59); and Winslow agreed that "Where was true love, there was no fear; and that my heart was so upright towards [Natives such as Corbitant] that, for mine own part, I was fearless to come among them" (*Good News* 556). Perhaps this "love" was dependent, as it was for Winthrop's "Model of Christian Charity" in 1630, upon a "ground...of resemblance," *i.e.*, the "proper" forms of Christian belief. Relevant to these issues of internal cultural dissent, economic hardship and Native "hostility" is de Rasiere's letter describing his visit to 1627 Plimoth, featuring the Governor's heavily armed processions especially to and from "church" in the fort; where "each sets his arms down near him. Thus they are constantly on their guard night and day." Plimothers enforced, he wrote, "stringent laws and ordnances," "very strictly indeed, even among the tribes which live amongst them"; and they were people to "speak very angrily" when they heard, from Natives, of some Dutch people's "lack" of sexual mores like their own. It would be interesting to know how the topic had come up in conversation.

reported to the Adventurers, it sought "to quitte the plantation of them" (1:363); and this no doubt effective threat among colonists with few "wilderness" skills is exactly what Morton reports as Plimoth's "Charity"---*i.e.*, "you may see what it is to be Without" (181).

From this point, problems predictably multiplied. For to banish the "unreformed" was to send them out to become rivals (like John Oldham, below) in that place most "unbelievers" called the world; and outside the pale was precisely where control, of behavior and so of trading-wealth, was impossible. As late as 1629-30, between Morton's first and second banishments, Plimoth discovered that their own newly-affiliated trade agent for Maine, one Edward Ashley, was reaping profits via the trade of guns on the Penobscot River. Because of his successful methods, and his sending the furs directly home (where they could not be used to discharge any Plimoth debt), Ashley came to be better-supplied than Plimoth (FBH2:85, 97)---and, not surprisingly despite Plimoth's shock, "by forward Bristoll men" (81). Beaver was the frontier-equivalent of ready cash, for which a man (like Weston for example, *Canaan* 106) would "want for no supplies." As usual, when merchants received the golden results of "old school" trade, they poured in more investment with ease. Plimoth's fabled economic "hardships" begin to appear like another scenario that underwrites much popular and academic colonial fantasy, that of the beleaguered isolates starving on a merciless shore. Food and help were all around them. Ships were passing by with mail.

Like Morton, Bristol's merchants apparently had no problem with arming "Indians" as Ashley had done, in spite of the 1622 proclamation (Canup 103: when Ashley before the Council said that his "crime" was "a common use" he probably embarrassed its members quietly profiting from gun-trade: qtd. in FBH2:109). If the "Bristol school" took any view of the American/English future, perhaps it was assumed that Native Americans, no matter how well-armed, could simply be bought from their attachments to the land (the matrix of its "commodities"); bought "like anybody else" in the Bristol world of trade, which reached the Mediterranean through factors such as Wollaston and Rasdall (the unsavory details in Holly and Ford).

No document shows that Plimoth arranged the "trap" arresting Ashley, but they did assist his prosecution and gain his enormous cache of forfeited furs. The windfalls of "justice" suggested vast rewards for would-be "governors," as Gorges had promised colonists they could become (*Narration* 64). Whether the land was "Satan's kingdom" or not, departures of Stranger and Saint alike for green pastures were not far off.

In such an environment, then, with Morton and other "equals" around, Plimoth colony *as conceived* could not endure without new action. Every planter who failed "reform"---in Puritan cosmology, sure to be almost every human being---was sure to become an economic rival. Winslow would call "special means to advantage" what came to the undertakers, a strategy stumbled upon "to enlarge the dominions of our State...and the church of Christ also" (*Hypocrisie Unmasked*). It was discovered, in the midst of the Weymouth affair, that fear of "Indians" could bolster or at least prolong economically-crucial cohesion of the "common" planters, where "Christian fellowship" could not compete with other desires, chiefly for private property and potentially-vast material wealth. Something more had to hold the "cultural mission" and its colony-debt-paying "work force" together.

"Private" land, and a visibly massed share of wealth, were already almost universal desires or goals for European people: these came to comprise their "American Dream." But those had not been the "Pilgrim" congregation's original goals: they had proclaimed the early intention to share America, in Christian-communal fashion, amongst themselves. But because their normal, powerful inheritance of those long-inculcated European desires had remained mostly unanalyzed, they were only deferred; and they resurfaced for Plimothers as soon as necessity, and the "opportunity" of "empty" land, dictated. And that was in the midst of their crucial first efforts to grow a surplus of food-crops.

How, then, were "hostile" Native people involved?

Bradford recorded that at first (1621-3), Plimothers would scarcely labor at all "in common" as they put it, "without any recompence" (FBH1:301). When each "his own perticuler" was then assigned certain land (resorting to custom in avoiding a disaster), he saw parents pulling children daily to the fields (FBH1:299-300).[73]

This was what produced Plimoth's own first capital for trade "investment," handled by Winslow at Kennebec. So we see how carefully controlled expansion, via parsed-out "private" stakes in the land, created the "capital" (in this case, corn) that began to allow Plimoth to purchase its way into previously "inaccessible" wealth. This, in turn, promised Plimoth's most invaluable rewards: increased freedom from English church and state, from bishop and businessman, from compromise with the realities of other peoples. As will appear, the process

---

[73] Morton's "family values" were Old English ones, with a West Country code of "neighborliness" connecting families and, in the larger world represented by New England, enabling (for ex.) his many nods toward practical American mixed marriages---conceived *within* a familiar hierarchy (man over woman, gentleman over common, Englishman over Native etc.). Even so, *Canaan* is impressed and convinced that Native American egalitarian ways *do* "work" (48-50).

As "Puritans" separated from Anglicans, many promised to "reform" English ways in radical Christian fashion. Wm. Bradford recorded that at earliest Plimoth, "The experience that was had in this common course and condition, tried sundry years...may well evince the vanity of that conceit of Plato's ["Commonwealth"]....For the young men...did repine that they should spend their time and strength to work for other men's wives and children without any recompense. The strong, or man of parts, had no more...than he that was weak....The aged and graver men...thought it some indignity [to be 'ranked and equalized...with the meaner and younger sort']....And for men's wives to be commanded to do service for other men, as dressing their meat, washing their clothes, etc., they deemed it a kind of slavery....[It] did at least much diminish and take off the mutual respects that should be preserved amongst them" (Morison ed. 133-4). "Reform" did not prosper well among the reformers.

"best of all" promised more sheer power to coerce new levels of private profit from the markets of American trade.

But, for the undertakers to maintain their "cultural mission" in America, "the trick" would be to maintain organized management of these forts, farms, churches and the spreading-out human elements of "mission" support. Since the most palpable and pervasive authority they already knew, the English government, had taught them that "religion" might be the best means, "ideological unity" would be demonstrated henceforth by compliance with a central authority (like the Crown), deriving steady financial shares of each "private" planter's profits. This was to be justified under only the most conscionable contingencies of "common good": the success of this system made a "commonwealth" of Massachusetts (exs. *Canaan* Bk. 3 Chs. 21, 26, 27).

"Common good" meant, for these Europeans, eternal expansion into more "undeveloped" wealth, to make more "American Dreams." And because the land already had human occupants, the whole process had to produce an unavoidable obstacle---Native American "hostility." What Plimoth discovered was that this obstacle could also serve as a most palpable "justification" for the strict discipline and control of its people. Plimoth's deployment of its "law and order" was a "religious" version of the more secular "martial law under capitalism" already in practice in England's Virginia, as in the Spanish West Indies before them.[74]

---

[74] The "praying towns" resulting from this had the same function as Caribbean *encomiendas*/ plantations: profitable labor and cultural extinction for Native peoples.
   Thomas Weston and other English "Merchant Adventurers" pioneered the "capital venture" here, which from the beginning (according to historians Ford, Deane *et als*), required the advantage of "monopoly and special exemptions given to them by law and royal grants." These the Crown granted to mercantile recipients, along with crucial powers to exercise "large political functions" over those who could literally be called the working people, because these were seen as "favorable instruments for extending the trade of the kingdom" (FBH 1-96). "Political functions" such as a daily, martial-law-style "curfew" for the less-elite, were designed to ensure profitability for one party of "undertakers" or another. Weston had found the exiled "Pilgrims" in Leyden, saw "potential" in them, and offered financing to America if the Virginia Co. failed them (99).

Under construction in, and as, "New England," then, was a circular dynamo---a Christian (religious), Capitalist (economic), Patriarchy (social/power structure). Its "disciplined" force, the common planters with their "training day" skills, would continuously establish and then defend access to raw resources and to trade. This would pay for churches, meaning towns of persons deemed religious, whose members were both democratically their own army, and their own elected aristocrat-commanders, deciding where next to exert their collective forces and how to divide the spoils.

The more this process took over land, and outlawed or extinguished (as it always did) every alternative to itself, the more power it gained to coerce its desired *increase* of profit---from both the increasingly-disciplined laborers within, and from exchanges with remaining others on the "outside." (The flight of settlers from such "communities" drove both the settler-gone-Native/traitor to family values, and America's imperial race to the Pacific.) Since none of this brought benefit to Native American peoples, Plimoth's sluggish early trade-years reflected that Native peoples, *because they still could*, were taking their wealth elsewhere where the "truck" was better for them (citations with Note 81 below, and Ch. 10).

We begin to see the substance of the Plimoth-Morton conflict---and who most paid the price of it. No source spoke more clearly than *Canaan* the connections between this new Puritan species of colony and the "image" of Native peoples:

> As an article of the new creed of Canaan, [they would] have received of every newcomer there to inhabit, that the Salvages are a dangerous people, sutle, secret, and mischievous, and that it is dangerous to live separated, but rather together, and so be under their Lee, that none might trade for Beaver, but at their pleasure, as none do or shall do there. Nay they will not be reduced to any other song yet of the Salvages to the southward of Plimoth, be-

> cause they would have none come there, saying that he that will sit down there must come strong. But I have found the Massachusetts Indian more full of humanity than the Christians....(109)

The "dangerous" Native was being created literally by the misunderstandings, ethnocentrism, and ineptitude detailed above; and figuratively by a "new creed" that wove economics and Plimoth's Christian "public covenant" together, in order to control trade and the "newcomers," who would be set to work upon American resources. These connections---and the "truth" about Native people---"every man was not of sufficiency to judge, nor fitness to know," Winslow's circle decided (562) as the "dangers" had reportedly mounted during the Weymouth episode.

Indeed, the undertakers' "secrecy" in making these mortal "public decisions" had been adopted exactly because certain "base" *English* people were themselves telling Natives of the rumored plots to seize their corn-supplies. In synch with Puritans waging increasingly-intense "cultural reform" against Morton's Old England back at home, the undertakers were struggling here to break a long tradition of neighborliness. In New England the break was a racial one as well.[75]

Morton, like his predecessors, labored just as consciously at the colonizer's task for England's elite, with his gun-trade, revels and cohabitations. But there were differences. Just after his May 1627 revels (more on them to follow), William Bradford wrote an appeal to the Council for New England. Plimoth could not compete as things stood. It was time for "moral" Englishmen (such as were taking over the Parliament addressed above by Gorges), to take or make

---

[75] This is not about " where "racism" began in North America: see the Preface to Richard Drinnon's *Facing West: The Metaphysics of Indian-Hating and Empire-Building,* which studies racism more as a long *continuum* of varying intensities.

sides over how to best "manage" America's wealth. Operations like Morton's let too much of it be "wasted":

> We cannot likewise forbear to complain unto your Lordships, of the irregular living of many in this land, who...begin to leave fishing, and fall wholly to trading, to the great detriment of both the small beginning here [at Plimoth], and the state of England, by *the unprofitable consuming of the victuals of the land upon these salvages*: Whereas plantations might here better raise the same in the land, and so be enabled both to subsist and to return the profit thereof into England...which would be so beneficial to the commonwealth. (Letters 56; emphasis added)

It was time to clean up the territory. In exchange for quasi-official support (which cannot have been easy to ask for), Plimoth offered what they thought would most appeal: pure profit: *total expropriation,* to the point that, in Bradford's mind at least, Native peoples could be denied food for the increase of profit.

It was "only" what English colonizers had tried already in Ireland (Carlin). Morton too had seen "Irish" in Native ways, but where his "how-to" writings argued "moderation, and discretion" (9), and supported this with multiple correction of those who thought that no place could "matter" so much as England (54), Plimoth was strictly scripted to establish and enforce the worldview exemplified *for them* by the Biblical "Israelite" conquest of ancient Canaan. And they came to support this with economics based in that ideology; with Biblical paradigms forbidding most kinds of relations with culturally-different people, Native American and English. A thousand years of JudeoChristian ritual, social mores, and practices reaching often into (or for some, "inscribing") the smallest detail of personal life, had come to dictate that the future of *this* Newfoundland be written in that same "meta-language" amongst all European cultures, that of The Bible. And its fundamental, self-defining historical scenario---the conquest and erasure of Canaanite/Philistine civilizations---the Puritans explicitly followed, and carried out in and against Native America. By 1646 (as much earlier in Virginia colony), "blasphemy" against any of this was a capital crime (Ch. 9).[76] With exactly these things, New English *Canaan* in its very first words confronts the reader.

The secular capitalism of "Bristol school" colonizers presented Native Americans with plutocratic "charms" and "fair means," and bribed wealth away by trading guns to sufficiently-influential numbers of hunters and warriors. These relations lacked a core-ideology except that of convenient profit, and so "allowed for" the kinship-based ways that Native participants brought to the equation. But the Plimothers had, indeed, an ideology: it was their "identity" to themselves in Holland, and to historians long after; and both parties foreclosed upon compromise of that ideology where and when they could. At Plimoth, the various Native responses warned clearly how "dangerous" those peoples, "outside" in *their* world, would in time become. By tracing out the workings of this "foreknowledge," we see better why Plimoth's early accounts so typically

---

[76] The *Pentateuch* or first five "books" of The Bible are replete with instructions for such conquest and erasure of "others": see Pribek 345-8 and Jennings *Invasion* 83 for more on these linkages, and Macalister and Dothan on the realities of Old Canaan's "others."
    The well-known anecdote of a fight inside the early Massachusetts church at Watertown between a mouse and a snake (told in Winthrop's *Journal* WJH1:84) was interpreted as a symbol of "a poor contemptible people, which God had brought hither, [who] should overcome Satan here, and dispossess him of his kingdom." Readers must decide whether Puritans were "conscious" of the fact that "Satan" was going to be dispossessed in Native American "form." Alfred E. Cave's *The Pequot War* (13-19) details traditions painting "Indians" as "Satanists," cannibals and immolaters of children for the Puritans—"traditions" that stem directly from The Old Testament's Israelite invasions of Cannan/Palestine. In how many ways can the following (for ex. The Bible, Wisdom 12:3-11) be understood?
    "The ancient inhabitants of your holy land you [Yahweh] hated for their loathsome practices, their deeds of sorcery and unholy rites, hated as ruthless murderers of children, as eaters of entrails at feasts of human flesh, initiated while the bloody orgy goes on....You determined to destroy them at our fathers' hands, so that this land...might receive a colony of God's children worthy of it. Even so, since these were men, you treated them leniently...to destroy them bit by bit...although you knew very well they were inherently evil...and fixed in their cast of mind; for they were a race accursed from the beginning."

register both intense fear of Native people, and on the same pages, sensitive observations of them as gracious, helpful and "civilized" beings.

Both statements were "true," sincerely written. But the latter were driven by what "undertakers-only" knew their "mission" had to entail; and their increasing need for the finances to support their cultural mission compelled Winslow to "explain" about "Satan" to the laborers, and to shape his narrative for readers to the same conclusion. These fictions, these images that kept the undertakers one step ahead of most English others, were a means to help them maintain a sense of paternalistic "guidance" of the lives within the palisade---despite economic realities there and outside it. If Brewster's, Bradford's and Winslow's long-fought-for ideals were to prosper, they "had" to counter and overwhelm both observations of Native humanity (which their honesty compelled them to report), and most of the "unreformed" newcomers' hedonic responses to it. Humanity on the "other" Native side was the worst-possible (in their terms, "Satanic") obstacle to the plan for a Biblical "Promised Land," which had led them from Scrooby to Plimoth, and to Weymouth.

"Bristol ships" maximized profit by daring the gun-trade, and found protection from Native resentments over colonization in at least minimal forms of kinship: cohabitation in the camps of both sides, sexual relations based in either affection, trade or both; intermarriage, the shared "revels" of seasonal traditions. (Morton recognized the need to assuage the "exasperated" minds of Native hosts, 109.) And cheatings, killings went on as they did around the world. That is not the same thing as the programmatic imposition of inequality upon members of an "outside" group as such; not the same thing as denying others the right to go on existing if they are or choose to be "outside" or "different."

The virtue of "Bristol" ships, slight as it was in the end to Native people, was that they "allowed" Native peoples some kind of place in America's future, "bringing them to civility" as Morton and so many pre-1620 peers had put it. After the early epidemics, some Native people, perhaps with confidence renewed by the guns in their hands, did speak their views of day-by-day colonial "development." Morton would not "forbear" their calling Englishmen "cutthroats" (111-12), but with his first six chapters of Book 3 he made it repeatedly clear that they had a right to their opinion and response.

Thus Morton became "subversive." Bradford, Winslow, Wood and others who disapproved the trade of guns (even Morton's servant Edward Gibbons, Ch. 10 below) tooks such remarks---from Natives and from *Canaan* alike---for threats, insults, and "insolence."

What, then, does this conflict so much centered in the trade of guns reveal? That the trade of guns was "immoral" only where "the historian" has decided that Native people (past or present) should have no voice or options in America's colonization.

At Plimoth, where Christianity's "cultural mission" outlawed and punished Bristol-style relations, and made as little as possible of Native viewpoint, that mission assured Plimoth's experience of "hostile" Natives as surely as Morton's "pagan" readings and other influences created his American days. A mission crucially dependent upon victorious Plimoth economics wrote that "bottom line" in Bradford's letter. In private with the Council there was no need to mention "vulnerable women and children," the justifying, family values symbol in the body of anti-Morton and anti-Native American writings. Positioned ideologically as "pure and helpless victims," and physically--- according to the rules of family togetherness---on the colonial machine's front lines, women and children are virtually never heard from in Puritan texts; except when, by their (coincidental?) exposure to "danger," they help to emotionally resolve or justify radical actions in "dangerous times." (Hence the useful "precedent" set by Weymouth just when, in both leading Plimoth accounts, inner "discontent" was afoot.) Before century's end, this was deeply inscribed upon the America nascent in these colonial microcosms. The experiences of an "innocent victim" of King Philip's War and her "captivity narrative"---of one Mary Rowlandson, a woman with children positioned just the same way on the Puritan "frontier," at Lancaster along the beaver-rich inland rivers---was to become *the* cultural script for what was called "maintaining an English-American identity and community" (Armstrong/Tennenhouse). It also helped generations of invaders to monologically mythologize themselves, into victims with a righteous calling to violence of their own; into God-preserved "Yankee peddlers," and the family-consumers of their goods, wrought from an America (under the new myth) "virtually unoccupied."

In the immediate wake of Morton's high tide at the Revel, omni-frustrated Plimoth was suggesting that with luck and help, Native Americans could be "cut off" to establish the "order" of maximum profit. Profit and more controlled plantations would be indivisible aspects of each other (Ch. 9). And their "business" was to propagate "family values": the circular dynamo comprised (with exceptions) of Christian mores, Capitalist economics, and Patriarchal social structure, eternally capturing natural wealth "for the sake of" morality, survival, freedom, winning the west, healthy competition, etc.

In Morton's legal fights against Puritans, he never suggested that they be starved or driven from the land. He approved Plimoth's efforts to "enlarge the territories of His Majesty's empire" (54), and his satire was usually aimed at simple ineptitude mixed with arrogance (exs. Bk. 3 Chs. 10, 12, 15). He spoke his major points in tiny footnotes: "Impatience confuted by example" (gloss to 119). Morton's success outside the palisade simply---but publicly, among the available servant-class---gave the lie to enforced ethnocentrism, being used by Plimoth's inexperienced undertakers to turn the wheel of their colonizing.

That method had developed as *the only possible New England one compatible with Plimoth's public covenant.* In New England, "our State...and the church of Christ also" had come to be powered by the profitable "reform" of newcomers, at Native American expense.[77]

---

[77] We have seen Puritan ideas and attempts toward the "reform" of the English in England. That *New* English differences treated herein were the chief ones deemed significant *at that time* between Morton's and the Puritans' methods, is borne out in methods of the other earliest Puritan beachheads on the Massachusetts' "north shore." Vaughan's *Frontier* (94-5) analyzes instructions from London agent Matthew Cradock to Captain John Endicott and company as they took over Roger Conant's (and Plimoth's!) former fishing-platform at Naumkeag/Salem. Cradock's first letter (2/16/1629) called for just, humane treatment of Natives as well as caution in the wake of Virginia's wars; but within two months, after the Mass. Bay charter had delegated "ample power to govern and rule," the instructions changed to what Vaughan termed "more specific" ones. All males were to henceforth be "exercised in...armes," Natives were forbidden access to the plantation except at assigned times, and a "stiff directive" promised "severe" punishment for any gun-trade. In 1630 King Charles I renewed his father's Proclamation against the same, and Mass. Bay passed such a law that year too (Shurtleff *Records* 1-76), against sales and firearms-training for Natives. It was a law "with its source principally in Thomas Morton's behavior" (Felt 47). Winthrop (WJH 1:90) records the whipping and "branding in the face" of one Hopkins of Watertown for selling a "piece and pistol" to the *friendly* "James Sagamore" of Saugus (1632).

Major (*Dissertation* 28) reveals the further fact that by March 1631, "all persons who had Indian servants were ordered to discharge them by May 1, and it was ordered that none should thereafter take Indians into their households without permission of the Court" (Shurtleff 1-83). Uncontrolled affiliations with Native people, especially those between trade rivals and hunters, were a problem on Mass. Bay's mind, since, as Major adds, Winthrop explicitly declared that "such laws would be fittest for us, which should arise pro re nata upon occasions" (WJH 1:323).

These departures from long previous practice were everywhere in the Puritan era. Recall Sir Humphrey Gilbert's 1580s plans to use music and other "delights" for "solace of our people and allurement of the savages" (qtd. above; and he was a soldier): by 1630 the Rev. Francis Higginson's *New-England's Plantation* (rpt. in Force 3) related the new forms of "solace." "We have great Ordnance," he wrote; "But that which is our greatest comfort [is] we have plentie of Preaching, and diligent Catechizing, with strickt and carefull exercise, and good and commendable orders *to bring our people into a Christian conversation with whom we have to doe withall*....If God be with us, who can be against us?" (14; emphasis added).

Finally, analysis of these changes must include the 17th century's larger historical context of radical cultural analysis and change. As New England Puritan ideologies like the above were imposed and daily enforced upon the "common people" settling there and the Native peoples around them, other people in England developed political analyses that often had originated in *their* own total exclusion, by early capitalism and other forces, from any rights in land and its lifegiving produce. Christopher Hill and David Petegorsky have explored the deeply spiritual, politically radical and socially inclusive philosophy in the Leveller/Ranter and Digger movements, especially as crystallized in the virtually "unknown" works of Gerrard Winstanley, the eventual "leader" of the Digger movement. This remarkable "untrained" thinker rose from the masses of "alehouse intellectuals" in the troubled 1630s (as Morton composed *Canaan*, and picked up the phrase "the light of nature" often seen in such Leveller and Digger tracts, as well as in humanist discourses, below). Winstanley's analysis of one of the main obstacles to a this-world "Glory" is directly relevant to the ideology imposed upon the Massachusetts territory:

"The conception of a personal God or devil, of an actual heaven and hell were the psychological result of the inability to understand the nature of the physical world, the refuge of those who felt impelled to substitute fancy and imagination for the knowledge they were unable to achieve: [in Winstanley's words], 'it is a doctrine of a sickly and weak spirit who hath lost his understanding...of the Creation[,] and of the temper of his own Heart and Nature[,] and so runs into fancies'" (qtd. in Petegorsky 179). See also the "Ranter Christmas Carol" c.1650 qtd. in Hill *World* Ch. 9: "They prate of God; believe it, fellow-creatures,/There's no such bugbear; all was made by Nature...."

Many humanists, often another "anti-Puritan" cultural force, held with Pomponazzi that "healthy" people should ideally require no "fictions" to make them behave properly toward each other (1516: text in Cassirer 365; see also Appendices). In Northern Europe, Erasmus (not to mention "alehouse intellectuals" in their own ways, *vide* Clark, and Wrightson) spoke of related ideas as "a wonderful elevation of mind...this in a man that only Acted by the light of Nature! ....*Sancte Socrates Ora Pro Nobis*" (qtd. in Davies 28-29). And this was the publication-time (1632) of Spinoza's landmark *Ethics*, which announced that there was "nothing" to be found "outside of Nature" (see Harris *Rise of Anthropological Theory* 19). Perhaps Protestant "literalism" was driven in part by the intent---what Susan Griffin's *Pornography and Silence* would call the *need*---to impose upon oneself and other people a model for "reform" which protected one from such tides of insight. (Morton: "he must out, lest he pollute the Land, and them that are clean," 192). Ch. 9 below presents primary evidence from both Morton's servant Edward Gibbons and John Winthrop for just such choices and the later "forgettings" (Griffin's term: denials) that such choices had been made. Others who refused or remained "indifferent" to "reform" made up the "mockers" warned about by Puritan divine William Perkins to his "true believers," qtd. above.

8: *Revel, Arrest & Return*

> *What is't you lacke, what would you buy,*
> *What is it that you need;*
> *Come to me, gallants, taste and buy,*
> *Here's that will doe the deed....*
> --Gesta Grayorum (1594: 60)

By May 1627, Thomas Morton had reorganized the failed "Mount Wollaston," extended its trade from Narragansett to Kennebec, and was preparing to make more of his transatlantic circumstances. The tensions troubling England since his boyhood, however, had worsened, and were now to be played out on New England soil.

This decade of his first American tenure[78] was marked by Kings James' and Charles' proclamations against "illicit" traders (1622/30); and the second publication specified confiscation of the property and goods of any English subject "whatsoever" found trading without a permit from the Council of New England. The move to begin excluding fishermen without these licenses and the "irregular" traders who had "opened" the New World was sure to increase already-intense competition. Since bona fide "authorities" were scarce along the American coasts to enforce such new non-statutory rules, a plantation with "permanent" intentions and "family values" would likely find itself de facto enforcer, with or without clear patent of its own. As with Ashley's stock of furs, the gains bestowed by confiscated commodities were the reward, and fishermen with slight resources or connections had small recourse. Adams and Ford detail the resentments of "old comers" associated with Morton, increased by the arrival of Winthrop's Mass. Bay Colony.

---

[78] Excluding his final, possibly four years in America (1643 to perhaps 1647), Morton's "experiment" of New England had been: June 1624-September 1628 (4 years 4 months); and April 1629-November 1630 (1 year 9 months)--- a total of 6 years 1 month (more or less).

In both Old and New England, new kinds of economics were moving people "away from a grounded site of exchange in a traditional and geographically locatable marketplace," toward a "growingly abstract" system whose "culturally incomprehensible" operations would be increasingly controlled and policed by anti-traditional, would-be social and moral elites (Miller 76). So the 80-foot Maypole erected by Morton's company in May 1627, "barked" to its bright yellow pine-timber and crowned with a rack of antlers to make it "a fair sea mark for directions" (135), was the deft effort of men "as few as might be" (113) to compete amid all these changes, by attracting New England's oldest traders with a symbol of the older, carnivalesque Elizabethan way: what Shannon Miller has analyzed as "old" England's hardly-utopian but "recognizable, community-based, and physical marketplace."

Here as in England, where money itself (that is, access to food and goods) was becoming a thing "more abstract," the anxious "desire to contain it" was made worse by the apparent collapse of felt or "believed in" connections of interdependence amongst England's social classes. The Thirty Years' War, too (1618-48), which shocked Europeans with the unprecedented deaths of 8 million "civilians," helped to create new Renaissance conceptions of relationship itself (political, economic, personal), in which any one party's gain (in power, wealth, etc.) was assumed to be every other party's loss (Greenblatt *Renaissance* 141). The assumptions that guided human social relations changed accordingly, as different classes of people sought to consolidate whatever they possessed against the "permanent carnival" of war and the new marketplace: to "sharpen boundaries, to render meanings more precisely" (Agnew 10).

Plimoth met these times in one way: Morton's hoary Maypole and the rising plantation's new name (Ma-re Mount: *Canaan* 135), as signifiers of "almost unlimited" meanings (McWilliams 7), were calculated to attract *numbers* rather than "reformed" trading partners. The name was not least a ribald promise that trade would somewhere go "amorally" on, without formal superimposition of law or ideology.[79]

Seasonal, boisterous revels based in the cycles of organic and agricultural time are older than Western "civilization." In times deemed oppressive, people often turned that boisterous tradition to the uses of protest. In early 1500s France, *societes joyeuses* would form to elect a *Prince des Sots* and stage actions "to avenge by satirical verse and drama and pageantry any offense against the social or fashionable code of the time" (Welsford 22). But "protest" was a secondary and external aspect of Ma-re Mount's days. As Morton's Englishmen used forms of country-dance (the Maypole) and court masque (Lord of Misrule, etc.) as literal staging for their New England business, they followed tradition and the trend of their countrymen too in adding "plot" or larger purpose to the entertainments.[80] Their "merry song" they constructed to invite Native women ("Lasses in beaver coats") to cohabit with them and thereby bring themselves closer trading-status (more detail in "The Riddle of May Day" following).[81]

---

[79] Book 3's Chapter 7 is a witty mock-epic run around "ideology" itself. Morton "bestows" some of his early days upon Plimoth; and when he and his servants are tasked for their "lack" of religious fervor on "that path so hard to keep," some are invited to be rid of him to join the congregation. Morton averts the "plots" "by discretion," and meets the attempt to maroon him with clever appeals to immediate needs (food/shelter) and simple pleasures. Repeatedly *Canaan* shows his awareness of the practical value of Devonshire neighborliness. (Another ex. on 196---he "cherished the poor sailors" with meat to gain intelligence.)

[80] As Italian social masquery evolved into French ballet, and ballet into English masque, "the dramatic instinct, which was so strong in England, made the masque writers incorporate the revels in a performance which had some kind of artistic unity, instead of allowing the masque to trail off into ordinary ballroom dancing" (Welsford 167).

[81] The social practices of West Country Englishmen and those of mostly Eastern-county Puritans seem important to their fortunes as traders. Marcus (*Politics of Mirth*: 290) offers a bibliography and survey of Morton's-day publications (from broadsides to poetry) arguing for and against "sports" and traditional English folk customs, which became such a cultural battleground between Royalists and Puritans, as well as between "masters" and "commons" in the coming Civil War. Petegorsky and Hill offer even more numerous primary sources.

As cited, Bradford does report Plimoth's aim to "cutt off" others' trade where possible: they made new resolve against Morton when he "gleaned away" all the Kennebec trade, but the

Revels and markets were multi-day affairs, talked up and attended for the benefits they brought, from trade and social connections to sheer pleasure and "free" food (paid for by whatever each brought themselves, from shellfish, venison, honey and chestnuts to Merrimac sturgeon, English biscuit and Native corn *nokake*; all washed down with either "the goodness of the waters" (89) or sailors' various wines (*rosa solis*) and brandies (*aqua vitae*). Native people doubtless did more than "help" erect the Maypole (134): Morton needed them, many of them wanted guns and goods at fair price, and so his meetings with different peoples from north to south leave their traces in *Canaan*, from the Kennebec (155) and French-affiliated peoples (40) to Passaconaway's Merrimacs, Chikatawbak's Massachusetts, the Nipmuc west of Mass. Bay (127), the peoples of Sowams and Narragansett (28; alleged receivers of Morton's guns in Bradford Letters 64), and even the "Pequenteenes" (as Morton originally spelled "Pequot," 45). He and others observed their seasonal and other times for meeting "in amity": if any of them saw Ma-re Mount as such a serious player as Plimoth did, it was in their interest to be there.

Likely present too were those "indifferent minded" planters (113) William Blackstone, Samuel Maverick, David Thompson, William Jeffreys and others, who had come to America much as Morton had and made the best of it. Fishermen perhaps with wives (or rather, women with multiple sailor-husbands, as was "notorious")---merchant sailors, lone trappers made up "the illiterate multitude" (164). A young English servant-woman accused by Plimoth of bearing

---

other parties around knew that it did not by *legal* right belong to Plimoth. Plimoth was still moving for a patent, motivated by the other Kennebec competitors from Piscataqua (FBH1: 439). Most revealingly, even as Plimoth began to make headway in the north, they complained that "others" "envied" them and "wente and fild the Indeans with corne, and beat downe the prise, *giveing them twise as much as* [Plimoth] *had done*, and under traded them in other commodities also" (Bradford FBH1:449; emph. added). Native people and other "outsiders" did not "understand" that they had been ordained to carry the load in the new program of someone else's increasing profit.

her master's child had run away with the man (FBH2:12-16), and, deserted by him, she found her way to Ma-re Mount, perhaps taking in some cheer for her own melancholy (Bk. 3 Chs. 9, 13: how long she stayed is not known).

There were also, as Morton recognized, "some dangerous persons" of all races present (113), but his confidence was high, and he used a panoply of means---gun-trade, home-brewed beer later turned by the "Song" into "Nectar,"[82] his expertise and status to keep, like Plimoth in his way, one step ahead of the uncontrollable economy all around him, with its swindlers and part-time pirate fishermen. Noticing that Native Sachems took "a great pride" in wearing a small "Tassell gent" (male hawk) "dried and stretched out" as an ornament "in the knot of his lock" (68), perhaps he paraded himself with a "Lannaret" on his arm which he had "reclaimed, trained, and made flying in a fortnight." Morton loved the great hunting-birds (66-8), and admired the title Sachem so that he used it (given or not) to bring himself help, as "a Sachem of Passonagessit" (148).[83]

The Maypole---surrounded by New England's brilliant spring weather, by the red and white bloom of gooseberry and dogwood tree---was the symbol of the "polytropic" Morton's power to attract and seduce. Plimoth "saw they [might be able to] keep no servants, for Morton would entertain any, how vile so ever, and all the scume of the country, or any discontents." These people, Bradford wrote, "would flock to him" in his "nest" from "all places" (FBH2:54; Letters 62-3).

---

[82] A collection of Harvard University-confirmed "Morton artifacts" intrepidly unearthed by G. Stinson Lord (1930) from the Ma-re Mount site in Quincy before it was quarried by "developers" ---including trade-axes and whetstones made from the deposits of it Morton reported on Maine's Richmond Island---also contained broken glass, possibly left from the "case of bottles" that was "spent" during the festivities. Source: Unpublished inventory of Lord's, including photograph of the collection [see illustrations], via Mr. William Bowman, geologist of Weymouth MA. New initiatives to display the items are under development at Quincy Historical Society.

[83] Naturalist and raptor specialist Mike McWade of the Blue Hills' Trailside Museum (Chikatawbak Hill station) feels that Native Americans must have been fairly impressed with the European art(s) of falconry, as there is no evidence of their own hunting with those species.

Indeed, Morton had early-recognized the essential struggle for manpower he had engaged, and the flavor of his countermoves leading up to these Revels can be inferred. For Morton the nominally-pious Anglican is "saying something" when he describes Christianity in a so-called "wilderness" as "that path so hard to keep" (116).

If Christian values are posed as "the path," then life (goes the proverb) is a forest---but not necessarily a "dark wood." Forest is neither evil nor frightening (let alone hostile or empty) if one is, or keeps close to, an experienced outdoorsman. Morton's remaining servants, "redeemed" or "converted" once already from the "Hell" in Virginia (Bk. 3 Ch. 7 is full of evangelical parody), listened to him about Plimoth's own forms of it before them. A few other young men, flattered or frightened by Plimoth's talk of their "poor souls," he outsmarted in their plot to maroon him on a rock off of Cape Anne. In these contexts, that was to threaten a man's life (and the first try for Morton's). But if we know the man at all now, his responses---sharp business moves and cultural play---should not surprise us as the animating spirits of May 1627. He was "part of all he had met": gentleman's justice and mockery mixed with the "pastoral realist" rewards of his Devon joys.[84]

---

[84] The only two of Morton's proteges known by name, Walter Bagnall and Edward Gibbons, were both fairly successful in their different American lives after Ma-re Mount: Bagnall, or "Great Wat," made a fur-trade fortune before he was killed in this hard "unscrupulous" life, while Gibbons "went Native" in the Puritan direction and made himself a soldier, merchant and eventual magistrate of Boston.

Below are full details/citations on each of these men; and the longer-lived Gibbons' parts in Morton's second arrest (1630), in the "Pequot War," and in Morton's final fate are documented in Chs. 9 and 10.

Nothing is known of Walter Bagnall before Morton refers to him as "A servant of mine" (73). He and Morton probably explored Maine's Richmond Island together for commodities: Book 2 Ch. 6 describes the large deposit of whetstone on the island's northern end, "very excellent good for edg'd tools" (80); and the artifacts referred to above, recovered by Lord "near the site of the present Church of Our Lady of Good Counsel, Merrymount" in Quincy, included some of it (McIntyre "Quincy"). Whetstone was valuable in 17th-c. Europe (AC 217n4), and it (besides access to the rich and lively beaver trade thereabouts) may have drawn Bagnall to settle there. According to Winthrop (WJH 1-69: 1631), Bagnall had been dwelling "alone in the said isle" "these three years" with a man named "John P---," meaning he went to live there in 1628 after Morton's first arrest by Plimothers. As to whether he was "alone" see *Canaan* Note 255.

Though Morton refused to plant "so Northerly" (80), the location was extraordinary: Champlain and De Monts had called it the Isle of Bacchus for its wild grapes and rich soil, it was connected to shore by a narrow bar at low tide which also protected its deepwater anchorage for trade-ships, and it lay near the fishing-grounds of Cape Elizabeth and the rivers of Saco Bay's plentiful herring, bass and eels (Duncan 112-13). There, Bagnall accumulated a fortune in "ready gold" of perhaps 1000 English pounds and another 400 "most in goods" (Winthrop 69). Adams (AC 218) reports that on May 11, 1855, "an old stone pot was turned up by the ploughshare, containing 52 coins," none stamped later than 1625 (Duncan 113; and MHSP May 1857, 183-88). Though it arrived after his death, Bagnall even obtained a patent for the island (on Morton's counsel to Gorges?) on Dec. 2, 1631 (AC 219; and *Records of the Council for New England* 51-2). Winthrop was aware that "This Bagnall" had been "sometimes servant to one in the bay," and considered him a "wicked fellow [who] had much wronged the Indians": perhaps Bagnall's wealth came from part of the trading there in which spoiled, disease-promoting foodstuffs (peas, bread, beans etc.) as described in FBH1:448, were used (as by the French there too) to maximize fur-trade profits. Jennings (*Invasion* 208) details how another trader deemed important to Native New England, John Oldham, was eventually killed because he was thought to have spread disease along his multi-village route to the Connecticutt River in 1633. Perhaps Bagnall was killed for similar reasons.

Adams (AC 218) cited a "theory...advanced in the Maine press, that Bagnall was an Episcopalian, and competitor in trade of the Mass. Bay Company; and that Winthrop and his associates, not being able otherwise to get rid of him, compassed his death by indirect means" (letter of S.P. Mayberry in *Portland Press*, Jan. 9, 1883). Whatever the facts, on Oct. 3, 1631, Bagnall and "John P" were killed by Maine Sagamore "Squidrayset" or "Squidraket" and "his company," who "burnt the house over them, and carried away their guns and what else they liked" (Winthrop 69); and the news reached Morton "when he died" (78). The English were unable to organize official retaliations, but they did hang anyhow a Native called "Black William" found living there not long after the attack. "William" had been a Massachusett said to have "sold Nahant [Mass.] for a suit of clothes" (A3EP 260).

Nothing explicit is known of Edward Gibbons before Morton's 1628 arrest and the full dispersal (by Endicott) of Ma-re Mount's company in 1629. Palfrey (2:225n1) says he was perhaps a brother of one Ambrose Gibbons, an early planter at Piscataqua: he may have been an original "Mount Wollaston" servant arriving with the 1624 *Unity*.

From Ma-re Mount, Gibbons went to Salem for "some little time" and "became converted from whatever Mortonism [!] he may have had" (Hale ed., *Lechford* 238n2). There, at a "gathering" for the 1629 ordination of Rev. Francis Higginson, Gibbons "fell down and Worshipped God, to their astonishment" (MHSC XXXIV, 289: full document Ch. 9). The first recorded result of this was Gibbons' employment as one of Morton's guards or jailers during his summer-1628 arrest by Capt. Standish: Ford ("Paid" 641) writes that "Endicott" performed that arrest and so was Gibbons' superior then, but Endicott was not on American shores till his and Morton's ship-of-first-exile had passed each other that autumn 1628.

By 1631 Gibbons joined the Boston congregation, whose first court of Election there made him a freeman (*Mass. Rec.* I-366). But as Palfrey notes in his careful list of records used here, that same August Gibbon was fined 20 shillings "for abusing himself disorderly with drinking" (*Mass. Rec.* 90). By 1632 Gibbon was a neighbor of Maverick and Blackstone (Johnson *Wonder* 64), and representing "Charlestown" in matters of raising a public stock (95). For 10 years (as of 1634) Gibbons served almost continuously as a court deputy (Hale 238), advancing to "ensign" under Capt. John Underhill that first year (*Mass. Rec.* 129) and taking part in actions against the French Aulnay at Penobscot (FBH2:208) by 1644.

But the career was bumptious. In March 1636 he was "discharged from service at the Castle [*Mass. Rec.* 165], perhaps for having incurred suspicion of being a partisan of Mrs. [Anne]

198   *Thomas Morton*

Samuel de Champlain and his frontier-lawyer-poet Marc Lescarbot had staged a "Theatre of Neptune" (1606) to welcome their backers and declare "that we lived joyously" (see "Masque" next section): they had also invented winter entertainments called *L'Ordre des Bon Temps* in which they and Native hunters competed to keep the table between them stocked with game. So did Ma-re Mount take measures to present magnanimous prosperity: besides brewing "beer" from the "hoppes" later found there (inventory below), they organized a drums-and-guns procession, drafted a manifesto of sorts with the "Poem" and a drinking-song including a "Chorus," and likely added English-traditional "masks or animal disguises" (James 273) to what was clearly planned performance.

They lived a life of few home-style distractions and here was a chance to refresh themselves and make headway with Native partners; whose own festive, ritual and competitive social ways included the display-uses of body-paints and

---

Hutchinson [*Mass. Rec.* 225]" as Palfrey states. Gibbons now became "lieutenant" to Underhill (himself in no great favor on similar grounds, *Mass. Rec.* 191) and took up work building and improving Fort Saybrook on the Connecticutt River, under the authority of John Winthrop Jr. and the engineer Lion Gardiner (Gibbons' letter from thence in full Ch. 10). There, he described himself as being in financial debt to Mass. Bay leaders and the Native peoples "very insolent" (Winthrop *Papers*, WPF3:323). Johnson (*Wonder* 161) writes that he was involved in negotiations to keep Narragansett warriors from siding with the Pequots against the English in the 1637 "War"; but it is possible Gibbons was absent from Underhill's and Mason's May attack on the village at Mystic. That year--despite suspicious trading, see below---he was again promoted, into the Ancient and Honorable Artillery Company of Boston, serving as its captain by 1641 and twice after (Morison *Builders* 147-8; Hale 239). As Boston's "spiritual warfare" (Johnson 227-9) and other conflicts increased, Gibbons helped to lead actions against French incursions at Penobscot and in fortifying Boston Harbor islands. 1649 saw him major-general of all Massachusetts forces: in 1650 he was a magistrate (*Mass. Rec* 3-182).

Johnson held Gibbons "a resolute spirit, bold as a Lion...very generous, and forward to promote all military matters" (229). There were also reports (WJH1:222; Palfrey 2:226) that his business-ventures were often held suspicious "for a Massachusetts official." By some secret involvement with New England's French rival LaTour, Gibbon was "quite undone"; but he soon managed to finance tobacco-voyages to Virginia. Sometime in the same period (c.1637) that he was in the Saybrook Fort, Gibbons was apparently aboard a "bark" trading in the West Indies when a French man-of-war captain raiding there (a "Mr. Petfree") found, amid their conflict, that he had known Gibbons earlier at Piscataqua. Gibbons "brought home an aligarto, which he gave the governor" (his further sea-adventures in Cotton Mather's *Magnalia Christi Americana* VI, I, 3). Gibbons died Dec. 9, 1654, leaving a son "Jotham" and a "considerable fortune," including lands deeded by the "Squa Sachem of Misticke" near Boston (Hale 228) for "many kindnesses and benefitts...received."

tattoos, crafted totem images in wood and stone, gorgets, feathers, skins (each with articulated systems of meanings and ranks), musical instruments and, not least, the woven belts and ornaments of wampum "black and white." Their feasting-customs, just now centered in the multi-course *Appanaug* or seafood "clambake" must have prevailed (richly treated in Peters, illustrated in Wilbur *Handcrafts*), since neither deer, fowl nor corn were truly in season. But English sports and hunting-games that kept the food coming were compatible: Wood describes the huge games of something like "football" played by Native peoples "on the sands," with "a mile" and sometimes "two days" between goals (Ch. 14). "Training day" exercises passed guns more or less openly between English and Natives (Bradford says Morton "taught" as well as supplied):

> [He] taught them how to use [firearms], to charge and discharge, and what proportion of powder to give the piece... and what shot to use for fowl and what for deer. And having thus instructed them, he employed some of them to hunt and fowl for him....They have also their molds to make shot of all sorts.... Yea some have seen them have their screw-plates to make screwpins themselves [to repair trigger-mechanisms] when they want them, with sundry other implements.... (Bradford *History*, Morison ed. 228-9)

Indeed near the center of it all stood "Mine Host" Thomas Morton at 50, the "washed up" attorney and worsted husband now at his height, surrounded by extremes of hardship and freewheeling atmosphere, by a crowd of many different cultures working together in secular self-interest, enlivened by "the unloosing effect of overseas coastal strip existence" (Galinsky 34). Perhaps he (as "Jupiter") and the young men ("Gammedes" 137) had known pleasures with each other before this attempt by some of them to acquire Native companions, connections and/or wives. But there also stood Morton the poet; fancying himself a "Proteus" (oracular island demigod) with "seven knights" (his 7 servants of record), just as in *Gesta Grayorum* years ago at the Inns. Given the message and manifesto within the company's "Poem" (next section), it is likely that Morton spoke it aloud at some point in the festivities. Here is a short "gloss" of its carefully-coded message, what the company was saying at the heart of the whole event.

"The Poem" (135) is "a little epic about love" or epyllion; and it tells both the "history" and the hopeful intentions of the Ma-re Mount company. It is a quite sympathetic attempt to use various mythical and magical kinds of language to act out or facilitate "healing" of, and "marriage" with, the plague-devastated Native peoples around Morton's plantation. A mixture of imperialist business ruse, artistic allegory, and literal attempt to promote "marriage" (intercourse among people, among cultures) to the races now inevitably sharing the continent, "The Poem" is unmistakeably concerned with human suffering due to epidemic, and with the serious need for some kind of healing---that will begin a new (and yearly) decisive action "by tradition" performed by all parties on the land, in favor of life anew. (Even a "little" epic's outcome concerns the origins and fate of a whole people.)[85]

The last two lines burst into clarity like a fought-for declaration---that some kind of annual "hollyday" connection expressing "love" must begin; between a woman who is widow, mother and attractive nymph, strongly identified with the land, and a sea-borne, multitalented, "Protean" male (an "old man of the sea" as Homer says), who must bluster his way into her attention. (And this woman *is* thinking her own thoughts: below). Of course, while there was much about Native gatherings (seasonal feasts, marriages, healings, etc.) to make Morton term them all "revels," these May Days were "not really" staged as

---

[85] As with Morton's imitation of and departures from Thos. Lodge's gentleman-literary example, so with his relationship to Edmund Spenser; whose "broadly conceived Christian humanism" produced the poetry and social agenda(s) of *The Faerie Queene* (1590/96/1606)---"at once patriotic, traditional, humanistic and religious," written "to make a poem, and to persuade and move (even, perhaps at length, to remake) a society" (Maclean ed., xii, 427, 431). On Morton's distinct meanings for mythical "Proteus" (more positive than Spenser's), see "Masque."

a promised cure for mortality. As in Native America *and* England, they were "only" a credible, encouraging social and metaphysical promise, to all participants, that "life" would, somehow, go on.[86]

It is not known whether Plimothers shared in the Revels, saw the "Riddle" and "Song" "fixed to the Maypole," (135) and/or expressed "defiance" *at* the event. But this very peak is the point where Thomas began a shocking discovery that would hurt him for the rest of his life---his civilization's traditional feelings for *poets* ("Antimasque" above).

Both Morton's and the undertakers' less ingenuous claims about their rivalry become apparent now. On one side, Morton foregrounds the cultural and religious differences which "from that time," he says (139), caused his persecution: economic competition is mentioned (113, 141), but he neatly omits how Ma-re Mount came to be "in a good way for gain in the Beaver trade." (He, like the "forward" investors seen above, will not admit or sanction the secret,

---

[86] Pratt (in AC17) refers to what we have seen in plenty, that May-time customs including Maypoles were already part of the life here, and that those involved seemed "very mery." James Axtell's research in the *Documentary History of the State of Maine, Collections of the Maine Historical Society* (2nd series 4, 1889, 298)---and in its *Province and Court Records*---shows that "neglect of public worship" was the chief Puritan accusation against Down Easters, many of whom were West Country people "out of the brawling seaports of Western England, of Cornwall and Devon, not the Puritan villages of East Anglia." See his "The Scholastic Philosophy of the Wilderness" in *The European and the Indian*, 157.

But this was not neglect of religion *per se*. Vladimir Propp's overview of customs like and related to those of May above is relevant, if we want to know larger human contexts ("The Commemoration of the Dead" in Turner, ed., *Time Out of Time*). The women's customs in Propp's cultural example include annual wailing and grieving at lost loved ones' and ancestral graves (Morton saw this done in Native New England too). Was this what "Scilla/Niobe" was doing when (one imagines) she and Morton first met? At the burial grounds "people prayed for the dead and lamented their loss, fed the dead and then feasted themselves. Sadness changed to merriment and sometimes revelry with song and dance, and even 'indecent amusements' as older reports suggest ....[The] cult of the dead was part of a general system of beliefs concerning nature, work and religion, all of which included the cycle of life-death-resurrection as one essential underlying pattern" (Propp 232).

According to John Langstaff, founder of Revels, Inc. (an American nationwide English-folk-theatre company specializing in Revels; qtd. in Dempsey *Morton* video), this same cycle is sometimes evoked by the figure of "Hobbyhorse," who in some traditions looks less like a man on horseback than a great black-shrouded figure---Life, or Death?---who dances a unique pattern of alternating rises and falls in the midst of "regular" dancers before the crowd.

most-profitable part of American business: gun-trade was indifferent to, contradicted the basic rarely-spoken assumption of public discourse, that America would gradually be conquered by force of arms followed by "conversion" (see Hakluyt 1582/1585, qtd. in *Canaan* 49).[87]

Plimoth, on the other side, makes arming Native peoples the core of its complaint against Ma-re Mount (FBH2:52; Letters 56-64; Winslow MHSP 5:133). But there is nothing to corroborate Bradford's two lists of "some of the chief of every plantation" (2:54; Letters 63) who supposedly held a first, unlocated, and never repeated parliament of their own, and (he says) resolved to "request" that Plimoth "suppress" Morton. Most on the list were known by other records as just the "indifferent" types of English to have enjoyed and appreciated "Mine Host." None of them left any gratitude on record to either Plimoth or Mass. Bay, which later prosecuted Morton, and under whose rule they did express themselves unanimously---as Company "slaves" (qtd. in Young 145).[88]

Bradford's claims cannot be disproven, but as will appear below, there are anomalies in these records whose acceptance has long been a "proof of loyalty" (Banks). Morton agrees that a 1627-28 "general collection of Beaver" was made

---

[87] William Bradford definitely shared the view of Native American relations as at least a battle or siege, if not war outright. Amid peace and stagnant trade---a condition on the landscape that to Morton made him a "Prince" not of Hell, but of "Limbo" (152) ---Bradford told Gorges (*Letters* 62) "we shall be beaten with our own arms" if the Council "abided" Morton's (and the Council's own profit-earning investors') practices. This naivete helps to explain Plimoth's shock that absolutely "nothing was done to" Morton when he arrived in England a "prisoner": Bradford had expected his letters to prosecute Morton by panicking the Council.
But it might be said that Plimoth panicked itself the most. As seen above, Plimoth's desire to "beat" Native peoples generated the totally uncorroborated claim that in 1627-28, the plantation was still "daily" (Letters 63) expecting to be "overrun and spoiled" by Natives at "great preparations" (62). These distinctions help relieve long-standing clouds over Native "New English" character, clouds widely assumed to have their substance in these documents.

[88] Bradford on both his lists included: William Blackstone (Shawmut/now Boston), Mrs. David Thompson (by 1627 a widow of Thompson's Island, Boston Harbor), Roger Conant (Naumkeak/Salem), John Bursley/Burslem (Wessagussct/Weymouth), John Oldham (Nantasket/Hull), and Edward Hilton ("Cocheco," now Dover, NH).

for funds against him, but he adds that "he was not thought a good Christian that would not lay much out for that employment" (162). This seems a plausible trace of coercion from the plantation "then of more strength than them all" (FBH 2:54); and which, Bradford adds curiously, "had least cause of fear or hurte" from Morton's practices.[89]

Meanwhile the months after May 1627 were acrimonious, Morton hearing "Many threatening speeches," which "his company...seemed little to regard" (141), and Bradford hearing Morton's "scurillous termes full of disdaine" (2:55) in answer to "neighborly" letters of warning to cease and desist. The Plimothers appealed to the authority of their oppressor James I's Proclamation on "illicit" trade, and Morton replied in Inns of Court fashion: "the king [is] dead and his displeasure with him" (qtd. in FBH2:55). Plimoth resolved that "ther[e] was no way but to take him by force," and Bradford, lacking official powers, set to work on letters to Gorges, the Council for New England and others of influence back home. Standish prepared his men.

Significantly, the only related document for this period besides Bradford's writings and the Ford "List" is one that was copied as an entry (Nov. 21, 1627) into future Mass. Bay governor John Winthrop's "Notebook of Cases before the Court of Wards and Liveries" (WPF2:44). *Purportedly*, this passed across Winthrop's desk between Morton's Revels and first (June 1628) arrest, this single "objective" register of the "murder charge" to come:

> Wm. Stuart of Stratfield turgisse in com. South: hant:
> Informed that one Tho:Moreton late of Swallowfield in
> Com: Wilt: one of the Attorneys of [blank] about vj yeares
> since, did combine with one Tho: Wigge, and certified
> this capias [a "writ or process commanding...arrest" of
> the person named---OED] of 100 *li.* and after about a

---

[89] Important matters relating to these lists, and to another later one, are treated below and in Ch. 9, for clarity's sake.

> yeare the said Wigge dyed, supposed to be made awaye by the said Moreton, and one Edwardes who was layd in prison for it, but Moreton fledd.

While nothing connects this directly to Plimoth's campaign, its timely pass through bureaucrat Winthrop's hands seems remarkable. History is, of course, full of coincidence. However, this appears to be Winthrop's entire entry concerning "Moreton." Exactly why this came to Winthrop in his particular office is not clear. Nor is why Winthrop copied *this* capias down for his notebook, out of all the documents he handled in the Court: in this regard Winthrop's writings are almost always clear, and above there is no hint---from himself. We see only editor Forbes' footnote for the page, suggesting that the capias refers to "Morton of Merrymount."

There is no evidence that John Winthrop had ever heard of Morton (or Bradford) before November 1627, above. By the time Winthrop and his Puritans migrated (1630), they did make a point of distinguishing themselves from Plimoth's "Separatists" (WJH1:12); but at *this* time, there was no way for Winthrop to have connected the above "Moreton-Wigge-Edwards" process to a gun-running "Lord of Misrule" in New England. Morton was not arrested till early summer 1628, and Winthrop's work at the Court of Wards was concerned with *internal* English affairs, ones related to minors' estates held in trust with the Crown. Winthrop and his editors offer no remarks on these matters.[90]

---

[90] The reader will recall Ch. 4's examination of the roots of this "made away/murder" allegation. This editor has examined original documents with the Massachusetts Historical Society; but as Librarian Peter Drummy confirms, there is only this entry of the capias "in Winthrop's hand," and no date for it except that *assigned by* the various editors. (The 1968 rpt. in Vol. 2:44, edited by S.E. Morison *et als*, offers nothing new; nor does the 1997 edition of Winthrop's *Journal* edited by Dunn/Yeandle).

Hosmer (1908 "Introduction" to Winthrop's *Journal "History of New England"*) writes that Winthrop's personal and gubernatorial "papers" passed from his Connecticutt descendants into the hands of New England historians "William Hubbard, Cotton Mather and Thomas Prince": further work on them was done by Jonathan Trumbull and Noah Webster, followed by the "quaintly provincial but sincere and vigorous" James Savage's 1825-26, 3-volume edition (based on the original manuscripts, Hosmer writes---16). Hosmer (17) "adopted without change the

New English spring of 1628 saw no second (recorded) revels. But in June Captain Myles Standish and perhaps eight men moved in Plimoth's behalf. The "truth" of this arrest lies somewhere between Morton's and Bradford's accounts (*Canaan* 143-8; FBH2:56). Morton claims he was taken by surprise while alone at Weymouth, and that he then escaped (and slammed the door behind himself, no less---showing something of his confidence in his skills and social connections even at this point). He rushed home across the Monatoquit wetlands under a night-sky full of thunder and lightning---He recalls this as comedy in his "Bacchanal Triumph," and paints himself as one raised on "wild meat," in sly cahoots with the land and "the way things are." At Ma-re Mount, he readied his guns with two "assistants" (as he'd warned he would, FBH2:55); and then he chose cautiously to "yield upon quarter," only to be beaten up and nearly stabbed (145-6). Bradford reports no battery. Morton, he says, charged out of his house not to parley but to shoot Standish, but was so "steeld" with liquor that the Captain merely "stept to" and "took" him. In both accounts the young "assistants" fared poorly: Morton reports one so "craven" that he only got drunk, and Bradford another who "lost but a little of his hot blood" when he somehow "ran" his nose upon a sword.[91]

---

transcript of the text made by Savage," adding that he made "Careful tests of the accuracy of Savage's work...in many parts between the original and the copy," making "some use also" of "the [which?] original manuscripts" at the Massachusetts Historical Society (19).

Until it can be shown how Winthrop *in 1627* could have "known enough" to enter this himself in his "papers," we must assume that one or more later editors gave it its present date/ position. As *Canaan* repeatedly demonstrates, enough American historians distorted "Morton matters" to make this another credible example of scholarly service to Puritan and puritanical causes. See Ch. 10's conclusion for another such anomaly in "Winthrop's" writings.

[91] The former Low Countries soldier Standish's previous experience against barricaded planters brought chuckles to S.E. Morison's account (29) of the conflict between Plimoth and Roger Conant's struggling company of men at Cape Ann in spring 1625 (FBH1:420). Standish's "temper," not what John Smith would call that of a "seasoned" man, and his lack of diplomacy (Plimoth's Rev. Robinson and Edw. Winslow's *Good News* detailed both) have inspired a heartwarming indulgence in some historians of New England.

Now the jocular Morton found how "much it stood" him to be "very circumspect": Standish "in a rage" (156) would have "dispatched" him, he wrote. Bradford---in his mid-30s with the older Morton before him---took counsel with "elder" Brewster, who reminded these "authorities" who "ruled the roost" back in England, and Bradford agreed only to ship Morton home "without any other thing to be done to him." This caution might at least give Plimoth a year to disperse the colleagues around the Maypole.

But, consistent with the rest of this story, no vessels passed through Plimoth that summer of 1628, even for trade (AC289). So Morton was marooned on the Isles of Shoals off the "New Hampshire" coast, "a month at least" (148; more precisely, it was June to early autumn). This moment in Morton's fortunes is where we can learn most from the anomalies between William Bradford's above two lists of "contributors to" this 1628 arrest and marooning, and a document or third list purportedly related to the same events (Ford ed., "Paid for Th: Morton" in MHSP 45: 642, rpt. below in Ch. 9).

The first sign of problems behind Bradford's long-accepted story is the rather striking absence from both his lists of that popular early planter and later public Morton-sympathizer Samuel Maverick (the "C of E man"). And yet, Maverick *does* appear on Ford's related document (reprinted in full below for readers' convenience). There is a reason for these documents' differences; and it will lead us to recognize that Plimoth grew suddenly aware of its errors toward Morton, and took steps to soften the consequences. Let us see what kinds of clues, records, and overlooked chronological facts support support these new shadings to the story.

The only date on Ford's "Paid for" list is "10 Aprilis 1629" (this editor has inspected the original documents: the list came to light in 1856 and the date is identical to all other writing therein). Even if we adjust "1629" by a year forward *or* backward in relation to modern calendars, it fits only into the most basic existing scenario of events---that Morton was arrested/marooned from June-September 1628, sailed to England and returned by "spring 1629" as seen above. More or less by "April 1629," he was again "at liberty" and moving freely about his "old nest in the Massachusetts."

Therefore, the activity we see in Ford's list---the paying-out of money to the same planters described by Bradford, plus Samuel Maverick---shows in its detail that those men had supplied Plimoth with specific (yet an odd collection of) merchandise and items; and that they were now (spring 1629) being paid in cash for those things.

The very means of these cash payments---through the person of Morton's own former servant Edward Gibbons---is another anomaly that (with the reader's patience) actually brings new understanding. Gibbons, known to Puritans first as indeed a "Merry Mounter," was now in the wake of Morton's first arrest very dramatically ingratiating himself with Plimoth's and Salem's authorities (documents below). Could it be that Gibbons was already "trusted" by them with sums of precious cash, in such an affair of theirs?

One further obvious fact helps us put together these payments and Gibbons' involvement. As shown below, Ford's document also contained a *second* list that "probably" (Ford said) showed the items taken from Ma-re Mount's houses before they were burned two years later, in 1630. Since Morton's young men remained "free" there between his first (1628-9) and second (1630) arrests, there must have been a period of "respect" or at least hesitancy on all the Puritans' parts that protected those servants from immediate dispersal, re-assignment to new "masters," and/or other standard procedures cited here. If Plimoth left Morton's Ma-re Mount alone even in his extended absence, they must have grudgingly acknowledged Morton to have been acting within existing law, and expected that he would, rightfully, be back to rejoin his men, property, and business, with all that tacit support from court and Council.

And so, after Plimoth had marooned Morton on the perilously barren Isles of Shoals in September 1628 in the hope he might conveniently die or quit the country altogether, something weakened Plimoth's belief in its own cause. They could not go so far as to fetch Morton back, not in front of their own people. But there was Edward Gibbons, who seemed serviceable and "spoke Morton's language"; and now we see why Ford's first list names such specific-yet-random-seeming merchandise.

Raisins, wine, sugar, a shirt, "a shute of clothes" (Morton complains he had only one "thin suit" on the Isles (148)---these are things that a "lone planter" might have to spare, to contribute for the succor and survival of a friend whom one could help in no other way. Gibbons was quietly appointed to collect a shallop's full of supplies like these, to gather contributions from the "C of E" men with whom Morton had shared his trade and Revels. And this scenario (rather than Bradford's list of "contributors to suppress" Morton) is quite in synch with what was in fact "mainstream New England neighborliness" at the time. Such a clumsy, awkward and unlikely series of events was necessary *because* the Puritans were trying to disrupt and terminate long-standing relationships; ones centered (to their fear, as Bradford details) in "a place like Ma-re Mount."

Interestingly, Morton's account of his marooning on the Isles of Shoals says that Native Americans, not Gibbons, delivered him his supplies (148). If Morton had known of Plimoth's change of attitude, he would have gloated and seized it as admission of wrong. Instead Morton leaves us the "anomaly" that his Native partners recognized him as a "Sachem" in "league of brotherhood"---yet they would not simply rescue him from his island prison. How, then, does this add up with all the rest?

Young Edward Gibbons, not surprisingly, dared not face Morton. He had cast his cultural bets and was now making money by working against his original company. He took the gathered-up planters' merchandise to the camps of Ma-re Mount's former "league" Native trading-partners; explained all about the new "authorities" at Plimoth, whom they had "best not contradict"; and asked Native people to deliver these merciful comforts themselves, to the dangerously improvident "Sachem" soon to be punished by the faraway English king.

It is also a mark of all three of Morton's arrests that his treatment improved when his rivals reminded themselves of his connections with the Council, with Gorges and the nobility (first due to Brewster: on the last time see Winslow's letter Ch. 10). Indeed, as will appear in detail, when his captors' 1630 hopes against him soured, they "sounded him secretly" (190) to come to terms and avoid embarrassment with "the vulgar people [who might] count them men unadvised." This was also the policy taken by Mass. Bay after its early antagonism with another aristocratic arrestee, Sir Christopher Gardiner; who received a contrivedly less-hostile sendoff than originally planned for him (Ch. 9).[92]

Ford points out that none of this document is in Gibbons' handwriting. But, if it is an authentic record of actions, it brings new shadings of the people around and against both Morton and Plimoth; and shows that the Plimothers subtly strove to keep from giving the English government more cause against

---

[92] Major's *Dissertation* was the first critical writing to examine these 1628-29 events (30, 87), and he felt that these lists reflected money "spent on Morton's behalf." He points out that this was just when new Plimoth laws were laid down against "disorderly living" and other kinds of "amoral" but practical "housekeeping" (he cites Pulsifer and Shurtleff I: 44, 68, 91).

Major (21) mentioned also that there is not a single specific recorded example of English "neigbours and freinds" being "daly killed" (as Bradford claims, FBH2:53) with guns. Even in Massachusetts territory alone, where Bradford claimed to know of at least 60 "peeces" in Native hands, it seems impossible to locate an example until perhaps the events leading up to the "Pequot War" c. 1633-37.

themselves, while holding fast to their intent to change the rules of intercultural contact in New England. Between their pride and Gibbons' avoidance of Morton, Mine Host never learned what these supply-items signified. He saw only that, as Adams put it (AC37), Plimoth's 1627-8 objective was to declare itself "a power on the coast, ready to assert itself in the work of maintaining order"---an "order" Morton wanted in neither old nor New England.

At last a ship also bearing John Oldham (another bumptious Plimoth-affiliated planter and business agent) picked Morton up from the Isles; and the pair were at Plymouth, England, by early autumn 1628 (AC31).

But Bradford knew that Plimoth's order was not that of standing statute or practice. So a second set of his letters went to Gorges and Council (61-64) by way of Oldham (FBH2:57). Bradford and Morton report that Oldham and/or a second "agent" were financed to "informe" authorities and "prosecute" Morton. Though this was a putative legal proceeding, Morton says he was nearly a target of the London "underworld" of magic and "cunning men" ("wise men" in Fletcher/Stevenson 8), who were often "public figures known over wide areas" and able to devise a "snare" with anything from herbal poisons to perjured affidavits (Thomas *Magic* 648 and Ch. 8). Outright bribes for a "cunning instrument" from a judge often backed up such "magic." But, where Bradford concludes disappointedly that Morton "foold" Oldham and was "not so much as rebuk[ed]," *Canaan* adds (163) that Plimoth's man in London, when the "facts" and gold proved "all too little," was indeed advised: *To let Mine Host alone.*

As the budding Massachusetts Bay Company (dominated by John Winthrop's variety of Puritans) began now to vie with the aristocracy-based Council for New England over a share of the latest reorganization of "English" territories, Oldham the ambitious Plimoth outcast (who eventually served Plimoth well and "made good") hoped himself to become a beneficiary of confusions in the various land-patents. Thus, he pressed not very hard in Plimoth's misguided cause before Gorges and the Council---who had no doubt reaped the profits of Morton's trade. He was "at liberty" (163), and he wasted no time getting passage and supply for his return.

The possible second "agent" above may have been Isaac Allerton, who had also boarded a fishing-ship back to England in fresh pursuit of a patent for Plimoth. For as he returned there "early in 1629" (that is as accurate as records allow), who but Morton stood at his side. This return has amazed historians as much as it dumbfounded Bradford (FBH2:74), though Allerton's own business-ventures were departing these days more and more from his "Brethren's" (to the point where he ended his days a secular merchant among the Dutch). Allerton accepted more of the norms of the world around him and made use of Morton, lodged him in his own house a few weeks ("as it were to nose them" of Plimoth), and employed him as a "scribe" until Bradford "caused [him] to pack [Morton] away."

Morton had delighted in their "terrible amazement to see him at liberty." But why *did* he return at all? What he did not record was his likely deep chagrin at still needing work, at his age, for all he had done. And his supposed backers had "in the meantime" come to a reorganization of Massachusetts territories, and were about to issue the Mass. Bay Company's charter to develop "foundations" laid at Naumkeag/Salem. Yet another Devon man and Morton's next major nemesis, Captain John Endicott, had passed by Morton's first-exile ship back in the fall of 1628, Endicott arriving to "order" lands between the Merrimac and Charles Rivers. The new geography of the Mass. Bay patent, by design, erased all previous land-claims; so perhaps Gorges and Council were consoling (further manipulating) Morton with some promised share of any lands *they* might win, as the land-disputes ground onward in the courts.

As with the above machinations, the roles of bribery and maneuverings amongst Charles' courtiers in bringing about the grant of Mass. Bay's charter fill pages of speculations (Palfrey Vol. 1: AC52); and they became important legal ammunition in Morton's later suit against Winthrop's Boston (Chs. 9-10). For now, all Morton could probably offer was his "agency" and experience in New England: the advantage of gun-trading was certainly over. As he walked out of Plimoth into America again, the Plimothers gave warning (13), and he derided "their practices, and loss of labor." They were "willful people that would never be answered," except by his disappearance.

At his "old nest" in the Massachusetts, Morton found that this new Captain Endicott (soon to be dubbed "Captain Littleworth") had already paid a visit: sometime between autumn 1628 and May 1629 (before he had jurisdiction, Mayo 17), Endicott had cut down the Maypole, "rebuked" the people still living there "for their profaneness," and "admonished them to looke ther should be better walking" (FBH2:49-51).[93] Still, Morton's somehow-liberated young men carried on there, the place now known by the Puritan nickname "Mount Dagon" (132).[94]

---

[93] Endicott reported "former traders" of "prophane and dissolute living" in a letter to Mass. Bay Company of May 27, 1629 (Shurtleff Records of Mass. Bay 1:48).

[94] "Dagon" was a male deity of Old Canaan's Philistine people(s), who, just before they began to encounter Israelite incursions into the "Promised Land" (Bible, *Judges* 16:23), had settled among their old trading-partners, the "Canaanite" civilizations long there. The Philistines' arrival c. 1200 BCE had been as "People[s] of the Sea" from Biblical "Caphtor," ancient Crete; which they had left upon its being conquered by the "Homeric Greeks." Passages of Bk. 1 Chs. 1-3, on the use of "loadstones" and mass migrations, show that Morton put thought into his ancient Mediterranean chronology; and he proved to be not far from the archaeological facts. See Macalister and Dothan.

Although the intended meaning of this name given by Plimothers to Passonagessit/Mare Mount seems clear enough, it is also interesting to imagine the ironic (as usual) senses in which the remaining "Mortonites" might have carried it. If Gibbons was not unique in their company as one "well accomplished" and only "divinely" illiterate (Scottow), they could have worn the name with mock-pride as "philistines"; that is, as people "civilized" by their own (and long-customary) definitions, but forced to live among newly arriving, antagonistic, self-professed "New Israelites" or Puritans; for whom, as Morton said, it seemed that "Church discipline [was] the most essential part of their Religion" (183). These are the cultural differences emerging from digs in the Middle

Perhaps now "Great Wat" Walter Bagnall departed for his trader's life in Maine (Notes above). But the servant headed in the opposite cultural direction, Edward Gibbons, reportedly began "Lamenting his Christless estate" (Scottow 289); or at least "his Ambition exceed[ed] what he could expect at home." Given the "Aprilis 1629" date on Ford's list above, it is possible that he now "went over" to Plimoth's side, and traveled with them when they paid their respects to fellow Separatists new-come to form the church of Salem. But there, as Francis Higginson and Samuel Skelton were made Salem's pastor and teacher respectively, and the Plimothers "laid on hands" in Christian solidarity, "a Saving Work upon a Gentleman of [eventual] Quality" began in their midst. Scottow continues with how Gibbons convinced the assembled "Brethren" that

> he was no Debauchee, but of a Jocund Temper, and one of the Merry Mounts Society, who chose rather to Dance about a Maypole[,] first Erected to the Honour of Strumpet Flora, than to hear a good Sermon; who hearing of this Meeting, though above Twenty Miles distant from it, and desirous to see the Mode and Novel of a Churches Gathering; with great studiousness, he applyed himself to be at it; where beholding their orderly procedure, and their method of standing forth, to declare the Work of God upon their Souls, being pricked at the Heart, he sprung forth among them, desirous to be one of the Society, who though otherwise well accomplished, yet divinely illiterate, was then convinc'd and judged before all; the secrets of his heart being made manifest, [Gibbons] fell down and Worshipped God, to their astonishment, saying, *That God was in them of a Truth*....(emphases original)

"God was in them." So decided Gibbons, and as he behaved accordingly, so began the respectable career of future Boston's Major of the Militia (he even made magistrate and became Myles Standish's superior officer, Ch. 10). Boston would agree that Edward Gibbons "was Born there" at Salem; and his climb to

---

East today, and in Morton's time there were enough literary traces of them to work with, if one with such a book in mind sought them out. Clearly they underwrite *Canaan*'s title.

Puritan prominence would later, it seems, help Morton after all to obtain a last crucial bit of mercy.[95]

"Mine Host," for now increasingly isolated, clung to hopes of land or at least a friendly colonial governor-general, through the continuing struggles between Gorges' Council and Mass. Bay's growing connections at court (FBH2:74; AC39). Morton's new liberty in New England was constant reminder of these threats to Puritan supremacy in America. But three events would soon seal Morton's fate for the next 13 years, and beyond.

Endicott was soon empowered and directed to see that henceforth "none be partakers" of American wealth except within Puritan constructions of "peaceable men...honest life and conversation...good order and government" (MHSP 1860: 2, 133; Young 145; Shurtleff *Records* 1, 361-94). Accordingly, he and perhaps Skelton ("Pastor Master Eager" in *Canaan* 164) drew up new "Articles" under those powers, to tighten the perfectly-circular project of "regulating the trade in beaver skins...to meet the charge of providing churches and forts" (AC39; Young 96, 146). They summoned all the planters they could reach to Salem that autumn of 1629, to sign and submit to their monopoly.

In the original charter, however, emphasis had been laid on "the fact that the [Salem] Governor and council were authorized" within terms "grounded on the power derived from His Majesty's Charter to ordain reasonable laws, *not repugnant or contrary to those of England*" (Rose-Troup, *Mass. Bay* 67; *Records* 1:361, emphasis added to terms Morton cites in *Canaan* 165). Monopoly Morton derided, but further, because of what he saw as the calculated and dangerous

---

[95] The dramatic benefits of submission to Puritan rule are seen as clearly in John Oldham's career; for after his bumptious beginnings in exile from Plimoth, he was almost drowned at sea, and from then on he "acknowledged the hand of God to be with them" of Plimoth (FBH1:412). Having "survived" life outside the stockade, he was soon one of the Puritans' most called-upon and prosperous "agents" for many purposes.

lack of these conditions in the Salem document, he refused to sign (although, he says, all the others did). His common law training showed him the "very mousetrap" designed to work along the same lines as European government in general. Against an American "construction of the Word" by an elite, increasingly backed up with the force to make "reality" of its interested definitions (Eusden 59), he "saved his stock," traded to "six and seven for one" on his own, and saw their scheme fail within 6 months (166). As he "derided the Contributors [not to mention Endicott] for being catched in that snare," Captain Littleworth's already-aching "tooth" grew worse.[96]

Accounts agree that as 1629's winter deepened, "scarcity of food" became a "chief difficulty" at Salem (amid this and "fevers" Endicott's wife perished: Mayo 19). In Salem's share of the Puritan appeal for renewal of the King's proclamation against Native gun-trade, it was explained that too many "poor people" with "no provisions" had come there that year; that too much dependence upon the "industry of their servants," and "slothfulness and neglect in planting corn" had caused many deaths; and that outside "provisions" alone could sustain those people "afraid of being surprised by savages who had been supplied with guns by interlopers" (clearly we see Morton's old and the Puritans' new "worlds of intercultural trade" still at contest in these years). Rose-Troup's *Mass. Bay Company* (quoting this document 71) found its familiar strains "very misleading" for reasons of her own; but Morton's report on the crisis is consistent with economic trends toward "abstraction" cited above.

---

[96] As Morton likely still believed New England's cultural future a matter of contention, he may indeed have tried to "stir up" during these months both planters and Native contacts, against the new would-be rulers (WPF1:57; Maverick *Clarendon Letter*). Adams (AC38, 41) and Young (145) agree on the "jealousy and discontent" of the planters against Mass. Bay's beginnings; yet the planters did submit, except for Blackstone's post-1630 exodus from "Boston" and Samuel Maverick's long but day-by-day negotiation of his life in the Puritans' factious midst (Ranlet Ch. 2).

For Endicott, he writes, "trucked away the vittles" (159), "improvidently trucked" (167) Salem's stores before the winter "for the present gain of Beaver": perhaps an amateur's move to make way with the Company. In consequence, Endicott and "Commissioners" (claims Morton, supplying more likely motive than the "arrest attempt" Adams sees in this "visit"), came by boat to Ma-re Mount; found that a forewarned Morton had hid his most needed survival tools (hunting-guns, powder, etc.) in the forest; and took all they could of Ma-re Mount's corn. This time, tellingly, Morton saved his "derision" for "when they were gone," and took himself hunting "in a country so much abounding with plenty of food for an industrious man." Whatever one makes of this, Salem needed food, and they knew which Englishmen had it. The "logic" of Morton's position now, being disliked the more for his "help," was a richer absurdity than the Inns could have scripted.

A second incident, if it happened, might have been part of Morton's "miscarriage," which before long gave his rivals "just occation" to arrest him (FBH2:74). Winthrop's associate Thomas Dudley (Letter 11) claims that Morton fired "hail shott" (small pellets for birds vs. a heavy single bullet) at "a troupe of Indians, for not bringing a Cannowe unto him to cross a river withal, whereby hee hurt one, and shott through the garments of another." Maverick wrote later that if this happened, "no hurt [was] donn" (Letter 41). Perhaps this tells at least of Morton's rising anger and sense of powerlessness; and that he too could vent his emotions on Native people. At his "trial" below, neither this nor "illicit trading" were mentioned.

And then came the beginning of the "Great Migration"---By May's end 1630, Mass. Bay Company ships were arriving in soon-to-be "Boston" Bay, their elected governor John Winthrop stepping ashore with his 400, and 600 more of these less "Separatist" Puritans on the way. It was the largest English enterprise yet, and with friends here and there now at court. As Thomas Morton stood watching from the Blue Hills above the Bay, he might have guessed himself again the first order of "business" for this new flotilla of "Saints" and would-be governors. With blistering "Canaanite" or anti-Biblical ironies underneath his words (169), he squinted at what would soon become the "traditional" American view of this "cosmically important" beaching:

> What, are all the 12 Tribes of New Israel come? No, none but the tribe of Issacar; and some few scattered Levites...and they make it a more miraculous thing for those seven ships to set forth together, and arrive at New Canaan together, than it was for the Israelites to go over Jordan drishod: perhaps it was....

"New Israel," like New Plimoth, was to be by familiar definition a place "rid...of all pollution" (170), excluding the "irreligious." And as part of the "parallell...in all points" which Morton (like these his rivals) perceived between New Canaan/New England and more ancient cultures of "the West," here the cultural "reform," the "ridding" was to commence with the many-cultured peoples of Canaan.[97]

---

[97] Calloway's "Borderlands" (19-20) provides one challenge to the long-accepted model of constant intercultural conflict and contest, pointing out that by this time the region had known over 100 years of "offspring" or children descended from "coexistence."
   Morton's ironies are literary as well as personal/political, reflecting his usual disappointments with Puritan tastes. As early as 1628, the Mass. Bay Company's advance-men of Naumkeag/Salem were enriching Puritan America's rhetorical soil, so to speak, for the seeds and the harvest to come. Scottow: "That so many Eminent Persons...should upon Sea-Bridges, pass over the largest Ocean in the Universe, by the good hand of their God upon them...[;] that each individual [ship] should have a caelestial Convoy, under the Flaming Swords of flying cherubim...."*A Narrative* (290).

"Come on, Come on...figure out the doubtful way
At which awhile all youth should stay...."

MASQUE:
The RIDDLE of MAY DAY

> *I ask the reader to excuse these rhymes*
> *if they are not as well-polished as a well-bred*
> *man would wish. They were made in haste.*
> *But nevertheless I have a wish to insert them*
> *here because they serve as a part of our history*
> *and to show that we lived joyously.*
>
> --French planter & attorney Marc Lescarbot,
> postscript to *The Theatre of Neptune*, performed in New France 1606

Until recent decades, most remarks about the career of Thomas Morton of Ma-re Mount have had two points of acrimonious departure: his New England plantation's relatively personal relations with Northeastern Native Americans, and his trading guns to them for the choicest pelts of the fur-trade. Objections against the interracial, erotic and economic practices of Morton's small group of straggling planters, inscribed in the criminal statutes and personal writings of his contemporary Puritan rivals and in the texts of critics and historians schooled in their values, explicitly made mortal sins of both "intermarriage" of any kind and gun-trade to "Indians": both were synonymous with subversion of Puritan-English empire.[98]

---

[98] Dozens of "critics and historians" are cited in the "Sampler." "Antimasque" above details further examples with one of the most influential editors of "American Literature," Moses Coit Tyler, who was first a Congregational minister; like another "major critic/historian" John Gorham Palfrey, who reproduces Wm. Bradford's entire version of the Plimoth/Ma-re Mount conflict, and ferociously attacks the very idea of Native "civilizations" (1:232 for ex.). Contemporary literary historian Nina Baym found that Tyler's influential work(s) were "followed because he was himself a follower"; and Baym agrees with many views of Tyler, as *the* early-definitive editor of what was deemed, by minister, secular ideologue and book-publisher alike, as "fit to read" in American classrooms. Another editor of so-called "forefunners of the Pilgrims," Levermore,

Unfortunately, the dismissal of these practices simultaneously crippled most understanding of the poetry and other kinds of performance in *New English Canaan*, a book that revels in the Renaissance more than most of its fellows. This crippling continues, now because of poststructuralism's all-but-exclusive focus upon the fundamental incoherence and domination-motives of all discourse (see "Antimasque" above). But *Canaan* has scarcely been read even according to previous methodologies. So these pages, as part of a first full-length Morton biography, work to establish if possible what author and book (both assumed to be reasonably intelligent) were *most likely trying to say*. And they leave more recent fundamentals to others more adept at their demonstration.

Erotic relations and gun-trade with Native people are central to the contexts of *Canaan*'s "The Poem" and "The Song," which Morton's company publicly performed and "fixed" to their Maypole over Massachusetts Bay during the May Day Revels staged there in 1627. Can we solve the long-standing "riddle" that the Ma-re Mount trappers and planters ("the authors of these Revels" (139) deliberately wove into these poems? The "Poem" and "Song" are their plantation's history and celebration, and a manifesto or formula for what this company of men conceived as successful colonizing. In order to consolidate their growing strength as a competitor for the Northeastern fur-trade, Morton and his colleagues took up discourses and popular cultural forms of the Renaissance, combined them with the most widespread practices of trade in the first 100 years of Northeast contact, and used these to address (in both self-

---

remarks (2:596) that Longfellow's equally Pilgrim-sanctifying *Courtship* (Pt. 7) "immortalized" the killings committed by Standish at Weymouth in 1622: these are strong lines of agreement round Mr. Morton across the American-critical ages.

interest and compassion) the people of Native American New England, who were then suffering the aftermath of catastrophic "plague."[99]

English trade of guns to Native Americans had begun by the late 1500s, with the earliest West Country fishing and fur-trade ships who stayed ashore long enough to salt their catches of cod, some of them wintering in crude encampments along the northern shores of the New-Found-Land. Traffic in firearms, whether "loaned" to Native men to expedite the flow of pelts from inland trap-lines, or traded outright, apparently did bring Morton the lion's share of New England trade for a brief time, between his post-1624 takeover of "Merrymount" and his first arrest in June 1628. It was, he hinted, his way of "comply[ing]" with America's pre-existing practices in order to "carry her," or outdo New England trading-rivals (140). Quinn's "Renaissance Influences" (79) details earlier attempts in Ireland and the Northeast to purchase "a loyal nucleus" of Native trading-partners; a practice borrowed from imperial Roman policy, by way of Macchiavelli.

As we have seen in detail already, Ma-re Mount's timing, too, was right: the demand for guns in Native southern New England had sharpened with the early 1600s and was fundamental to the Ma-re Mount settlement and early

---

[99] The charges against Morton are not "legal" ones but derive from Bradford's *History* (2:52); his *Letters* (56-64 to the Council for New England); and Winslow's 1635 accusation in a "Petition" (1635: *Mass. Hist. Soc. Procs.* 5:133). Though there is no record of a hostile act by a Native New Englander with a gun from Morton or any other trader between 1624 and 1630, a recent example of the continuing "conviction" standing against Morton and, more importantly, against Native peoples, is Vaughan's *New England Frontier* (Boston 1965: rpt. 1995: 89-90), which invokes C. F. Adams Jr.'s hostile 1883 *Canaan* in order to reaffirm the prevailing view of "the Morton affair."

The view has been that, while the Puritans of Plimoth supposedly would have been glad to leave Morton alone on the landscape (which they knew they did not legally govern), all the early Massachusetts planters did have "cause for apprehension" from the "poor [Native] survivors" of the "plague" to whom Morton traded guns. Hence Plimoth's duty to behave "responsibly" as the sole party in the region capable of "interracial diplomacy" (Vaughan's phrase for keeping guns solely in European hands), "while behind the impenetrable veil of the forest," he adds, "were [also] the dreaded Narragansetts"---the peoples of what James Axtell ironically called "darkest Connecticutt."

success. It does appear the case that they complied with "the occurrents of the time" (135) on both English and Native sides of transatlantic trade.

With those contexts, we come to the poetry produced there with the realization that the intercultural human behaviors most prominent in descriptions of those earliest American fish-and-trade ventures were also the most prominent Puritan charges against Morton's style of settlement. These included "irregular" trade (especially in guns); cohabitation with Native women (to Bradford "abusing the Indian women most filthily," Letters 62); and community practices often indulged by both Native peoples and Europeans "many days together," under the general terms "revels." (Bradford centered his rival's misdeeds round a "May-pole," FBH2:48; and Morton dubbed "revels" a number of different Native social gatherings, from healings to feasts to marriages (22, 29, 33 for exs.).

We have reconstructed how this complex of activities evolved, where "two nations" in "traffic together...[are] endeavoring to understand the other's meaning" and try to create and speak what Morton called "a mixed language," brought about by "the covetous desire they have to commerce with our nation, and we with them" (17). And we have seen that Morton was a well-read, "Old England" West Country gentleman and Inns of Court-trained attorney, who had reached his late forties before he saw "New English" shores. To best comprehend his "Poem" and "Song," we must keep clearly in mind, then, both their practical origins in "irregular" trade, and the literary and cultural languages inscribed upon Morton by his early life.

Providing witty, magnanimous diversions to a sophisticated audience in exchange for social and economic favors was a strategy Morton learned in London's courts and practiced on the frontier, with an astute literary and cultural memory. Readers will recall his Inns tenure marked by 1594's *Gesta Grayorum*

("Entertainments at Gray's Inn"), a days-long and spectacular assemblage of performances for Queen Elizabeth I that included the creation of an entire mock-Court, lyricists and orators such as Thomas Campion and Sir Francis Bacon, processions and government-cavalry reviews through the streets of London, arrays of torch-lit barges on the Thames, and indoor presentations of brief poetic narratives mixed with dances, which were from this point to crystallize into the English court masque in the hands of young Ben Jonson and younger Shakespeare (Welsford 162-3).[100]

Early in these performances for the Queen, once the mock-court had been established (of "Mighty Prince Henry, Prince of Purpoole"), offices, arms and "royal" pardons were issued, and then various bizarre orations concluded with "dancing till late," till the Queen retired. As the days of shows wore on an "altar" was set up for "sacrifices" and incense to the "Goddess Amity," round which "ladies" danced as "Nymphs and Fairies, with instruments of musick, and...very pleasant melody with viols and voices...hymns and praises to her deity" (18). Again an array of "counselors" delivered ridiculous orations on "learned mysteries" and the secrets of "Trismegistus" (24); and by midway through the its proceedings came the performance most relevant to Morton's poetry, "Proteus and the Adamantine Rock."

Its wisp of a story concerned *the* Renaissance figure of change and of human potential, the seaside Greek demigod Proteus (Homer's "Old Man of the Sea," *Odyssey* IV), and his magical island, with whose written-in "magnetic" powers he had imprisoned the Prince and his "seven knights." An "Esquire" arrived to rescue the men and delivered a speech proving to the willful Proteus that the "true attractive Rock of Hearts" was Elizabeth herself (46). Proteus

---

[100] The reader will notice and hopefully excuse several repetitions of materials from Chapter 3: these are to add practical ease for critical readers.

admitted himself outmatched and, with no choice but to set her seven knights free, he struck the island-scenery with his staff. And as he looked on (with his "attendants" including one named "Amphitrite," below), the men emerged from within it "in a very stately mas[que]...in couples, and before every couple came two pigmies with torches....[They] danced a new-devised measure....After which, they took unto them ladies; and with them they danced their galliards, courants....And they danced another new measure" (49). This performance-adjourning-to-dance is the structure of *Canaan*'s "Revels" chapter too. *Gesta* then shifted its shape again: an "Antimas[que] of Mountebanks" took form in which "The greatest master of medicine Aesculapius" appeared with his "fellow artists of severall nations" (60), to perform a healing by means of "musical charms," songs sung with a "Chorus":

> *What is't you lacke, what would you buy,*
> *What is it that you need;*
> *Come to me, gallants, taste and buy,*
> *Heer's that will doe the deed...*

Ailments addressed included old age, "Lost maidenhead," "greife of the spleene": verses spoke to each ailment with a comic incantation of cure, and the Chorus cautioned at last, "Yet let us not [in] too much lyccor delight" (62), a fine pun somewhere between "liquor" and Homer's *ichor*, the substance of divine beings. In *Gesta* this referred to a "powder" mixture distributed by the healer that "preserved" one from "fate" (60): "Nectar" was to be Morton's term for such a substance in his "Song," the second half of Ma-re Mount's Revels performance.

Finally in *Gesta*, a "player" named "Parradox" appeared, to mock virtually everything from the learned circles of ancient Athens to current religious factions ("my father a Jesuite, my mother an Annabaptist...." 65). So closed this generation-and-more's most impressive Inns of Court entertainment, with a few short lyrical songs in honor of "the Kinge of Love and Pleasure" and the raising of a "May-pole" onstage. Players were to "circle it with your caprians [fertility-related] daunces" in honor of the "Feast of Venus Citherea" (72), "Parradox" in the lead with "his Disciples." *Canaan*'s rich intertextual relation with all this will emerge.

Gesta was a rainbow of literary genres and rhetorical styles, of symbolic actions and powerful displays of language that commanded attention and respect.[101] The compelling exhilaration of performing/watching it came from its being *as* an "emblem" of actual Elizabethan power, as an often-daring dialogue with as well as entertainment for the ruling class. With no over-arching "plot," its unity lay in its manifold skillful approaches along the frontiers between celebration and satire; and the young men both performing and watching it were exhorted by *Gesta* to "make emblems" of their own (21). In this sense, *Gesta* shared what William Keach has shown to be a part of much Inns of Court poetic production for this period---a kind of poetry densely woven from mythology and esoterica but, nonetheless, rooted in an "articulated consciousness of the immediate historical context" (*Elizabethan Erotic Narratives* 40).

In this dynamic and learned atmosphere Morton gained his mythic vocabulary, and to make "emblems" from them of people and events near at hand. For example, he inscribed his and his indentured servants' American situation in *Gesta*'s terms. Like "Prince Henry" stranded with seven knights on an "attractive" yet confining "rock," Morton had found himself by 1626 in New England with *seven* servants of an original company of 30: he then re-organized this failing "Mt. Wollaston" into his own successful "Ma-re Mount" by means described above (voyage-documents in Holly). By 1627's Revels, the youths had

---

[101] As noted (Ch. 3), the focus of the entire program, a royal woman in the person of Queen Elizabeth, with her years of lavish court-spectacles such as at Kenilworth, was impressed by the "Proteus" performance so that, when the "lesser courtiers" joined the players to dance, she exclaimed "What! Shall we have bread and cheese after a banquet?" (*Gesta* 49).

grown seasoned enough to want to settle down, desiring to have wives "brought over to them, [which] would save them a voyage" (*Canaan* 139; and on the early, widespread practice of cohabitation and/or intermarriage see Canny "Permissive").[102]

As his fur-trade profited further from those youths' close relations with Native women, Morton smiled in a phrase no longer so cryptic---that "He that played Proteus (with the help of Priapus) put their noses [at Plimoth] out of joynt." He had set those seven knights "free" to pursue their desires for life and wife, and this (with the gun-trade) had spelled Ma-re Mount's success as a plantation.

Together, these general elements---firearms, rivalry for Native American trade-partnership, England's Inns culture, intercultural/interpersonal attractions in America---equip us to read Ma-re Mount's sophisticated productions in context; and to perceive Morton's training in what attorneys do, appropriate all available means (here, young men's desires, Native demands and lifeways, one's cultural education) for winning ends.

What ends? And how does "The Poem" speak to and involve its hearers to achieve them? As we explore this baffling esoteric oration, we notice the sudden clarity of its final couplet, which breaks away from that pied language into a "proclamation" for all to hear and understand.[103] Indeed, the "Poem" is more than

---

[102] The concept of intermarriage as the most advisable way for Europeans to colonize America was old by this time. Many documents in the collection *Early Images of the Americas* (Williams and Lewis, eds., 1993) testify that the English (such as Sir Thomas More with his *Utopia*) kept abreast of ideas such as those of the early Spanish colonizer Las Casas; who, in a *memorial de remedios* ("brief of appeals") to the Spanish Crown, proposed a plan for the creation of colonies/communities where "Indians" and "ennobled" Spanish "peasants" were to intermarry and share the coast of "Cumana" (now Venezuela). At the opposite geographic end of Europe, Scotsman Sir William Alexander praised John Rolfe's marriage to Virginia's Pocahontas because he believed that "by admitting equality" one might help to "remove contempt" from the attitudes of some English (qtd. in Kupperman *Settling With the Indians* 104).

[103] Morton writes that these poetic works were "performed" (139), including such signs of significant organization as a "Chorus"; and Bradford's account of these activities by "all the scum of the

concerned with "some contemporary occurrence": it is constructed to address what in 1627 appeared to be America's very malleable future, both its promise and the threats to it. You, the colonist/reveler/reader, are the one who must "Rise Oedipus," and grasp, even practice the mysterious subtleties read aloud, danced, and "fixed to the Maypole"[104]---that embodiment of long-standing colonial formulas for life and prosperity in New England.

THE POEM

Rise Oedipus, and if thou canst, unfold
What means Charybdis underneath the mould,
When Scilla, solitary on the ground
(sitting in form of Niobe) was found;
Till Amphitrite's Darling did acquaint
Grim Neptune with the tenor of her plaint,
And caused him send forth Triton, with the sound
Of trumpet loud; at which the seas were found
So full of Protean forms that the bold shore
Presented Scilla a new paramour,
So strong as Samson, and so patient
As Job himself---directed thus, by Fate
To comfort Scilla so unfortunate.
I do profess, by Cupid's beauteous mother,
Here's Scogan's choice for Scilla, and none other;

---

country" (FBH2:77) at least agrees that the poetry was made quite "public." Scottow ("Narrative" 1629: 289) wrote that servant Edward Gibbons had some experience of letters, being only "divinely illiterate." It will appear that Native Americans present could have comprehended the poems. They were at least half of the most crucial audience being addressed.

[104] As noted above/below, Morton both follows and departs from usages (incl. mythical Niobe and Proteus) in Edmund Spenser's *Shepherd's Calendar* (1579) and *Faerie Queene* (1590s). Like Spenser, Morton's impulse is to both "make a poem" and "persuade and move" people toward his idea of a "virtuous and gentle discipline," and considers it "So much more profitable and gratious" to present "doctrine by ensample, [rather than] by rule" (Spenser qtd. in Maclean ed., 427, 2). Where they chiefly differ is on the nature of "Proteus" in human nature and best interests. For Spenser he is "father of false prophecies" (*FQ* III, viii) and, as in Boccaccio's influential *De Genealogia Deorum*, symbol of a "changefulness" associated "with forces opposed to order and harmonious unity" (Maclean 297). The reader can easily compare Morton's.

> Though Scilla's sick with grief because no sign
> Can there be found of virtue masculine.
> Aesculapius come: I know right well
> His labor's lost when you may ring Her knell,
> The Fatal Sisters' Doom none can withstand
> ---Nor Citherea's Power; Who points to land
> With proclamation that the first of May
> At Ma-re Mount shall be kept hollyday.

A few chief aspects: "The Poem" consists of three complete sentences (of 13, 4 and 6 lines), and is laced with many "triplicities" that show these authors involving their audience by playing upon many different traditions and kinds of written and spoken language (including Native American ones). We must bear in mind that "The Poem" was *written to be read and perhaps acted-out,* before a multicultural crowd on a hilltop overlooking the sea; and that its first words demonstrate to that crowd why they (and we) are assembled---to call upon a "spirit," for information on a matter "underneath the mould," literally at the feet of the person declaiming. (No doubt this was done with the Inns' special blend of true formality and pure play.)

Some of those "threes" in "The Poem" would have evoked, then, a seance or public consultation of an oracle. Its rising pitch and ardor, as it calls upon figure after figure for an answer to its question, makes "The Poem" something of a three-part incantation or prayer (in whose Christian, "pagan" and Native American traditions the number 3 is of endless significance). There is also a narrative here that moves in threes: its story-aspect unfolds spatially, from sea to shore to land ("'Scilla' was found by speaker 'I' and then..."), and from past to present to future time (she *was* found; here *is* a choice; we *shall* keep this day).

Further, "The Poem" invokes three famous healers for the world of human troubles it describes (Oedipus vs. "plague" in Thebes; "forms" of "Proteus," who gave remedy for a diseased ancient-world plantation; and Asklepios, whose cult in Rome began with his help against epidemic: more on each below). These "threes" that make up the three main sentences, a structure not unlike the good riddle asked of Oedipus himself, work together to drive "The Poem" toward a "comfort," if not exactly a cure, for the "sick." They build up and bear their rhetorical fruit in a *couplet* which is also a very understandable proclamation. Thus, "The Poem," as a piece of written, spoken form, appropriates many kinds of shared language-acts, toward inspiring further human actions. It entices and would order those actions according to long-prevailing customs of literal and figurative coupling, within springtime's "hollyday" tradition.[105]

Prayer, riddle, story, healing, proclamation---These kinds of speech, these most-evident appeals and concerns can guide us through the next step of piecing-together the chief components of "The Poem," its many symbolic

---

[105] These Revels' most obvious appropriation of tradition to attract/engage with New Englanders is of course the "fertility rite" aspect of May Day tradition. Marcus (2): "May Day had been an official feast day of the Catholic and Anglican churches. It carried associations of fertility [healthy increase of children, crops and livestock], renewal, frolicks in the green-wood, and restored community." Thomas (61, 65) elucidates the English sense of "fertility rite" within folk-customs: the term has been a familiar one in existing Morton studies, beginning with Bradford's likening these Revels to the "beastly practices of the mad Bacchanalians" celebrating the "Roman Goddess Flora" (*FBH*2-48). Marcus lists a wealth of Renaissance texts (*pro*-sports and *con*) linking these agriculture-centered customs back to Classical and pagan-European cultural sources. Adams' 1883 *Canaan* adopted the Puritan critique of them (18) found in Phillip Stubbes' 1583 *Anatomie of Abuses*, while Slotkin, Zuckerman and Shea have each explored some aspects/concerns listed above.

It would have been easy, useful, and important to a central *reason for* the Revels, for a person with a few Eastern Algonquian words at his command to relate what was "in the attempt" of these various "speech acts" within "The Poem." Citations below and easily available will show Native New Englanders practicing and interested in such actions (of religious, political and other function) performed upon significant land-forms such as this hill. For examples and overviews see Bragdon "'Emphaticall Speech,'" and Mavor & Dix's 1991 *Manitou: The Sacred Landscape of New England's Native Civilization* 160-1. The latter and Vastokas' *Sacred Art of the Algonkians* (1973: 107, *passim*) have collated numerous archaeological and other evidences of marked "fertility" and erotic "concerns" (among many others) in Eastern Algonquian artifacts, from petroglyphs to the many unmistakably phallic "effigy pestles" in Mass. Archaeological Society (Middleboro) and private collections. The careful anatomical detail in these "grinding tools" is obvious, and one example dates from a Paleolithic site at Squibnocket (Martha's Vineyard) c. 6-4000 B.C.E. Fruitlands Museum (Harvard MA) has also exhibited a small stone "fertility figurine" found in Connecticutt.

fragments and allusions, which now demand of us information about a number of humans and demigods of myth, history and folk-culture.

Morton says he "raised" Oedipus as "the absolute reader of riddles" (139). Oedipus is also, in Ovid's *Metamorphoses* (VII, 176; as in older works by Sophocles and Apollodorus) triumphant against two "plagues" of disease afflicting his city. Morton's Oedipus seems called upon to read a riddle concerning epidemic. He and (by identification) the speaker on the hill want to know "What means" that "whirlpool" of the mortal body's dissolution, death "underneath the mould"---with reference to conditions "Here," and at this time ("When" this "Scilla" was "found" and it led to May Day's "proclamation").[106]

But the answer, though "we" are led on with all the implicit gratifications of "hollyday," will be known one step at a time: without "Scilla...in form of Niobe" we cannot begin to learn what this epidemic "means" for us, as a crowd of different peoples atop the hill. The "order" promised by this "hollyday" is to be neither brutish nor anarchical: to get there, she must be our first concern. Who is "Scilla-Niobe," and why does she sit "solitary" in grief?[107] The "authors of these Revels" needed Renaissance imagery to address the 1627 character and condition of Native America.

Morton and company, in their effort to understand Native peoples at least enough to enlist their help, noticed and responded in these Revels and poems to

---

[106] The other obvious way to read Oedipus might be as a figure of parricide/incest; though how that would mesh *with all the other* figures in "The Poem" in a reasonable coherence of meaning (granting Morton intelligence), or in consistency with historical and other contexts, remains to be shown. On "the mould" and "Charybdis" as death: Morton was apparently told by Native New Englanders that, in their cosmology, at least some deceased or "destroyed" human beings "went to Sanaconquam, who feeds upon them," and as he heard this his informants were "pointing to the Center of the Earth" (42). Charybdis was a mid-ocean whirlpool avoided by Odysseus' ship (but not by others') in Homer's *Odyssey*.

[107] The word "solitary" is a first identification of this woman with a natural and a human landscape: see the Bible's Jeremiah, *Lamentations* (1:1)---"How the city doth sit solitary, that was full of people! How is she become a widow!"

the most catastrophic human event in 17th-century New England: the "Great Mortality" of "plague" and/or other diseases that between 1616 and 1619 killed as many as ninety percent of an estimated 90-135,000 Native Americans inhabiting lands from Maine to Connecticutt.[108] This grieving woman is inscribed "in threes" herself, as attractive "nymph" (like Scilla, below), as widow (gloss 139, and as mother Niobe): indeed both Scilla and Niobe resonate strikingly with the colonial events that brought mass death by epidemic from England to the Northeast.

In *Canaan*, Natives "it seems boasting of their strength" to some resentful French captives, "said that they were so many that God could not kill them" (19). This "innocent arrogance" resembles Niobe's claim in Greek myth. This "loveliest of women" in Ovid's Roman telling, boasted that her wealth and many beautiful children rivaled those of the Gods; and Niobe lived to lament their loss.[109] This woman's "first name," however, is Scilla: we must turn back to Classical myth, to

---

[108] Many recent population estimates are reviewed in Salisbury *Manitou* (36) and Bragdon (*Peoples* 25). On what disease these "plagues" were, see Spiess and Spiess: for many specific reasons Cronon (87) suggests not bubonic plague but chicken pox. In any case, Higginson (1630: in Force II, 16) agreed with Bradford (FBH2:208) that epidemic had left scarcely "one in a hundred" Native New England people alive by about 1620.

A number of textual sources, besides long-standing oral traditions shared with this writer by numerous living Native scholars, agree that a matrilineal and/or matrifocal social structure was the rule in Morton's southern New England. Sources include Salisbury's and Bragdon's careful studies of primary evidences as well as those by Grumet, Etienne and Leacock, Simmons ("Narragansett" and *Spirit*), Salwen (170), Allen (*Hoop* 30-42), and Leland. The oldest-known limestone carving found in the region, too (now in Harvard's Peabody Museum) represents a mother with a child on her back (Davis 2-5) and "probably served as some sort of ceremonial object." The "Great Squa Sachem" mentioned in *Canaan* (132) had powers real enough to bestow upon her three land-granting "Sachem" sons in the 1620s-30s: Morton's one sample of Native oratory was Chikatawbak's anger over desecration of his mother's grave (*Canaan* 109); and before Morton, William Morrell's poem *New-England* described Native women as go-betweens among feuding tribal groups. Typically, Morrell wrote, their diplomacy led to intermarriage ("Hymen" was his word, and Morton's too in "The Song" that followed performance of "The Poem").

[109] "Wherever I turn my eyes, everywhere throughout my home, I see unlimited wealth. Moreover, I am as beautiful as any goddess. Add to all this my seven sons and seven daughters....Can you still ask what cause I have for pride?" (*Metamorphoses* VI, 139)

Thomas Lodge and the Inns, and to the Native American landscape for help on how to read this fundamental first sentence of the three.[110]

In Ovid's influential telling, young woman Scilla's seaside refusals of many suitors' advances were *not* a reason to punish her: when "paramour" Glaucus made his bid (himself "only recently" a man of the sea, 309), Scilla went her way, with less fortunate friend Galatea noting that "at least the men who seek your love are not ruthless...and you can refuse them, as you do, with impunity" (305). Scilla's own interests and "interiority" consisted mainly of enjoying her pleasant natural surroundings, and Ovid gave us this uncomplicated life as neither idyllic nor doomed. It simply went on, until Glaucus sought out sorceress Circe for a love-charm. Circe herself fell in love with Glaucus and, when refused, she spitefully made Scilla "monstrous" by poisoning her favorite tidal pool. This created a circle of fierce "dogs" about Scilla's lower abdomen. And she, in sympathetically-rendered anger of her own, became a danger to passing sailors such as Odysseus' crew. At last, for her attacks on sailors who were still nonetheless drawn to her, Scilla was transformed into a great stone land-form by the sea.

A redoubtable woman, victimized by others' needs and problems, with respectable feelings of her own: a danger, affiliated with "fierce animals" yet irresistable to those neophyte sailors who all wanted something from her---The metaphor grows clearer in light of the earliest encounters in the region (well-documented in relation to Champlain, Capt. Thos. Hunt, Plimothers *et als* in

---

[110] It is integral to "The Poem" that this mortal woman Scilla-Niobe's triple-aspect as nymph, mother and widow corresponds to the poem's three invocations of the Goddess of Love Venus/Aphrodite---as "Amphitrite's Darling" (nymph), "Cupid's...mother," and as an aspect of The Parcae or "Fatal Sisters." Such a divine-mortal linkage is carried further in "The Song" with its invitation to share in "Nectar."

Carpenter), which were increasingly characterized by violence, kidnap and "poisonous" liquors and disease, as Morton's American decade wore on.

Morton's Scilla is also in keeping (and more) with Thomas Lodge's epyllion about her at the Inns. For as Keach has shown, where Inns writers might have been expected to produce "frivolous" and "decadently Italianate" poetic reactions against Petrarchan and neoChristian valuations of Scilla's story (such as is found in *Ovide Moralise*), Lodge and others displayed "sensitivity to the violent pathos and psychic torment" in Scilla's mistreatment. Lodge's treatment, and Morton's after him, went beyond any simply-crude "parody of orthodox moralizing" (Keach 43, 50). This distinction fostering sensitivity was, Keach writes, Lodge's aim: his send-up of the self-absorbed Glaucus was the "dig" he aimed at the Inns' very audience of "penny-knaves," with their cynical sexual mores. It is notable also that while in Lodge's telling, Scilla sits at first coyly displaying her attractions before a gathered company, in "The Poem" she sits grieving and impassive, sick and silent except perhaps for her "plaint" taken up by others. Her emotions are the first things told of her; they originate in independent events before the speaker's arrival; and her silence speaks, because we revelers/readers know the stories of Scilla and Niobe. "Oedipus" must discover the cosmic "reason" for her sufferings.

Finally, we note other versions of Niobe's tale. For example, within Sophocles' *Antigone*, the latter heroine is told that, like Niobe, "your self-sufficiency has brought you down"---and Niobe here is *turned to stone* after weeping for her lost children (lines 872-5: qtd. in Grant 213). In several sources available to Morton's generation, Niobe's final fate is as a statue that "still weeps" (primary texts listed in Graves *Myths* 1-259). But these variants resonate not only with Morton's Renaissance.

A half-morning's walk north of the site of Ma-re Mount in Quincy, facing the islands of Boston Bay at the very end of the peninsula called Squantum, stands Squa Rock, an imposing 35-foot high granite outcrop with an unmistakable likeness to a woman's high-cheeked features. (See Illustration 21: and/or, follow the beach-side trail at midday's low tide, or the waters rise high enough to obscure this "face" in the cliff.) A number of Native and other legends relate how it became known as "Weeping Rock" or "Squa Tumble," after a Native woman who "fell" into the sea there.

The earliest meanings of *Squantum* itself, however, take us back to tales of the gigantic "Indian" couple, Maushop and Old Squant/Granny Squant (Crosby 35; Simmons *Spirit, passim*). They say that Maushop (for several "reasons") devoured and/or transformed all their children; and that Granny Squant, in grief for them, was herself changed into a tearful stone beside the ocean. Morton did not miss the rock-formations called "Squanto's Chapel" at Moswetusett near his home (noted earlier), and he cannot have missed Squa Rock so close to his plantation. Scilla-Niobe "is" America, its land and peoples: these are figured also in *Canaan*'s "Author's Prologue" as attractive bride and widow grieving "fruitlessly" over a "tomb" that was her "womb" (*Canaan* 7).[111]

---

[111] According to Horner ("Squantum" 1), the word *Squantum* is "derived from *Musquantum*, a place of awesome significance now known as Squantum Head....In 1635 the prefix *Mu* was dropped, at least from the recording of the land deeds": Horner continues that Native residents there told of "a most awesome male/female spirit" by that name. In Higginson (13) *Squantum* is "their evill god."

For other possible influences on Morton's imagery here, see the "Ditchley" portrait of Queen Elizabeth, shown standing upon/identified with (a map of) England; and the Belphoebe-like Native figure on John Smith's 1612 map of Virginia (rpt. in Arber, *Travels*), both pointed out to me by Paul Caton of Brown University. A visual identification of Scilla with a seaside standing rock appears in Keach (41): this is *de Glauco* from Nicholas Reusner's *Picta Poesis Ovidiana* (Frankfort 1580), one of many influential "mythological handbooks" circulating at the Inns. That Morton was influenced by such manuals will further appear below. He also seems repeatedly taken with widowed or grieving women: witness his brief marriage to widow Alice Miller (documents in Banks) and his "curative" writings on and to the melancholy "Barren Doe of Virginia."

Given the strong clues that Morton came from West Country Devonshire, he may have been interested by peculiar and historic land-forms, Devon itself being thickly "inscribed" with them, from Neolithic barrow-tomb petroglyphs to the markers left by Vespasian's 2nd Roman

All this represents an unsurpassed inclusion of Native history and experience in four lines of early English-American poetry. These things, Ma-re Mount's "authors" tell us, happened *before* ("Till") the work of "Amphitrite's Darling" in the next line, who carried Scilla-Niobe's "plaint" to "Grim Neptune."[112] He, in turn, filled New England's "bold shore" with "Protean forms" (multilingual fishermen, trappers and traders, lone planters, would-be

---

Legion (Hoskins 9; Whitlock 106; Fox Chs. 1, 2, 7). Sachem Chikatawbak's Neponsets moved there just as Morton arrived, and may well have shown their new trade-partner around. Long exposure to such non-English landforms and pre-English cultural ideas would help a man of the Renaissance to appreciate the same things in his New Canaan neighborhood.

[112] "Amphitrite's Darling" is Roman poet Virgil's nickname for the sea-born Goddess of Love, Venus/Aphrodite (*Aeneid* Book V: Arner 161), who was attended by many sea-nymphs such as Amphitrite. In the same verse-chapter Venus is also dubbed "Citherea" after the Greek island long-known for her worship. "Venus" as a synonym/signifier for "Love" Morton may have borrowed from (among hundreds of sources since Classical times) Spenser's 1595 *Colin Clout's Come Home Again*: other examples of this equation follow.

"Neptune" was the force forbidding, then allowing (thanks to Venus) the hero Aeneas to reach his intermarital, nation-founding destiny in the new-found-land of Italy (*Aeneid* Book V). For Morton Neptune may signify James I, figured thus in Ben Jonson's unperformed 1624 masque *Neptune's Triumph for the Return of Albion* (in which a "Proteus" and other characters "solicit the ladies" with "strange obsession"; Fumerton 169). Or Neptune may be Morton's more immediate colonial employer Sir Ferdinando Gorges, who also "filled" the seas with ships before Morton's *Unity* in 1624; and whose Council for New England built a vessel for Gorges' use called *The Great Neptune* in the 1630s (Preston 247-8).

"Triton" was a benign seahorse-like "river god" and herald of Greek sea-king Poseidon (the Roman Neptune: see Graves *Myths* 1-44, 59). In New France planter Marc Lescarbot's 1606 *Theatre of Neptune*, the boat bearing his masque's main character is drawn by "six tritons" with "trumpets" (Richardson ed., 17, 19). Grafton (64) reprints a woodcut showing Triton in Johannes Galle's *Speculum diversarum imaginum speculativarum* (Antwerp 1638); which in turn represents Columbus on a ship surrounded by such fish-tailed beings, themselves much like the Glaucus-figure in Keach (41) noted above. In "The Poem" Triton seems a reference to the numerous musters of Devonshire men wanted for service in American enterprises, since the 1580s days of Sir Humphrey Gilbert. Details of Morton's exit to America are presented in Chapter 4.

Robert Graves' 2-vol. *Greek Myths* remains the best reference-work on the subject, with its lucid listings of primary-textual variants for each myth and their historical and other contexts. For every mythological figure used in Morton's "Poem" and "read" in these pages, I have taken primary-source variants and Renaissance handbooks into account including Charles Stephanus' popular 1553 *Dictionarium Historicam*, Starnes' and Talbot's *Classical Myth and Legend in Renaissance Dictionaries*; *Ovid moralisé*; Tottell's 1557 *Miscellany*; Natales Comes; works by Boccaccio; and the broad selection of handbooks in Kermode.

missionaries, *et als*); out of whose midst Scilla's "new paramour" had stepped when he "found" her sitting "solitary on the ground."[113]

And what does this learned counsel *posted on the Maypole* immediately say about the winning qualities needed ("to carry" America) by any hopeful New World paramour? Not surprisingly for poetic offspring of the Inns, this hero's strength must be his weakness. Samson, first, stands where one expects an example of power; but in Morton's words, the new American man must have "Samson's strength to deal with a Delilah" (140). In Morton's own day, Samson was most often an example of how *not* to behave in racial, religious, cultural and marital affairs (Kermode 1396): the wonderful irony behind this Biblical strongman is that *he could not resist* the women of Philistine and Canaanite races, who (like the Native Americans still in control of New England, 113) in ancient times had "dominion" over the landscape (*Judges* 13). Samson was a precariously rash and transgressive figure on the cultural frontier called Old Canaan---and he enjoyed the challenge of being "bound" and made vulnerable to Delilah, caring little that his elders disliked his choice in love ("she pleaseth me," he shrugs to them; *Judges* 14: 3-4).

Job, too, was then widely read and "performed" as a figure of "despair and impatience," rather than as a man who bore patiently with sufferings beyond his understanding (Lewalski 189). These were both "flawed protagonists" whose very imperfections were part of the "deliberate allegory" created among men by God, to serve his edifying ends in the world (Astell 179, 189: this partly describes Milton's later *Samson Agonistes* as well). Each figure's "fall" was part of the show

---

[113] As *Canaan* notes, Native New England funereal customs included frequent grave-visitations in which relatives would "lament and bewail" their losses. As this was a practice no doubt too common in the epidemics of the 1610s-1620s, the poem's "finding" of Scilla-Niobe may refer to an actual event between Morton's company and a "solitary" Native woman. Winthrop met one (and had a very different response) while lost near his Boston Bay house: *Journal*, ed. Hosmer 1-68.

in morality plays, giving "fallen nature its due" by voicing (for example) Job's "What is my strength, that I should wait? And what is my end, that I should be patient?"---thus enlisting more powerfully the audience's "undisciplined" energies, for safe-return to "normative" standards of behavior. To wander was still to be headed home.

Thus, a young planter of Morton's company, like him nominally Christian but without the will or compulsion to "fetch" over an English wife (and with a Native "lass" close by), might feel encouraged to enjoy what Marcus called "a condition of happy ambiguity in which the license and lawlessness [sic] associated with [May] customs could be interpreted as submission to authority" (3).[114] Hence too the happy moral ambiguity in the final phrase of the poem's first sentence: one is *"directed thus,* by Fate/To comfort Scilla." "Comfort"---"whatever form it may take between you," smiles Morton the trader and chief poet---is moral, appropriate, "heroic" action in such circumstances of mutual need. As "The Song" to follow agrees: "Nectar is a thing assigned/By the Deity's own mind/To cure the heart oppressed with grief...."

---

[114] Of course a different reading is possible: Job's story does conclude with a humbling divine epiphany that restores his "health and household" (Astell 2): Samson's suicidal destruction of the Philistines' temple helps to purge the landscape of "pagan" cultural rivals, and this is consistent with Morton's remarks on New England's epidemics being good for colonists' purposes. But as Morton told "Pilgrim" readers (137), we must not read only "a part" of "The Poem." Construe Samson, then, as an exemplary killer of heathens for God's purposes, or as a mock-heroic "anti-Puritan" who slays *those* "philistines" with the jawbone of a "fool." And/or read Job here as a man whose deepest faith takes him past the afflictions (boils etc.) that defeat others, and confirms his "chosen" status. But how can such readings cohere with *the rest of* "The Poem"? The undecidability of Samson and Job---the only two JudeoChristian signifiers in the poem except for Scogan the fool---makes them yet another invitation to wander or experiment, especially on a frontier with virtually no authorities either to reward conformity or enforce it. Neither of the two Ma-re Mount servants known historically displayed enthusiasm for either Puritanism or Christianity. Walter Bagnall definitely lit out for the "ungodly" territories of Sir Ferdinando Gorges' Maine (see Winthrop's *Journal*), while the better-documented Edward Gibbons became a merchant of no great ethical repute in Puritan Boston (his career summarized in Hale, ed. Lechford 238). Ma-re Mount's other servants (between five and seven men at least) remain what European-style records call "unaccounted for."

Indeed, at this point in performance of "The Poem," the speaker (likely Morton as the highest-ranked" gentleman" present) emerges as "I," as if to demonstrate the way to complete this unfolding narrative, the poem's "cure" and its proclamatory "manifesto of Ma-re Mount." With a ceremonious oath to Venus and Love itself, "Here" is made an emphatic *choice* or decision to "court" the New World. Yet, why is this important gesture rendered in terms of a "fool"?

John "Scogan" was one of the best-known English court harlequins or fools; and of his many "squibs" the only one Morton refers to (140) was his clever evasion of a death-sentence from his king. Sentenced to hang, Scogan "failed" to find a gallows-tree to his "liking" (Adams lists several sources, Prince Society *Canaan* 278). This "fool" not only dared offend, but used a form of tradition, the last wish, to play up a pretense that he had a "choice" at all; and the fiction turned (his) death back into life. Morton and his audience knew that "Scogan's Choice" meant virtually none---such a predicament amounted to about the same nothing as the average human being's will to deny, or resist, the almost-universal "destinies" of "marriage" (sex-relations of some kind); and "unjust death," represented by "hanging," doom at the hands of overwhelming power, political, natural or other. (See Whiting 189, Harvey 276 on this proverb quoted in *Canaan*'s "gloss" to "The Poem": consider that "where one settles down is also where one meets doom.")

So, while there appear to be virtually no options for the "choice" required of Ma-re Mount's company, there is an enticement here, suggesting that by practicing "Scogan's" wit, one may elude any consequence of the social taboos being broken. But, with the enticement, "The Poem" gives a warning, to embrace here and now what choice there is: it reminds readers then and now that each man (including Morton) had, no doubt, less attractive options back home than here, and that each stood relatively blessed with opportunity from the "Fate" and/or "Love" which had "directed" their lives to New England. It might seem foolish formality to insist on affirming, by (pretense of) choice, one's American lot; but this could make all the difference in a life here. The soon-to-arrive poet of Andover Anne Bradstreet learned this, after feeling her "heart rise" at first sight of the "wilderness."[115]

This choice and "cultural courting," however, must be performed *"Though Scilla's sick."* This line says many things; but note first that the poem's final sentence calls out suddenly for help---as if things may fail---to a third and "ultimate" (in the "pagan" world) healer, Asklepios. Virgil's Aeneas is an aspect (ironic and otherwise) of our poem's speaker---who at Ma-re Mount is trying, as Aeneas did, to organize a new "country" in humble circumstance. But here in New England the possible "new community" is on the edge of doom from epidemic. Ma-re Mount reaches further into early Rome for help: "Aesculapius" and his cultus saved the capital in 292 B.C.E. (Kerenyi *Asklepios* 5-9; and he was thanked with a waterside-temple on the Tiber). This anxious summons of a doctor was also to draw upon standard English mummers'-play tradition, by which, near the end of plays involving preChristian themes of death-and-rebirth, he was called to restore "dying" players (Arner 158; James 273-5; Thomas 72).

---

[115] Recall Ch. 1's "Padstow Mayers' Song" from 17th-c. West Country Cornwall: it also chided celebrants to make their choices, by mention of the grave ("whither we are going") in the midst of their dance: "Unite and unite...For summer is a-comin'...And whither we are going, we all will unite...." Welsford details long European traditions of the court fool's dances and struggles with Death, such as those of "Pauvre Pierrot" after a wave of epidemic: *"Enfin voila le cholera ...Bim-Boum, Zoum-Zim. Toujours comme ca"* (387). "He makes love to a rose by moonlight, and the moon has the face of a skull."

With final regard to the benefits of what was later called *amor fati* (choosing one's fate), Morton was familiar with Horace's *Satires*; and an Italian folktale behind Horace's "II" (line 6) refers to a peasant laborer in his fields, who asks Hercules' help in improving his life. Hercules brings the man before the wealth-savvy god Mercury, who promises to help the man find "buried treasure"; and when the man agrees, he finds himself back in his field with the same work ("planting") before him (rpt. in Knox 635).

We have seen Asklepios' appearance in *Gesta Grayorum* above; and in Morton's well-thumbed Cicero, Asklepios was one who "healed with his oratory, not medicine" (*De Oratore* 159). If each indentured "paramour" fails to make Native American Scilla-Niobe recover and respond, warns "The Poem" (with refreshing candor for both a male and a colonizer), "His" New World "labor" will be as "lost" as this woman to the forces of mortality---to "the mould." She is "now to be taken up[,] or laid down" (*Canaan* 139).

Scilla's final disposition either will or will not enable the poem's ultimate proclamation to become human action. But we see by now that Morton learned his lessons at the Inns. For "The Poem" enlists its audience with skillful appeals: now it "brings them to the edge" by voicing human anxieties beneath the overwhelming forces of "doom," which all can "relate to" because "none can withstand." And, straight into this moment before the void, comes an enjambment which, like "the nick of time," brings resurrection.

"Doom" is met with "Citherea's Power"; and, via that tiny *equating* conjunction "Nor," "The Poem" yokes together death and desire. "None" can withstand *either* force. "Venus" is an equal power among the Parcae or "Fatal Sisters." And, though Death began this oration, now it is Venus (Love) "who points" to American land and peoples; and she speaks "with proclamation," whose fulfillment, in *regular practice* by this nascent community, will carry Ma-re Mount's peoples away from that edge of doom where they stand, and take their "narrative" into the future. Their own actions will (hopefully) embody an answer to this prayer and riddle. "Cure" will come in time, through annual "keeping" of "hollyday." Scilla-Niobe's "grief" can heal only with the acted-on promise within most social ritual---that "life" will, somehow, go on.

"The Poem" asks for "new" understanding, and "points" the New World as the place where the twin inevitabilities of death and desire will join together in a powerful regenerative alchemy. There is no subtext of anxiety from what Bakhtin (432) called "official culture" that, as in Christian eschatology, these two "devouring" forces must lie down together as lion and lamb. Morton delivers their Ciceronian or ancient "pagan" circular configuration, as they were typically joined in philosophy and ritual in the temples of Cythera (see for example Pausanius' *Description of Greece* I, 3, 23: Cicero recommended "solace" rather than "solution" for the "problem" of death, in actions "partaking of a common *humanitas*"; qtd. in Lorch 78-80).

Ma-re Mount's proclamation speaks from and to a cosmos that, like Native New England's, is not "just" but infinitely malleable to those with shamanistic skills: it is a cosmos of "brass," in Sir Philip Sidney's famous terms, but with plenty of "gold" available, in the form of pleasant year-round consolations to those with the skills to exploit them.[116] It dictates that, while none can resist either death or desire, one can build a human(e) community amidst them, via "hollyday"---what Katherine Albanese termed the "balancing act" of nature-inclusive religious practices (23).

In Anglican Church terms, "the body is where God communes with us, where we show our worship" (Blunt *vii*). Choices are made in organization of a community, and through custom and ritual each community signifies, to itself, to others, to the universe, its choices: historical identity. Ma-re Mount, beginning with its 80-ft.-high horns "as a fair sea-mark" to bring in people and the bulk of the traffic in American wealth (134), signed to its neighbors in the vocabularies of

---

[116] Connors 78: "Morton's implied comparison [*Canaan* 53-4] of a real country" to Sidney's "golden ideal" world "is not altogether farfetched: it seems to be an example of what Tillyard would call an 'Elizabethan hovering between equivalence and metaphor,' (an instance of 'equivalences shaded off into resemblances')." All of which goes to say that Morton was suggesting America as about the closest thing to a paradise one might realistically expect.

seasonal rhythm, market-town economic intercourse, trade-sustaining human relations.

There were consequences for Native Americans in this trade and poetry, however, that must be recognized. Most invasively, "The Poem" and the Revels themselves carry on "*Though* Scilla's sick." Indeed, as with *Canaan*'s early remark that the epidemic "angel of the Lord" had made the land "more fit" for the English, "The Poem" and Revel capitalize in every sense on Native New England's human devastation. Scilla will be courted by these English, whether or not "she" (her desired community of fur-traders and "marriageable" women) understands what these "paramours" are saying with their words and dances. And they will "court" her at a time of grief she suffers partly because there is a supposed lack of "virtue masculine" in these still-populous Native American surroundings. The last verse of "The Song" to follow the solemnities of "The Poem," with its more accessible round dances, performs this colonization in an erotic cajoling of Native daughters for the sake of their wealth, as it calls for "Lasses" to follow their own warm-weather custom (Wilbur 83) and remove upper-body wraps, especially of course their "beaver coats."

But the invasive offenses within the "cultural work" performed by "The Poem" (that is, extension of "His Majesty's Empire," Native American subjection) are as integral to it as its "humane virtues" and "fair means." Morton's central metaphor of a "widow" for Native American land and peoples, an almost singular metaphor in colonial texts, puts in plain sight the loss of Native men rather than their fictive and convenient absence, as it "courts" Scilla-Niobe. And the phrase "virtue masculine" has something more cosmic than biological about it, more of the medieval apothecary or alchemical formula (as "The Song" does with its line, "This physic will soon revive his *bloud*"---*his* race---any male's---and *his* "melancholy" humor). Reading Morton's syntax carefully, we see that what keeps Scilla "sick," what keeps her from any hope of a future amid the wreckage of all she has known, is not, at last, the lack of a male at all.

"It" is specified as a "sign." Scilla remains silent, unable to answer "Scogan's choice," because she has been crushed by the apparent failure of her civilization and its apparently-displaced system of "signs" of meaning, perspective, understanding; by the failure of every traditional healing-practice that Native peoples must have tried to save themselves. Scilla's cosmos, once assumed fundamentally hospitable (Speck *Penobscot Man* 311), has rendered no cure, no countersign to the ritual appeals made by shamans, *sages-femmes*, and broken circles of Native kin-relations.

Morton's culture knew as little about "plague" as its American hosts. But in that void ripped open in Native reality, Ma-re Mount would place not simply its own Transcendental Signifier (the phallic "speaking" Maypole), but the entire Revel itself and its energies: "The Poem" and "Song" are three-dimensional speakings, performance-texts whose characters are living bodies; and they are moved by multiform American desires (for profit, freedom, eros). The Revel *is* the company's improvised offering of European "medicine," the best collective means for regeneration of the "tribe" through whom they want to get rich.

There is no question of the company's imperialist motive: there is room for new critical and historical appraisal of *all* aspects here. For Cronon, Morton was "almost alone" (80) in grasping the Native sense of living "richly": Goldberg (65) remarked the "egalitarian" cultural mixture here; and for Jennings (*Invasion*) the "widow" image alone was extraordinary. Ma-re Mount was in a contest with Plimoth for the New England fur-trade, and used ritual itself as "a present act which historically recalls the past for the purpose of reordering---even predetermining---the future" (Cope 170). Where the intrusive aspect of that "Though" in "The Poem" registers the colonialist project, an anthropologist of ritual like Victor Turner would simultaneously observe a rather typical "forcible aspect" noted in most rites that must call for a break with the past (*Celebration* 202).

Most importantly on this point, "The Poem" does not "act" as if Scilla *has* cooperated automatically; but ends with a warning and a hope for shared renewal. Constructed out of the *interdependence* of both trading-partners and of male/female, it plights a public "troth," to move "her" toward speech. The Revels both are, and call for from Scilla, a language and speech of connection rather than of lack: what one writer has understood in our own time as "acceptance," "of the irrevocability of absence by putting...death into words" (Wyatt 477).

Only if Scilla responds can the Revels achieve the opposite of a simple imperialist ventriloquism. It is an act more grave than, but not unlike, one of Wampanoag Sachem Ousamequin's, when he wondered to his Pilgrim guests that their King James "would live without a wife" (*Mourt* 66). The Revels, responding to and/or "reading in" the same "predicament," present the same question to a person understood to be suffering.

The early trade that followed inevitable contact was not so different from previous relations of trade that prevailed on both sides pre-contact, amongst the "races" or nations of Europe and those of America. Cohabitation, sex relations, intermarriage, seasonal rituals were all employed to *smooth over* the constant contests and offense-expiations that make up human intercourse; and these were salted everywhere with profit and fighting, cheating, dancing, murder, reconciliation and reveling. In early-colonial New England these helped the Mare Mount company over the resentments *they* inevitably roused in Native peoples for their intrusion into the land and its power-relations. Perhaps the only

Ma-re Mount distinction in Native eyes might be its lack of a *programmatically-applied* racial discrimination.[117]

At Ma-re Mount the typical early-New England "rule" had been pleasure expedient to short-term profit, the "haste" Lescarbot described above; which also produced the same imagery in French histories, of health and medicine found in shared activities.[118] A later colonial phase more characterized by outright violent conquest departed from these early forms of "gradualism" ("bringing them to civility"), such as Hariot spoke for in Virginia. The Dutch, treating for New Amsterdam trade through Algonquian Canarsee "daughters" (see Capt. de Vries' *Historiae* qtd. in Raesly 174), also came to scorn syncretism and intermarital methods, as did the French by the 1700s (Dickason 277).

But as we study the poetry at the center of "The Revels of New Canaan" we cannot discount the cultural reaching-out to Native peoples that was part of the Ma-re Mount colony. Young New England missionary Thomas Mayhew, 14

---

[117] See Shurtleff, ed., *Records* of the Mass. Bay Colony, whose courts in March 1631 (not long after Morton's 2nd exile) ordered "all persons who had Indian servants...to discharge them by May 1," and that "none" should thereafter "take Indians into their households without permission of the Court" (1-83). In his appeals for Council support against rival "irregular" traders, Governor Bradford of Plimoth offered to increase profits by trying to stop "the unprofitable consuming of the victuals of the land" by "these salvages" (1628: *Letters* 56).

[118] "We spent this winter very pleasantly, and fared generously by means of the *Ordre de Bon Temps*, which I introduced. This all found useful for their health, and more advantageous than all the medicines that could have been used" (Champlain c.1604-7, *Voyages* [1907: Grant ed.] Ch. 16, p. 110). See the same "health/medicine" metaphor in Lescarbot's *New France* Bk. IV Ch. 16.

Note that Huron peoples also devastated by epidemics understood enough of Champlain's offer of French-Huron intermarriage in order to reject it (Thwaites *Relations* 5:211, 14:17-21). Native contexts do put *English* "ritual behavior" in interesting light. Dozens of Renaissance scholars write of masques and court-revels as above all concerned with making "subjects" (in every sense) of their participants. Native New Englanders were not without forms of "subjection" correlating with material and other status (Simmons "Shamanism"). But they must have looked wonderingly at rituals that deployed every kind of normally-restricted pleasure (*haute cuisine*, music, dance, magic, "emblems," drama, eroticism etc.) in order to invest "leaders"---by illusion, confusion, transference---with powers that meant participants' own increased subjection. (Lavish masques bankrupted aristocratic England toward Civil War.) At another ritual, Mohawk people reacted thus: "When we pray they laugh at us....and... ask me what I am doing and what I want, that I stand there alone and make so many words, while none of the rest may speak...." (Rev. J. Megapolensis, 1644: rpt. in Jameson ed., 175-180).

years after Morton, saw likewise on Martha's Vineyard "that a way to gain the confidence and respect of the Indians, and so further settlement by the English, was to compete with the powwows, as they competed with one another, as healers" (Mavor and Dix 157).[119] Many sources on just the visible, structuring aspects of Native public ceremonies suggest a Ma-re Mount attempt to connect with those traditions.

A shaman or powah guided people through a ritual *acting-out*, to envision, diagnose the problem and remedy it with the group's participation. The aim was a ritual, sometimes including the use of narratives[120], which "dramatized" the fact of sickness, the powah's power to heal it, and the cure of the patient whose "energies" had hopefully been thus galvanized. Music, dance, call-and-response ---"These do begin and order their service and Invocation of the Gods, and all the people follow, and joyne interchangeably in a laborious bodily service," Williams observed (189-92). Winslow described "arbors" or "bowers" of rushes raised at

---

[119] Scholars of Northeast Native American cultures including Frank G. Speck, Elisabeth Tooker, Bruce Trigger and William S. Simmons have shown both variety and "great conformity" in the religious and shamanistic practices of the region (Speck, "Penobscot Shamanism" 242): they and others (Fogelson, Hallowell *Conjuring*, Vogel, Wallace *Death and Rebirth*) also provide useful detail on the varieties of shamans/"powahs," their purposes and practices. Some healers specialized in herbal medicine: compare with *Gesta*'s and Ma-re Mount's distribution of "Nectar" to heal ailments listed in their respective "Song[s]." A second kind of powah organized and conducted rituals centered on magical counter-spells, dancing and audience-interactions (Heidenreich 373); and a third variety cured via the interpretation of dreams. The two principal acts in all were diagnosis and treatment. Speck's description of a powah's "penetration in a dream vision" to the "spiritual forces" that underlay a material condition (260) was not far from early Europe's "Asklepian" school rooted in Bronze Age magic/medicine. Winslow's *Good News* (583), Williams' *Key* (128) and Wood's *Prospect* (101) supply observations on these Native New England practices.

[120] These might include retellings of myths, recountings of tribe-historical acts or achievements by other healers, or a use of short "anecdotes" that communicated healing-helpful incidents of "common people" using magic powers. Not only an attempt to "raise healing energies," this constituted an analytical use of language (as opposed to trance-inducing "vocables"), which could help to identify sources of disease related to breach of taboo, or to behavior or ethical issues. Broader contexts: studies by Toelken and Zolbrod in Swann, ed., *Recovering the Word*. The former shows how, in Navajo tradition, "words and narratives have the power to heal" (396), while Zolbrod studies Western "chantway" customs, in which rituals/narratives "merge" patient with myth-protagonist, the former thereby "taking up quest" for cure.

Native ceremonial places "as Apollo and Diana had temples" (583-4; see also Bragdon *Peoples* 219). Wood wrote that "all the auditors" of the powah's performance "with one voice utter[ed] a short canto," a sound "like a quire" to Williams (192). There were also, his *Key* added consistently with *Canaan*, other kinds of "Solemne speeches and Orations," "Lectures...concerning Religion, Peace, or Warre and all things," heard "sometimes" by "neere a thousand."

Surely all these cultural forms (not to mention the round-dances to follow with "The Song") were deliberately blurred together within Ma-re Mount's colonial purposes. Through them, a crystallized moment of early-intercultural human history, one very much worth knowing about (and exploring further), comes into view.

9: *Banned in Boston: Second Exile,* Canaan, *and Revenge*

> Most Loving and Kind Father and mother, my humble duty remembered unto you trusting in God...to let you understand what a country this new England is where we live.... Here are but few indians and a great sort of them died this winter, it was thought of the plague...They are a crafty people and they will cozen and cheat, and they are a subtle people ... And whereas we did expect great store of beaver, here is little or none to be had, and their Sagamore John [a Massachusetts son of the Great Squa Sachem of Mystic] weigheth it....
>
> Here is some good ground and marsh ground but here is no Michelmas spring...Here are good store of wildfowl but they are hard to come by...It is harder to get a shot than it is in old England...And people here are subject to disease, for here have died of the scurvy and of the burning fever two hundred and odd, besides many lie lame...Here is nothing to be got, without commodities to go up into the east parts amongst the indians to truck...We cannot live here without provisions from old England...We do not know how long this plantation will stand....
>
> (edited letter of "Walltur toone in
new eingland the 15 of marche 1630";
in WPF3: 17-19)

This, a morning's walk up the shoreline from Thomas Morton's Ma-re Mount, was the state of the Puritan vanguard that had deployed ahead of John Winthrop's Mass. Bay Company and the vessels of the "Great Migration." With their arrival and their stocks of outside supplies, conditions about "the hill" in nascent Charles' Town and "Boston" Neck improved, but with a mortal slowness unfortunately typical of plantations begun by these east-England yeomen, gentry, urban merchants and craftspeople (Fischer 27, 32). Leaders Winthrop, Dudley, and Prince wrote of their disembarking people that, though well-provisioned, many stepped ashore already sick, "which increase[d] for want of houses, and...no fresh food to cherish them" (their various texts qtd. in Young *Chronicles* 316-319).

Game was still plentiful, much because of the epidemics decimating Native communities, but the crucial colonial turn came only after Winthrop's hundreds fanned out and planted the surrounding "champion grounds" with food-crops (Morgan 56-65). Morton of Devonshire watching this tableau must have felt bitterly confirmed about some things, which would not help him to hide his scorn when he finally did meet Winthrop and company. Considering their opinion of Morton's "cultural type," and of others considered "without" their church-congregations (including the helpful Blackstone and Maverick), there was little chance of cooperation either way between these colonizers. Not even of "imployment" for the probably-floundering, skilled but "carnal" hunter, to provide "fresh victuals" (180).[121] Too many of England's and America's conflicts stood between them.

John Winthrop was 12 years Morton's junior, born in 1588 at Groton, Suffolk: this was an "old monastic estate" purchased, under England's dissolution of Catholic monasteries, by Winthrop's father a London cloth merchant, and which had grown prosperous on land-rents and "the rising metropolitan demand for foodstuffs" from nearby London (Hosmer 1:5; Morgan 5). As a young country gentleman Winthrop shared in his way Morton's confident assumptions on the rightness and need (or not) for hierarchies social and religious. A journal-writer from early days, Winthrop considered himself very sensually "disposed" as a youth ("Christian Experience" 154). The "notions of God" within his family's Christianity demanded a "spiritual combat" against this,

---

[121] Blackstone and Maverick guided Boston's colonists to better sites than Endicott had chosen: they (and Thos. Walford) became early claimants that "they were as good live in Turkie as live under such a government"---qtd. in Rose-Troup, *Mass. Bay* 55.

but he remained (he wrote) "very wild, and dissolute, and as years came on my lusts grew stronger, but yet under some restraint of my natural reason."

From this period Winthrop emerged with the same significant knowledge that Morton had grasped from between the lines of his education: Winthrop discovered that he "had the command of myself that I could turne into any form. I would as occasion required write letters etc. of meer vanity; and if occasion were I could write others of savory and godly counsell." He saw that he was going to have to learn to "fashion" himself, as people said it then; to *participate creatively* in constructing the man he would become, as well as yield to the traditions and compulsions of culture and country.

But young Winthrop was not, apparently, helped as Morton had been (by his early physical and intellectual educations, by moots and pageants alike at the Inns, by the cosmography and cosmopolitan travel literature of Classical and Renaissance Europe), to feel at ease with such insights; to become creative in the midst of a "troublingly" relative or "fictional" human universe, where "vanity" and the "godly" are equally subjective and produced. (Shea 53 finds this awareness of "fictionality" in Morton, while Shakespeare had as usual said it for the age: "nothing good or bad but thinking makes it so.")

Winthrop's social class may have provided him with the same quality of education, but his writings reflect zero enthusiasm for the existential comforts of secular culture.[122] Morton had learned to delight and find "solace" in the "mere play" of wit (becoming a so-called "cynic" or "atheist" like his Inns fellows---"Hell is in Westminster" etc.). Winthrop searched and suffered for a more external and

---

[122] Bercovitch claims that "the emigrants derived their concept of errand [that is, their "errand into the 'wilderness'"] from the Elizabethan premises for national election"---*Puritan Origins of the American Self* 72. Yet Winthrop's words relating to Morton, as well as his writings, echo far more of the ethnocentrism ("election") found throughout The Old Testament's Israelite invasion of Canaan/Palestine. Morton could imagine his rivals ironic English "knights" (149), but he dubbed Winthrop "Joshua" for reasons.

literal sense of control over his powerful mind and passions; and as he matured, he realized where his nature was mostly at peace. Despite all his confessed "wickednesse" he had never felt himself "scorning religion" (meaning his father's Puritan variety of Christianity). "I had no temptation unto [such scorn] in regard of my education" ("Experience" 154).

Married with children by 18, trained to preside over his father's manorial court for tenant-disputes by 21, Winthrop spent the next four years (1613-17) at Gray's Inn, seen above as the site of *Gesta* two decades before, and now an increasingly Puritan-affiliated body. He returned home a justice of the peace, man of property and growing social connections. William Perkins, the celebrated Puritan divine quoted in Ch. 1, was an influence Winthrop recalled in his spiritual notebook (156) as his thirties wore on, between his passionate sensuality and aspiring-Christian values.

The same economic depressions that drove Morton's choices in the 1620s took Winthrop to work as a "common attorney" in the Court of Wards and Liveries (managing lands and rights of minors for the Crown). But as he and Morton moved through England's systems, society, and situation toward America, early events and choices began to tell for their experiences there. Deeply in love with his wife and (like Morton) enamored of field sports, his inner torment over his pleasure with hunting reflected perhaps a common need for deep relation with the world, while keeping himself also (in his words) "dead unto" it ("Experience" 165: Morgan 13-17). After accumulating his arguments, Winthrop resolved to quit hunting and to take up disapproval of it, his final point being that his skills were so poor that he "most commonly" brought "nothing" home in the game-bag. One assumes that, in synch with above-seen trends toward economic "abstraction," he began paying money to others to put meat on his daily table.

This choice not to work at or maintain those skills may have proved Winthrop's intensifying Christian practices, but it deprived him and others of "victuals" full-within their grasp in New England. It was one of the ways in which this period's challenges turned into crises, and "confirmed" Old World assumptions about "wilderness"---ideas of America avowedly more embattled than the fishermen's and traders'.

Winthrop was also the man to set down the central first documents of the "Great Migration." He along with Rev. John Cotton was called upon to satisfy the sensitive and sincere consciences of thousands of emigrating countrymen, who were explicitly aware of the need to explain and justify their impending, massive appropriation of Native American lands. (Remember that in Virginia this had already resulted in thousands of English deaths by ineptitude, harsh labor, and "Indian wars": the Crown was eager for profit, not for more quasi-Spanish colonial guilt and embarrassment.) But Winthrop found little in his background to motivate any effort to balance this duty of conscience for his people, with the fact that Americans had *their* time-honored ways of inhabiting, "investing in," and enjoying "rights" in their land. It was not difficult in England then to learn about worlds and peoples of unquestionable achievement who had reached it without any regard to "modern" European cultures and religions. Greek and Roman sources as well as a marketplace of New World texts were plentiful.

Instead, the young governor's "Reasons" (*Papers* 2:141) decided that a "Civil" or legal right to land had originated in European-style cattle-breeding (which included manuring, enclosure of pasture, etc.); and that this created rights in land superior to Native Americans' merely "naturall" rights. (This construction of his own acts into something "higher" than nature, critics today would call a "trace" of Winthrop's boyhood with The Bible.) On this basis and surrounded mostly by fellow "believers," it was not necessary to explain how Native

Americans could have been expected to "develop" into Palestinian pastoralists without cattle. (Jennings' *Invasion* 80-81 traces the development of this self-entitling discourse in Samuel Purchas' and Captain John Smith's influential writings after the 1622 Virginia "Indian uprisings.") But, as we have seen, if Winthrop *had* wished to know more before dispossessing unseen civilizations, informtion was available. Martyr's, Hakluyt's and others' widely-read collections, and other pamphlets of the day (see for exs. Cox and Hodgen) would have informed him of the reality of other realities.[123]

Instead, by 1630 Winthrop's much-revised writings described *the ground of love* (the "ground," that is, of a full place and share in "the" community) as *a resemblance*. Metaphorically, this meant resemblances instantly understood, like those often felt between children of the same mother (Winthrop's terms). In the new life being constructed by the "migration" and by Puritan writings like this ("A Model of Christian Charity"), resemblances meant qualities that could only be known ideologically, between mutually-recognized members of a church; who together, like the Biblical Tribes of Israel, "put a difference" between themselves and others deemed insufficiently "godly" ("Charity" 284, 290).

While this made relations workable among Salem, Charlestown, Plimoth and Boston Bay, England's larger social struggles increasingly concerned the reform-program *decrease* of resemblances between the English worlds of Winthrop and Morton. Chapter 1's historians have debated whether the "old England" longed for in sources was "utopian," but the first Mass. Bay Court did

---

[123] Another lawyer turned colonist, then-noted historian of New France Marc Lescarbot: "For more than twenty-five years, the English have retained a foothold in a country called...Virginia....Soon after I published my *History of New France* [1609], there was an embarkation of eight hundred men to be sent there. It is not reported that they bathed their hands in the blood of those people, for which they are neither to be praised nor blamed; for there is no law nor pretext which permits us to kill anyone, whosoever he may be, and especially the persons whose property we have seized." "The Conversion of the Savages" (1610) in Thwaites, ed. *Jesuit Relations* 1:62.

legislate twice against *some*thing in an early three-year period, by way of economic wage-and-price controls to "protect the colony" against the consequences of labor-shortage (WJH1:112). Only certain men were to enjoy certain profit-margins. Already there were "idle" people about, who seemed "at leisure" because they had indeed begun to find their American way, could provide for their needs without "carking" (Morton's term for "anxious toil") every day of the week. The Court was unsatisfied that four days' labor appeared to meet people's needs; and as in Old (reformed) England, "sports" and Christmas (illegal by 1659) had no place in New. Native Americans, deemed "other Sonnes of Adam" by the Christian theory of a single Creation that had "degenerated" into diversity (O'Gorman 55, *Canaan* Book 1 Ch. 2), could offer the new Mass. Bay planters even less resemblance to themselves than a Thomas Morton.[124]

Seven weeks were left Morton between Winthrop's landing and Mass. Bay's first (August 23, 1630) Court, the Governor and Assistants gathering at Charlestown. Essentially because Morton stood for, if no longer practiced, the last century's "amoral" ways of getting New World wealth, he was the Court's first action "by process": "It was ordered, that Morton, of Mount Woolison, should presently be sente for" (Shurtleff *Records* 1:74: in its next business the Court ordered limits on what "carpenters, joyners, bricke-layers, sawers and thatchers" could charge for their labor). But till Morton was brought before them

---

[124] Winthrop's "unabashed presumption of superiority which was to carry English rule around the world" was formed through his early enjoyment of presiding at his father's manorial court, where the disputes of social inferiors (such as those who did his hunting) were "settled" (Morgan 13, 60). His "solemnity of manner" alone won Native "respect," Morgan writes, "and he took care that relations should be on his terms, not theirs" (Jennings' *Invasion* concluded its detailed study the same way 40 years later). See also Winthrop's 1631 night spent lost in woods less than a mile from his house (WJH1:68), through which he sang psalms and sheltered in a Native *wetu*. Morton with his outdoorsman's pride saw no reason to take moral direction from a spatially-disoriented "Joshua." At the *wetu* (probably like Morton earlier), Winthrop "met" a Massachusetts Native woman: that is, she came there to use the bark shelter herself for some reason, and he somehow closed the "door" and kept her out until she left. She may have been performing what Vaughan (347) called "the old ceremony" of a woman "walking alone" during her menstrual period.

two weeks later, they were unable to develop any charges based in English statutes or (for that matter) proclamations. Adams suggests that Morton was first captured and held at Salem for the Court, and "made regularly to attend divine service" while there (AC326).

Outside of Court records, Winthrop said Morton had been "exciting jealousy and discontent" among the old planters (WPF1:57). Maverick mentioned Winthrop's further claim of a Morton "design to sett the Indians at varience with" the new colonists (Letter 40). But neither Adams (AC40-44), Ford (FBH2:74-77), nor anyone else has substantiated a crime that the Court might have seen fit for public record. The action was "in fact summary" (Adams), officially the first of its kind in Massachusetts. Morton, Ford wrote, "fell under" the new legal system, "fell into" the Court's custody, appearing on September 7; and the Court settled for this language:

> It is ordered by this present Court, that Thomas Morton, of Mount Wolliston, shall presently be sett into the bilbowes, & after sent prisoner into England, by the shipp called the gifte, nowe returneing thith[er]; that all his goods shalbe seazed upon to defray the charge of his transportacon, pay[ment] of his debts, & to giue satisfaccon to the Indians for a cannoe hee uniustly tooke away from them; & that his howse, after the goods are taken out, shalbe burnt downe to the ground in the sight of the Indians, for their satisfaccon, for many wrongs hee hath done them from tyme to tyme. (*Records* 1:75)

By this (complete) entry, the charges are the defendant's unspecified "debts," and a kind of canoe-rustling. No Native plaintiff is named, as they are in later cases of record; though there is Wood's description (91) of another gentleman's arrest not long after Morton's, Sir Christopher Gardiner's (*Canaan* Bk. 3), which was managed at last by intimidated deputies when he "commanded waftage" over a river in some Native people's "ticklish wherry," and they tipped him over. Morton, then, may well have been running from Mass. Bay antagonists when he unjustly borrowed a ride across an obstacle---and laughed at them into the bargain, just as he'd slammed the door loudly behind himself in giving Standish the "slip" in 1628.

History must not excuse Morton's own undoubted offenses against Native peoples. But is important to weigh in both his relative record, and the fact that so little (even this) is certain.

Not till the next Court session (Sept. 28) were any laws written against Native gun-traffic and training. Yet Morton was not allowed to "capitulate" or discuss with the Court "wherefore they [were] so violent to put such things in practice against a man they never saw before" (170). Standing stiffly, and hailing like Winthrop from the Inns, he tried to "decline" the Court's jurisdiction, trusting (as with Endicott before) that these Assistants respected the essential condition of the Crown's grant, that they institute no legalities "repugnant" to English law (see FBH1:330n1). But this was exactly not the place for lawyerly distinctions and maneuvers to receive anything but "discountenance" (Hale ed. Lechford xv: Eusden Ch. 3). Head of the Court John Winthrop, like Edward Gibbons standing guard nearby, had chosen the world in which he would build his identity.

The Court "all with one assent put [Morton] to silence, crying out, *Hear the Governor*" (171) and enforced its orders, "because"---in language Adams (AC44) attributes to Winthrop's "admonitory remarks"---"the habitation of the wicked should no more appear in Israel." There were no terms left but these, plus eristics, with which to "convict" and so banish Morton as the first "legal" act of "reforming" America.[125]

---

[125] This lack of substance behind Morton's "crimes" is also the finding of the two best-equipped, dedicated scholars ever to study his case. Nevertheless, the reader will marvel at the implied "necessity" and rightness created for this Court's actions in the prose of these scholars (for ex., Adams AC48: Morton's case was "strong," and yet there was "absolutely nothing to be said in his favor"). Their own careful accounts of the records and "facts" repeatedly admit very little warrant for the "anti-Mortonism" in American letters. Even the supposed "murder warrant"---detailed above, and seen by not one person then or after---these scholars granted was "nothing," and/or

Accounts agree he was set in the stocks: these must have been Boston's originals, built by a carpenter who christened them himself when caught overcharging the "state" for them (in Willison's notes). Maverick (*Description* 238) and Deputy Gov. Dudley (*Letter*) said that the order to burn Ma-re Mount "in the sight of the Indians" was carried out. Dudley adds the likely "message to the Indians" detail that Morton's hands were at some second public opportunity "bound behind him": this was probably part of proceedings that have been very much confused among the sources. Most basically (as will appear from details), Ma-re Mount was burned with Native people and Morton present. Having there heard Native people's remonstrations with his foes, Thomas was taken back to Boston by boat (from whose deck, he said, he saw the smoke rising); and then Boston was stuck with this "Lord of Misrule" in their midst.

---

utterly illegal for justice-of-the-peace Winthrop to have used, had it existed, in New England---let alone in Scotland or colonial Ireland (AC47).

Below is the first of *two* lists preserved in the documents published by Ford in "Paid For Th: Morton." As stated, the date on this *first* list---"Due to Ed. Gibons 10 Aprilis, 1629, upon his accompt, 17 *li* of beaver"---is a problematic one for existing "facts" of Morton's story.

The *second* list (printed in this book's *main text* to come) is left equally unclear by Ford. As for the goods, he only says that they were "probably" taken from Ma-re Mount houses and from "Nantasco," a site "across the water" at Nantasket where ex-Plimoth minister Layford, Oldham and others had gathered after 1623. There Morton likely had goods in a second storage, which someone reported. The *second* list's date is unspecified; but since Endicott in 1629 found, and did not disperse, the remaining company living at Ma-re Mount, it is unlikely that the houses (plural on *Canaan* 51) were "emptied" until the actual 1630 burning.

Here is the list printed *first* in Ford, word for word (monetary values excluded).

PAID FORTH: MORTON BY ED. GIB[BONS].

To Mr. Conant for vinegar	To Mr. Layford	To Pasco for a shirt	To Richard
To Frost for lether	To Mr. Bursley	To the store	For a shute of Clothes
For 3 pound of suger	For j gallon of Resaselis [wine]		For 10 lb. of Reasons [raisins]
Due upon an accompt...0.2.2		in mony...4.0.0	To Mr. Maverick...6.6.0
The parte of trade is sould to........10.10.6		More of debt.......................... 0.15.0	
More of Mr. Blackstone.................. 0. 6.0		More of Mr. Cribbe [Crabbe?]....... 0.18.0	
More of goodes sould......................... 2. 8.4		Lent 30 wt. of beaver....[supposed total] 14 . 7.10	

No doubt with the help of budding citizen Edward Gibbons, the houses were emptied of all goods, and these (along with more from an insufficiently-wary, separate store at Nantasket across the water) were all confiscated, before the burning of New Canaan. ("j" likely signifies 1).

j: fowling peece	j: pistolj: barrell of lyme	j: barre of lead
J: sithe [scythe?]	2 Rubbers 1 spade	18 trencher plates
2 meltinge ladles	It[?] 5 rugges used 2 traded	78*li* of leads
1 skim[m]er	1 saucer 21 hatchetts	21 *lb* of pewter @ 10*d* p
1 beaker	9 *lb* of powther	30 *lb* of shott
1 saw at Wessaguscus Sheete lead	j calking Iron	
j barbers bason 2 wast coate	4 lether botteles	4 ould howes [hoes]?]
j dram bole 3 *lb* of beades	hoppes	ji how [?]

As Morton describes his hard-fought efforts in flames (171), he cannot resist a parting shot at righteous ineptitude: he claims that Native people (condescended to by himself as "poor silly lambs") protested his treatment, and mocked the "Eliphants of Wit" for burning houses so "needful" at winter's door. As it turns out, Josselyn confirms that 1630 was an especially cold winter (Lindholdt 176).

Morton's and Winthrop's accounts here agree that the shipmaster of the intended *Gift* refused to carry Morton back to England, and that no replacement could be found except *Handmaid* (WJH2:267-9; MHSP XLIV, 255; AC45)---which limped, unlooked-for, into port weeks later (October 29), "Jo: Grauntes master," with all her masts "spent" or broken from sea-storms. The ship was unfit to sail until December; but Morton's is the one record of this agreed 4-month interval, when he likely malingered in Boston's first jail. (Dudley confirms he was "kept...prisoner *till* we sent him" (Letter).[126]

After *Gift*'s refusal, *Handmaid* seemed to bring the Court relief; but it also bore (apparent) news about anti-Morton colleagues back in England:

> [They] were enforced (contrary to their expectation)
> to be troubled with his company...wherein at length
> it was discovered that they...had run themselves
> headlong into an error....If they sent Mine Host away
> by banishment, he is in possibility to survive, to
> their disgrace for the injury done: if they suffer him
> to stay, & put him in status quo prius, all the vulgar
> people will conclude they have been too rash in
> burning a house that was useful, and count them men
> unadvised....(*Canaan* 190)

Perhaps like Oldham as Plimoth "agent" before, Boston's allies in England found "all too little" to work with, and suddenly Morton's social standing loomed large again, to the point that Boston began to collect 40 shillings from every "hand in this black design" (191). But then "In comes Master Wethercock [*Handmaid*'s John Grant] a proper Mariner"; and apparently Boston decided to try a previous strategy.

---

[126] If Morton's record stands alone on this interval of time (Book 3 Ch. 29), there is no incredible human behavior in it, nor anything inconsistent with the rest of what can be called his story.
  There may have been "lost" pages from other accounts: several documents concerning him have been found to be exactly the ones "lost" or "missing" from larger, still-existing archives. For example, the records of his admission to the Inns of Court (John Donne's and others' of the time exist); the pages from the records of the Council for New England which correspond to the years in which Morton possibly obtained a patent for New England land (Holly 8-9); the petition of "many pages," containing what Winthrop called "some truths misrepeated" (WJH 1:112), that Morton composed for his, Gardiner's and Ratcliffe's legal suit against Mass. Bay in 1634 (see below); any record of the "murder warrant"; the original 1634 "victory letter" he wrote from England to planter Wm. Jeffreys (its text survived in Winthrop's papers); Morton's final *series* of petitions for speedy trial and/or release from Mass. Bay's Boston jail in 1644-5; and, of course, the early "sheets" and at least 400 original copies of *Canaan*, mysteriously "taken" and/or confiscated between 1632 and 1638.
  On Master Grant's tack with his sailing-crew: while improvisation (such as Morton's in 1624-27) was an assumed part of almost every ship's voyage, Grant's maneuver (through Morton's lens) resembles others later recorded by Josselyn (*Second Voyage* 1674: 145) against the poorer and more needy sailors and fishermen, cozened by powerful supply-merchants into virtual "slavery," or driven by debts to them off their attempted "mortgage" land altogether, "to begin the world again" elsewhere---usually in the next "Indian Territory."

Back in 1628, the Plimothers had exposed Morton on the Isles of Shoals, a move that defensibly looked like frontier-standard confinement, but contained as well a gamble that he might conveniently perish. The same was tried now in December 1630: Grant, like Oldham, was given both "letters of credence" and instructions to "rid" New England of Morton "by one means or another." All this is alleged by *Canaan*: Puritan sources say nothing.

Grant was to "play the miserable wretch" (197), convince his sailors that their "master," driven by economic and seasonal factors, had somehow envisioned their best interests in a poorly-vittled winter voyage back to England, following along the southern "Indies" route "from island to island" (196)---and this with supplies "but for a month when they weighed anchor." If numbers of Puritans were still dying on their well-stocked emigration vessels, then a 9-month planned ordeal "shifting" for subsistence, with nothing at times but "a bisket a day, and [at last] a few Lymons" taken in at the Canaries (197), was something more than second-class legal process.

Morton knew these things. And so because he valued his own life, this time, he forced his captors to *hoist* him, by force and in public, aboard the exile-ship using block-and-tackle. He was trying not to amuse historians, but to make it clear to *some* witness that there was neither a defensible "mistake," nor anything like his own choice, in his being forced into the likely death-trap of a voyage (Maverick alone recorded the scene, Letter 42). It was a display, in case he did die, to help Mass. Bay to founder, amid allegations like the ones brought against himself.

Now he had another reliable strategy. He made sure to "cherish" the "poor sailors" with a few "pieces of pork" and with banter "merrily disposed," and so kept himself informed on Captain Grant's plans and moves, while keeping eyes open for French "enemy." (1626 had brought back war, and the "slug" of a ship lacked for powder "if they had met them.") The kinds of American experience soon to take up Morton's angry pen---"lessons" found in many texts around *Canaan*, that New World suffering and danger came mostly from ignorance, ineptitude, greed, willfulness, and malice---burned into his memory under the "Torrid Zone's" winter sun:

> [When] they let drop an anchor near the Island S. Michael's [in the Azores], not one bit of food [was] left for all that starving allowance of this wretched Wethercock [Grant]....Mine Host of Ma-re Mount (after he had been in the Whale's belly) was set ashore to see if he would now play Ionas...so metamorphosed with a long voyage that he looked like Lazarus in the painted cloath....(197-8)

A later, minor document reveals that Morton felt the lack of his "goods, monies and writings" (95) as he landed; that soon after his return he "repaired to Axbridge" (the Somerset town where historical record had found him---Ch. 4); and that he understood "it would be work enough now [c. Sept. 1631]...to pursue his complaint" against Puritan New England (94).[127] Scholars Baxter (283) and Ranlet (17) suggest that Morton's sure complaints to Sir Ferdinando Gorges and the Council for New England made "little impression" right away, but this is to hurry over the fact that Morton was 55 now: after a voyage that metamorphosed "Samson" ("Poem") into "Lazarus," he may well have needed to regain his habitual strength and vigor.

---

[127]Minor Wallace Major's groundbreaking 1957 *Dissertation* on Morton (much-cited but unpublished) brings forth this Morton-document cited nowhere else: a "petition" of Morton's to King Charles I's Court of Requests ("Bundle XXXVII, 1636, rpt. in *MHSP* LIX [1926], 92"), dated June 21, 1636---just as Morton was putting last touches on *Canaan*. In the petition Morton tries to date events with the phrase "in or about the year of our Lord God 1624" and adds that "your said subject [was] then minded to travaile and to make a Voyage into New England aforesaid, which he shortly after performed" (qtd. in Major 9). Further language there reinforces the 1624 arrival-date as Morton adds that "your said subject about twelve yeares since departed out of the Realme of England, and travelled into New England in the parts beyond the seas."

Bradford wrote that Morton now "lay a good while in Exeter" jail, but Banks (above) found no such record or complaint; and Adams and Ford agree it was unlikely (AC49; FBH2:76). Nothing came of any warrant, for "murther" or anything else (though just ahead in 1635, Morton's court-foe Edward Winslow still felt need to invoke it before the Council: no one seemed to notice).

For Sir Ferdinando, however, Morton's angry reports would have promised new ammunition for his, Captain John Mason's, the Earl of Warwick's and others' new motions to reinvigorate the Council for New England itself. With Morton amongst them by autumn 1631, in November these gentlemen "determined that there should be no repetition of the process by which the Massachusetts colony had come to exist (Preston 283): Gorges was eager to meet the "demand" of the Privy Council round King Charles for a clarified and newly-limited concept of "proper legal authority in New England" (284).

Charles, like his subjects, was part of a time when assumptions about power implied that others' gains were one's own losses: having dismissed Parliament ("I only threaten my equals"), Charles now meant to keep even Puritans across the Atlantic from even imagining themselves as "liberated" from his throne and its Anglican religious domination. Morton's complaints could prove useful as his and the New England Councilors' maneuvers commenced against Mass. Bay's charter.

Still, it took a year (into summer 1632) to achieve matters of legal record. If Gorges perceived a new chance to combine his ambitions for New England governorship with the discomforts of his aristocratic friends over Mass. Bay, he may have preferred to wait for witnesses besides his Mr. Morton: having profited from his doings, they needed more complainants not so vulnerable to the "morality" arguments that increasingly dominated public debates and collective proceedings. (This was a symptom both of Puritan "reform" and of the religious terms in which Charles, so far, was expressing his repressions of demands for rights and powers.)

These began to arrive. As Gorges's own Councilors worked to convince Privy members of their New England interests, one of his most traveled "spies" arrived back at Bristol an "exile" as well, Sir Christopher Gardiner (August 15, 1632: MHSP XX: 74, and below). By that November 6, the enlarged Council for New England decided (among many resolves) to engage a lawyer "to follow up the business of obtaining a new patent for the Council"---meaning that "all land grants made in the past were to be called in" and reconsidered, if not revoked (Preston 288).

In Morton's terms (198) this was "Jove's" first thunder. Given the ardor, labor, sacrifice and suffering that had so far built Plimoth, Salem and Boston, the threat of charter-revocation was just the nightmare that made Adams (AC48) agree with Morton on the "unadvised" aspect of banishing an angry and skilled attorney. Gorges' and the New England Council's new petition ("many sheets of paper" in Winthrop's words) was ready to lay before Charles' Privy members by December 19, 1632. Morton, residence unknown, may have worked overtime at this legal-brief-prototype of Book 3's narrative: he appreciated significant dates (as seen below), and this would be to return old Captain Littleworth something "to keep Christmas with" (168).[128]

---

[128] Morton was not the attorney of record till May 1635's *quo warranto* proceeding against Mass. Bay (*Records of the Council for New England* 129, qtd. in full below). But he was surely "the man" to compose that first complaint-petition of 1634. This document must have anticipated *Canaan*'s prose even more than the *warranto* does, and that it cannot be found is a loss to scholars of early American writings. A fourth witness was said to have been Dixie Bull, one of the earliest named "pirates" of New England waters (Winslow "Petition" 1635). First affiliated with the 1631 "Aquamenticus" (York, Maine) plantation attempt, Bull was a coastal trader and "interloper" on French territories: when they caught him and confiscated his vessel he garnered new operating-capital by plundering his colleagues' Pemaquid fishing-station, and he performed other perfidious actions which made him no friend of Mass. Bay. He was eventually driven back to England, where he died. See FBH2:142n1; and *The Trelawny Papers* (2 *Maine Historical Collections* III, 23). Bull's testimony, if any, has not survived.

Sir Christopher Gardiner, an English soldier of fortune and reputed "knight" (perhaps a "commoner" with a foreign coat of arms, like John Smith)---a man with "26 yeares" of "travailes in France, Italy, Germany, and turkey" (Dudley Letter) and "not unwilling...to take any paynes for his living" (FBH2:137), had gone to New England "to live a private life" just before Winthrop's flotilla in 1630, and settled on the Neponset River near Ma-re Mount. Before long, word had reached Winthrop of Gardiner's two extant marriages back in Europe, even as he "cohabited" at Neponset with a "comely" servant Mary Grove.

From that point in this nearly-erotic gossip, and when it appeared that Gardiner had been in contact with Gorges---Gardiner was hunted (Wood 91) and arrested. With his house ransacked and his servant married off to another before long (FBH2:138-40), he braved enough anger to make Boston think twice about its actions, and considering his connections too they tried to make his release more amicable. Gardiner left for Maine's fishing-stations and thence for England. In both countries he and Morton became friends enough to share poetry, and supported each other's anti-Puritan claims; but after Jan. 1633's Privy Council meeting (below), Gardiner disappeared from records. He and a Philip Ratcliffe, however, lent the complaint some volume.

Ratcliffe had gone to New England (likely in May 1629 with 20 other servants) as an advance-agent of Mass. Bay Company's Mathew Cradock, a merchant with a "semi-independent plantation in the colony to which [he] never emigrated himself" (Preston 435). If Ratcliffe was at heart an Anglican who "disdained" most of Puritan Separatism (177), he may have represented to the Bay some "center of disaffection" already troubling the leaders in their first year of hardships (Sept. 1630-June 1631). He certainly was made a public example. Winthrop records that he was "convict, *ore tenus* [by his own words], of most foul, scandalous invectives against our churches and government" (June 14, 1631:

WJH1:64). *Canaan*, like this first petition, offers more detail, recounting that when Ratcliffe sought to collect business-debts owed by Salem, he was "sick and weak, and stood in need," but was told "not to mind these transitory things."

Ratcliffe (less "circumspect" than Mine Host) had then "cast out" words to the effect that the Devil was the "setter up" of such a "church": Salem's Endicott prosecuted him before Winthrop, and Ratcliffe was "censured to be whipped, lose his ears, and be banished the plantation, which was presently executed" (WJH1:64). Morton's prose on this (Book 3 Ch. 25) is obviously part of his efforts for legal redress. But there is no portrait of such combined colonial sanctimony, greed and sadism that rings so far and frighteningly true across later periods of history and literature. Gardiner's poem (in *Canaan* 5) says he was "amazed" at Morton's accuracy, and Morton (179) praises the knight "then present" for interceding with Winthrop to save "part of [Ratcliffe's] ears." In the hands of editors Adams, Ford, Deane and others, Gardiner receives much the same scholarly discredit as Morton, while Ratcliffe is represented---as he was by his enemies at the time---as a "lunatic man" (for ex. editor Savage's note qtd. in WJH1:56).

If Ratcliffe was "lunatic," the less reason for Endicott's and Winthrop's actions. Savage notes that they pressed ahead despite knowing that English authorities would find out. Such "defiance" in the colonies gave Gorges and his lawyer momentum.[129]

---

[129] Ford (FBH2:141) termed Ratcliffe "demented," and Adams (A3EP 259) gave the "poor wretch" the excuse of being a "bondsman in a strange land and under a hard rule," and the "unsettled mind" of a "coarse, crazy, homesick Englishman." But as Adams (259-63) details how "typical" Ratcliffe's brutal treatment was, it grows difficult to tell one dementia from another. Salem's Endicott had recently been fined for "executing his own process" (260) by beating one Thos. Dexter for a "defiant speech" with "his arms on kembow"; while in England Puritan "radicals" were also being publicly mutilated by the Star Chamber and "ecclesiastical authorities," leading up to Archbishop Laud's "thorough" policies against dissenters against the Anglican Church in the 1630s. The 1640s brought the Lancashire and other "witch trials," Laud's own beheading (1644), and the English Civil War. In Europe, meanwhile, the Inquisition had recently entertained Galileo in Rome (1633).

On November 26, 1632, his witnesses ready, Gorges called upon the Privy Council's appointed "referees" to convene for investigation of Mass. Bay's alleged abuses of powers, powers which he believed threatened to make New England's Puritans too much a "free people" with "a jurisdiction independent of the Council," let alone that they were raising a "church without a bishop."[130] The dangers of sedition and rebellion against the Crown, and the laws of England, Gorges claimed, were plain to see. The witnesses were not heard until December 19, and from there the Privy Councilors made their own "preliminary" investigations; but in January, they issued a most unexpected decision. Despite

> ...the faults or fancies (if any be) of some particular men upon the general Government, or principall adventurers (which in due time is further to be inquired into), [we] have thought fitt in the meane time to declare, that the appearances were so faire, and the hopes so great that the Countrie would prove both beneficial to this Kingdome, and profitable to the perticular Adventurers, as that the Adventurers had good cause to go on cherefully with their undertakings. (*Acts of the Privy Council* 1:184, Grant/Munroe eds.; rpt. in FBH2:144-5)

The New England colonies had "faults," but these were not to be allowed to interrupt Charles' and the aristocracy's shares of American wealth if it could be avoided. In private, Mass. Bay's transgressions were painted small in comparison with the English moneys already invested in it, and with the lucrative future doubtless about to commence through unhindered "development." (Morton agreed that these colonists' "industry" would "very suddenly" shower their children with wealth, 55.) Adams (in his *Canaan* and

---

[130] Adams (AC51; A3EP265): That "even now" Mass. Bay "only needed a little more consciousness of strength to ripen on occasion into rebels" was "probably asserted in the document"; and "however Winthrop might deny it, the developments of three years later [fortifying Boston against government seizure of the charter, etc.] showed conclusively that this was true. In the light of their sympathies and sufferings, Gardiner and Morton probably saw the real drift of what they had heard said and seen done in New England a good deal more clearly than Winthrop." *Canaan* (142): "they were become...masterless people." See also Preston 291, 299.

Three Episodes) best explores how Boston brought this about against Gorges' formidable faction: Cradock himself (Ratcliffe's master), Sir Richard Saltonstall, John Humphrey and other Puritans well-connected with "high quarters" (A3EP266) had filed written responses; while Edward Winslow and Captain Thomas Wiggin (early Piscataqua planter) predictably familiarized the Councilors with "moral" transgressions behind each Gorges witness.

Winthrop (WPF1:103) felt that written testimonies had done the work. But Wiggin and Winslow, working with Sir Christopher's, Ratcliffe's and Morton's "crimes," added a letter to Sir John Coke (then Privy Council Secretary and a judge who had ruled against a king's power to make law); and it brought in none other than now-Puritan George Miller, Morton's former son-in-law, to "witness" the "murther" charge (FBH2:76: Preston 292). Further, Winthrop, concerned about those "some truths" in what Morton might say even if "misrepeated" (WPF1:101), got his brother-in-law Emmanuel Downing also to write to Coke, and had him stress (via Mass. Bay's many emigrated shipwrights) the colony's potential value as a source of naval stores and new ships. This was a powerful appeal in a country so lacking in natural resources of commodity value.

But it was another courtier, Sir Thomas Jermyn, an old Parliament-opponent of Gorges (FBG2:145), also of the Privy Council and a Virginia investor---who shuttled most effectively between the Council faction for profit-first, and King Charles himself, whose financial needs and religious piety were both stronger than his father James'. Charles, in fact, "said, he would have them severely punished, who did abuse his governor [Winthrop] and the plantation (WJH1:101; FBH2:142). In Preston's words, "the powerful interests which had enabled the Puritans to obtain their charter in 1629 were still operating on their behalf" (293; also Palfrey 1:391). For the moment, Winthrop and Bradford rejoiced (WPF2:120).[131]

Morton (now 57) appears nowhere but in the papers of the power-struggles: we have nothing for his next 15 months (while Gorges' stymied Council pondered) except a hint in *Canaan* that, when not working, he tended to disappear into whatever family life he possessed.[132] Except for his book, will, and minor documents, his one other writing comes from this period (below); and though it shows how dynamic a time this was for him despite initial defeat, it is not clear whether Gorges' high-level pressurings, or King Charles' own situation, most led to the next turn in Morton's career.

Back in 1628 a Puritan-dominated Parliament had forced Charles to sign the Petition of Right (against arbitrary arrest and taxation): in 1629 Charles had somehow granted Winthrop's Mass. Bay Company its charter for the "Great Migration," and now the 1630s continued to multiply tensions between them. In 1630 Charles had drawn his line and declared "personal rule," dissolving Parliament to deprive Puritans of every political power he could: Puritan ministers were ousted, whipped and/or jailed, their writings banned or burned. A cloth-industry depression had also hit Puritan gentry hard, increasing public

---

[131] Adams (A3EP282), Preston (292) and Ranlet (18) seem certain that Charles' rebuke to Gorges' attack on Mass. Bay included indignation "for [Gorges'] association with individuals like Morton and Gardiner"; but *they* are citing only Bradford and Winthrop (citations given above), in whose language on *this* incident this editor finds no mention of either Gardiner or Morton by name. See also *Records of the Privy Council* 1-184. As noted below, when Morton and Winslow *later* tangled face-to-face before the Commission of 1635-36, Morton *was* rebuked (on likely grounds detailed below, not necessarily for his "moral character"), and Gorges and Mason were chided for "countenancing" the work he had been professionally retained to do. It may seem "poetic justice" but it is factually inaccurate to apply this rebuke to the earlier episode.

[132] He punned, as he began to write in this period of Bishop Laud's ascendancy, that he used *The Book of Common Prayer* "in a laudable manner amongst his family" (142); and that his will tried to provide only for a "neece" suggests that Morton had only a single sibling's family as his nearest relations. Alice Miller (Note above) died sometime between 1623 and 1636. If she was alive in the 1630s perhaps Morton paid a visit and this renewed George Miller's interest in helping the "murther warrant" along. It went nowhere.

disorders among the now further-unemployed working classes; and as Charles strove to maintain "divine right" with dubious money-raising policies that worsened most troubles, his Courts of Star Chamber and High Commission prosecuted all opposition to himself and the Anglican Church's forms of worship. Preston (Ch. 14) assembles many letters and private papers to show that Gorges took shrewd new stock of Charles now (1633-34), and devised a plan for "his" New England that fit the King's ways hand-in-glove.

By the time the conservative Anglican Bishop of London William Laud was appointed Archbishop of Canterbury (Sept. 1633), Gorges had all but convinced him to inform the King that only a new "Commission for Foreign Plantations" could restore in America the conformity demanded in England. Without such measures---including "persons of honor" like himself to forward respect for the divine origins of royal power---New England's church and political independence would cause its natural wealth to fall in the end into French or Dutch hands. It was true that English-Dutch rivalry was about to intensify over the Connecticutt River Valley's manifold riches, with Native peoples caught between: Morton's old friend John Oldham led Englishmen overland to its banks in 1633 (spreading epidemic along the way, Natives later claimed); and the Cotton and Hooker congregations said their goodbyes this same year, the latter destined for Pequot lands on the Connecticutt River.

And so by early 1634 Gorges' ambitions, and Charles' and Laud's "thorough" purposes together began to act on what was "at last...a definite policy" (A3EP277). In February several ships with more Puritan emigrants were allowed to leave only after posting bonds with the Privy Council for their oaths of allegiance to Crown and Church: the same week, the Council issued orders for the physical return of the Mass. Bay charter, a most-telling sign of minds changing behind the scenes. Within two months (April 28) the new Commission was a reality, ready and ardent to continue under Laud that "preliminary" investigation into the 1629 grant of Mass. Bay's powers. As New England's Roger Williams stepped up his defiant denials of the magistrates' demands for oaths to themselves, the Commission further thundered at Boston's backs, announcing its new empowerment to prosecute, even to execute---any nonconformists.

On May 1, 1634---seven years after his Ma-re Mount Revels, four since his second banishment---Morton composed the following letter to announce the turning of the tide. He sent its remarkable echoes of *Canaan* and other wit to a dependably unreliable party he knew, Weymouth "old planter" William Jeffreys in New England. In those hands, with luck, it would be most provocative all-round, and thereby enlarge the author's revenge.[133]

> My Very Good Gossip,
>
> If I should commend myself to you, you reply with this proverb, *propria laus sordet in ore*[134]; but to leave impertinent salute, and really to proceed. --You shall hereby understand that, although when I was first sent to England to make complaint against Ananias and the brethren, I effected the business but superficially (through the brevity of time). I have at this time taken more deliberation and brought the matter to a better pass.[135]
>
> And it is thus brought about, that the king hath taken the business into his own hands. The Massachusetts Patent, by order of the council, was brought in view; the privileges there granted well scanned upon, and

---

[133] Morton had few good things to say about Weymouth planters: they seemed to lack his "old England" social code (for ex. Bk. 3 Ch. 11), though they also lacked a Puritan religious one. In the light of his intentions Morton was "right" to mistrust Jeffreys with the letter, but "wrong" to think there would be no consequence to himself for it (Ch. 10).
NOTE: The original letter is "lost": Winthrop's Journal (WJH2:194), followed here, has been the source of all reprints (such as MHSC 2nd series VI, and Hubbard 428-30). Text is not collated with those reprints. Some punctuation, all paragraphing modernized.

[134] *propria laus sordet in ore*   No source consulted includes this "proverb" but its Latin roughly translates, "One's own praises make a shabby speech"

[135] **Ananias**   as in *Canaan* (164), likely Increase Nowell, Mass. Bay "collector"

at the council board in public, and in the presence of Sir Richard Saltonstall and the rest, it was declared, for manifest abuses there discovered, to be void. The king hath reassumed the whole business into his own hands, appointed a committee of the board, and given order for a general governor of the whole territory to be sent over.

The commission is passed the privy seal, I did see it, and the same was 1 mo. Maii [on May 1st] sent to the Lord Keeper to have it pass the great seal for confirmation; and I now stay to return with the governor, by whom all complainants shall have relief. So that now Ionas being set ashore may safely cry, Repent you cruel Separatists, Repent, there are as yet but forty days. If Jove vouchsafe to thunder, the charter and kingdom of the Separatists will fall asunder. Repent you cruel Schismatics, Repent.[136]

These things have happened, and I shall see (notwithstanding their boasting and false alarms in the Massachusetts, with feigned cause of thanksgiving[137]) their merciless cruelty rewarded, according to the merit of the fact, with condign punishment for coming into those parts like Sampson's foxes with fire-brands at their tails.[138]

The king and council are really possessed of their preposterous loyalty and irregular proceedings, and are incensed against them; and although they be so opposite to the catholic axioms,[139] yet they will be compelled to perform them, or at leastwise suffer them to be put in practice to their sorrow. In matter of restitution and satisfaction, more than mystically, it must be performed visibly, and in such sort as may be subject to the senses in a very lively image.[140]

---

[136] **Ionas** *etc.* As in *Canaan*'s conclusion [198], this is Morton's nickname for himself after his 1630 exile voyage: **forty days** is from The Bible's tale of Jonah/Jonas, who told "heathen" Nineveh that Yahweh would destroy their city after 40 days if they did not "repent."
Jove King Charles I

[137] Boston held public "days of humiliation" in prayer for legal victory.

[138] **Sampson's foxes** In The Bible *Judges* 15:1-17, Samson sent the animals thus to set fire to the Philistines' harvest.

[139] **catholic axioms** poss. "traditional cultural ways" or "approved Anglican practices"

[140] **mystically...visibly** poss. terms from the metaphysics of Christian Holy Communion, for ex. that the offering-bread is the "visible" sign of the "mystical" body/presence of Christ
    subject...image poss. terms from aesthetic/poetic theories of Sidney and others

My Lord Canterbury having, with my Lord Privy Seal, caused all Mr. Cradock's letters to be viewed, and his apology in particular for the brethren here, protested against him and Mr. Humfrey that they were a couple of imposterous knaves; so that, for all their friends, they departed the council chamber in our view with a pair of cold shoulders.[141]

I have staid long, yet have not lost my labor, although the brethren have found their hopes frustrated; so that it follows by consequence, I shall see my desire upon mine enemies; and if John Grant had not betaken him to flight, I had taught him to sing clamavi in the Fleet before this time, and if he return before I depart, he will pay dear for his presumption.[142] For here he finds me a second Perseus: I have uncased Medusa's head, and struck the brethren into astonishment.[143] They find, and will yet more to their shame, that they abused the word and are to blame to presume so much,---that they are but a word and a blow to them that are without.[144]

Of these particulars I thought good, by so convenient a messenger, to give you notice, lest you should think I had died in obscurity, as the brethren vainly intended I should, and basely practiced, abusing justice by their sinister practices, as by the whole body of the committee, una voce, it was concluded to [have been] done, to the dishonor of his majesty.

And as for Ratcliffe, he was comforted by their lordships with the cropping of Mr. Winthrop's ears; which shows what opinion is held amongst them of King Winthrop with all his inventions and his Amsterdam fantastical ordinances, his preachings, marriages, and other abusive ceremonies, which do exemplify his detestation of the church of England, and the contempt of his majesty's authority and wholesome laws, which are and will be established

---

[141] **Canterbury** that is, Archbishop Laud   **Lord Privy Seal** Thomas Lord Coventry. See FBH2:183 and A3EP278 on these Council meetings. **Cradock and Humfrey**, Mass. Bay agents, had been ordered to arrange the charter's return, and it never arrived.

[142] **Grant** That is, "Master Wethercock" of Morton's 1630 exile voyage   **Sing clamavi** poss. "dog Latin" related to *clamitatio*, "a bawling noise"   **the Fleet** London's principal public jail

[143] **Perseus** Greek hero who learned the "Gorgon's" secrets, slew her, and used her head to turn his own enemies to stone (Graves GM1:237).

[144] **word, blow, without** Possibly, as *Canaan* repeatedly charges, this refers to uses of The Bible to justify policies etc.; so Mass. Bay is no sacred "Word," but a "blow" of "wind." Also, compare this different use of the term "without" with *Canaan* 177, 181.

in those parts, invita Minerva.[145]

With these I thought fit to salute you, as a friend, by an epistle, because I am bound to love you as a brother by the gospel.

Resting your loving friend,

THOMAS MORTON

After all else, the second appearance of mutilated witness Philip Ratcliffe and the Committee's outrage had turned the tide, and Morton rode it hard for all he had been through. Were the words about Winthrop's own ears a vicious threat from Morton, or legal justice for Ratcliffe?[146]

Given the literary echoes or anticipations of *Canaan* above, Adams thought that by this "heady" period the book was mostly composed (AC62; though 9 years later in A3EP285 he decided on after the letter). But despite hints of creative production it was unlikely Morton had time to turn his first "brief" and American notes (below) into something more, for he believed he would be back in New England by spring 1635 at Gorge's well-appointed side. Gorges (in his own late 60s) was already building himself a new ship and mustering soldiers for the enforcement of government judgments.

---

[145] These last sentences conflate various charges against both Plimoth and Boston: see Book 3 of *Canaan*.   **invita Minerva**   Latin proverb (ex. in Horace *Satires* 385)---"Contrary to the bent of one's [here, the Puritans'] genius" (Smith/Lockwood)

[146] Adams (AC60n2) calls the letter "a childish outbreak of delight and vanity" from a man "elated with a sense of his own importance" and "sure of his position": on 65 he shows that Morton was later "confirmed" in "everything material" he had written. Preston also finds this "vindictive boasting" (297). But it is normal for the man who (again) slammed the door behind himself in giving "the Worthies" the slip at Weymouth.

Bradford (FBH2:54 and *Letters*) says that William Jeffreys, perhaps originally of Robert Gorges' second Weymouth-expedition (1623), was a contributor to Morton's 1628 arrest: he is not on Ford's "Paid" list above. Adams (AC60) speculates that Morton and Jeffreys grew closer as Mass. Bay Company moved into the "old comers'" territories (citing MHSC VI, 3--a letter from Jeffreys to Gorges); but Ranlet emphasizes Morton's "deeper meaning" (19), his assumption that the "good gossip" would indeed deliver the letter to Mass. Bay. He did so by August (WJH1:130).

Those echoes show Morton with some poetics on his mind, and in his own hours he may have begun to take umbrage and inspiration from William Wood's just-published *New England's Prospect*, the then-clearest and most complete text on the subject.[147] But within two months of Morton's letter, as Boston's Governor Dudley was ordering the first fort at Castle Island, Morton also got a chance for revenge more directly upon the Plimothers who had jailed him first. As Gorges drew up requirements for a license and loyalty-oath from every emigrant (Preston 300), now-Governor Edward Winslow arrived in London on behalf of both plantations, and bearing careful procrastinations about the return of Mass. Bay's charter.

Morton was "procured" as Gorges' attorney, to oppose Winslow's request before the Commissioners that Plimoth and Boston be authorized to take defensive military steps against French and Dutch intrusions (FBH2:199). Gorges fought the idea because, while he wanted well-defended colonies, he feared helping to create a more expert Puritan force that might stand against his own next spring. This he poorly concealed, by having his attorney repeat their borrowed "morals and conformity" attack on church-practices at Winslow's Plimoth; which (they claimed) signified the same disloyalties as in Boston. Several charges did accurately describe Plimoth departures from Laud's strict Anglican forms (see itemized notes to Bk. 3 Ch. 27). But at this hearing, it must have emerged that these had mostly been made needful by the government's and Adventurers' *own* refusal to allow Plimoth's rightful and beloved minister, John Robinson, to join them in America. The Plimothers' poor luck with finding suitable "lawful" replacements had not helped them.

---

[147] As we compare Wood's sometimes punning, drily ironic jokes and carefully "plain style" prose with the "voluptuous discourse" of even Morton's man-of-letters letter, it grows easier to see why Morton dubbed *Prospect* a "wooden" production.

To Morton's accusing face Winslow "made answer, to the good satisfaction" of the Councilors, "who checked Morton and rebuked him sharply, and allso blamed Sir Fer'd Gorges, and Mason, for countenancing him" (FBH2:202).[148] Morton, rebuked for pressing his client's case, and Winslow close-behind, became scapegoats. Though Winslow (for the nonce Boston's spokesman) had answered nothing about Ratcliffe, the Commission was still unwilling to risk losing New England to satisfy Gorges (Winslow had spoken of "spring" invasion-rumors from French and Dutch). They were about to grant New England's request, when Archbishop Laud "now begane to question" Winslow about those church-practices. In moments, perhaps with a reminding wink from Morton regarding all his and witnesses' reports, Plimoth's governor was on his way to Fleet Prison for over four months. And so Morton found some satisfaction against both his New England antagonists---but the tables would turn yet again.

Meetings in early spring 1635 reflected Gorges' intensity, for in February new geographical partitions of "New England" were drawn up (Maine to Gorges, New Hampshire and Cape Ann to Mason, and to Lord Edward Gorges a cousin, all lands between Narragansett Bay and Salem). This was to take effect when Gorges officially surrendered the old Council for New England's Grand Patent: that was set for June and meant to erase every previous charter and land-claim. The move simultaneously relieved Mass. Bay (and the jailed Winslow) of pressure through the next year to return the charter as commanded, but this was

---

[148] Winslow's later petition for release from jail probably repeated what he said here: that Morton, first among "enemies to all goodness," had been "twice sent hither as a Delinquent"; once for trading and teaching firearms to Native people, and once for "murther" under a warrant from "Chief Justice [Hyde]" ("Petition" 133: see Note above on Banks' search through Hyde's records). Winslow also accused witness Gardiner as a "Jesuited gentleman" and mentioned the proto-pirate Dixie Bull as a Gorges ally: there was no word in Winslow's petition document, or in Bradford's *History*, about Ratcliffe.

also a promise of that document's extinction. Meanwhile, Winslow's petition for defenses against the French had been arrested too: near-total inaction resulted from a suddenly-apparent shortage of government funds,[149] and Gorges' faction fared little better just now. His grand new ship *Great Neptune*, built on the cheap, fell to pieces at launch.

But as Europe's gentlemen planned their investments, Native Americans kept losing land in all directions. New Netherlanders pressed their interests against several factions of New English along the Connecticutt River, and the Pequots there sued for peace and/or alliance (Jennings *Invasion* 196-7). New France-man Monsieur de Aulnay's forces took over Penobscot River trading-posts, while others drove Sir William Alexander's New Scots from Nova Scotian shores. Epidemics had "cleared" the land for Native survivors to be overrun, and in a second phase, the trade-commodities of "convenience" they accepted rendered them ever more dependent upon their invaders.

The Council compensated their colonizing-ally Alexander (Morton had read his bad poetry and approved his negative answer as to whether Native Americans "had religion"). They granted Alexander new tracts of land already claimed by France, generating fresh international confusions and realignments; and all this conspired with Morton's world of English politics to fully doom the Mass. Bay charter (Duncan 94). In June 1635, Morton and the Attorney-General filed a writ of *quo warranto* ("by what warrant") against Mass. Bay, "Mr. Attorney" still charging abuses of powers but, more fundamentally now, showing that the offenses had been committed under an assumption of "liberties" that the King

---

[149] 1635 was the year of the "ship money" case that revealed and worsened King Charles' financial problems, his legal dilemmas, and his tottering popularity.

had never intended to grant.[150] This writ was the legal curtain-call for arguments (if any) in Mass. Bay's favor: some small hearings went on, but by July 1635

---

[150] For scholars' convenience the complete text is below (rpt. in Hutchinson 101-3). It clearly reflects "Mr. Attorney's" personal conflicts with "the orders and constitutions of [Puritan] society" and so reveals ways in which his thinking and *Canaan*'s prose developed.

**A Quo Warranto brought against the Company
of the Massachusetts Bay by Sir John Banks Attorney-General.**

London: That Sir Henry Rosewell and all the Massachusetts Company named in the patent and others of the said Company in New England, for 3 yeares last past and more, used in London and other places, as alsoe in severall partes beyond the seas, out of this kingdome of England, without any warrant or royall grant, the liberties, priviledges and franchises following, *viz.*:

1) To be a body corporate and politique by the name of the Governor and Company of the Massachusetts Bay in New England, and by that name to plead and be impleaded, answer and be answered in all courts and causes.

2) By that name to be capable of purchaseing and retaining any lands, herditaments or goods from his Majesty or any other in England or elsewhere, and of aliening the same to any person.

3) Have severall common seales alterable at theire pleasures.

4) To make and sweare a Governor and Deputy governor, of themselves, and to name and sweare any persons either out of themselves or others, to be assistants of the said society, and to appoint and sweare out of themselves soe many officers in England, and abroad in Massachusetts Bay, as they please, and at their wills to displace and change any of them.

5) To admit whom they please into the said Company, as well aliens as others, and to take severall [sums] of money for such admissions, and at their wills to disfranchise whome they please, and turn them out of that Company.

6) To hold to themselves and successors all that his Majesty's territory of Massachusetts Bay in New England, and the same to sell, give or dispose of as they please, and to have the sole government of all that country and all persons there or coming thither or trading thither, by the orders and constitutions of their society.

7) To keep a constant councell in England of men of theire owne Company and chooseing, and to name, choose and sweare certaine persons to be of that counsell, and to keepe one councell ever resident in New England, chosen out of themselves and to name[,] choose and sweare whom they please to be of that councell.

8) To appoint councell houses in England and beyond seas and there, when they please, to hold a court of such of the said company as they please; and in such courts to make such lawes and statutes concerning the lands[,] goods and chattells of that company and other persons beyond seas, against the laws and customes of England, and all such, as well of the said company as others who are disobedient to the same, to imprison[,] fine and amerce and them [sic] to leavy and convert to their owne use.

9) To transport out of England beyond the seas his majestys subjects and others and them, at theire wills, to governe on the seas and on partes beyond the seas.

To have power, against the lawes and statutes of England, to transport thence into partes beyond the seas all merchandizes and othe things whatever prohibited by the lawes and statutes of England and all weapons and instruments of warr[,] powder[,] shott[,] victuals[,] horses[,] mares and all other merchandize custome free.

10) To exact of all persons tradeing there, his majestys or others, of the said company or other, certaine [sums] of money, at theire wills, and to imprison such as refuse or neglect to pay the same.

Boston's efforts were full upon their own frightened public meetings and the resolve to resist any "foreign" or newer-English governor's forces, by fortifying harbor islands.

Before long Morton was more officially "entertained to be Solliciter for confirmation" of the new patent-plans, and to keep driving the repeal of Mass. Bay's. He was promised "twenty shillings a [court] terme, and such further reward as those who are interested in the affaires of New England shall thinke him fitt to deserve upon the Judgement given in the Cause" (qtd. in A3EP284). The language may show Morton well-aware that this legal work was going to erase any land-claims he might have or pursue: his later claims in word and will (Ch. 10) must issue from promises made at this time. But whatever he was found "fitt to deserve" was either nothing, or erased against his heirs by the Civil War to come. Morton's victories by and large always seemed to evaporate in his hands.[151]

---

11) To have the sole importation, from thense, of all merchandizes into England and, by their owne authority, prohibiting any of theire company to export out of England any merchandizes or other things thither.

12) And to lay fines and amercements on such persons trading with any goods thither and to imprison theire persons and lay such lucts on theire merchandize as they pleased.

13) To use, in those partes beyond seas and upon the high sea, at their pleasures, martiall law.

14) And to examine on oath any person in any cause touching life and member and to proceed to try all[,] sentence[,] judgment and execution touching life and member[,] lands[,] tenements[,] good and chattells, against the lawes and customes of England.

All which franchises[,] libeties &c. the said Sir Henry Rosewell and others of the said company have, for all that time, and still do usurp in contempt of his majesty &c.

And Mr. Attorney prayes process against the said persons to answer by what warrant they held the same.

[151] The minor document discovered by Major (Note 29 above) shows Morton demanding payment of a small debt and spending plenty of time in court(s) through 1636 as attorney and citizen. Major, while working with a copy of *Canaan* and other papers then in the Boston Athenaeum, found another such document: it had appeared in *The Boston Herald* on July 9, 1930 and purported to be at least part of a letter from Thomas Morton "To His Niece, Sara." Major (77-8) thought it reflected "some sort of order for restoration at Merry Mount"; but when and where this "letter" was found was not stated in the original news-clipping in the Boston Athenaeum (told this editor by John Lannon, Curator of Rare Materials). In it, "Morton" says:

"His Majesty, Charles Rex, did give me this demand on the precise

Gorges doggedly saw to all the New England preparations he could, sending even kinsmen to Maine's Saco and Agamenticus. But in December 1635 the much-followed Mason died, crippling Gorges' faction further, and Morton like him was marooned in England by lack of resources. What he felt amid this impotence, even as Mathew Cradock let Mass. Bay's case slide into "default," is not recorded. The powers of Mine Host's New English rivals lapsed extinct. He had won what might be called the legal struggle: restitution "subject to the senses" remained beyond his reach.

Morton's hectoring hint in the Jeffreys letter, that he might soon return at the side of the King's new governor, gave Mass. Bay (and its historians after them) nightmares; but it was Morton's hint alone. Mason had been sure to receive any second's post (Rowse *Elizabethans* 118). French lawyer, American planter and writer Marc Lescarbot had never been "buttered" (Morton's phrase) with defamatory charges, his books had been applauded; and yet he received nothing but a vague brief "naval commission" and obscure retirement (Biggar *History* xv). The observed "self-importance" in Morton's letter may derive from acute knowledge of his middling station and social dependency---aggravated by the in-fighting and inept failures round him on all sides, and by the nostalgic memory of a freewheeling outdoorsman's best American days.[152]

Other signs of the times he probably disliked were the "end of the masque" signaled by 1634 production at court of Puritan John Milton's *Comus*;

> Puritanical Winthrop....This demand may more benefit you than me since were it to come to his hands he would verily burn both it and me."

If this is at all a true fragment of a Morton letter, it would fit well both with his high professional/social circles at this time, and with his later claims to be passing on genuine land-titles to this "neece" (details Ch. 10).

[152] Nevertheless the very last allusive phrase of *Canaan* shows that Morton kept indeed his own counsel about the gentlemen whose bidding he performed for a living. On worries of a "Mortonite" or Royalist domination see Adams (A3EP286; AC77-8) and Ford (FBH2:201).

and the death of Ben Jonson, not far off in 1637 as he worked on *The Sad Shepherd*. Morton kept abreast of Jonson's works and imitated his use of Greek myth to give human perspective to his very personal satires. Mine Host had the time for it now, he and Gorges waiting at the King's Bench for new and renewed commissions. As this took all the way to early summer 1637, Morton might at last put *New English Canaan*'s scattered parts into some satisfying, perhaps self-advancing form. This chapter concludes with *Canaan*'s immediate contexts of composition and publication.

With Morton's apparent goal a Court-ordered restitution of his New England *status quo prius* (190), and given the deep traditional dislike for Puritan cultural change that he shared with Gorges---"reform" to one party, "fantastical ordinances" to the other---Morton deployed every tried-and-true tool and body of knowledge he could manage (common law and equity courts, Anglican doxa, popular social customs of England and America, satire in poetry and prose), to maximize the appeal of his claims. Book 3's Chapters 24-28 and 30 against Plimoth, Salem and Boston emerged from the original petition with Gardiner and Ratcliffe: of the whole book, there Morton's anger and convenient shavings on "the facts" are most evident, and least balanced-out by *Canaan*'s overall literary wit and good-humored liberality.

He was now (1635-37) living on a kind of plateau, both stalled and anticipating full triumph. The harshest feelings for pure revenge had been vented in Morton's proto-Book 3 legal fights. Now he was able (calculated or not) to commend, in Book 2's first pages, Plimoth's colonizing energy, and to make of it an accurate promise that fantastic wealth would come of it (55). This was tacit assent to Puritan colonies' and progeny's right to exist and prosper, so long as they functioned first (as Gorges intended) to extend the King's Empire.[153]

The Plimothers, Morton surely knew, were finding their way at last, now shipping home the decade's largest consignments of "coat beaver" such that they drove the prices down in London (FBH2:173; WPF3:150). But there was little gloating in *Canaan* that, as early as 1632 with "undertaker" Captain Standish, both Saints and Strangers were leaving Plimoth behind for New England "elbow room." (Reverend Cotton had expressed the Boston leadership's disdain for "democracy" in 1636: WJH2:125). Equal numbers were leaving for the green pastures in which Mass. Bay's own needs for produce now spelled "opportunity" (Willison 291-312). It is not clear how closely Morton followed developments in Massachusetts thorugh this period, but there was no reason not to enjoy himself with his scathing portrait of "Joshua" Winthrop. He appears to have missed the melting-in-the-rain of Boston Harbor fortifications and of Winthrop's "building" at Mystic (Medford: WJH1:69), due to the needless lack of lime which he had found plentiful at Weymouth (79).

More gravely, the religious and social tumult in Boston Bay that peaked with Anne Hutchinson's trials at this time, the blistering accusations of exile Roger Williams (now of "Providence"), and the 1635 exodus of former Inns Master Thomas Hooker's congregation (which had also proceeded despite Winthrop's two-year resistance)---these heavy burdens of Winthrop's Morton breezily left to the "limitless endowments" of America itself to resolve. To him it

---

[153] The "old hand" Capt. John Smith had said much the same by 1630's *Generall Historie* (Arber ed. 2: 892). He mocked Plimoth's early disasters as "selfe-willed" (not least because they studied Smith's books "cheape" rather than hire *him* as "point man"), and admired their endurance of "a wonderfull deale of misery...with an infinite patience." Morton knew Smith's works enough to imitate the 1616 *Description of New England* (Barbour 1: 323) as he began *Canaan*'s Book 2: "In the month of April 1614 with two Ships from London, of a few Merchants, I chanced to arrive in New England...."

was all too ideological, too much like the notorious in-fighting that had brought down the fledgling Kingdom of Israel after the conquest of Canaan/Palestine. Of course, Winthrop and Hooker tried at least to articulate the politics of relationship among America's Christian "new creatures," but deeper expansion into Native American lands was their common non-resolution to English internal problems. "The land is so apt for Fountains, a man cannot dig amiss: therefore if the Abrahams and Lots of our times come thither, there need be no contention for wells" (90).[154]

And "for the natives in these parts," Winthrop had written home in September 1634, "God's hand hath so pursued them, as for 300 miles space, the greatest parte of them are swepte awaye by the small poxe, which still continues among them: So...God hathe hereby cleered our title to this place," leaving "not 50" under Mass. Bay's direct "protection" (WPF3:172). This second-most-deadly wave of European diseases killed Morton's former Sachem Chikatawbak, plus countless other leaders and people; who died "like rotten sheep" despite some colonists' efforts to help (FBH2:170, 194).

So, although Morton filled *Canaan* with uniquely powerful celebrations of New England beauty, and emphasized the human, cultural and ethical presence there of Native Americans by moving them to first place in his final text, his encouragements to more English colonizing---including his statements that "plague" had made the land "more fit" for the English---worked against Native peoples to the same effect as the Puritan "wilderness" ideology; which figured

---

[154] *Canaan* is full of evidences that Morton took active interests in both oratorical and poetic theory. He likely held the erudite Hooker a worthy Abraham: "Lot" seems more satirical and likely falls upon Cotton, with his more ardent Separatist speeches and publications. Details on these times are efficiently had in WJH1: 90, 105-6, 132-3. Plimoth's and Boston's parting of the ways over Connecticutt are detailed there too (165), and Hosmer's note on 232 relates other examples of how "unpleasant" a place Boston Bay had become. See also Jennings' *Invasion* 196-7 on the English affairs so crucial to Pequot and other Native peoples at this time.

America as either a place needing "order" by conversion or conquest, or as an "uninhabited, Thank God" land of refuge for nonconformists.

The "Paradise school" of colonial writers, drunk with the "kind of narcotic or aromatic liquor" of this garden and its potential profit (Verrazzano, Rosier, Brereton, Smith, Levett, even Higginson)---their works are not just "textual traces" of European "yearnings for paradise" (Kolodny *Land*), but the main register we have, outside of Native peoples' own orature, of the magnitude and depth of Native Americans' losses after 13,000 years on the land. "[T]hey replied...saying they were almost Beaver's Brothers" (*Canaan* 96). Narragansett Sachem Miantonomi spoke it first "on record" when he tried to rally *all* Native peoples to resistance in 1637: "You know our fathers had plenty of deer and skins, our plains were full of deer, as also our woods, and of turkies, and our coves full of fish and fowl..." (qtd. in Drinnon 60).

It may be that few other forces did *as much* as European romanticism to help protect the Western Hemisphere from what the colonizers called their inevitable capitalism, even while such early "counterculture" sang for its supper at the tables of conquerors. But, as we realize (with help from Thomas Morton and *Canaan*) the true range of people's awareness and options at the time, we cannot avoid history and its judgment of choices. Full respect, true practice of "moderation, and discretion," were more than wanting.

Was Morton in England informed of the excesses of "The Pequot War" (1637: Ch. 10)? It registered nowhere in *Canaan*; and unless sheer timing can excuse, this seems a notable omission from an argument for "moderation" towards the human beings whose points of view it includes in nearly three-fifths of its chapters. The poise and paradoxes of Book 1 (even the constant frank critique of Christians, not just Separatists) were either never seen by most buying readers in St. Paul's Churchyard (reasons below), or were too obscure, too "literary," too disguised for Morton's own polemical purposes and audience. The colonial juggernaut grew. And again, where Puritans worked to develop "justifications" and thoughtful if conveniently ethnocentric policies, Morton took an "artful" approach and posed, repeatedly, the fact of Native "content" with their own civilization (50).

In context of his peers and predecessors, Morton's was an outstanding move toward the multicultural (that is, culturally relativistic) practice and history of "the frontier." Like the Renaissance itself, *Canaan* was a breaking of new ground that revived older bodies of knowledge, buried beneath the feet of Christian, English (and especially Puritan) superiority, self-entitlement, and extremes of monologic. But beyond his many-styled literary breakthrough in the presentation of American facts and points of view, Morton had few serious practical proposals to offer, beyond the call for a general governor in New England: he mustered only a specious wager that the familiar evangelical follow-up to conquest would fail.[155] Perhaps, as *Canaan* said of businessman Andrew Weston (Bk. 3 Chs. 1-3), seven years' association with England's elite had led Morton to consider Gorges' plans to be "as much as he need to care for" (106) in the future of American lands and cultures.

Concluding this chapter are the facts-as-presently-known about *Canaan's* composition and publication.

Scholars note contradictory clues on the order of composition of *Canaan's* three main "books." It now appears that, as Morton began to create *Canaan* in the mid-1630s, he had before him at least a copy of his first long legal petition from

---

[155] "Butter and cheese will be cheaper [in New England] than ever it was in [Old] Canaan," he safely wagered, "as soon as the Brethren have converted one Salvage, and made him a good Christian" (91). Lechford (c.1641: 131) saw "much neglect of endeavors" to "teach, civilize and convert" Native people "about the plantations": the "Apostle to the Indians" John Eliot's first organized efforts toward missionizing came in 1646.

his ongoing suit against Puritan New England---that which was to become "Book 3." At this point he also "first" drafted/developed his notes and lists of New England "commodities," the raw material for "Book 2." (A minor document of his says that "writeings" had been taken from him in New England c.1630: his harsh 2nd-exile voyage likely prevented him from putting his lists back into "a rude lump at sea" as Roger Williams did.) These drafts of 2 and 3, he set aside long enough to draft all of Book 1 on Native New England; and then Morton continued to develop 2 and 3 into form coherent with Book 1's announcements of themes and subjects---most generally, the attractiveness of America and the need for "moderation, and discretion" in colonial affairs there.

With this manuscript-scenario, the tiny clues fit together. In Book 2 he refers (93) to coastal trees bent by the wind "as we have heard before" (that is, in Book 1 Ch. 1); so this must be Morton's at least-second "pass" through his commodities-lists as he develops them into Book 2. Indeed, on the next page he makes two references to "the front of this abstract"---meaning that Book 1 must "by now" be at least laid out in draft; and on the same page again, he refers *forward* to Book 3, in fact already before him in quasi-legal form: "before I do show you what Revels they have kept in New Canaan." And thus, when he does bring Book 3's novel-like chapters forth from the legalistic document (what Winthrop called "a petition of many pages"), Morton inserts mention (120) of things he has "showed you before in the second part"---even though (to scholarly confusion) Book 3's proto-chapters were written "first."

Connors (35) reviews arguments that Morton originally meant to position Book 3 first. A further clue treated there, Book 1's reference to the incident of the defacing of Sachem Chikatawbak's mother's grave, seems to confirm the above process; for the incident is told as if for the first time in Book 3 (106), but said in Book 1 (44) to have "been before related."

The entry for *New English Canaan or, New Canaan* appears in *A Transcript of the Registers of the Company of Stationers of London: 1554-1640*. London 1877: Edward Arber, ed., Vol IV: 283 (also reprinted in Bradford's *History*, FBH2:77). The few clues suggest this series of events roughly between the first legal petition by Sir Ferdinando Gorges, Morton and others (rejected January 1634) and *Canaan*'s "Printed at Amsterdam...1637."

By Nov. 18, 1633 (eight weeks before their initial court-failure), Morton had a "3 Books" form in mind for *Canaan*. On that day he (or his printer/agent "Charles Greene") described it thus as they registered a *Canaan* in some form with the Stationers Register of London. This---followed soon by temporary legal defeat---is a good sign of Morton's will to convert all his papers into literary "cultural capital."

Sometime after April 1634, when Archbishop Laud's and Gorges' new Com-mission was created to override that early defeat, Morton inscribed the budding *Canaan* to its members (2). As he now (1634-5) composed and revised, engaged with sources and rivals around himself, he hammered at Wood's just-printed *Prospect* (probably envying the fine map of Mass. Bay therein), got hold of Inns-men Robert Hayman's *Quodlibets* and Sir William Vaughan's *The Golden Fleece* to see what had been done (and not done) poetically on America; and he refined all he remembered since the loss of his first "writings." Also dating most of Book 2's composition to 1634 or later is that Book's concluding mention of the New English expedition of Henry Josselyn, financed by Gorges' partner John Mason. Mason died in December 1635; so Morton (as he neared 1637 printing) either decided against revising the passage to include it, or he left it unacknowledged deliberately, to deny that it might affect the triumph of Gorges' and his hopes. The closing page of *Canaan* refers to Morton's own May 1634 "victory letter(s)" back to New England---and so the clues within and around the text accrue that *Canaan* was composed in several phases, from 1634 to 1637, that assembled, revised and unified earlier components, from legal brief to commodities-abstract, from proto-anthropology to a rainbow of poetic experiments in lyric, satire and would-be epic.

There are surprising reasons why Morton's often-graceful prose was first-printed with such wretched typography. While DeCosta (4) and Adams (AC100) had to believe that Amsterdam was *Canaan*'s original place of publication, Connors (136n5) cited several opinions that this was a ruse, "frequently practiced to avoid jurisdiction in case of prosecution for libel." Morton and his printer, in fact, tried to create the *appearance* that *Canaan* had been printed in Holland---and this caused what did in fact happen to the book. This fiasco explains a long-misleading part of scholarly records: why does *one* of the 16 surviving original copies (now in the British Museum PBMIC39042) have a cover of different date ("1632"), different paper, different decorative art, printer, and even what modern English would term "improvements" of spelling and style?

Weighing all evidence in 1986, Sternberg (371) drew upon a complaint from "Charles Greene bookseller" to Archbishop William Laud, signed by Greene on Feb. 13, 1637. (Document in *The Complete State Papers Domestic* [Brighton, c. 1981], Ser. II, Pt. 6, reel 129). Sternberg connects two recorded events that decided so much of *Canaan*'s fate. First, 1637 was the year of the "Decree of Starre Chamber Concerning Printing" (July 11), meant to tighten strict publishing controls, especially over the "importation" of "seditious" books such as the many Puritan tracts and Bibles printed in the Low Countries. (See Johnson on putative printer "J.F. Stam": Stam's typical work was much more painstaking with English than *Canaan*'s typesetting reflects.) According to Foster (74), Stam printed bulk Puritan propaganda in the 1630s, including at least 7000 English Bibles in the same 1637.

Secondly, under this government-censorship Act, although *Canaan* was written and registered by a man of known service to Laud, perhaps "1 in 6 were dispersed without being questioned"---but then "the Wardens of the Stationers in their search after prohibited bookes tooke away about 400" of the copies, perhaps almost the whole edition. Why? This was an officially-licensed book! But to a perhaps less-than-literary "warden," it looked like one of those outlawed printings of "Stam" of Amsterdam. This is wholly consistent with detailed investigations by DeCosta; who notes further (without being able to explain) that, if "Stam" in Holland *had* been the true printer, the name would have read "Jan" instead of "Jacob" (94). The unlikely seems to be the fact, and best pulls together a long-confused heap of tiny clues.

As Sternberg shows, printer Charles Greene, who had registered a *Canaan* back in Nov. 1633, also filed a petition in Feb. 1637 on Morton's and *Canaan*'s behalf---ardently asking for return of those wrongly-confiscated books. But these were badly-entrenched times for the Crown: Greene and/or Morton would need good arguments to get back their edition. Making their position worse, however, was their own quasi-legal "shift" made *already* to protect themselves from libel. It strongly seems to be the strange case that Greene's printshop made a *deliberate* botch of the work, "as a foreigner would" with English; and added a *false* "Printed at Amsterdam" besides to the cover, to protect their client and shop from the possible consequences of "savage" candor.

The strangest piece of evidence most supports this. For among all the world's original copies of *Canaan*, only one has a cover different from the rest. Why? Because when it appeared to Greene and Morton that the "Amsterdam...J.F. Stam" imprint was what had caused confiscation, they slapped together an item in their defense.

They took a "true original" 1637 copy of *Canaan* still in hand (hence with paper and text identical to all the rest, as the British Museum's one "1632" copy is). They tore off this copy's "Amsterdam" cover, and printed up a new false cover that read---as scholars have puzzled at since---"Printed for Charles Greene and...sold in Paul's Church-yard." Compare the different art-decoration and information on this supposedly "original and approved" cover of "1632." The original 1637 covers bear a quasi-pagan male/female pair of "tritons" or heralds in a stylized wreath-bower, and proclaim the book's foreign origins; but the (false concocted) "1632" cover displays no less than a Crown or Bishop's mitre with the Cross prominent in its art, and claims to have been produced by a known English printer and sold in that mainstream-hawker's paradise, Paul's Churchyard. The "1632" cover, they now tried to tell the Wardens, was a lucky piece of unsold proof found somehow round the shop, that "1632" had been the classic licensed English edition of *Canaan* (now sold out); and this "1637" botch a foreign *reprint*, made like many other English texts over there, for respectable capitalist reasons. Good Mr. Morton's book, they claimed, came of a tried and true vassal.

This is why this British Museum copy's front-page paper is different from the rest of that copy's pages, as well as from the entire balance of the (actual and only 1637) edition. Indeed that "1632" date is *written in by hand* (as DeCosta observed but could not explain without Sternberg's documents). Because a handwritten entry could hardly convince that this had truly been the "original" publication date, the written "1632" must simply be a trace of the human events ---someone writing it out for emphasis during discussion, bringing the date before officials "from records back at the shop," etc. They dared not set the lie in type with Crown and Cross; but this was worth a try.

Greene and/or Morton tried to make their only edition of *Canaan* (1637) appear to be a harmless, if foreign, *reprint*, of the *Canaan* already approved with the Crown's Register. Their "Amsterdam" disguise of the book's English origins they now claimed to have been a cost-cutting practical move that had come back a typesetter's botch besides. (Note the repeated yet inconsistent "printer's error" in all original copies, that often misprints *u* for *n* and vice-versa: it is not an unconscious or dyslexic "tic," because it does not happen even nearly every time it might---it happens instead like a false error *salted in* on some pages, not on others.) But the Greene/Morton claim was rejected; or perhaps Archbishop Laud and/or his Wardens proved more "thorough" readers than Mine Host had bargained for. The petition was never answered.

A few of those "1 in 6" copies did reach New England (next chapter). But confiscation by his very "masters," outrage from Puritan New England (plus a bit of "countercultural" admiration), and a place in the fire beside his worst rivals' books, appear to have greeted most of Morton's "memorial to after ages" (134) while he lived.

Victory had vanished again, but the book would write his fate in New England and beyond.

10: *Land of the New Creed*

from Saybrook [Fort on the Connecticutt River]
the 29 of the 9 mounth [then December], 1636
ED: GIBONES to the Worshipful John Winthrop esquier Junior at Boston

Loving Sur,

My tender louf to you remembered. Sir, I know that you would be glad to hear of the welfare of this place and these proceedings: I can give you but little light into things; and that, in my own judgment, will not be much beneficial to the honors thereof.

The place is strong enough, with good watch and direction to put many Indians to the worst. Mr. [Lion] Gardiner [engineer for Lords Say and Brook] is careful, so far as I am able to judge. But work goes heavily of hand, and the work that was begun when you were here, looks old for want of finishing: [the men] find their stomockes to be good, their business much.

But I fear the profit little, and if some speedy course be not taken, the burden will be so heavy that I know not how it will be borne. And if it should be [given] up, we must [search for sustenance] up the whole river, and keep our houses if we can; for the Indians are very insolent: the Lord direct this way.

Sur, I have inquired for your thinges but can get but a small passle: I hope you will understand the reason.

Thus desiring that you would be pleased to remember us and our occasions to the God and Father of Christ Jesus, my humble service remembered to your father and mother, your wife and all the rest. I leave you in the bosom of a wise God, to guide you in all your godly employments; and so I rest, your poor 22li 20s debtor, or thereabout

ED: GIBONES
(in WPF3:323; edited, complete text)

In his former master's absence, one-time Ma-re Mount man Edward Gibbons had found himself on the cutting edge of a virtual invasion of Native American Connecticutt. He was now part of a post at "Saybrook" financed by the Earl of Warwick and others against further Dutch competition: the English river-towns (Wethersfield, Windsor, Hartford, Springfield) had all been developed by migrants from Mass. Bay by 1636, and early Plimoth traders there were angrily seeing their efforts superseded from many directions. As soldier Gibbons posted his appeals for support, "very insolent" Pequot braves were beseiging the wintry outpost, as part of their already-long resistance to the "overt subjection" planned for them (and their Narragansett and other relations) by the fractious Europeans and Englishmen of the coastal colonies.[156]

Gibbons had watched Boston burgeon, from the day when Morton's company had seen John Winthrop's ships drop anchor, through the recent years of resistance to the King's demands, to the present---in which Bostonians found, despite Morton's and Gorges' sense of victory, that most of the English government's will to enforce its decrees now "fell on sleep, so as ships came and brought what and whom they would, without any question or control" (WJH1:181).

But those ships had also been delivering church-congregations and more secular-minded patentees whose own lack of perfect "resemblances" brought them to challenge and compete with Boston's state and economy: such was the expansion assisted by Gibbons the man-at-arms. There had been diplomacy to

---

[156] "Overt subjection" is from the most thorough documentary examination of the foregrounds, various parties' motives in, and primary accounts of "The Pequot War"---Jennings' *Invasion of America*, esp. Chs. 11-12 (201 qtd.). Richard Drinnon's *Facing West*, Neal Salisbury's *Manitou and Providence*, Alden T. Vaughan's *New England Frontier*, Hauptman/Wherry's *The Pequots* and Cave's *Pequot War* also contain important studies.

ease the clash of forces. The Pequots, Narragansetts and Mass. Bay government had concluded a treaty designed to avoid a much-expected war (November 6, 1634: WPF1:1:148-9). Rivalry-killings, abductions of Native persons and vengeances, intertribal conflicts and "elbow room" for planters had almost seemed to have been contained as threats to the peace, until rivalries *within* English settlers' communities intensified (Jennings 196-199). And, following Hooker's exodus in 1635 and the killing of trader/agent John Oldham by Natives of the Block Island region in 1636, the situation soon exploded.[157] Gibbons was part of the line against revenge-attacks by Pequots, soon to be further angered by the much-criticized John Endicott expedition against Block Island peoples the following August. (It was carried out in revenge for Oldham's death; which had followed Native deaths by disease). Peace had all but no chance.

Yet, according to Lion Gardiner's own "Relation" (MHSC 3rd series III, 145-6), the Pequots outside Gibbons' fort were trying to negotiate terms (if war *was* to come) that would keep, as we have seen it was New England tradition to keep, women and children out of hostilities. In a sense these Native peoples could not imagine the gravity of their situation. Even Roger Williams, an exiled critic of Mass. Bay over (among other things) English titles to American land---and welcomed to "Providence" country that same year---now worked hard to undermine a nascent alliance against "all the English" by the Pequot and Narragansetts (WJH1:200-201: Drinnon 41-41). As Boston made its plans for a serious spring offensive, Williams supplied Winthrop with a sketch and plan showing that Boston might accomplish its intentions in a stealthy dawn attack on a main Pequot village (Letter in WPF 1637: sketch in MHSC 3rd series I, 161).

---

[157] It now appears that Oldham, relatively well-liked by the southern New England peoples as a trade-contact, may have been considered responsible for the wave of epidemic that devastated villages along his inland route to the Connecticut River in 1633, and was perhaps "executed" rather than killed in criminal circumstances. See, Cave *War* , Drinnon, Jennings *Invasion* 208.

This was the year of Harvard's founding and of the first profitable return of Boston's first slave-ship, named *Desire*. War was prosecuted against the Pequots on May 26, 1637, with an assault not on Pequot Sachem Sassacus' well-defended fort at Weinshauks, but at Mystic, a less powerful village filled with mostly old men, women and children. At least 300 Native people at the fort were trapped in their thatch-houses and burned to death, shot or stabbed as they fled; and a later total of at least 900 (WJH1:227-230) were pursued to death in "Fairfield" swamps, herded into West Indies slavery, or "mercifully" taken into New England households as "servants" (as Winthrop and Williams called their shares of spoil: Winthrop's "servant" later ran away, and no more is known of Williams' "boy"). This and the savage hand-to-hand violence of "mopping up" through that summer are documented in Winthrop's *Papers* (WPF3:453-511).

Would Morton and his West Country colleagues of "the Bristol school" have conducted "business" differently, if their cultural approach to America had been dominant in the 1630s? A rival courtier of Sir Ferdinando Gorges' had criticized his attempts to be increasingly diplomatic about dominating Massachusetts, with the remark that "Romans, Spanish and Dutch did and do conquer, not plant Tobacco and Puritanism only, like fools" (qtd. in Preston 314). Since the 1620s wars in Virginia, too, Captain John Smith had revised early counsels and recommended outright conquest of "treacherous and rebellious Infidels" who did not enjoy the colonizers' "drudgery work" (*General History* 1624: Arber ed. 579).[158]

---

[158] Beothuk peoples were literally hunted by the Northeast's earliest regular "visitors," the trappers and fishermen, for supposedly stealing tools, etc.; more likely for resisting fur trade itself (Brasser 83). But these "business reasons" for genocidal activities are not the same "cultural formation" as the denial-ridden colonial ideologies that emerged in the 1620s and 1630s in New England. What the two methods unfortunately had in common was described within Patricia Fumerton's remarks (*Cultural Aesthetics* 112-123) on the emergence of a "more selfish," post-Elizabethan model of subjectivity at this time; one intimately tied to the rise of capitalism, and characterized most by violent "cannibalistic" behavior-patterns, even in the guise of "high-culture" activities such as court masques, with their "voidings" of choice desserts.

Examples relevant to "The Pequot War" and aftermath: Rev. Hooker's speech to the troops as they "went aboard" ship for Mystic, "that they [the Pequots] should be bread for us"

The 1630s "Great Migration" of Puritans (about 20,000 strong) had begun to slow down as England's Civil War drew near, but religious and political turmoil in Mass. Bay kept dissidents and exiles moving as colonizers into the land. Connecticutt river-towns managed relations with Williams' "Rogue's Island": the "Antinomian" factions opposing Winthrop and Dudley from 1634-38, led by Anne Hutchinson and John Wheelwright,[159] had taken English culture into Long Island and New Hampshire; and the irascible visionary Samuel Gorton (landed 1637) had found himself (and his Gortonites, who said among other things that "Hell" was not a real place) another "explorer" when banished by the Court of "ye just asses" of Boston and Plimoth. Besides its "Indian troubles," then, the Puritan establishment had not had much success in its own terms against waves of "radical" criticism from many different kinds of people, just when Morton's *Canaan* briefly appeared before the world.

The book's "voluptuous discourse" (Wood's phrase), woven from cosmography and Classics, from unsanctified observation, poetry and ribald satire, had to displease: whether or not he saw a copy, Bradford called it an "infamous and scurrilous" book, typically "against many godly and cheefe men of the cuntrie," "full of lies and slanders, and fraight with profane calumnies against their names and persons, and the ways of God" (FBH2:76). Where Ranlet (21) claims that Mass. Bay agent Mathew Cradock saw or forwarded to Winthrop a

---

(qtd. in Underhill, *Good-Newes*); Bradford's thought that the Pequots' burning flesh seemed a "sweet sacrifice unto God" (FBH2:250); and Roger Williams' 1646 statement in verse that "Christ's little ones must/...eate up those which now a while/Their fierce devourers be" (*Key* Ch. 19, 184). On the other side, in one of Morton's metaphors for what happened to *him*, he compares himself to a "buttered" loaf (192); and when Standish's men first attacked him in 1628 he said it was "as if they would have eaten him" (146). On the continuation of such tradition see the final Note below.

[159] Wheelwright was the next recorded resident of "Mount Wollaston" or Ma-re Mount after Morton's company: after Braintree became a town, the site was purchased by one Henry Adams, a planter with 8 sons. *Mass. Records* 1:291; Lechford 41n42.

"manuscript copy" from London,[160] Adams doubted "that a single copy" was actually sent to New England (AC79). The West country old comer Samuel Maverick wrote two of very few "reviews" in *Canaan*'s time: to him it was "the truest description of New England as then it was that ever I saw," a book whose "offense" was that it "had touched...too neare" the Massachusetts Bay Colony.[161]

Canaan's late 16th-century style, its merciless "realism" mixed with fantasy, its demanding paradoxes quickly made it a book out of step with the demands upon its patron or "Solomon," Gorges. Not only was he turning 70 and doubtful that his health would survive an American voyage, even as he accepted official appointment (1637) as governor-general. Gorges was all but bankrupt, like many another adventurer. He took action to meet his problems and preserve his ambitions. By June 1638 he completed a long proposal to Secretary of State

---

[160] In a letter (WPF3:379) from Cradock to Winthrop of March 15, 1637, Cradock said he was approached in London by Maine planter George Cleeve (below), who desired his "approbacion" of some obscure thing the latter "intended": Cradock was then shown "a writing" which he "utterly disliked and disavowed for having aught to doe therein." But "taking it to perusse" before giving an "answere" on this "writing," Cradock "Caused a coppy to bee taken"---another "manuscript copy"or something different?---which he did send Winthrop. Was it a *Canaan*?

Adams (AC79) seems certain Winthrop had "never" seen it by the time Morton was haled before him again in 1644. The very next language in Cradock's letter mentions "Moreton" approaching Cradock "on the exchange"---and this leads Ranlet into error. For Morton was approaching Cradock "*from them* [Cleeve and others]," and wanted Cradock as Mass. Bay agent to "pay the Chardge or promiss...in taking out somewhat under the Seale"---the "taking out" or landclaim made "on or about the January 9 last." In short, as seen below, Cleeve had already hired Morton as attorney to help arrange *his own* patent under Gorges' new Feb. 1635 charter from the Council for New England (WJH1:224-5). The "writing" was not a copy of *Canaan*, for Cradock had shared no "part" in it to "disavow" except that he was satirically dubbed in it "Mathias Charterparty" in Book 3. He *would* have wished to disavow new attempts to settle rivals to Mass. Bay in New England. Since no other source mentions *Canaan*'s circulation in "manuscript" form, the affair must have concerned a legal-papers maneuver among Cleeves, Gorges and Morton---of whose expenses or implications Cradock wanted no part, but about which he thought fit to keep Winthrop informed.

Major (*Dissertation* 77): "Morton and Cleeves wanted financial help from Cradock in getting some document through the seals, but Cradock was so unwilling to be associated with Morton in any way that he did not learn the details of the business."

[161] Maverick repeated these remarks in his *Letter to the Earl of Clarendon*, 40-41: "a good description of the Country....only in the end of it [Morton] pinched too closely on some in authoritie there." There was one less "literary" comment from a New Englander---see below.

Windebank (Preston 314-17) detailing a more Puritan-tolerant plan for New England's governance, toleration a refinement created by the impossible expense of force-of-arms, and by Gorges' fear of the Crown's losing the colonies altogether. Gorges had again reversed himself on how to render New England most submissive and profitable, now recasting Maine as a "proprietary province" which would (with royal financial help) become the foundation for Royalist rule there. But this in turn demanded some degree of rapprochement with Mass. Bay (who held aloof and bided their time)---as well as more money to put Royalist manpower to work. The latter came first to hand.

Over that winter of 1637-8, "one George Cleves" or Cleeve arrived back in England, a 1630 planter near Richmond Island whose time there had overlapped with Morton's servant Walter Bagnall's ("Great Wat" had died in October 1631). Cleeve---called by some a "firebrand of dissension" (MHSC IV, II, 343; and AC85n2)---now looked up Thomas Morton, and hired him in an effort to confirm himself a patent within Gorges' lands (as Bagnall had been seeking when he died). Cleeves was already operating as Morton eventually would be, as an agent of English gentlemen now obtaining "large circuits of lands," who were "very ready to grant them out to such as will become their tenants, and, to encourage them, do procure commissions, protections, etc." (WJH1:224-5).[162]

Cleeve was "assured" and made "promises" by Morton the experienced prosecutor that his claim would succeed against another planter (detailed in Preston 338-40), and it did; and Gorges named Cleeve the experienced planter to take up Maine (or now, "New Somersetshire") governance as his proxy. But Gorges, quickly reminded that Cleeve had long been disliked as a "Gorges man" in Mass. Bay, changed his strategy; and he "casheerd" Morton for the Puritans'

---

[162] The word "protections" is very important for understanding how Morton dared return to New England in his final days, below.

delectation instead. In an August 1637 letter to Winthrop, Dudley and others, in which Gorges hoped "to attaine to the oppertunity to make...some kind of requital" (WPF3:492), he apologized for the agitations of Cleeve and "Moorton his agent":

> who since is wholely casheerd from intermedlinge with any our affaires hereafter; but this I write to you in perticuler that you maie take private notice thereof, and howe much I am offended with my selfe for being over credulous....Consideracion being had to the sincerity of one, and the fraude of others....I will approove my selfe Your true friend....

This was about all Gorges had to offer. The total impact of Morton's legal victories against Massachusetts Bay could be described by the fact that "there are no extensive records" of a heavy hand's activity by the dreaded Laud Commission (Preston 313).[163] The oppression of Puritans never had been Morton's goal: *Canaan* argued most simply for a New England administration "not contrary or repugnant to the laws of the Kingdom of England."

But with both Gorges and the Crown close to bankruptcy, the "control" of America now stood second to Charles' and Laud's control of dissent, at home in Parliament (about to reconvene at last in "Short" and "Long" sessions in 1640, which would see Laud in jail); and in Scotland, where religious issues now threatened open rebellion and even an invasion of English soil. Amidst this, Gorges took full (English) legal title to Maine (April 1639); but took it subject to the much-older, obscure "Plough Patent" of 1631, which somehow survived all

---

[163] Although as Thomas Lechford reports (Trumbull ed. 33n), Laud's Ecclesiastical Commissioners prosecuted Puritans in 1634 for allowing persons excommunicated by the Anglican "ordinary" to come to church services, this remains another fact out of balance with the excoriation of Morton's legal maneuverings by later historians. Cleeve and Morton may be meant by the two phrases ending Gorges' letter (sincerity and fraud); though the "fraud," unlike "sincerity," refers to more than one party. Adams makes much of this "fall" of Morton's from his height in England, and adds a few pages later what a meaningless "straw" move the dismissal was.

these reorganizations and came to end all his hopes (Moody ed., *Letters of Thomas Gorges* 60n17).

Yet Gorges, still insisting (by apologies for his delay) that he would personally govern New England, sent ahead a distant and somewhat Puritan-sympathetic cousin, Thomas (all of 22 years), to supervise the "province" in 1640, and employed Morton anew to witness a minor land-grant.[164] At the respectable age of 64, Morton, still close to Gorges in some sense, was scraping by on work he could find among all these men: one other document of the time shows that he signed (April 10, 1641) the charter for Agamenticus, and that these "letters of Incorporation" were "committed" to his lawyerly care.[165]

The gesture suggests his and Gorges' agreement that the best place now for Morton, as both agent in further causes and individual, was America (with of course some kind of Royalist protection). But where? In Virginia the far less Puritan English culture was more congenial; but in New England---with protection---he could hearten factions of "King's men" there, and/or gain a windfall of land. Thomas' will (below) shows that he had such hopes.

He had to raise his own funds for the voyage, although his first purpose in going was to deliver the Agamenticus charter to Thomas Gorges "the boy" in Maine. Morton (in Moody ed. *Letters* 55) wrote to him demanding "20 nobles...for

---

[164] Document showing Morton's 1640 signature in Banks' *History of York* 435-9.

Moody (xi and *passim*) shows that although Inns of Court-trained Thomas Gorges was dubbed "the boy" by the contentious planters around him, he was a relatively even-handed administrator during his tenure in America (1640-43). Thomas also (51) gives this study a parting 1641 glimpse of "the bringing in of the [Abenaki] natives to the Kingdome of Christ. The truth is it is in my conceit a most difficult thinge....I cannot perceave any more [Christianity] in those that are bred up in the English houses than the others. For the others, when they come to me they will discourse about their fashions and desier to know the fashions of ould Ingland [;] but propound a word of God to them[,] it strikes them mute. They answer noe[,] stammering that word [...]turne away theyr head loathing any mention of it....Prayers are continually made for them in the [Mass.] Bay...."

[165] The Agamenticus charter is in Hazard, *Historical Collections* 1:470-474.

his great payns and travell." Thomas Gorges complained that he "knew not" why "such a sum of money" was required; but having stayed in Boston upon his own arrival (*ix*) he had been told things---for he added, "I conceave Mr Moorton to be an able man, yet I know not whither it be a policy for a Lord of a province in [New England] to countenance him that hath declared himself an enemy to the land."

The money Thomas Gorges ordered sent; but evidently Morton was none too sure of any Gorges' ability or will to protect him, for even amid the Civil War's outbreak in 1642, he remained in England. Bradford (FBH2:77) is circumstantially right that Morton's return came about "when the warrs were hott in England," but as it proved, Morton was in Parliamentary employ at least for awhile (below), and found more to fear from Mass. Bay and Plimoth than from soldiers. Hoskins (*Devon* 86) relates that Morton's home-county endured "much sacking," that heavy "fines" were imposed upon King Charles' supporters; but Oppenheim (64) adds that while Devon's gentry with their tenants stood "strongly Royalist" at this time, the "maritime merchants and traders" there were mostly Parliament men. Still believing reasonably that law prevailed at last, even in New England, Morton kept looking for a solid patron to take him there in safety, and within a year he managed it.

If Gorges in his 70s could raise and ride with a West Country Royalist troop of horse in July 1642, so (perhaps) Morton: almost nothing is known of either as the war began, but Gorges' forces lost control of the West's main city Bristol and saw it become a lasting outpost for Parliament troops. Now Gorges lost touch with America, perhaps with Morton too; for Mine Host next surfaced in a way that suggests his finding his passage by manipulating old client George Cleeve, still at his patent-suits. First, "One Mr. [Alexander] Rigby, a lawyer and Parliament man, wealthy and religious" (WJH2:157), was "inspired by" Cleeve to purchase and enforce the old "Plough Patent" (Moody 60n17), a long-standing license to settle that included the land Cleeve wanted. Within a few years, together the pair took full title to the region called "Ligonia," and thereby split, irreparably, Gorges' own territories (Banks *History* 1:59, 174-5; Duncan 40, 93).

Second, by April 1643, Puritan-dominated Parliament was itself looking into this affair (the land-title was confirmed in 1647), and Ranlet (23) found a document revealing the uncomfortable co-appointment of Morton and none other than John Winthrop to "investigate" its legalities together.[166] Ranlet suggests from this, however, that Morton was "changing over" to a Parliament "allegiance" that was "clear," and that "No Royalist would have been given such an assignment."

This neglects, however, the fact that the quasi-Puritan Thomas Gorges had confirmed Morton's bad reputation as an "able man." When Parliament authorities began looking into Rigby's New England acquisitions, they gave Rigby good reason to make the experienced Morton his agent in defending them, and to afford Morton protection from Parliament's more enthusiastic members. Parliament's creating such unlikely partners as Morton and Winthrop at this late date showed not so much that Morton had fooled anybody, or changed his spots (the war was anything but decided yet)---but that Cleeve and Rigby had simply retained one of the best-known New England land-patent attorneys for their needs; one whose indeed-Royalist sympathies scarcely mattered given his age, resources, and anything but militant personality.

To meet and balance Morton, Parliament specified Winthrop as the opposite "type": a Puritan of almost as old New England experience as "Mine Host." So again Morton found a function or service that served his own needs,

---

[166] Ranlet cites Stock, ed., *Proceedings of Parliaments* 1:143-144 on this appointment.

though he was now quite dependent upon Rigby. Morton must have relished a day in high court with "brother" Winthrop.

They would meet again, in court, but never as brothers in either man's mind. That April of 1643 also saw Archbishop Laud's Commission officially dissolved; and though King Charles issued the condemned Laud a royal pardon, Puritan authorities rejected this, and Laud was reduced to requesting a simple beheading, not the traitor's being hanged, drawn and quartered. Within 9 months this was granted in full. No doubt Morton as one-time Commission prosecutor began to feel that he had better take up "Rigby's" business in foreign parts as soon as possible. Gorges himself, the man whose ambitions had all but established the English Northeast, was fading fast somewhere. Thomas' old client died in confinement after capture by Puritan forces at this very time. As battles spread death, there was less room all around for the passionate moderate.

Morton hung onto Rigby (if we project back from Winslow's late letter below), and, on May 23, he signed his name as witness of Rigby's grant of lands around Casco Neck to George Cleeve (Baxter 124). Connors (27), Adams and Banks believed that out of these involvements came most of Morton's claims---founded in these gentlemen's "I.O.U.'s" for legal services perhaps---that he possessed title to four separate New England tracts of land. Winthrop had written that many wealthy Englishmen were promising protections and grants to people who became their "tenants" to establish possession of territories. Morton was likely expected to act not as owner but as distributor of lands in Rigby's and others' names: from this he derived verbal and paper assurances for his safety and his chances of real estate ("which I now have or ought to have," he says in the will below).

Thomas scraped together his Atlantic passage and, amid final arrangements through that summer, made his will. Morton likely made a last visitation with family, too, to make them aware of his efforts to gain them land: he tries to bequeath properties (real or unreal) to a "neece" mentioned nowhere else. Thomas Morton, nearly 70 years old now, was consciously leaving England forever to end his days in another land which, he later said, "he loveth."[167]

> In the name of God Amen. The 23th day of August 1643. I Thomas Morton of Clifford's Inne London gent being in perfect health of body yet takeing into my serious consideracon the transitory estate of this Mortall life and being minded to settle my estate in such sorte that the benefitt thereof may be for the advaincment and advantage of my Nearest of Kindred hereafter in these presentes named and theire posterity whensoever it shall please Almighty god to take me hence, I doe therefore ordaine make and create this my last will and Testament in manner and forme following that is to say Imprimis
>
> I doe bequeath my soule unto Almighty God trusting assuredly that in and through the Merittes of Jesus Christ my savioure and Redeemer to be made partaker of the Kingdome of heaven with all believers and I bequeath my body to the earth from whence it came.
>
> Item as touching my estate Reall and personall I Doe hereby ordaine devise and bequeath unto my Loving Cosen german Tobias Milles and unto my neece Sara Bruce widowe[168] All that my estate right title and interest of what nature and quality soever, of in and unto all those my Landes tenementes or hereditamentes whatsoever in New England in America hereafter in these

---

[167] This text of Morton's will is Banks' transcription of the original: photostats of will and Morton's goat-headed seal in Banks, "Morton of Merry Mount," MHSP (1924-5), LVIII: 163-4.

[168] Banks "Morton" 158-9: "Thus far [1922] I have been unable to learn any particulars of Mrs. Bruce who may be the daughter of a brother or a sister of Morton. The 'Cozen German,' Tobias Milles, is undoubtedly the son of Edmond Milles of Eastrop Highworth, Wiltshire, gentleman. The parish registers of Highworth disclose the baptism of Tobias, son of Edmond and Margaret (Trember) Milles, 4 November, 1602, and the Prerogative Court of Canterbury (Book 'Lee' folio 100), contains the will of Edmond Milles dated 12 May 1638, in which he makes a bequest to Tobie Milles 'my loving and obedient Sonne,' to whom he leaves the residue of his estate and makes him executor of the will. It is to be noted that the probate of the will of Thomas Morton was not allowed until August 9, 1660, seventeen years after its execution, when 'Sara Wilson *als.* Bruce' was given authority to administer and power was reserved to Tobias Milles, the other executor. On April 10, 1661, Tobias Milles was given authority, as co-executor. The Administration Act Book of the P.C.C. for 1663 (fol. 97) contains the note that George Charlewood, principal creditor, was granted administration of the estate of Tobias Milles *als.* Mihill 'Nuper in Partibus Transmarinis defuncti.'"

presentes menconed. That is to say All that my estate Right title and interest of in and or unto All that one parcell of Lands within the Province of Carlile containing five thousand acres scituate on the East Side of the River Quillepiock[169] and extending foure Miles along by the side of the said River from the foote therof into the Landes[.] And also all that my estate Right title and interest in an other parcell of land in the said Province of Carlile Containing other five thousand acres scituate on the west side of the said River Quillepiock and extending from the foote thereof foure miles along by the side of the same River upwardes[.] And also all my estate right title and interest in one parcell of Land in the Province of Ligonia containing two thousand acres lying in Casco Bay next unto the River Pesumskegg[.][170] And also all my estate Right title and interest of in and unto all those two Islandes in Casco Bay neere to Pesumskegg River called the Clapboard Islandes[.] And also all that my estate Right title and interest of in and unto All that one Island Called Martin's Vineyard, scituate and being on the southerne side of Cape Codd, and neere unto the Narohiganset Bay.

To have and to hould all the said severall parcells of Landes unto them the said Tobias Millis and Sara Bruce theire heires executors and assignes forever Together will all the estate Right title and interest whatsoever which I now have or ought to have in the same or any part or parcell thereof[.] And for the better assurance and [sure] makeing of all and singular the said Landes and Islandes unto them and theire posterity hereby I doe by these presentes Nominate ordaine and appoynt them the said Tobias Milles and Sara Bruce and either of them to be Mine executors of this My last will and testament[.] In testimony whereof I have hereunto set my hand and seale

THOMAS MORTON   [seal]

Witnesses: *William Woodward sarvant to Mr. Fryer*   *Thomas Fryer*   witness

---

[169] On the location of "Carlile" (a grant of lands overlapping much of Connecticutt) see Preston's map 463: the Earl of Carlisle's tract included lands of "Quinnipiac" (that is, of Native peoples by that name living along that River---Banks 158).

[170] "Ligonia" named a region of Maine (1646-52) between Casco Bay and Cape Porpoise (Duncan 93). The "Pesumskegg" is now called the Presumpscot River, while the Clapboard Islands next mentioned were "part of ancient Falmouth" (Banks 163). The geographical spread of Morton's claims (including Capawac/Martha's Vineyard, later"legally" deeded to Thomas Mayhew by Gorges and others in 1649) may at least describe the parameters of lands he actually saw in his best New England trading-days.

The next trace of Morton comes from Winthrop's journal: between entries for December 2, 1643 and for January 18, 1644, Winthrop marked the arrival of *Hopewell*, "a ship of Boston" laden with West Indies wines, spices and sugar; and then he noted that "At this time came over Thomas Morton, our professed old adversary, who had set forth a book against us, and written reproachful and menacing letters to some of us" (WJH2:154).

Somehow, by January Morton had found himself at none other than Plimoth, where 14 midwinter years before he had been banished; and where now still resided such formidable adversaries as Edward Winslow, jailed not long ago at Morton's real or imagined instigation. As a Boston messenger waited, Winslow dashed off reports to Winthrop (some concerned killings and new rumors of war related to the Mohawks and Narragansetts), and at the last moment he added this news and comment:[171]

> Concerning Morton, our Gover[nor] gave way that he should winter heer, but begon as soon as winter breaks up. Capt. Standish takes great offence theerat, [especially] that he is so neer him at Duxburrow and goeth sometimes a fowling in his ground. [Morton] cannot procure the least respect amongst our people, liveth meanely at 4s per week, and [is] content to drinke water, so he may dyet at that price. But admit he hath a proteccion yet[:] it were worth the while to deale with him till we see it.
> The truth is, I much question his pretended employment: for he hath heer onely shewed the Frame of a Commonweale [the Agamenticus charter?] and some old sealed Commissions, but no inside knowne. As for Mr. Rigby, if he be so honest, good, and hopefull an Instrument as report passeth on him, he hath good hap to light on two of the arrantest knaves that ever trod on new English shore to be his Agents East and West as Cleves and Morton. But I shall be jealous on him till I know him better and hope others will take heed how they trust him, who investeth such with power [as those] who have devoted them selves to the ruine of the Countrey, as Morton hath.
> And for my part (who, if my hart deceive me not, can passe by all the evill instrumentally he brought on me), would not have this serpent stay amongst us who out of doubt in time will gett strength to him[self] if he be

---

[171] Text is from WPF4:428-9, with some changes in spelling, punctuation and paragraphing for clarity. "This serpent": The Bible, *Revelations* 13:9-11: "And the great dragon was cast out, that old serpent, called the Devil, and Satan, which deceiveth the whole world: he was cast out into the earth, and his angels were cast out with him....for the accuser of our brethren is cast down, which accused them before our God day and night."

> suffered, who promiseth large porcions of land about Newhaven, Narro-
> higg[anset, or Carlisle's grant] etc. to all that will goe with him, but hath
> a promise but of one person, who is old, weake, and decrepid, a very atheist
> and fitt companion for him. But, indeed, Morton is the odium of our peop[le]
> at present, and if he be suffered (for we are diversly minded), it will be just
> with God who hath putt him in our hands, and we will foster such an one
> that afterward we shall suffer for it. But the messenger calls for my letter....

Morton's return at 68 was that of a spirited man without much to lose: by all accounts he near-instantly went about settling scores as he could. Fiery Standish (now retired to the work of tax-collector) part-time captained a company of riflemen equipped with the latest "snap-hance" guns: next year against the Narragansetts he would be under the orders of no less than "Generall over the whole" Edward Gibbons (FBH2:381). Likely aware that Standish hated being "neer him" still, Morton rode his "protection" and put it in Standish's face that he was yet hale enough for sport on Duxburrow's frozen marshlands. So Morton was even "suffered" to use a fowling-piece: perhaps he paid or thanked his hosts with some "hard to come by" game.

A later letter from gentleman-colonist William Coddington to Winthrop suggests that Morton may have landed at Portsmouth (Rhode Island) "at his first comeing" (WPF4:490): the letter "quoted" Morton "insinuating who was for the king, and [that he] would report to such as he Judged to be of his mynd"---he had been "glad" to meet with "so many Cavaleres" about the southern New England plantations. Coddington wrote that Morton "discovered" to planters there that "he had lands to dispose of to his followers in each province[,] and from Cape Ann to Cape Codd was one."

We have seen the terms under which Morton "carried" these land-interests and those by which he described the tracts he "ought to have." Clearly, Morton's enormity sailed over the heads of Puritans then, and historians after (for ex. Mayo 180, who like Adams used it to justify Captain Endicott's and Boston's actions below). It is not credible that the attorney who had just spent 13 years wiping out all the "title" he could in New England, even his own as noted, now "believed" that he personally had any power to "dispose" of the now most-thickly-settled region of the Northeast (Cape Ann to Cape Cod). In *Canaan*, with Mason's help, he had estimated 12,000 English there, and the number had since increased to about 14-16,000 (Willison 385).

Morton had little or nothing but his old man's health and life-long pride. His tall words went to mock the fears projected onto him.[172] It had been Coddington's spy in Portsmouth, "Tenant Gould," serving briefly as Morton's "host howse"; and this Gould, "being much taken with" the old man, had listened to more of his talk. Though Morton "had wronge in the bay [to the] value of 200*li* and [had] made bitter Complaints thereof," he now intended (in Coddington's gossip) to "*let it rest till the Governour came over to right him*, and [Morton] did intimate he knew whose roste his spits and Jackes turned etc." (491, emphasis added).

Whether or not Morton believed that any governor was coming, no rational official of any faction would have handed Massachusetts Bay over to an individual due 200*li* of damages. A rational attorney knew this. If Morton still needed to humble himself for shelter at Plimoth after such brave talk, he was not much of a Royalist favorite to lead the New England faction supposedly gathering. Had he been, he would have ensconced himself in the class-traditional treatment he had usually managed (including genial drink) among New England's men of his own Christmas-keeping, old-English ilk. He was hale enough for all that if he could enjoy fowling in the icy seaside marshes of Duxburrow in January.

---

[172] Major (Dissertation 85): Even now Morton "was no man to submit to sanctimonious invasion of his legal rights or to pretend a piety that he did not feel."

"His" people were more numerous northwards, and had been since the "first permanent settlements" (by English people) had taken hold: West Country people had called Dover "Bristol" till 1641 (Bowden 114). There, Cleeve and Rigby now worked to extend Rigby's "government," that spring of 1644 appointing "commissioners," a legal Court, and sending another agent around, one "Tucker," with "a paper perswading all such as he findes any way inclyning to innovation, to sett there handes to it, for the better approving of what they have begun" (Richard Vines to Winthrop, WPF4:429). Morton's job was the same, to gather up and capitalize on disaffected people willing to "innovate" rather than be confined and limited by Puritan law, religion and culture.[173] As he did so, another old enemy tracked him. John Endicott's collected intelligences (June 23) told Winthrop that Morton had gone "by sea to Gloster on the sixth day last[,] hoping from thence to get a passage to the Eastward," to Maine; that in "all" whose "partes" there was "a great partie for the Kinge," particularly gathered at Cleeve's homestead of Richmond Island.

Two of Endicott's spies, "fayning" the Cavalier customs of "love and good cheer" there, reported "preparations for some designs": Endicott suggested that Morton had "endeavoured [tried to form or encourage?] a partie to the Southward" in Rhode Island, and was now coming north to "doe the like." "I sent a warrant to Gloster to apprehend him," he told Winthrop without mention of a legal charge. So dimly could he complete the details of Morton's Royalism that he fetched out warhorses: "most likelie [sic]...the Jesuites or some that way disposed have sent him over to doe us mischiefe[,] to raise up our enemies round about us both English and Indean" (WPF4:464).

---

[173] Vines, though Puritan like Winthrop, does not imagine that *Tucker* is an ideological guerilla. Like Morton, Tucker is just a breathing impediment to Mass. Bay, in this case for a Maine "landfall," such as "the Court" had hoped for before and after the 1640s.

Endicott pressed for "speedy advi[ce]" to "put in execution"; and the pressure increased on Winthrop on the 26th. One "John Browne" of Taunton (close to the Rhode Island colony), wrote to demand that something be done about fellow settlers' walking away from their designated workplaces, in spite of "warnings" about dangerous Native people (WPF4:464). To this not-unfamiliar problem Mr. Browne added "one thing more":

> I pray you thinke on it...that you would not permit
> that vyle person Morton to pas[s] without some due
> punishment[,] for he hath in my Jud[g]ment Abused the
> cuntry very much and that In print....

The July letter of Coddington's above reached Governor Winthrop soon after Brown's. Whatever Morton was doing, within five weeks he "fell into" (as Ford put it) the hands of Winthrop's Court of Assistants at Boston (September 9, 1644: WJH2:194-6).[174] Given what was about to be presented as "criminal evidence" against Morton, it is reasonable to think that old planter William Jeffreys took part (perhaps a second time) in arranging Morton's capture. That first ambush by Standish's "worthies" had been sprung at Weymouth (141), Jeffreys' residence of record; and *Canaan* had said nothing good about Weymouthers, claiming they had cozened Ma-re Mount fur-trade with Massachusetts Natives (125-6).

Now, as the old nemesis he had called "King Winthrop" glared his resentments at Thomas from across the Boston courtroom, lawyer Morton must have circumspectly smiled at the new "charges." Would they fetch out the old

---

[174] Adams (AC86) claims that Morton made it past Endicott's deputies to Maine, but was back in Rhode Island by the time Winthrop heard from Coddington ("August"). But this is not explicit or implied in any record. It is also quite an itinerary. Hutchinson 92: Morton had brought "letters from the Earl of Carlisle and Mr. Rigby which did not protect him."
  "Fell into" (FBH2:77n) echoes Ford's earlier phrase (74) for how Morton back in 1629 "fell under," as well, Captain Endicott's powers: Connors (28) follows suit. Adams is more detailed: Morton's 1644 arrest meant he was likely "pounced upon by Endicott's officers as he was furtively passing through" the Cape Anne area.

"murther warrant"? But then, a certain letter was produced and read aloud before the court (the record edited for clarity below from WJH2:194). As Morton's own words about cropping "Mr. Winthrop's ears" came back to him, and the ghastly memory of Philip Ratcliffe's mutilations, old Thomas must have stood mortified with fear.

> At the court of assistants, Thomas Morton was called forth presently after the lecture, that the country might be satisfied of the justice of our proceeding against him. There was laid to his charge his complaint against us at the council board, which he denied [as "his" complaint, having prosecuted it for Gorges]. Then we produced the copy of the bill exhibited by Sir Christopher Gardiner, etc., wherein we were charged with treason, rebellion, etc., wherein he was named as a party or witness. He denied that he had any hand in the information, [saying] only [that he] was called as a witness.[175]
>
> To con[vict] him to be the principal party, it was showed:
> 1. That Gardiner had no occasion to complain against us, for he was kindly used, and dismissed [from New England] in peace,[176] professing much engagement for the great courtesy he found here.
> 2. Morton had set forth a book against us, and had threatened us, and had prosecuted a quo warranto against us, which he did not deny.
> 3. His letter was produced, written soon after to Mr. Jeffery, his old acquaintance and intimate friend....

Winthrop had saved the letter for 10 years. Now Morton was to pay for having been right about his "Very Good Gossip" Jeffreys; and who could have expected to answer for it this way, in a putative court of law? Now Winthrop had at mercy the man and high-government prosecutor who had frightened him, and all of Boston, brought on its days of "humiliation" and prayer for their charter—the so-called "Lord of Misrule" (Bradford) who had troubled their personal, political, and families' sense of well-being for 15 years.

---

[175] This must refer to a Puritan-circulated copy of the original 1633 petition "of many pages" filed by Gorges/Morton *et als*, referred to earlier by Winthrop himself. Its "some truths mis-repeated" (as he called them) have not survived. DeCosta (94) felt that it "cannot" have borne Morton's name because he was not "convicted" here of writing it.

[176] Winthrop still didn't get it. Gardiner's complaint was that Puritans *had* no right to "dismiss" him from New England.

But perhaps the court's desperation in satisfying "the country" of their justice now grew more obvious with each item Winthrop recited and "charged" aloud. For Morton was now led away with no (recorded) statement-in-answer beyond Winthrop's pen. Thomas may have circumspectly abided all he could; for once again, these authorities could bring themselves to inscribe no legal public record of their own charges or findings. They simply locked Thomas Morton up.

"Nothing," recorded Samuel Maverick, was "laid to his Charge." Morton was "keept in the Comon Gaole" as New England autumn set in (*Description* 238).

Yet, remarkably for a man with little money and few friends willing or able to sympathize in public, Thomas still managed by that November 13 to get a ("lost") petition to "ye Cort," no doubt with a hope to get out before the worst of winter (Shurtleff *Records* 2:90). The court's response was:

> For answer to Thomas Mourtons petition, ye magistrates have called him publiquely, & have layde diverse things to his charge, which hee denies; & therefore they thinke fit that further evidence be sent for into England, & that Mr. [Emmanuel] Downing may have instructions to search out evidence against him, & [Morton] to lye in prison in ye meane time, unlesse hee find sufficient bayle.

"Bail" was unlikely where the Court held it treason to help a Royalist (Ranlet 26), or to appeal to the King (AC88). In 1646 Mass. Bay would build on this with a death-penalty for "blasphemy" by any "Christian or pagan"---*Records* 2:176). "Mr. Downing," Winthrop's son-in-law, went about his role with now-predictable lack of success, and "Captain Littleworth" Endicott sought the "respite from urgent business" that he had "earned" (Mayo 182).

Thomas Morton remained imprisoned that "whole winter" (Maverick 238); "about a year, in expectation of further evidence out of England," as Winthrop mused in his journal (196). Morton's confinement was "without fire or beddinge...[through] a very cold winter" (Maverick Letter 41); and Morton (below) said he had been besides "laid in Irons[,] to the decaying of his Limbs." "That really broke the old rascal's spirit," quipped Samuel Eliot Morison (*Builders* 1952:217n1).[177]

The next document Adams found was "yet another petition from Thomas Morton, bearing no date, but, from the endorsement upon it, evidently submitted to the General Court of May 1645, six months later, when Dudley was governor" (AC89).[178]

The author of *Canaan*, and of these words, was now 69.

To the honored Court at Boston assembled:

The humble petition of Thomas Morton, prisoner.

Your petitioner craveth the favour of this honored Court to cast back your eies and behould what your poore petitioner hath suffered in these parts.

First, the petitioner's house was burnt, and his goodes taken away.

Secondly, his body clapt into Irons, and sent home in a desperat ship, unvittled, as if he had been a man worthy of death, which appeared contrary when he came there.

Now the petitioner craves this further[,] that you would be pleased to consider what is laid against him: (taking it for granted to be true) which is not proved: whether such a poore worme as I had not some cause to crawle out of this condition above mentioned.

Thirdly, the petitioner craves this favoure of you, as to view his actions lately towards New England, whether they have not been serviceable to some

---

[177] Adams thought the use of irons "Wholly probable" (AC92). At the bottom of a 1640s Boston prison a "circumspect" Morton would avoid false accusations about his treatment. This was now at least the fourth indirect attempt on his health or life: see 1) his attempted marooning off Cape Anne c. 1625 (Bk. 3 Ch. 4); 2) his 1628 marooning on the Isles of Shoals; 3) his December 1630 exile voyage home. The petition following shows him aware of the intent behind all these actions. He kept trying "to crawle out of this condition."

[178] This editor has examined the original document at Mass. Historical Society and it does "bear no date"; and there is as usual no official court record of Morton's release. So this last period of his life is known completely through a few last bits of hearsay, as will appear. Adams found the petition "certainly humble enough in tone" for the great men of the court.

gentlemen in the country; but I will not praise myself.

Fourthly, the petitioner coming into these parts, which he loveth, on godly gentlemen's imployments, and your worshipps having a former jelosy of him, and a late untrue intelligence of him, your petitioner has been imprisoned manie Moneths and laid in Irons to the decaying of his Limbs; Let your petitioner finde soe much favoure, as to see that you can passe by former offence, which finding the petitioner hopes he shall stand on his watch to doe you service as God shall enable him.

At the bottom of this document (in Illustrations) are these "endorsements":

> The house of Deputies desire the honored magistrates to return them a reason, wherefore the petitioner came not to his triall the last quarter Courte according to graunte (as they conceave) of a former petition presented to the Courte by him.
> ROBERT BRIDGES

> The reason why he came not to his tryall was the not cominge of evidence out of england against him which we expect by the next ship.
> THO; DUDLEY   *Govr*

> The house of Deputies have made choyce of Major Gibbons, and Captain Jennison to treat with the honored magistrates about this petition of Morton.
> ROBERT BRIDGES

Winthrop's journal (2:196) took up Morton's being "again called before the court, and...some debate what to do with him." Morton's meals and prison-guards were making him "a charge to the country," for "he had nothing." The court ("we") decided he was "not fit to inflict corporal punishment upon," for Morton stood before them "old and crazy" (that is, in decrepitude). So it was "thought better to fine him ["100 pounds"] and give him his liberty, as if it had been to procure his fine, but indeed to leave him opportunity to go out of the jurisdiction."[179]

The significant presence of the "choyce" Major Edward Gibbons "treating with the honored magistrates" above may have played a part in this particular sentence of the court's. While they knew that the decisive slaughters of Royalist armies had begun the previous summer at Marston Moor, England, the court presently had to somehow overlook its own previous concerns about Morton as a Cavalier security-threat.

It had not changed its view of Gorges' "province" "beyond Pascataquack," where Morton might be expected to go. There was a body-politic "not received nor called into the Confederation [formed after 'The Pequot War'], because they ran a different course from us both in their ministry and civil administration": indeed they had "lately made Acomenticus (a poor village) a corporation and had made a taylor their mayor, and had entertained one Hull, an excommunicated person and very contentious, for their minister" (WJH, May 1643, 99).

Gibbons, perhaps, helped the court nearer the actual extent of Morton's powers now. This is likely in one sense, at least, beyond any simple guilt of Gibbons' for his years of work against Mine Host's hard-won plantation. Gibbons' own career (detailed above) had taken him to the Caribbean too, and into more than one "shady deal" talked about in Boston. Perhaps the once-merry Edward had realized at last the need for "humanity" in the "complicated" new world all around his chosen Puritans.

---

[179] This "liberty" was also extended to Miantonomi, one of two leading Sachems (the other was Uncas) who, in the wake of "the Pequot War," took their peoples in different directions relative to English interests. Miantonomi, who spoke much of a "pan-Indian" alliance against "New England," was also allowed after imprisonment to "go out of the jurisdiction," so he could be murdered discreetly against further "agitations" (Winthrop 2:134-136).

Recall that Winslow's letter on Morton above described a mysterious individual *with* Thomas: someone "old, weak and decrepid[,] a very atheist and fitt companion for him" who had "promised" to go along with his new American plans. Did that individual now rejoin Morton in his last departure from Massachusetts Bay in the spring of 1645?

Perhaps sly Samuel Maverick managed to "keep Christmas with" him in jail, or Morton bumped into Maverick off the beaten paths, as he headed out. For an echo of speech seems to linger in Maverick's brief statement, our last glimpse of Morton before he disappears from record. "The offence was he had touched [the "Magistrats"] too neare[:] they not proveing the charge he was sett loose...haveing as he said and most believed[,] received his bane by hard lodging and fare in prison" (*Description* 238). After those words, Thomas Morton spoke no more to "after ages."

Whatever his "crazy" condition, he left the area "soon after, and he went to Acomenticus" (WJH196). Of Morton's "living there" we have only three uncorroborated words, purported to be Winthrop's: "poor and despised." Morton's conditions are debatable, however, for more than the obvious reasons why Winthrop might choose such words. It is not clear how Winthrop, recording this in 1645, could next record the "fact" that Thomas Morton then "died within two years after." If Morton did not die until 1647, this information---presented in all editions as a spontaneous 1645 journal-entry without revision---was possibly added later (accurate or not) by Winthrop, in his Connecticutt "retirement," to his own papers. This would be although no editor accounts for first/second "versions," etc. Of the Winthrop editors treated in Ch. 8 above, none would have lacked motive or means to create what Morton and *Canaan* indeed proved to be, a highly "socially instructive model of cultural closure" for the "troubling" story of the likes of Mine Host.

"Winthrop's" three words are all that speak of Thomas Morton's last days ---how many he had, and what kind. But Thomas was a man of life-long healthy strength, skilled in social and survival skills. He would have smiled at the "No, No!" heard from the Native peoples of that north country, "under" Thomas Gorges. With a bit of benign revenge according to the old code of "quietness," in the raising of a Maypole (or perhaps even two) in the springtime company of old fishermen-friends, Native traders in the seaside meadows of "Maine"---There "Mine Host" might yet have found his rest.

Maverick said only that Thomas died "soone after" being "sett loose." No grave, marker, record or remains can presently be found in Agamenticus (York), Maine. For a long time there was only what Banks (*History* 1:160) had last been able to learn in 1931 of Morton's remains, that he lay in "the little cemetery in Clark's lane on the banks of the river Agamenticus[,] where the first settlers are buried....unhonored but not unsung among the town's distinguished dead." But this graveyard itself no longer exists.[180]

Is it possible that Mine Host cared to compose some further lost "memorial," out of his last days in the land "which he loveth"? One certainty among very few can be that Thomas Morton---West Country English adventurer, attorney, poet of America---passed away like "Job himself" (136): old, and full of days.

---

[180] According to Ms. Virginia Spiller, Librarian of the Old York Historical Society (July 1997), neither the Clark's Lane Burial Ground, nor any remains recovered from it, now exist. Banks had traced this "old burial yard" through an early land-transfer (York Deeds Vol. 7, Folio 149): it was located on the first "York harbor" site, "at the early Anglican Church there in 1632" and "in back of the 'Old Chapel'" (Spiller). In the 19th century the site was "developed" into The Emerson Hotel: numbers of bones and artifacts were found, and their photographs were sold on postcards for a few years; but there were no headstones, and all the remains were "lost," or "simply thrown away." The site is most recently St. George's Church, moved there in the 1950s. See also *Canaan* (Preface) on "The Archaeology of Ma-re Mount."

BIBLIOGRAPHIES

Abbreviations used throughout

AC	"Adams' *Canaan*" or the 1883 edition of *Canaan* by Charles Francis Adams Jr. (Prince/Mass. Historical Society)
FBH	*Of Plimoth Plantation*, by William Bradford (Worthington C. Ford *et als'* 2-volume edition)
WPF	*The* [John] *Winthrop Papers*, edited by Forbes
WJH	*Winthrop's Journal*, edited by Hosmer
A3EP	C. F. Adams Jr.'s *Three Episodes of Massachusetts History*
Key	Roger Williams' *Key Into the Language of America*
TV	John Josselyn's *Two Voyages to New England*
SV	John Josselyn's *Second Voyage*
ENEV	*The English New England Voyages* by David Beers Quinn
MHSC, MHSP	Massachusetts Historical Society: *Collections* and *Publications*
H15	Vol. 15 (*The Northeast*) of *The Handbook of North American Indians*, Bruce G. Trigger, ed.
JAF	*Journal of American Folklore*
Bio	Part 2's biography *Thomas Morton*

Acosta, Jose de, *The Natural and Moral History of the Indies*. Madrid 1589. London 1604, trans. Edward Grimston. Rpt. London: The Hakluyt Society, Clements R. Markham, ed. 1930

Adams, Charles Francis, Jr., ed., *Prince Society Edition of New English Canaan*. New York: Burt Franklin 1883

---, *Three Episodes Of Massachusetts History: The Settlement of Boston Bay*. 2 vols., New York 1892. Rpt. New York: Russell & Russell 1965

Adams, Robert M., ed., *The Prince by Niccolo Machiavelli*. New York: Norton (1977) 1992

---, ed., *Ben Jonson's Plays and Masques*. New York: Norton 1979

Aesop, *Fables*. In *Caxton's Aesop*. R.T. Lenaghan, ed. Cambridge: Harvard University Press 1967

Agnew, Jean-Christophe, *Worlds Apart: The Market and the Theater in Anglo-American Thought 1550-1750*. Cambridge: Cambridge University Press 1986

Albanese, Catherine L., *Nature Religion in America: From the Algonkian Indians to the New Age*. Chicago: Chicago University Press 1990

Alexander, Sir William, *An Encouragement to Colonies* and other works collected in Prince Society, eds., *Sir William Alexander and American Colonization*. Boston: Prince Society 1873. Rpt. Burt Franklin 1967

Allen, Paula Gunn, *The Sacred Hoop: Recovering the Feminine in American Indian Traditions*. Boston, Beacon Press 1986

---, "Where I Come From God Is A Grandmother." *Prisma: A Multicultural Forum*. Boston: University of Massachusetts Publications, Vol. 2 #1, Spring 1991

Amussen, Susan Dwyer, "The Gendering of Popular Culture in Early Modern England." In Harris, ed., *Popular Culture in England c.1500-1850*

Anderson, Benedict, *Imagined Communities: Reflections on the Origin and Spread of Nationalism*. London: Vero 1983

Andrews, K.R., N.P. Canny and P.E.H. Hair, eds., *The Westward Enterprise: English Activities in Ireland, the Atlantic and America 1480-1650*. Detroit: Wayne State University Press 1979

Arber, Edward, ed., *Travels and Works of Captain John Smith, President of Virginia and Admiral of New England 1580-1631*. 2 vols., Edinburgh: John Grant 1910

---, ed., *The Story of the Pilgrim Fathers as Told By Themselves, Their Friends and Their Enemies 1606-1623*. Boston: Houghton Mifflin 1897

---, ed., William Webbe's *Discourse of English Poetrie* [London 1586]. London: A. Murray 1871

Armstrong, Nancy and Leonard Tennenhouse, *The Imaginary Puritan: Literature, Intellectual Labor and the Origins of Personal Life*. Berkeley: University of California Press 1992

---, eds., *The Ideology of Conduct: Essays on Literature and the History of Sexuality*. New York: Methuen 1987

Armstrong, Virginia I., *I Have Spoken: American History Through the Voices of the Indians*. Athens: Ohio University Press 1991

Arner, Robert D., "Mythology and the Maypole Of Merrymount: Some Notes on Thomas Morton's 'Rise, Oedipus.'" In *Early American Literature* 6, 1971, #2

---, "Pastoral Celebration and Satire in Thomas Morton's New English Canaan." *Criticism* Vol. 16 #3, Summer 1974, 217-231

Ascham, Roger, *Toxophilus*. 1545. Edward Arber, ed. London: Southgate 1868

---, *The Schoolmaster*. 1570. Lawrence V. Ryan, ed.. Charlottesville: University Press of Virginia 1967

Ashcraft, Richard, "Leviathan Triumphant: Thomas Hobbes and the Politics of Wild Men." In Dudley, ed., *The Wild Man Within*

Ashley, Leonard R.N., *Elizabethan Popular Culture*. Bowling Green State University Press, Ohio 1988

Astell, Ann W., *Job, Boethius and Epic Truth*. Ithaca: Cornell University Press 1994

Atkins, J.W.H., *English Literary Criticism: The Renascence*. New York: Barnes & Noble 1968

Auden, Wystan Hugh, ed., *An Elizabethan Song-Book: Love Songs and Madrigals*. New York: Anchor 1955

Aurelius, Marcus. *Meditations*. In Meric Causubon, trans., *The Golden Book of Marcus Aurelius*. New York: Dutton 1906

Axtell, James, *The European and the Indian: Essays in the Ethnohistory of Colonial North America*. New York, Oxford University Press 1981

---, *The Invasion Within: The Contest of Cultures in Colonial North America*. New York, Oxford University Press 1985

Ayres, Harral, *The Great Trail of New England*. Boston: Meador Publishing 1940

Bacon, Francis (Sir), *Essays or Counsels, Civil and Moral*. London 1597. 3rd edition rpt. (1625) in Witherspoon/Warnke

Bailey, Alfred Goldsworthy, *The Conflict of European and Eastern Algonkian Cultures 1504-1700*. Toronto 1969

Bain, George W., and Howard A. Meyerhoff, *The Flow of Time in the Connecticutt Valley: Geological Imprints*. Springfield MA: CT Valley Historical Museum 1963

Baker, Brenda J., "Pilgrim's Progress and Praying Indians: The Biocultural Consequences of Contact in Southern New England." In *In the Wake of Contact: Biological Responses to Conquest*. Larsen, Clark Spencer and George R. Milner, eds. New York: Wiley-Liss 1994

Bakhtin, Mikhail, *Rabelais and His World*. Bloomington: Indiana University Press 1984

Bald, R.C., *John Donne: A Life*. Oxford University Press 1970

Banks, Charles Edward, "Thomas Morton of Merrymount." (Incl. the Will of and early English records on Thomas Morton) MHSP Vol. 58, 147-93

---, ed., "To the King's Most Excellent Majesty." (1636 English legal petition for recovery of a minor debt, by Thomas Morton). MHSP Vol. 59 (1925-26), 92-95

---, *History of York, Maine*. 2 volumes. Boston 1931. Rpt. Baltimore: Reginal Publishing 1967

Baraga, Frederic, *A Dictionary of the Ojibway Language*. Minnesota Historical Society Press 1984

Barbour, Philip L., ed., *The Complete Works of Captain John Smith*. Chapel Hill: University of North Carolina Press (3 vols.) 1986

Barck, Oscar T. Jr., and Hugh T. Lefler, eds., *Colonial America*. New York: Macmillan [1958] Rpt. 1968

Barker, Francis, Peter Hulme, Margaret Iverson and Diana Loxley, eds., *Europe and Its Others: Proceedings of the Essex Conference on the Sociology of Literature*. Colchester: University of Essex 1985

Baron, Hans, "Cicero and the Roman Civic Spirit in the Middle Ages and the Early Renaissance" in *Lordship and Community in Medieval Europe*, F.L. Cheyette, ed. New York: Holt Rinehart & Winston 1968

Barrett, Louise K., *The Ignoble Savage: American Literary Racism 1790-1890*. Westport CT: Greenwood Press 1975

Barsh, Russell Lawrence, "The Nature and Spirit Of North American Political Systems." In *American Indian Quarterly*, Vol. X #3, Spring 1986

Baxter, James Phinney, *George Cleeve of Casco Bay 16301667*. Portland, ME 1885

Baym, Nina, *Feminism and American Literary History: Essays*. New Brunswick: Rutgers Univesity Press 1992

Beauchamp, W.M., Onondaga Tale of the Pleiades." In JAF (1895) 13: 281-2

---, "Indian Corn Stories and Customs." In JAF (1898)11:195-202

Beck, Horace P., *Gluskap the Liar and Other Indian Tales*. Freeport ME: Cumberland Press 1966

Bellamie, Jerome, *The Simple Cobbler of Agawam*. London 1647. Rpt. in Force *Tracts* 3:8

Belsey, Catherine, *The Subject of Tragedy: Identity and Difference in Renaissance Drama*. New York: Methuen 1985

Benes, Peter, ed., *New England/New France 1600-1850*. Vol. 14 of The Dublin Seminar for New England Folklife. Boston University 1992

---, ed., *Medicine and Healing*. Vol. 15 of The Dublin Seminar for New England Folklife. Boston University 1992

---, ed., *Algonkians of New England: Past and Present*. The Dublin Seminar for New England Folklife. Boston University 1993

---, ed., *New England's Creatures: 1400-1900*. Vol. 18 of The Dublin Seminar for New England Folklike. Boston University 1995

Bennett, H.S., *English Books and Readers 1558-1603: Being A Study in the History of the Book Trade in the Reign of Elizabeth I*. Cambridge: Cambridge University Press 1965

---, *English Books and Readers 1603-1640: Being A Study in the History of the Book Trade in the Reigns of James I and Charles I*. Cambridge: Cambridge University Press 1970

Bennett, John W., *The Ecological Transition*. New York: Pergamon 1976

Bennett, Linda A., and Genevieve M. Ames, eds., *The American Experience with Alcohol: Contrasting Cultural Perspectives*. New York: Plenum Press 1985

Bennett, M.K., "The Food Economy of the New England Indians 1605-1675." In *Journal of Political Economy* 63 (1955), 369-397

Bercovitch, Sacvan, *The American Puritan Imagination: Essays in Revaluation*. Cambridge: Harvard University Press 1974

---, *The Puritan Origins of the American Self*. New Haven: Yale University Press 1975

Bermudez, Jose Luis, *The Paradox of Self-Consciousness*. Cambridge: Massachusetts Institute of Technology Press 1998

Biggar, H.P., ed., *The Early Trading Companies of New France*. University of Toronto Library 1901

Bilharz, Joy, "First Among Equals? The Changing Status of Seneca Women." In Klein, ed., *Women and Power in Native America*

Black, Hentry Campbell, *Black's Law Dictionary*. 3rd ed. St. Paul, MN: 1933

Bland, D.S., *A Bibliography of the Inns of Court and Chancery*. London: Selden Society Publications, Supplementary Series 3, 1965

Blunt, John Henry, ed., *The Annotated Book of Common Prayer; being an Historical, Ritual and Theological Commentary of the Devotional System of the Church of England*. London: Rivingtons Press 1866

Bolgar, R.R., ed., *Classical Influences on European Culture AD 1500-1700*. Proceedings of an International Conference Held at King's College, Cambridge, England April 1974. Cambridge University Press 1976

Borque, Bruce and R.H. Whitehead, "Tarrantines and the Introduction of European Trade Goods in the Gulf of Maine." In *Ethnohistory* 32: 327-341

Bovie, Smith Palmer, ed., *The Satires and Epistles of Horace*. Chicago: University of Chicago Press 1959

Bowden, Martyn J., "Culture and Place: English Sub-Cultural Regions in New England in the 17th Century." In Benes, ed., *The Dublin Seminar for New England Folklife*. Boston University

Boyce, Smith Palmer, trans., *The Satires and Epistles of Horace.* Chicago: Chicago University Press 1959

Boyd, Susan H., "This Indian Is Not An Indian: Labeling Play in Powwowdom," in Michael A. Salter, ed., *Play: Anthropological Perspectives. Proceedings of the Association for the Anthropological Study of Play*, West Point, NY: Leisure Press 1977

Bradford, William, *History of Plimoth Plantation 1620-1647.* Charles Francis Adams, Arthur Lord, Morton Dexter, Gamaliel Bradford Jr., and Worthington C. Ford, eds. 2 vols., Boston: Houghton Mifflin Co 1912

---, "A Dialogue" in Young, *Chronicles* 416-17

---, "Letter Book" in MHSC I, series III (1794), 27-76

---, "A Descriptive and Historical Account of New England in Verse, from the Manuscripts of Williams Bradford," (a.k.a. "Verse History"). In MHSC I, series III (1794), 82-3

Bradley, James W., "Native Exchange and European Trade: Cross Cultural Dynamics in the Sixteenth Century." In *Man in the Northeast* 33 (Spring 1987): 31-46

Bradstreet, Anne, *Contemplations.* London 1650. In Meserole, ed., *American Poetry*

---, "To My Dear Children." In McElrath and Robb, eds., *The Complete Works of Anne Bradstreet*

---, poetry: see entries under Hensley, McElrath/Robb, and Piercy

Bragdon, Kathleen J., "'Emphaticall Speech and Great Action': An Analysis of 17th-Century Native Speech Events Described in Early Sources." In *Man in the Northeast* 33 (1987), 101-11

---, "Vernacular Literacy and Massachusetts World View 1650-1750." In Benes, ed., *Algonkians* (1993), 26-35

---, *Native People of Southern New England 1500-1650.* Norman: Oklahoma University Press 1996

--- and Ives Goddard, *Native Writings in Massachusett.* 2 vols. Philadelphia: American Philosophical Society 1988

Brasser, T.J., "Early Indian-European Contacts," in H15

Braun, D., "Explanatory Models for the Evolution of Coastal Adaptation in Prehistoric Eastern New England." *American Antiquity* 38 (4:1), 582-96

Brooks, Cleanth, R.W.B. Lewis, R.P. Warren and David Milch, eds., *American Literature: The Makers and the Making.* New York: St. Martin's Press 1973

G. Brotherston, ed., "How Salmon Are Lured Inland." In *Image of the New World: The American Continent Portrayed in Native Texts.* London: Thames & Hudson 1979

Brown, Judith K., "Economic Organization and the Powers of Women Among the Iroquois." *Ethnohistory* 17 (Summer-Fall 1970), 151-67

Bruchac, Joseph, and Michael s. Caduto, eds., *Keepers of the Earth: Native American Stories and Environmental Activities for Children*. Golden CO: Fulcrum 1988

---, eds., *Keepers of the Animals: Native American Stories and Wildlife Activities for Children*. Golden CO: Fulcrum 1991

---, eds., *Native American Gardening: Stories, Projects and Recipes for Families*. Golden CO: Fulcrum 1996

Bull, John, John Farrand Jr., and Susan Rayfield, eds., *The Audubon Society Field Guide to North American Birds: Eastern Region*. New York: Knopf 1977

Burrage, Henry S., ed., *Early English and French Voyages*. New York: Scribner's, Original Narratives of Early American History 1906

Burton, Robert, *The Anatomy of Melancholy*. 1621. Dell, Floyd and Paul Jordan Smith, eds., New York: Tudor (1927) 1955

Bush, David, *Mythology and the Renaissance Tradition in English Poetry*. New York: W.W. Norton 1963

Bush, Douglas, "Spenser's Treatment of Classical Myth." In Maclean, ed., *Edward Spenser's Poetry*

Calloway, Colin G., "The Abenakis and the Anglo-French Borderlands." In Benes, ed, *New England/New France*

Camden, William, *Remains Concerning Britain*. 1605. R.D. Donn, ed., University of Toronto Press 1984

Cameron, Euan, ed., *Early Modern Europe*. Cambridge: Oxford University Press 1999

Canny, Nicholas P., "The Ideology of English Colonization." In *William and Mary Quarterly*, 3rd series vol. XXX (OCt. 1973) #4, 575-98

---, "The Permissive Frontier: The Problem of Social Control in English Settlements in Ireland and Virginia." In Andrews, *The Westward Enterprise* 17-44

Canup, John, *Out of the Wilderness: The Emergence of An American Identity in Colonial New England*. Middletown CT: Wesleyan University Press 1990

Carpenter, Dolores Bird, ed., *Early Encounters: Native Americans and Europeans in New England. From the Papers of Warren Sears Nickerson*. East Lansing: Michigan State University Press 1994

Carlin, Norah, "Ireland and Natural Man in 1649" in Barker, ed., *Europe and Its Others*

Carlson, Catherine A., "The (In)Significance of Atlantic Salmon in New England." In Benes, ed., *New England's Creatures*

Carlson, Richard G., ed., *Rooted Like the Ash Trees: New England Indians and the Land*. Naugatuck, CT: Eagle Wing Press 1987

Carroll, Joseph, *Evolution and Literary Theory*. Columbia: University of Missouri Press 1995

Carson, Dale, *Native New England Cooking*. Madison CT: Sachem Press 1986

Cassirer, Ernst, P.O. Kristeller and J.H. Randall, Jr., eds., *The Renaissance Philosophy of Man*. Chicago University Press 1948

Castiglione, Baldasar, *The Book of the Courtier*. 1528. George Bull, trans. New York: Penguin 1967

Castor, Grahame, *Pleiade Poetics: A Study in Sixteenth-Century thought and Terminology*. Cambridge University Press 1964

Cave, Alfred A., *The Pequot War*. Amherst University of Massachusetts Press 1996

Cave, Terence, *The Cornucopian Text: Problems of Writing in the French Renaissance*. Oxford: Clarendon Press 1979

---, "'The Triumph of Bacchus' and Its Interpretation in the French Renaissance." In Levi, *Humanism in France* 249-265

Caven, Brian, *The Punic Wars*. New York: Barnes & Noble 1980

Ceci, Lynn, "Native Wampum as a Peripheral Resource in the 17th Century World System." In Hauptmann *Pequots* 48-63 (1990)

--- "Squanto and the Pilgrims: On Planting Corn 'in the manner of the Indians.'" In Clifton, ed., The Invented Indian 71-90 (1994)

Chamberlain, Barbara Blau, *These Fragile Outposts: A Geological Look at Cape Cod, Martha's Vineyard and Nantucket*. Garden City NY: American Museum of Natural History Press 1964

Chambers, Mortimer, Raymond Grew, David Herlihy, Theodore K. Rabb and Isser Woloch, eds., *The Western Experience to 1715*. New York: Knopf 1974

Champlain, Samuel D., *Voyages of Samuel de Champlain 1604-1618*. W.L.Grant, ed. New York: Scribner's 1907

---, *The Works of Samuel de Champlain*. 1626. Hentry P. Biggar, ed. 6 vols. Toronto: The Champlain Society 1922-1936

Charvat, William, *The Origins of American Critical Thought 1810-1835*. Philadelphia: University of Pennsylvania Press 1936

Chiappelli, Fredi, Michael J.B. Allen and Robert L. Benson, eds., *First Images of America: The Impact of the New World on the Old*. 2 Vols. Berkeley: University of California Press 1976

Chilton, Elizabeth S., "In Search of Paleo-Women: Gender Implications of Remains from Paleoindian Sites in the Northeast", in *Bulletin of the Massachusetts Archaeological Society*, Vol. 55 (1), Spring 1994, 8-17

Cicero, Marcus Tullius, *On The Character of the Orator (De Oratore)*, Rome c. 55 B.C.E. London: Henry G. Bohn 1855, J.S. Watson, trans.

---, *Brutus.On The Nature of the Gods. On Duties*. Hubert M. Poteat, trans. Chicago: University of Chicago 1950

---, *On Supreme Good and Evil*. In M. R. Wright, ed. and trans., *Cicero on Stoic Good and Evil*. New York: Aris & Phillips 1991

---, *Tusculan Disputations*. A. E. Douglas, ed. 2 vols. Chicago: Aris & Phillip 1985

Clapham, Henoch, *An Epistle Discoursing Upon the Present Pestilence*. London. T. C[reede], 1603

Clark, Peter, *The English Alehouse*. London: Longman, 1983.

Clendinnen, Inga, *Ambivalent Conquests: Maya and Spaniard in Yucatan 1517-1570*. Cambridge: Cambridge UP 1987

Clifton, James, "Alternate Identities and Cultural Frontiers." Editor's Introduction to *Being and Becoming Indian: Biographical Studies of North American Frontiers*. Chicago: Dorsey Press 1989

---, ed., *The Invented Indian: Cultural Fictions and Government Policies*. London: Transaction Publishers 1994

Coleman, Robert, ed., *Virgil: Eclogues*. Cambridge: Cambridge University Press 1977

Combellack, Frederick M., *The War at Troy: What Homer Didn't Tell*. New York: Barnes & Noble 1996

Connor, Sheila, *New England Natives*. Cambridge: Harvard University Press 1994

Connors, Donalf F., *Thomas Morton*. New York: Twayne 1969

Cook, Sherburne F., "The Significance of Disease in the Extinction of the New England Indians." *Human Biology* 45 (3) (1973): 485-508

Cooke, Jacob E., gen. ed., *The Encyclopedia of the North American Colonies*. 3 vols. New York: Scribner's 1993

Cooper, John M., "The Culture of the Northeastern Indian Hunters" in Johnson *Man in Northeastern North America*

Cope, Jackson I., *The Theatre and the Dream: From Metaphor to Form in Renaissance Drama*. Baltimore: Johns Hopkins University Press 1973

Cowan, William, ed., *Papers of the Seventh Algonquian Conference*. Ottawa: Carleton University 1976

Cox, Edward G., ed. *A Reference Guide to The Literature of Travel* (3 vols: Old World, New World, England). Seattle: University of Washington Press 1935-49

Cox, Donald D., *Common Flowering Plants of the Northeast*. Albany: State University of New York Press 1985

Cronon, William, *Changes in the Land: Indians, Colonists and the Ecology of New England*. New York: Farrar Straus & Giroux 1983

Crosby, Connie, "The Algonkian Spiritual Landscape." In Benes, *Algonkians of New England*, 35-41 (1993)

Crosby, W.O., *Physical History of the Boston Basin*. Boston: J. A. Crosby 1889

Crossley, Hastings, trans., *The Golden Sayings of Epictetus* (c. 50-100 AD). Danbury CT: Grolier Harvard Classics Series 1980

Cummins, John, *The Hound and the Hawk: The Art of Medieval Hunting*. New York: St. Martin's Press 1988

Curliss, Bruce (Nipmuc Native community leader). Interview in Dempsey, videodocumentary *Nani*

Curry, Patrick, *Prophecy and Power: Astrology in Early Modern England*. Princeton University Press 1994

Curtin, J. and J.N.B. Hewitt, *Seneca Fiction, Legends and Myths*. Washington D.C.: Smithsonian Institution 1918. Bureau of American Ethnology Annual Report 32

Dailey, R.C., "The Role of Alcohol among North American Indian Tribes as Reported in *The Jesuit Relations*." In Marshall, ed., *Beliefs* 1979

Daly, Robert, *God's Altar: The World and the Flesh in Puritan Poetry*. Berkeley: University of California Press 1978

Dame, Lorin L, and Henry Brooks, *Handbook of the Trees of New England*. Boston: Athenaeum Press 1904

Danby, John F., ed., *Elizabethan and Jacobean Poets: Studies in Sydney, Shakespeare, Beau-mont and Fletcher*. London: Faber & Faber 1975

Daniel-Ropp, Henri, *Daily Life in the Time of Jesus*. Ann Arbor: Servant Books 1980

Davenport, Francis Gardner, *European Treaties Bearing on the History of the United States and Its Dependencies*. Washington D.C.: Carnegie Institute Publication 254. 3 vols. 1917

David, Richard, ed., *Hakluyt's Voyages*. Boston: Houghton Mifflin 1981

Davies, Horton, *The Worship of the American Puritans 1629-1730*. New York: Peter Lang 1990

Davies, Stevie, ed., *Renaissance Views of Man*. Manchester University Press 1979

Davis, Mary Bird, ed., *Old Growth in the East*. Richmond, VT (05477): Wild Earth Publications. 2nd edition 1999

Davis, Natalie Zemon, "Boundaries and the Sense of Self in 16th-Century France." In Heller, Sosna & Wellbery, eds., *Reconstructing Individualism*

Davis, William A., "Digging It In Massachusetts." *The Boston Globe* June 6, 1992

Day, Gordon M., "Western Abenaki" in H15 148-159

---, "The Indians As Ecological Factor in the Northeast Forest." In *Ecology* 34 (2): 329-46

Deagan, Kathleen A., "Spanish Indian Interaction in Sixteenth Century Florida and Hispaniola." In Fitzhugh, ed., *Cultures in Contact*

DeCosta, B.F., "Morton of Merrymount." *Magazine of American History* Vol VIII #2, February 1882, 81-94

---, DeCosta, B.F., "Morton's *New English Canaan.*" *New England Historical and Genealogical Register* 48 (1894)

Delgado-Gomez, Angel, "The Earliest European Views of the New World Natives." In Williams, ed., *Early Images of the Americas* (1993)

de Molina, Don Diego, "Letter of Don Diego de Molina." 1613. In Tyler, ed., *Narratives of Early Virginia.* New York: Scribner's 1907

Dempsey, John, *Thomas Morton and the Maypole of Merrymount: Disorder in the American Wilderness 1622-1647.* 2-hr. video documentary (1992) distributed by the producer.

---, Jack, *Nani: A Native New England Story.* 1-hr. videodocumentary (1998) distributed by V-Tape, 401 Richmond St. West, Suite 452, Toronto, Canada M5V 3A8 (456-351-1317; *or*, video@total.net

Densmore, Frances. *How Indians Use Wild Plants for Food, Medicine, and Crafts.* New York: Dover 1974

De Vries, David P., *Korte Historiael ende journaels aenteyckeninge,* 1610-1633. 1655 Rpt. in Myers, ed., *Narratives of Early Pennsylvania*

Dexter, Lincoln A., *Maps of Early Massachusetts: Prehistory Through the 17th Century.* rev. ed. 1986

Dickason, Olive Patricia, *The Myth of the Savage and the Beginnings of French Colonialism in the Americas.* Edmonton: University of Alberta Press 1984

Dincauze, Dena F., "A Capsule Prehistory of Southern New England." In Hauptmann and Wherry, *The Pequots*

Donald, Leland, "Liberty, Equality, Fraternity: Was the Indian Really Egalitarian?" in Clifton, ed., *The Invented Indian* 145-168

Dothan, Trude, and Moshe Dothan, *People of the Sea: The Search for the Philistines.* New York: Macmillan 1992

Dowling, Maria, *Humanism in the Age of Henry VIII.* London: Croom Helm 1986

Drinnon, Richard, *Facing West: The Metaphysics of Indian-Hating and Empire-Building.* New York: Schocken 1980

Dudley, Edward and Maximilian E. Novak, eds., *The Wild Man Within: An Image in Western Thought from the Renaissance to Romanticism.* University of Pittsburgh Press 1972

Dudley, Joseph, "Letter to Bridgit Countess of Lincoln". 1631. Rpt. in Force *Tracts* Vol. 2

Duff, J.D., trans. *The Civil War* (by Lucan c.39-65 AD). New York: Putnam's 1928

Duncan, Roger F., *Coastal Maine: A Maritime History.* New York: Norton 1992

Dunn, Jerome P., "Squanto Before He Met the Pilgrims." In *Bulletin of the Massachusetts Archaeological Society*, Vol 54, #1, Spring 1993

Dyer, Gwynne, *War*. New York: Crown Press 1985

Eastman, Charles A. (Ohiyesa), *Indian Scout Craft and Lore*. 1914. Rpt. New York: Dover 1974

Eccles, W.J., *France in America*. East Lansing: Michigan State University Press 1990. [Ch. 1: "False Starts 1500-1632"]

Edmundson, George, *Anglo-Dutch Rivalry During the First Half of the 17th Century*. Oxford University Press, 1911

Eliade, Mircea, *Cosmos and History: or, The Myth of the Eternal Return*. W.R. Trask, trans., Princeton UP 1954

Elias, Thomas S., *The Complete Trees of North America: Field Guide and Natural History*. New York: Book Division 1980

Elson, Ruth Miller, *Guardians of Tradition: American Schoolbooks in the 19th Century*. Lincoln: University of Nebraska Press 1964

Emerson, George B., *A Report on the Trees and Shrubs Growing Naturally in the Forests of Massachusetts*. 2 vols. Boston: Little Brown 1887

Empiricus, Sextus, *The Outlines of Pyrronhism* (c. 150-225 AD) Rpt. in Hallie, Philip P., ed., and Etheridge, Sanford G., trans., *Scepticism, Man and God: Selections from the Major Writings of Sextus Empiricus*. Middletown CT: Wesleyan University Press 1964

Epictetus, qtd. in *The Golden Sayings of Epictetus*. Hastings Crossley, trans. Danbury CT: Grolier Harvard Classics Series 1980

Erasmus, Desiderius, *Twenty Select Colloquies of Erasmus.*. Louvain 1519, London 1680: R. L'Estrange, trans. In Davies, *Renaissance Views of Man*

Erickson, Vincent O., "Maliseet-Passamaquoddy" in H15 123-36

Etienne, Mona, and Eleanor Leacock, eds., *Women and Colonization: Anthropological Perspectives*. New York: Praeger 1980

Eusden, John Dykstra, *Puritans, Lawyers and Politics in Early 17th Century England*. New Haven: Yale UP 1958

Evans, Humphrey, *Falconry For You*. London: John Gifford Ltd. 1960

Feest, Christian F., "North Carolina Algonquians" in H15, 271-81

---, "Virginia Algonquians" in H15, 253-270

Felltham, Owen, "Of Poets and Poetry" in *Resolves*. London 1628. Rpt. in Witherspoon/Warnke

Felt, Joseph B., *Annals of Salem, From Its First Settlement*. Salem: W. and S.B. Ives 1827

Fenton, William N., "Northern Iroquoian Culture Patterns" in H15, 296-321

Fernald, Merritt Lyndon and Alfred Charles Kinsey, *Edible Wild Plants of Eastern North America*. New York: Idlewild Press 1943

Finkelpearl, Philip J., *John Marston of the Middle Temple*. Cambridge: Harvard University Press 1969

Fischer, David Hackett, *Albion's Seed: Four British Folkways in America*. New York: Oxford University Press 1989

Fiske, John, *The Dutch and Quaker Colonies in America*. 2 vols. Boston: Houghton Mifflin 1903

Fletcher, Anthony, *A County Community in Peace and War: Sussex 1600-1660*. New York: Longman 1975

--- and John Stevenson, eds., *Order and Disorder in Early Modern England*. Cambridge: Cambridge University Press 1985

Fitzhugh, William, "Early Contacts North of Newfoundland Before 1600: A Review." In Fitzhugh ed., *Cultures in Contact*,

---, ed. *Cultures in Contact: The Impact of European Contacts on Native American Cultural Institutions*. Washington D.C.: Smithsonian Institution Press 1985

Fogelson, Raymond D., "Change, Persistence and Accomodation in Cherokee Medico-Magical Beliefs." In *Symposium on Cherokee and Iroquois Culture*, W.N. Fenton and J. Gulick, eds,. Smithsonian Institution, Bureau of American Ethnology, Bulletin 180. Washington D.C. 1961

Foley, Stephen Merriam, *Sir Thomas Wyatt*. Boston: Twayne Series, G.K. Hall 1990

Force, Peter, ed., *Tracts and Other Papers Relating Principally to the Origin, Settlement, and Progress of the Colonies in North America, From the discovery of the country to the Year 1776*. Washington: 3 vols., Peter Force printer, 1836

Ford, Worthington Chauncy, "Morton of Merry Mount: Paid for Th: Morton." In MHSP Vol. 45 (Oct. 1911-12), 641-3

---, "Captain Wollaston, Humphrey Rasdall and Thomas Weston. In MHSP LI (1917-18), 219-232

Foster, Stephen, *Notes from the Caroline Underground*. Hamden CT: Archon Books 1978

Friedman, Jerome, *Blasphemy, Immorality and Anarchy: The Ranters and the English Revolution*. Athens: Ohio University Press 1987

Fowler, Alistair, *The Country House Poem*.

Fowler, Barbara Hughes, trans., *Vergil's Eclogues*. Chapel Hill: University of North Carolina Press 1997

Fox, Aileen, *South West England*. New York: Praeger 1964

Freeman, Stan, and Mike Nasuti, *The Natural History and Resources of Western Massachusetts*. Florence MA: Hampshire House 1994

---, *The Natural History of Eastern Massachusetts*. Florence MA: Hampshire House 1998

Friedman, Jerome, *Blasphemy, Immorality and Anarchy: The Ranters and the English Revolution*. Athens: Ohio University Press 1987

Frost, Jack, ed., *Immortal Voyage....And Pilgrim Parallels: Problems, Protests, Patriotism 1620-1970*. North Scituate, MA: Hawthorne Press 1970

Fuertes, Louis Agassiz, "Falconry, The Sport of Kings." *National Geographic Magazine* article (c.1920) provided by Mike McWade, Trailside Museum, Canton MA. This material is also found in Fuertes' revised *Birds of Massachusetts and Other New England States* (1925: 3 vols.): see Forbush, Edward H., ed., *Natural History of the Birds of Eastern and Central North America*. Boston: Houghton Mifflin 1939

Fumerton, Patricia, *Cultural Aesthetics: Renaissance Literature and the Practice of Social Ornament*. University of Chicago Press 1991

Funk, Robert E., "Post-Pleistocene Adaptations" in H15, 16-27

Gaines, J., "Life Behind the Mohawk Lines." *The Boston Globe*, July 22, 1990 (19)

Galinsky, Hans, "History of the Colonial American Humorist: Thomas Morton and the Burwell Papers" in *Forms and Functions of History in American Literature*, W. Fluck, ed. Berlin: Erich Schmidt Verlag 1981, 21-43

Gardener, Henry, *New England's Vindication*. London 1660. Charles Edward Banks, ed. Portland ME 1884

Gardiner, Harold C., *Mysteries' End: An Investigation of the Last Days of the Medieval Religious Stage*. New Haven: Yale University Press 1946

Gardner, Russell H. (*aka* Great Moose: Wampanoag Tribal Historian/Gay Head Aquinnah), "Genesis of New England's Sacred Landscape and Our Spiritual Legacy." Unpublished text of lecture to Massachusetts Archaeological Society, Robbins Museum, Middleboro MA: April 5, 1997; read from aloud by Gardner in Dempsey, *Nani*

---, "Anthropomorphic and Fertility Stoneworks of Southeastern New England: A Native Interpretation." Illustrated. To be published 1999 by *The Massachusetts Archaeological Society Bulletin*. Generously shared in mss.

Gascoigne, George, *Notes on English Verse*. London 1575. In John W. Cunliffe, ed., *The Complete Works of George Gascoigne*. Cambridge, England: The University Press 1907-10

Gathorne-Hardy, G.M., *The Norse Discoverers of America: The Wineland Sagas*. 1921. Rpt. London: Oxford University Press 1970

Gatrell, V.A.C., *Hanging Tree: Execution and the English People (1770-1868)*. New York: Oxford University Press 1994

Geertz, Clifford, "Religion as a Cultural System" in *The Interpretation of Cultures: Selected Essays*. New York: Basic 1973

Gefou-Madianou, Dimitra, *Alcohol, Gender and Culture*. New York: Routledge 1992

Gerard, John[?], *Gerard's Herball, or General History of Plants*. London (1597) 1633

Gesta Grayorum, or, The History of the High and Mighty Prince Henry, Prince of Purpoole...Who reigned and died A.D. 1594. Together with a Masque.... Multiple anonymous authors at Inns of Court, London. Rpt. in John Nichols, ed., *The Progresses and Public Processions of Queen Elizabeth*. 2 Vols. Society of Antiquaries of London, Printers 1788

Gifford, William, trans., *Satires* (of Juvenal, c. 38-70 AD). London: G. & W. Nicol 1817

Gill, Sam D., and Irene F. Sullivan, eds., *Dictionary of Native American Mythology*. New York: Oxford University Press 1992

Gilligan, Carol, "Remapping the Moral Domain: New Images of the Self in Relationship." In Thomas C. Heller *et als*, eds., *Reconstructing Individualism: Autonomy, Individuality and the Self in Western Thought*. Stanford UP 1986

Ginzburg, Carlo, *The Night Battles: Witchcraft and Agrarian Cults in the 16th and 17th Centuries*. 1966. John and Anne Tedeschi, trans. Baltimore: Johns Hopkins University Press 1983

Girouard, Mark, *Life in the English Country House*. London: Yale University Press 1978

gkisedtanamoogk, and Frances Hancock, *Ceremony Is Life Itself*. Portland, ME: Astarte Shell Press 1993

Goldberg, Jonathan, "Bradford's 'Ancient Members' and "A Case of Buggery Amongst Them.'" In *Sodometries: Renaissance Texts, Modern Sexualities*. Stanford University Press 1991

Golding, Arthur, trans., *Ovid's Metamorphoses*. London 1627. In John F. Nims, ed. New York: Macmillan 1965

Goldman, Marcus S., *Sir Philip Sydney and The Arcadia*. Illinois Studies in Language and Literature Vol. XVII, Numbers 1&2. Urbana: University of Illinois Press 1934

Gookin, Daniel, *Historical Collections of the Indians in New England*. 1674. 1806 Rpt. in MHSC 3 series vol. 1, 141-229

Gookin, Warner F., and Philip L. Barbour, *Bartholomew Gosnold: Discoverer and Planter*. London: Archon 1963

Gorges, Sir Ferdinando, *A Brief Relation of the Discovery and Plantation of New England*. London 1622. MHSC 2nd series ix (1823), 1-25

---, *A Brief Narration of the Original Undertakings, for the Advancement of Plantations in America*. [1658]. Maine Historical Society Collections, I ser II, 1847, 1-65

Gradante, William J., "The Message in the Mask: Costuming in the Festival Context." In Kendall Blanchard, ed., *The Many Faces of Play*, Champaign, IL: Human Kinetics Publications 1986

Grafton, Anthony, *New Worlds, Ancient Texts: The Power of Tradition and the Shock of Discovery*. Cambridge: Harvard University Press 1992

--- and Lisa Jardine, *From Humanism to the Humanities*. Cambridge: Harvard University Press 1986

Grant, Michael, *Myths of the Greeks and Romans*.New York: Signet 1962

Grant, W.L., and James Munroe, eds., *Acts of the Privy Council, Colonial Series 1613-1783*. Hereford, England: 2 vols. 1908

Graves, Robert, *The Greek Myths*. 2 vols. New York Penguin 1960

---, *The White Goddess: An Historical Grammar of Poetic Myth*. New York: Farrar Straus & Giroux (1948) 1980

Gray, Edward F., *Leif Eriksson: Discoverer of America AD 1003*. New York: Oxford University Press 1930. Rpt. New York: Kraus 1972

Gray, Philip Howard, "Thomas Morton as America's First Behavioral Observer (in New England 1624-1646)." In *Bulletin of the Psychonomic Society*. 1987, 25 (1), 69-72

Green, A. Wigfall, *The Inns of Court and Early English Drama*. New Haven: Yale University Press 1931

Greene, Thomas, *The Light in Troy: Imitation and Discovery in Renaissance Poetry*. Yale University Press 1982

Greenblatt, Stephen J., *Sir Walter Ralegh: The Renaissance Man and His Roles*. New Haven: Yale University Press 1973

---, *Renaissance Self-Fashioning: From More to Shakespeare*. Chicago: University of Chicago Press 1984

Grossman, Mary Louise and John Hamlet (photography by Shelly Grossman), *Birds of Prey of the World*. New York: Clarkson N. Potter 1987

Grumet, Robert Steven, "Sunksquaws, Shamans and Tradeswomen: Middle Atlantic Coastal Algonkian Women During the 17th and 18th Centuries." In Etienne *Women and Colonization*

---, ed., *Northeastern Indian Lives 1632-1816*. Amherst: University of Massachusetts Press 1996

Guazzo, Stefano, *The civile conversation of M. Steeven Guazzo*. Brescia 1574. George Pettie, trans. 1581. Rpts. London: Constable & Co.; New York, Knopf 1925

Guilbert, Charles Mortimer, ed. (Custodian of), *The Book of Common Prayer*. [1549] New York: Seabury Press 1979.

Guillette, Mary E., ed., *American Indians in Connecticutt: Past to Present. A Report Prepared for the Connecticutt Indian Affairs Council*. State of Connecticutt, Department of Environmental Protection 1979

Guillory, John, *Cultural Capital*. Chicago: University of Chicago Press 1993

Guterman, Norbert, ed., *The Anchor Book of Latin Quotations with English Translations*. New York: Anchor 1966

Hakluyt, Richard, ed., *Divers Voyages Touching the Discoverie of America and the Islands Adjacent Unto the Same*. London: T. Woodcocke 1582. Rpt. John W. Jones, ed., London: Hakluyt Society 1850

---, ed., *The Principall Navigations, Voyages, Traffiques, and Discoveries of the English Nation*. Rpt. (12 vols). Glasgow: 1903-05

Hale, Edward Everett Jr., ed., *Notebook Kept by Thomas Lechford, Esquire: Lawyer in Boston, Massachusetts Bay 1638-1641*. Camden, ME: Picton Press 1988

Hall, Anne Drury, *Ceremony and Civility in English Renaissance Prose*. Pennsylvania State Univeristy Press 1991

Haller, William, *The Rise of Puritanism*. New York: Columbia University Press 1938

Hallett, Leaman, F., "Medicine and Pharmacy of the New England Indians." *Mass. Archaeological Society Bulletin*, Vol. 17 #3 (1956)

Hallowell, A. Irving, "Ojibwa World View and Disease." In *Contributions to Anthropology: Selected Papers of A. I. Hallowell*. Chicago 1976

---, *The Role of Conjuring in Saulteaux Society*. New York: Octagon 1971

Halpern, Richard, *The Poetics of Primitive Accumulation: English Renaissance Culture and the Genealogy of Capital*. Ithaca, NY: Cornell University Press 1991

Hamilton, William J., Jr., *The Mammals of Eastern United States*. New York: Hafner 1963

Hammond, Jeffrey A., *Sinful Self, Saintly Self: The Puritan Experience of Poetry*. Athens: University of Georgia Press 1993

Hammell, George, "Mythical Realities and European Contact in the Northeast During the Sixteenth and Seventeenth Centuries." In *Man in the Northeast* 33 [1987]: 63-87

Hanke, Lewis, *The First Social Experiments in America: A Study of the Development of Spanish Indian Policy in the 16th Century*. Cambridge:Harvard University Press 1935

Harbage, Alfred, gen. ed., *William Shakespeare: The Complete Works*. Rev. ed. New York: Penguin 1969

Harris, John, *Saga of the Pilgrims: From Europe to the New World*. Chester, CT: Globe Pequot [1983]1990

Hariot, Thomas, *Brief and True Report of the New Found Land of Virginia*. London 1588. Rpt. New York: Dover 1972

Harris, Marvin, *The Rise of Anthropological Theory*. New York: Crowell 1968

Harris, Tim, ed., *Popular Culture in England 1500-1850*. New York: St. Martin's 1995

Harpur, James, ed., *Great Events of Bible Times: New Perspectives on the People, Places and History of the Biblical World*. New York: Doubleday 1987

Hart, Alfred, ed., *Shakespeare and The Homilies, and Other Pieces of Research into the Elizabethan Drama*. Melbourne: Melbourne University Press 1934

Harvey, Sir Paul, ed., *The Oxford Dictionary of English Proverbs*. Cambridge: Oxford Univeristy Press 1948

Haskins, George, *Law and Authority in Early Massachusetts*. Hamden CT: Archon 1960

Hauptmann, Laurence M. and James O. Wherry, *The Pequots in Southern New England: The Fall and Rise of an American Indian Nation*. Norman: University of Oklahoma Press 1990

Hayman, Robert, *Quodlibets*. London 1628. Original copy in the John Carter Brown Library, Brown University, Providence RI USA

Hazard, Ebenezer, ed., *Historical Collections*. 2 vols. Philadelphia: 1792

Hazlitt, W.C., *Faiths and Folklore of the British Isles*. New York: B. Blom 1965

Headlam, Cecil, *The Inns of Court*. (Illustrations by Gordon Home) London: Adam & Charles Black 1909

Heard, J. Norman, *Handbook of the American Frontier: Four Centuries of Indian-White Relationships*, Vol. II *The Northeastern Woodlands*. Metuchen, NJ: Scarecrow Press 1990

Heckewelder, John, *History, Manners and Customs of the Indian Nations Who Once Inhabited Pennsylvania and the Neighboring States*. Philadelphia 1818. Rev. ed. Bethlehem PA 1876: Publication Fund of the Historical Society of Pennsylvania. W.C. Reichel, ed.

Heiberg, Marianne, *The Making of the Basque Nation*. Cambridge University Press 1989

Heidenreich, Conrad E., "Huron" in H15, 368-88

Heller, Agnes, *Renaissance Man*. Richard E. Allen, trans., London: Routledge & Keegan Paul [1967] 1978

Heller, Thomas C., Morton Sosna and David Wellbery, eds., *Reconstructing Individualism: Autonomy, Individuality, and the Self in Western Thought*. Stanford: University of California Press 1986

Heninger, S.K., Jr., *A Handbook of Renaissance Meteorology*. Durham: Duke University Press 1960

---, *The Cosmographical Glass: Renaissance Diagrams of the Universe*. San Marino: Huntington Library 1977

Hensley, Jeannine, ed., *The Works of Anne Bradstreet*. Cambridge: Harvard University Press 1967

Higginson, Francis, *New England's Plantation*. London 1630. Rpt. in Force, *Tracts* 1

Hill, Christopher, *The World Turned Upside Down: Radical Ideas During the English Revolution*. [1972] New York: Viking 1973

---, *Change and Continuity in Seventeenth Century England*. Cambridge: Harvard University Press 1975

Hitchcock, Edward, ed., *Final Report on the Geology of Massachusetts in Four Parts: Econom-ical, Scenographical, Scientific and Elementary Geology*. Amherst: J.S. and C. Adams Publishers 1841

Holly, H. Hobart, "Wollaston of Mount Wollaston." Quincy [MA] Historical Society Publication. Rpt. from *The American Neptune*, Vol. XXXVII, #1, Jan. 1977

Holmgren, Virginia C. *Racoons*. Santa Barbara CA: Capra Press 1990

Honour, Hugh, *The New Golden Land: European Images of America from the Discoveries to the Present Time*. London: Allea Lane 1976

Horner, George R., "Squantum, Moswetusett, Mattachusett, Massachusetts, Neponset, Chikkatawbut." In *Quincy History*. Quincy, MA: Historical Society #21, Winter 1989, 1-4

Hoskins, W.G., *Old Devon*. Devon, England: David & Charles, Publishers [1954] 1972

---, *Devon*. Devon, England: David & Charles, Publishers 1968

Hosmer, James Kendall, ed., see *Winthrop's Journal "History of New England"*

Howatson, M.C., ed., *The Oxford Companion to Classical Literature*. New York: Oxford University Press 1989

Howell, W.S., "Poetics, Rhetoric and Logic in Renaissance Criticism." In Bolgar, ed., *Classical Influences* 155-162

Hubbard, William, *The History of the Indian Wars in New England*. 1677. (1865) Samuel G. Drake, ed., Roxbury: W. Eliot Woodward. Rpt. 1969, New York: Kraus Reprint Co.

Huddleston, Lee, *Origins of the American Indians 1492-1729*. Austin: University of Texas Press 1967

Hulme, Peter, "Polytropic Man: Tropes of Sexuality and Mobility in Early Colonial Discourse." In Barker, ed., *Europe and Its Others*

Hunter, G.K., *John Lyly: The Humanist as Courtier*. London: Routledge & Keegan Paul 1962

Hurstfield, Joel and Alan G.R. Smith, *Elizabethan People: State and Society*. New York: St. Martin's 1972

Hutchinson, Thomas, *A Collection of Original Papers Relative to the History of the Colony and Province of Massachusetts Bay*. Boston: Fleet 1769 Original copy in John Hay Library, Brown University, Providence RI . Rpt. Cambridge: Harvard University Press 1936

Hutton, Ronald, *The Rise and Fall of Merry England: The Ritual Year 1400-1700*. New York: Oxford UP 1994

Ingram, Martin, "From Reformation to Toleration: Popular Religious Cultures in England, 1540-1690." In Harris, ed., *Popular Culture in England*

James, E.O., *Seasonal Feasts and Festivals*. London: Thames and Hudson 1961

Jameson, J. Franklin, ed., *Narratives of New Netherland 1609-1664*. New York: Barnes and Noble 1909

Jantz, Harold S., *The First Century of New England Verse*. (1944) Rpt. New York: Russell and Russell 1962

Jennings, Francis, *The Invasion of America: Indians, Colonialism and the Cant of Conquest*. Chapel Hill: University of North Carolina Press 1975

---, *The Founders of America*. New York: W.W. Norton 1993

Johannessen and Hastorf, eds., *Corn and Culture in the Prehistoric New World*. Boulder: Westview Press 1994

Johnson, A.F., "J.F. Stam, Amsterdam, and English Bibles." *The Library* 5th series, 1954, 185-7

Johnson, Edward, *Johnson's Wonder-Working Providence 1628-1651*. [1653] J. Franklin Jameson, ed., New York: Scribner's, 1910

Johnson, Frederick, ed., *Man in Northeastern America*. Andover, MA: *Papers of the Robert S. Peabody Foundation for Archaeology* 3, 1946

Johnston, Alexandra F., "English Puritanism and Festive Custom." *Renaissance and Reformation* (New Series) 1991, Vol. XV, #4, 289-99

Jones, Ann Rosalind, "Nets and Bridles: Early Modern Conduct Books and 16th-Century Women's Lyrics" in Armstrong, ed., *The Ideology of Conduct*

Jones, Colin, "Plague and Its Metaphors in Early Modern France." *Representations* 53 (Winter 1996): 97-127

Jones, James Rees, *The Anglo-Dutch Wars of the 17th Century*. New York: Longman 1996

Jones, Louis Thomas, ed., *Aboriginal American Oratory: The Tradition of Eloquence Among the Indians of the United States*. Los Angeles: Southwest Museum 1965

Jonson, Ben, *Timber*. London 1641. Rpt. in Witherspoon/Warnke

Jorgensen, Neil, ed., *A Sierra Club Naturalist's Guide to Southern New England*. San Francisco: Sierra Club 1978

Josephy, Alvin M., Jr., ed., *The American Heritage Book of Indians*. New York: Simon and Schuster 1961

Josselyn, John, *New-Englands Rarities Discovered*. 1672. In Transactions and Collections of the American Antiquarian Society [Archaeologia Americana], IV (1860), 130-238

---, *An Account of Two Voyages to New-England*. 1674. Rpt. in Lindholdt, ed., *John Josselyn, Colonial Traveler*

Juvenalis, Decimus Junius, *Satires*. William Gifford, trans. London: G. & W. Nicol 1817

Kahn, Victoria, "Humanism and the Resistance to Theory." In Patricia Parker and David Quint, eds., *Literary Theory/Renaissance Texts*. Baltimore: Johns Hopkins University Press 1986

Keach, William, *Elizabethan Erotic Narratives: Irony and Pathos in the Ovidian Poetry of Shakespeare, Marlowe and Their Contemporaries*. New Brunswick: Rutgers University Press 1977

Kearney, Hugh, "The Problem of Perspective in the History of Colonial America." In Andrews, ed., *Westward Enterprise* (290-302)

Kelly-Gadol, "Did Women Have a Renaissance?" In Bridenthal, Renate and Claudie Koonz, eds., *Becoming Visible: Women in European History*. Boston: Houghton Mifflin 1977

Kelso, Ruth, *The Doctrine of the English Gentleman in the Sixteenth Century*. University of Illinois Press 1929

Kennedy, J.H., *Jesuit and Savage in New France*. New Haven: Yale University Press 1950 (Ch. 2: "Canada 1608-1629")

Kerenyi, Carolyn, *Asklepios: Archetypal Image of the Physician's Existence*. New York: Pantheon 1959

Ker, C.A., trans., *Martial, Epigrams*. New York: Putnam's 1919

---, *Dionysos: Archetypal Image of Indestructible Life*. R. Manheim, trans. London: Routledge & Keegan Paul 1976

Kermode, Frank *et als*, eds., *The Oxford Anthology of English Literature*. Cambridge: Oxford University Press 1973

Klein, Laura F. and Lillian A. Ackerman, eds., *Women and Power in Native America*. Norman: University of Oklahoma Press 1995

Knox, Bernard, ed., *The Norton Book of Classical Literature*. New York: Norton 1993

Kohl, Benjamin G., "Humanism and Education." (Vol. 3: 5-22) in Rabil, ed., *Renaissance Humanism*

Krech, Shepard III, ed., *Indians, Animals and the Fur Trade: A Critique of Keepers of the Game*. Athens: University of Georgia Press 1981

---, ed., "Native American Medicine." In Cooke, ed., *Encyclopedia of the North American Colonies*

Kricher, John C., *A Field Guide to Eastern Forests*. Boston: Houghton Mifflin 1988

Kristeva, Julia, "Oscillation Between Power and Denial," in *New French Feminisms: An Anthology*, E. Marks *et als*, eds. New York: Schocken 1981

Kupperman, Karen Ordahl, *Settling With the Indians: The Meeting of English and Indian Cultures in America 1580-1640*. Totowa NJ: Rowman and Littlefield 1980

---, *Captain John Smith*. Chapel Hill: University of North Carolina Press 1988

---, "'Brasse without but Golde within': The Writings of Captain John Smith." In *Virginia Cavalcade* (Winter 1989), 38:3, 134-43

---, "Thomas Morton, Historian." *The New England Quarterly*, Vol. 50, Dec. 1977, 660-64

LaFrance, Marc. R. and Yvon Desloges, "Game as Food in New France." In Benes, ed., *New England's Creatures*

Lamphere, Kim and Dean Snow, "European Contact and Indian Depopulation in the Northeast: The Timing of the First Epidemics," in *Ethnohistory* 35, #1, 1988: 15-33

Langbaum, Robert, ed., *The Tempest by William Shakespeare*. New York: New American Library (Signet Classic Shakespeare Series) 1964

Langstaff, John, founder/director of Revels, Inc., Cambridge MA-based performance company: personal interview (1992) in Dempsey, *Thomas Morton* video-documentary

Leacock, Eleanor, "Montagnais Women and the Jesuit Program for Colonization" in Etienne and Leacock, eds., *Women and Colonization*

Leahy, Christopher, John H. Mitchell and Thomas Convel, eds., *The Nature of Massachusetts*. Reading MA: Addison Wesley 1996

Ledger, P., ed., *The Oxford Book of English Madrigals*. London: Oxford Univeristy Press 1978

Lee, Sidney, *The French Renaissance in England: An Account of the Literary Relations of England and France in the 16th Century*. New York: Scribner's 1910

LeGoff, Jacques, *The Medieval Imagination*. Arthur Goldhammer, trans. Chicago: University of Chicago Press 1985

Leland, Charles G., *Algonquian Legends*. Boston 1884. Rpt. New York: Dover 1992

---, *Kuloskap the Master and Other Algonkin Poems*. New York: Funk & Wagnalls 1902

Lentricchia, Frank, "Michel Foucault's Fantasy for Humanists" in *Ariel and the Police*, Wisconsin UP 1988

Lescarbot, Marc, *Nova Francia, or A Description of Acadia*. 1606. Henry P. Biggar, ed., London: George Routledge & Sons 1928

---, *The History of New France*. 1618. W.L. Grant, trans. Toronto: Champlain Society 1907-14

---, "The Conversion of the Savages." Paris 1610. Rpt. in Thwaites, ed., *The Jesuit Relations* 1

---, *The Theatre of Neptune in New France*. [1606] Harriette T. Richardson, ed. Boston: Houghton Mifflin 1927

Levermore, Charles Herbert, ed., *Forerunners and Competitors of the Pilgrims and Puritans*. 2 Vols. Brooklyn NY: New England Society 1912

Levett, Captain Christopher, *A Voyage into New England*. London 1628. Rpt. in Levermore, ed., *Forerunners* Vol. 2

Levi, Anthony H.T., ed., *Humanism in France at the End of the Middle Ages and in the Early Renaissance*. Oxford: Manchester UP 1970

---, "The Neoplatonist Calculus: The Exploitation of Neoplatonist Themes in French Renaissance Literature." In Levi, ed., *Humanism in France*

---, *Pagan Virtue and the Humanism of the Northern Renaissance*. London: Society for Renaissance Studies, Occasional Papers #2, 1974

Lewalski, Barbara K., *Milton's Brief Epic: The Genre, Meaning and Art of Paradise Regained*. Providence: Brown University Press 1966

Lewis, Clifford M. and Albert J. Loomie, eds., *The Spanish Jesuit Mission in Virginia 1570-1572*. Chapel Hill: University of North Caroline Press 1953

Lindestrom, Peter, *Geographia Americae, with an Account of the Delaware Indians Based on Surveys and Notes Made in 1654-1656*. Amandus Johnson, ed. Philadelphia: Swedish Colonial Society 1925

Lindholdt, Paul J., ed., *John Josselyn, Colonial Traveler: A Critical Edition of Two Voyages to New-England*. Hanover: University Press of New England 1988

Loftfield, Thomas C., "The Adaptive Role of Warfare Among the Southern Algonquians." In Cowan, ed., *Papers of the Seventh Algonquian Conference*

Loftie, W.J., *The Inns of Court and Chancery*. Illustrations by Herbert Railton. New York: Macmillan 1893

Lodge, Thomas, *The Complete Works of Thomas Lodge* (3 volumes, no editors specified). New York: Russell & Russell 1963

Longrigg, Roger, *The English Squire and His Sport*. New York: St. Martin's 1977

Lorch, Maristella, "Petrarch, Cicero and the Classical Pagan Tradition." In Rabil, ed., *Renaissance Humanism* Vol. 1, 71-94

Lucan (Marchus Annaeus Lucanus), *The Civil War*. J.M. Duff, trans. New York: Putnam's 1928

Macalister, R.A.S., *The Philistines: Their History and Civilization*. Chicago: Argonaut 1965

Macchiavelli, Niccolo, *The Prince*. 1513. Robert M. Adams, trans. New York: Norton [1977]1992

Maclean, Hugh, ed., *Ben Jonson and the Cavalier Poets*. New York: Norton 1974

---, ed., *Edmund Spenser's Poetry*. 2nd edition New York: Norton 1982

Major, J.M., "The Moralization of the Dance in Elyot's *Governour*." In *Studies in the Renaissance*, Vol. 5 (1958), 27-36

Major, Minor Wallace, "Thomas Morton and His *New English Canaan*." Unpublished Ph.D. Dissertation, University of Colorado 1957

---, "William Bradford Versus Thomas Morton." *Early American Literature* Vol. V, #2, Fall 1970, 1-13

Malone, Patrick M., "Changing Military Technology Among the Indians of Southern New England 1600-1677." *American Quarterly* 25 (1973), 50-53

---, *The Skulking Way of War: Technology and Tactics Among the New England Indians*. New York: Madison Books 1991

Mancall, Peter, C., *Deadly Medicine*. Ithaca: Cornell University PressP 1995

Manning, Charles and Merrill Moore, "Sassafras and Syphilis." *New England Quarterly* IX (1936), 473-475

Marcus, Leah, *The Politics of Mirth: Jonson, Herrick, Milton, Marvell and the Defense of Old Holiday Pastimes*. Chicago: University of Chicago Press 1986

Markham, Gervase, *The Pleasures of Princes: or, Good Mens Recreations. Together with The Experienced Angler by Robert Venables.* [c.1570s] London: Cresset Press 1927

Marsh, Christopher W., *The Family of Love in English Society 1550-1630.* New York: Cambridge University Press 1994

Marshall, Mac, ed., *Beliefs, Behaviors and Alcoholic Beverages.* Ann Arbor: University of Michigan Press 1979

Marten, Catherine, *Occasional Papers in Old Colony Studies #2.* December 1970. Plimoth Plantation Inc. publication

Martial (Marcus Valerius Martialis), *Epigrams* (c. 40-104 AD). Walter C. A. Ker, trans. New York: Putnam's 1919

Martin, Calvin, "Fire and Forest Structure in the Aboriginal Eastern Forest." In *The Indian Historian* 6 (1973), 23-26

---, "The European Impact on the Culture of a Northeastern Algonquian Tribe: An Ecological Interpretation." *William and Mary Quarterly* 31, #1 (1974): 3-26

---, *Keepers of the Game: Indian Animal Relations and the Fur Trade.* Berkeley: University of California Press 1978

Mason, Carol I., "A Sweet Small Something: Maple Sugaring in the New World." In Clifton, ed., *The Invented Indian* 91-106

Mates, Benson, ed. and trans., *The Skeptic Way: Sextus Empiricus' Outlines of Pyrrhonism.* New York: Oxford University Press 1996

Mathes, Valerie, "A New Look at the Role of Women in Indian Society." *American Indian Quarterly* 2 (Summer 1975), 131-9

Maverick, Samuel, *A Brief Description of New England and the Severall Towns Therein, together with the present government thereof.* Rpt. in MHSP, second series Vol. 1 (1884-5), 231-249

---, Letter to the Earl of Clarendon. 1661. In "The Clarendon Papers." *New York Historical Society Collections II*, 1869, 40-41

Mavor, James W. Jr., and Byron E. Dix, *Manitou: The Sacred Landscape of New England's Native Civilization.* Rochester VT: Inner Traditions 1991

McBride, Kevin A., "'Ancient and Crazie': Pequot Lifeways During the Historical Period." In Benes, ed., *Algonkians of New England* 63-75

---, "The Legacy of Robin Cassacinamon." In Grumet, ed., *Lives*

McCann, Franklin T., ed., *English Discovery of America to 1585.* New York: Octagon 1969

McClane, A.J., ed., *McClane's Standard Fishing Encyclopedia and International Angling Guide.* New York: Holt, Rinehart & Winston 1965

McCluhan, T.C., ed., *Touch the Earth: A Self-Portrait of Indian Existence*. New York: Simon and Schuster 1971

McElrath, Joseph R. Jr., and Allan P. Robb, eds., *The Complete Works of Anne Bradstreet*. Twayne Publishers: Boston 1981

McElroy, Harry C., "Aspects of the Lanner Falcon." In *Journal of the North American Falconers Association*. Vol 17. Oklahoma City OK: Mercury Press 1978

McGrath, Patrick, "Bristol and America, 1480-1631," in Andrews, ed., *The Westward Enterprise*

McIntyre, Ian, "Quincy May Obtain Relics From Morton Trading Post." In *Quincy Patriot Ledger*, Sept. 1, 1955, 34-35

McMullen, Ann, "Native Basketry, Basketry Styles, and Changing Group Identity in Southern New England." In Benes, ed., *Algonkians of New England* (1993) 6-88

--, "Soapbox Discourse: Tribal Historiography, Indian-White Relations, and Southeastern New England Powwows." In *The Public Historian*, Vol. 18, #4, (Fall 1996) 53-74

--- and Russell Handsman, *A Key Into the Language of Woodsplint Baskets*. Washington, CT: American Indian Archaeological Institute 1987

McPherson, John and Geri McPherson, *Primitive Wilderness Living and Survival Skills*. Randolph, KS: Prairie Wolf Press 1993

McWilliams, John P., Jr., "Fictions of Merrymount." *American Quarterly* 29, 1977, 3-30

Merchant, Carolyn, *Ecological Revolutions: Nature, Gender and Science in New England*. Chapel Hill: University of North Carolina Press 1989

Merrill, George P., *The First One Hundred Years of American Geology*. New Haven: Yale University Press 1924

Merrill, Robert V., *Platonism in French Renaissance Poetry*. New York University Press 1957

Merrill, Samuel, *The Moose Book*. New York: Dutton 1916

Meserole, Harrison T., ed., *American Poetry of the Seventeenth Century*. University Park: Pennsylvania State University Press 1985

Miller, Lee, ed., *From the Heart: Voices of the American Indian*. New York: Knopf 1995

Miller, Perry, ed., *The Puritans: A Sourcebook of Their Writings* (1938). Rpt. (2 vols.) New York: Harper & Row 1963

Miller, Shannon, "Consuming Mothers/Consuming Merchants: The Carnivalesque Economy of Jacobean City Comedy." In *Modern Language Studies* Vol XXVI, #2 & 3, Spring-Summer 1996, 53-72

Minot, H.D., *The Land-Birds and Game-Birds of New England*. 3rd edition William Brewster, ed. Boston: Houghton Mifflin 1903

Mirandola, Pico della, "Oration: On the Dignity of Man." (1486). Rpt. in Davies, ed., *Renaissance Views of Man*

Mitchell, Alan, *The Trees of North America*. New York: Facts on File 1987

Montaigne, Michel de, *The Essayes of Michael Lord of Montaigne*. (1580-1588) London 1603, John Florio, trans. 3 vols. London: J.M. Dent & Sons 1910

Moody, Robert E., ed., *The Letters of Thomas Gorges, Deputy Governor of the Province of Maine 1640-1643*. Portland: Maine Historical Society 1978

More, Sir Thomas, *Utopia*. 1516. Northbrook IL: AHM Publishing 1949, H.V.S. Ogden, trans.

Morgan, Edmund S., *The Puritan Dilemma: The Story of John Winthrop*. Boston: Little Brown 1958

Morison, Samuel Eliot, *Builders of the Bay Colony* . New York: Macmillan 1952

---, ed., *Of Plimoth Plantation, by William Bradford*. [1952] New York: Random House 1981

Morrell, William, *Nova Anglia; or New-England*. London 1625. Rpt. in MHSC Vol I, 1792, 125-139

Morton, Nathaniel, *New-England's Memorial*. [1669] 5th ed. John Davis, ed., Boston: Crocker & Brewster 1826

Mourt's Relation: A Journal of the Pilgrims at Plimoth (anonymous, London 1622). D.B. Heath, ed., Chester CT: Globe Pequot Press 1963

Myers, Albert C., ed., *Narratives of Early Pennsylvania, West New Jersey and Delaware*, 1630-1707. New York: Scribner's 1912

Nabokov, Peter, ed., *Native American Testimony: A Chronicle of Indian-White Relations from Prophecy to the Present 1492-1992*. New York: Penguin 1992

Nanepashemet (*aka* Anthony Pollard), personal interview in Rolbein, Seth, "The Thanksgiving Myth: The head of Plimoth Plantation's Wampanoag site gives his people's view of this popular American feast." *Boston Sunday Herald*, "Sunday People Magazine," Nov. 17, 1991; p. 6 (incl. "jumps" to pp. 8 and 19)

---, personal interview on Native New England culture and history in Dempsey video-documentary, *Thomas Morton* 1992

---, "Smells Fishy to Me: An Argument Supporting the Use of Fish Fertilizer by the Native People of Southern New England." In Benes, ed., *Algonkians of New England* (1993)42-50

---, "Hobbomock: A Special Instrument Sent of Massasoit for Their Good Beyond Their Expectation." Unpublished paper delivered at Northeastern Anthropological Association, Danbury CT March 1993

New England Begins: The Seventeenth Century. Vol. 1. Boston: Museum of Fine Arts, Department of American Decorative Arts and Sculpture Publications 1982 (no listed authors)

NOVA. *The Lost Red Paint People*. Film production of the WGBH-Boston Educational Foundation 1987 (Program #1420)

Nova Britannia: [attrib. Robert Johnson *Offering Most Excellent Fruites by Planting in Virginia. Exciting all such as be well affected to further the same.* Printed for Samuel Matcham, London 1609. Rpt. in Force, *Tracts* 1

Numbers, Ronald L., ed., *Medicine in the New World: New Spain, New France and New England.* Knoxville: University of Tennessee Press 1987

O'Gorman, Edmundo, *The Invention of America: An Inquiry into the Historical Nature of the New World and the Meaning of Its History.* Bloomington: Indiana University Press 1961

Oleson, Tryggvi J., *Early Voyages and Northern Approaches 1000-1632.* Canadian Centenary Series: Toronto: McClelland & Stewart 1963

Oppenheim, M.M ., *The Maritime History of Devon.* Exeter, England: University of Exeter 1968

Orgel, Stephen, *The Illusion of Power: Political Theater in the English Renaissance.* Berkeley: University of California Press (1975) 1991

---, ed., *The Complete Masques of Ben Jonson.* New Haven: Yale University Press 1969

Ortiz, Alfonso, "Some Cultural Meanings of Corn in Aboriginal North America." In Johannessen, ed., *Corn and Culture*

Osborn, James M., ed., *The Autobiography of Thomas Whythorne.* New York: Oxford University Press 1961

Ovid, *Metamorphoses*. M.M. Innes, trans. New York: Penguin 1955

Pagden, Anthony, *Spanish Imperialism and the Political Imagination.* New Haven: Yale University Press 1990

Palfrey, John Gorham, *The History of New England During the Stuart Dynasty.* (3 vols.) Boston: Little Brown 1890

Patter, Lois, *Secret Rites and Secret Writing: Royalist Literature 1641-1660.* Cambridge: Cambridge University Press 1989

Patterson, Annabel, *Censorship and Interpretation: The Conditions of Writing and Reading in Early Modern England.* Madison: University of Wisconsin Press 1984

Payne, Edward John, ed., *Voyages of the Elizabethan Seamen to America: Select Narratives from the 'Principall Navigations' of Hakluyt.* Oxford: Clarendon Press 1900

Pausanius, *Description of Greece.* W.H.S. Jones, trans. Cambridge: Harvard University Press 1978

Peacock, John, "Principles and Effects of Puritan Appropriation of Indian Land and Labor." *Ethnohistory* 31, #1 (1984): 39-44

Pearce, Roy Harvey, *Savagism and Civilization: A Study of the Indian and the American Mind.* (1953) 2nd ed. Baltimore: Johns Hopkins University Press 1965

Pennington, Loren E., "The Amerindian in English Promotional Literature 1575-1625" in Andrews, ed., *The Westward Enterprise*

Perkins, William, *The Arte of Prophesying*. [1613] Rpt. in *Works of That Famous and Worthie Minister of Christ in the University of Cambridge, M. William Perkins*. 2 vols. Cambridge, England: John Legat 1608-9. Original copy in the Brown University Hay Library, Star Collection

Petegorsky, David W., *Left-Wing Democracy in the English Civil War: A Study of the Social Philosophy of Gerrard Winstanley*. New York: Haskell House 1972

Peters, Russell, *The Wampanoags of Mashpee: An Indian Perspective on American History*. Somerville: Media Action Press 1987

---, *Clambake: A Wampanoag Tradition*. Minneapolis: Lerner Publications 1992

Peterson, Harold L., *Arms and Armor in Colonial America 1526-1783*. New York: Bramhall House 1956

---, *Arms and Armor of the Pilgrims 1620-1692*. Plymouth MA: Plimoth Plantation Inc. and Pilgrim Society 1957

Piercy, Josephine K., *Anne Bradstreet*. New York: Twayne Publishers 1965

Plane, Anne Marie, "Childbirth Practices Among Native American Women of the Northeast and Canada, 1600-1800." In Benes, ed., *Medicine and Healing*

Plato, *The Republic*. B. Jowett, trans. New York: Vintage 1972

Poe, Edgar Allan, "The Philosophy of Composition." (1850) Rpt. in Brooks, ed., *American Literature*

Pollard, H.B.C., *A History of Firearms*. Boston: Houghton Mifflin 1933

Pomponazzi, Pietro de, *On the Immortality of the Soul*. Venice 1516. Rpt. in Cassirer *et als*, eds., *The Renaissance Philosophy of Man*

Popkin, Richard H., *The History of Scepticism from Erasmus to Spinoza*. Berkeley: University of California Press 1979

Potter, Harry, *Hanging in Judgment: Religion and the Death Penalty in England from the Bloody Code to Abolition*. London: SCM Press 1993

Powledge, Tabitha and Mark Rose, "The Great DNA Hunt, Part II: Colonizing the Americas." *Archaeology Magazine*, Nov./Dec. 1996, 58-67

Pratt, Phineas [attrib.], "Relation." (c.1622) In MHSC IV, 476-491

Prescott, Anne Lake, *French Poets and the English Renaissance*. New Haven: Yale University Press 1978

Prest, Wilfred R., *The Inns of Court Under Elizabeth I and the Early Stuarts 1590-1640*. London: Longman 1972

Preston, Richard Arthur, *Gorges of Plymouth Fort*. Toronto: University of Toronto Press 1953

Pribek, Thomas, "The Conquest of Canaan: Suppression of Merrymount." *Nineteenth Century Literature*, Dec. 1985, 40:3, 345-54

Price, Richard, *Ethnographic History, Caribbean Pasts*. Working Papers #9. Department of Spanish and Portuguese, University of Maryland, College Park 1990

Puttenham, George, *The Arte of English Poesie*. London 1589. Rpt. Kent, OH: Kent State University Press 1970

Rabb, Felix, *The English Face of Machiavelli*. London: Routledge & Keegan Paul 1964

Qualls-Corbett, Nancy, *The Sacred Prostitute: Eternal Aspect of the Feminine*. Toronto: Inner City Books 1988

Quinn, David Beers, *The Newfoundland of Stephen Parmenius*. Toronto: University of Toronto Press 1972

---, *England and the Discovery of America 1481-1620. from the Bristol Voyages of the 15th Century to the Pligrim Settlement at Plimoth*. New York: Knopf 1974

---, "Renaissance Influences in English Colonization." In *Transactions of the Royal Historical Society*, 5th series, XXV 73-93

---, *North America from Earliest Discovery to the First Settlements: The Norse Voyages to 1612*. New York: Harper & Row 1977

Quinn, David Beers and Alison M. Quinn, eds., *The English New England Voyages 1602-1608*. London: Hakluyt Society 1983

Rabb, Theodore K , *Enterprise and Empire: Merchant and Gentry Investment in the Expansion of England, 1575-1630*. Cambridge: Harvard University Press 1967

Rabil, Albert Jr., ed., *Renaissance Humanism: Foundations, Forms, and Legacy*. 3 Vols. Philadelphia: University of Pennsylvania Press 1988

---, "Petrarch, Augustine and the Classical Christian Tradition." In Rabil, ed., *Renaissance Humanism*

Rae, Wesley D., *Thomas Lodge*. New York: Twayne Publishers 1967

Raesly, Ellis Lawrence, *Portrait of New Netherland*. New York: Columbia University Press 1945

Ralegh, Sir Walter, H*istory of the World*. C. A. Patrides, ed. New York: Macmillan 1971

---, *The Discoverie of...the Empire of Guiana*. London 1595. In Hakluyt, *The Principall Navigations* Vol. 10

Rancour-Laferriere, Daniel, *Signs of the Flesh: An Essay in the Evolution of Hominid Sexuality*. Indiana University Press 1988

Ranlet, Philip, *Enemies of the Bay Colony*. New York: Peter Lang 1995

Rapoza, Andrew V., "The Trials of Dr. Phillip Reade, 17th-Century Itinerant Physician." In Benes, ed., *Medicine and Healing*

Rasieres, Isaac de, "Letter to Samuel Blommaert." (1628) Rpt. in Jameson, ed., *Narratives of New Netherland*

Ray, Arthur J., *Indians in the Fur Trade*. Toronto: University of Toronto Press 1974

Reynolds, Barrie, "Beothuk" in H15, 101-108

Ribner, Irving, ed., *The Complete Plays of Christopher Marlowe*. New York: Odyssey Press 1963

Riggs, David, *Ben Jonson: A Life*. Cambridge: Harvard University Press 1989

Ritchie, William A., "Archaeological Manifestations and Relative Chronology in the Northeast." In Johnson, ed., *Man* 96-105

---, *The Archaeology of Martha's Vineyard: A Framework for the Prehistory of Southern New England; A Study in Coastal Ecology and Adaptation*. Garden City NJ: Natural History Press 1969

Ritzenthaler, Robert E., "Southwestern Chippewa," in H15, 743-59

Robinson, David, *From Drinking to Alcoholism: A Sociological Commentary*. New York: Wiley 1976

Rostenberg, Leona, *The Minority Press and the English Crown: A Study in Repression 1558-1625*. The Hague: Nieuwkoop B. De Graaf 1971

Rosensteil, Annette, *Red and White: Indian Views of the White Man 1492-1982*. New York: Universe Books 1983

Rothenberg, Diane, "The Mothers of the Nation: Seneca Resistance to Quaker Intervention" in Etienne, ed., *Women and Colonization*

Rowe, John Howland, "Ethnography and Ethnology in the 16th Century." Kroeber Anthropological Society Papers 30, 1-19

Rowse, A. L., *The Elizabethans and America*. New York: Harper & Rown 1959

---, *Shakespeare: A Biography*. New York: Harper & Row 1963

Russell, Howard S., *Indian New England Before the Mayflower*. University Press of New England 1980

Said, Edward, *Culture and Imperialism*. New York: Knopf 1993

Sale, Kirkpatrick, *The Conquest of Paradise: Columbus and the Columbian Legacy*. New York: Knopf 1990

Salisbury, Neal, *Manitou and Providence: Indians, Europeans and the Making of New England 1500-1643*. New York: Oxford UP 1982

---, *The Indians of New England: A Critical Bibliography*. Bloomington: Indiana University Press 1982

Salwen, Bert, "Indians of Southern New England and Long Island: Early Period." In H15, 160-176

Sandys, George, trans., *Ovid's Metamorphosis* [sic] *Mythologiz'd, and Represented in Figures*. Oxford, England: John Litchfield, Printer 1632. Original copy in John Hay Library, Brown University, Providence RI 02912 USA

Sasek, Lawrence A., *The Literary Temper of the English Puritans.* Baton Rouge: Louisiana State University Press 1961

Sattler, Richard A., "Women's Status Among the Muskogee and Cherokee." In Klein, ed., *Women and Power in Native North America*

Saunders, Charles Francis, *Useful Wild Plants of the U.S. and Canada.* New York: Robert McBride 1920

Saum, Lewis O., *The Fur Trader and the Indian.* Seattle: University of Washington Press 1965

Scaglione, Aldo, "A Note on Montaigne's 'Des Cannibales' and the Humanist Tradition." In Chiappelli, ed., *First Images* 1976

Scarry, C. Margaret, ed., *Foraging and Farming in the Eastern Woodlands.* Gainesville: University Press of Florida 1993

Schama, Simon, *The Embarrassment of Riches: An Interpretation of Dutch Culture in the Golden Age.* New York: Knopf 1987

Schoeck, Richard J., "Humanism in England." (Vol 2:5-39) in Rabil, ed., *Renaissance Humanism*

Scholes, Robert, *Textual Power: Literary Theory and the Teaching of English.* New Haven: Yale University Press 1985

Scottow, J., "A Narrative of the Planting of the Massachusets-Colony &c" [1628] Rpt. in MI ISC XXXIV, 279-330

Seznec, Jean, *Survival of the Pagan Gods: The Mythological Tradition and Its Place in Renaissance Humanism and Art.* B.F. Sessions, trans. New York: Pantheon 1953

Shea, Daniel B., "'Our Old Professed Adversary': Thomas Morton and the Naming of New England." *Early American Literature*, Vol 23 #1, 1988, 53-69

Shurtleff, Nathaniel E., *The Records of the Governor and Company of the Massachusetts Bay in New England.* (5 Vols.) Boston: William White 1853

Shrewsbury, J.F.D., *A History of Bubonic Plague in the British Isles.* London: Cambridge UP 1970

Shuffelton, Frank, ed., *A Mixed Race: Ethnicity in Early America.* New York: Oxford UP 1993

Siebert, Frederick, *Freedom of the Press in England: The Rise and Decline of Government Controls 1476-1776.* Urbana: University of Illinois Press 1952

Simmons, William S., *Cautantowwitt's House: An Indian Burial Ground in the Island of Conanicut in Narragansett Bay.* Providence: Brown University Press 1970

---, "Southern New England Shamanism: An Ethnographic Reconstruction." In William Cowan, ed., *Papers of the Seventh Algonquian Conference*, Ottowa: Carleton University Press 1976

---, "Narragansett" in H15, 190-197 (1978)

---, *Spirit of the New England Tribes: Indian History and Folklore 1620-1984.* University Press of New England 1986

Simpson, P. ed., *Cassel's New Compact Latin-English, English-Latin Dictionary*. New York: Macmillan 1977

Singman, Jeffrey L., *Daily Life in Elizabethan England*. Westport CT: Greenwood Press 1995

Slack, Paul, *The Impact of Plague in Tudor and Stuart England*. Boston: Routledge and Keegan Paul 1985

Slafter, Edmund F., ed., *Sir William Alexander and American Colonization*. Boston: Prince Society 1873. Rpt. New York: Burt Franklin 1967

Slavin, Arthur J., "The American Principle from More to Locke." In Chiappelli, ed., *First Images*

Slotkin, Richard, *Regeneration Through Violence: The Mythology of the American Frontier 1600-1860*. Wesleyan University Press 1973

Slow Turtle (a.k.a. John Peters; Medicine Man of the Wampanoag Nation [Mashpee], Director of Massachusetts Center for Native American Awareness), personal interview in Dempsey video-documentary *Thomas Morton* 1992

Smith, Abbot Emerson, *Colonists in Bondage: White Servitude and Convict Labor in America 1607-1776*. Chapel Hill: University of North Carolina Press 1947

Smith, John, *Description of New England*. London 1616. Rpt. in Arber, ed. *Travels and Works*

---, *New Englands Trials*. London 1622. Rpt. in Arber, ed., *Travels and Works*

---, *Description of New England*. London 1616. Rpt. in Barbour, Philip L, ed., *The Complete Works*

---, "The Sea Marke," in Barbour, ed., *Complete Works* 3:265

Smith, William and John Lockwood, eds., *Chambers Murray Latin-English Dictionary*. London: Chambers 1995

Snow, Dean R., *The American Indians: Their Archaeology and Prehistory*. London: Thames and Hudson 1976

---, "Late Prehistory of the East Coast," in H15, 58-69

---, "Eastern Abenaki" in H15 142-147

---, "The Solon Petroglyphs and Eastern Abnaki Shamanism." In Cowan, ed., *Papers of the Seventh Algonquian Conference* 281-288

Speck, Frank G., "The Family Hunting Band as the Basis of Algonkian Social Organization." *American Anthropologist* 17 (1915)

---, "Medicine Practices of the Northeastern Algonquians." In *19th International Congress of Americanists: Proceedings* (Dec. 27-31, 1915) Washington D.C., 1917: 303-321

---, "Penobscot Shamanism." *Memoirs of the American Anthropological Association*, Vol. VI #4, Oct.-Dec. 1919

---, *Penobscot Man: The Life History of a Forest Tribe in Maine*. Philadelphia: University of Pennsylvania Press 1940 (rpt. 1970)

Speck, Grank G., and R.W. Dexter, "Utilization of Marine Life by the Wampanoag Indians of Massachusetts." Washington D.C.: Washington Academy of Sciences, *Journal*, XXXVIII (1948), 257-265

Speiss, Arthur J. and Bruce D. Speiss, "New England Pandemic of 1616-1622: Cause and Archaeological Implication." In *Man in the Northeast* 34 (Fall 1987), 71-83

Spencer-Wood, Suzanne M., "Feminist Issues Involved in Recognizing Gender in Historical and Archaeological Contexts." In *Bulletin of the Massachusetts Archaeological Society*, Vol. 55 (1), Spring 1994, 24-30

Spengemann, William C., *A Mirror for Americanists: Reflections on the Idea of American Literature*. Hanover NH: University Press of New England 1989

Spenser, Edmund, *The Faerie Queene*. London 1590-96. Rpt. New Haven: Thomas P. Roche, ed., Yale University Press 1978

Starkey, David, *The Reign of Henry VIII: Personalities and Politics*. New York: Franklin Watts 1986

Starna, William A., "The Pequots in the Early 17th Century." In Hauptmann and Wherry *The Pequots* 33-47

Starnes, D.T. and E.W. Talbert, eds., *Classical Myth and Legend in Renaissance Dictionaries*. Chapel Hill: University of North Carolina Press 1955

Sternberg, Paul R., "The Publication of Thomas Morton's *New English Canaan* Reconsidered." *Papers of the Bibliographical Society of America* Vol. 80 #3, 1986

Stone, Lawrence, *The Crisis of the Aristocracy 1558-1641*. New York: Oxford University Press 1967

---, *The Past and the Present*. Boston: Routledge & Keegan Paul 1981

Stoneham Historical Commission, *Stoneham, Massachusetts: A Shoe Town*. Cambridge MA: Landscape Research Publication 1981

Strathmann, Ernest A., *Sir Walter Ralegh: A Study in Elizabethan Skepticism*. New York: Columbia UP 1951

Streitberger, W.R., *Court Revels 1485-1559*. Toronto: University of Toronto Press 1994

Strong, Pauline Turner, "Captivity in White and Red: Convergent Practice and Colonial Represenation on the British-American Frontier, 1606-1736." *Crossing Cultures: Essays in the Displacement of Western Civilization*, Daniel Segal, ed. Tucson: University of Arizona Press 1992

Stubaus, Karen R., *'The Good Creatures': Drinking Law and Custom in 17th Century Massachusetts and Virginia*. Ann Arbor MI: University Microfilms International 1985

Swann, Brian and Arnold Krupat, *Recovering the Word: Essays on Native American Literature*. Berkeley: University of California Press 1987

Sydney, Sir Philip, *The Defence of Poetry*. London 1595. Rpt. in Kimbrough, Robert, ed., *Sir Philip Sydney: Selected Prose and Poetry*. Madison: University of Wisconsin Press 1983

Tacitus (Publius or Gaius Cornelius Tacitus), *On the Origin, Geography, Institutions, and Tribes of the Germans* (c. 55-116 AD) In Alfred John Church and William Jackson Brodribb, trans., *The Complete Works of Tacitus*. New York: Modern Library 1942

Tantaquidgeon, Gladys, *Folk Medicine of the Delaware and Related Algonkian Indians*. (1972) 2nd ed. Harrisburg: Commonwealth of Pennsylvania: Pennsylvania Historical and Museum Commission 1977

Temple, Sir William, "Of Poetry." London 1689 in *Miscellanea* (II: 1692). Rpt. in Witherspoon/Warnke

Tetel, Marcel, *Montaigne*. New York: Twayne Publishers 1974

Thirsk, Joan, ed., *The Agrarian History of England and Wales 1500-1640*. 5 vols. London: Cambridge University Press 1967

Thomas, Keith, *Religion and the Decline of Magic*. New York: Scribner's 1971

Thomas, Peter A., "The Fur Trade, Indian Land, and the Need to Define Adequate 'Environmental' Parameters." *Ethnohistory* 28, #4 (1981): 359-79

Thwaites, Reuben Gold, *The Jesuit Relations and Allied documents: Travels and Explorations of the Jesuit Missionaries in New France, 1610-1791*. 73 Vols. Cleveland, Ohio: Burrows Brothers 1896

Tillam, Thomas, "Upon the first Sight of New England June 29 1638." In Meserole, ed., *American Poetry*

Tompkins, Jane, *West of Everything: The Inner Life of Westerns*. New York: Oxford University Press 1992

Tooker, Elisabeth, "The League of the Iroquois: Its History, Politics and Ritual" in H15, 418-441

---, *Native American Spirituality of the Eastern Woodlands*. New York: Paulist Press 1979

Trigger, Bruce G., *The Children of Aataentsic: A History of the Huron People to 1660*. 2 Vols. Montreal: McGill-Queen's University Press 1976

---, editor of *Volume 15: The Northeast. The Handbook of North American Indians*. William C. Sturtevant, General Editor. Washington, D.C. 1978

Trinkaus, Charles, "Renaissance and Discovery" in Chiappelli, ed., *First Images of America*

Trumbull, J. Hammond, ed., *Plain Dealing or News from New England*, by Thomas Lechford. Boston: Wiggin & Lunt 1897

---, *Natick Dictionary*. Smithsonian Institution Bureau of American Ethnology Bulletin #25, 1903

Tuck, James A., "Regional Cultural Development 3000 to 300 BC" in H15, 28-43

--- and Robert Grenier, *Red Bay, Labrador: World Whaling Capital A.D. 1550-1600*. St. John's University Press, Newfoundland, Canada 1989

---, "The Maritime Archaic Tradition." Publication of the Newfoundland Museum 1996. Internet *source:* http://www.stemnet.nf.ca/-cshea/note12.html

Tuchman, Barbara, *The First Salute*. New York: Knopf 1980

Turner, J.G., *One Flesh: Paradisal Marriage and Sexual Relations in the Age of Milton*. New York: Oxford University Press 1987

Turner, Victor, ed., *Celebration: Studies in Festivity and Ritual*. Washington, D.C.: Smithsonian Institution Press 1982

---, "Carnival, Ritual and Play in Rio de Janeiro." In *Time Out of Time: Essays in the Festival*, A. Falassi, ed., University of New Mexico Press 1987

Tyler, Moses Coit, *A History of American Literature*. (2 Vols.) New York: G.P. Putnam's Sons 1880

Underdown, David, *Revel, Riot and Rebellion: Popular Politics and Culture in England 1603-1660*. New York: Oxford University Press 1985

---, "The Taming of the Scold: The Enforcement of Patriarchal Authority in Early Modern England." In Fletcher and Stevenson, eds., *Order and Disorder* 1985

Underhill, John, *Newes from America; or a New and Experimentall Discoverie of New England*. London 1638. MHSC 3 series VI (1837), 1-28

Vanderbilt, Kermit, "The Literary Histories of Moses Coit Tyler." In Voloshon, Beverly R., ed., *American Literature, Culture and Ideology: Essays in Memory of Henry Nash Smith*. Series XXIV, Vol. 8. New York: Peter Lang 1990

Vanderwerth, W.C., ed., *Indian Oratory: Famous Speeches by Noted Indian Chieftains*. Norman: University of Oklahoma Press 1971

Vann, Joseph, ed., *Lives of Saints*. New York: Crawley & Co. 1954

Van Wassenaer, Nicolaes, *Historisch Verhael*. 1924. Rpt. in Jameson, ed., *Narratives of New Netherland*

Vastokas, Joan M and Romas K. Vastokas, *Sacred Art of the Algonkians: A Study of the Peterborough Petroglyphs*. Peterborough, Ontario: Mansard Press 1973

Vaughan, Alden T., *New England Frontier: Puritans and Indians 1620-1675*. Boston 1965. Rpt. Norman: University of Oklahoma Press 1995

Vaughan, William. *The Golden Fleece*. London 1626. Original copy in the John Carter Brown Library, Brown University, Providence RI USA

Vecsey, Christopher and Robert W. Venables, eds., *American Indian Environments* Syracuse 1980

Verrazzano, Giovanni da, *The Voyages of Giovanni da Verrazzano 1524-28*. 2 Vols. Lawrence C. Wroth, ed., New Haven: Yale UP 1970

---, "Soderini Letter, The": *Letter to Piero Soderini, Gonfaloniere, the year 1504*. Princeton: Princeton UP 1916, George Tyler Northrup, trans.

Virgil, *The Aeneid*, T.H. Delabare May, trans. New York: Bantam 1963

---, *Eclogues*. Robert Coleman, ed. Cambridge: Cambridge University Press 1977 (see also Fowler, trans.)

---, *Georgics*. Smith Palmer Bovie, trans. Chicago: University of Chicago Press 1956

Vogel, Virgil J., *American Indian Medicine*. Norman: University of Oklahoma Press 1970

Wagner, David R., "The Ekonk Hill Petroglyphs." January 1996 unpublished article (available from the author at Box 373, Thompson CT 06277)

--- and David Ostlowski, "The Stone Mounds of the Eastern Woodland People." January 1997 unpublished survey/article (available as above *Wagner*)

Wallace, Anthony F.C., "Woman, Land and Society: Three Aspects of Aboriginal Delaware Life." *Pennsylvania Archaeologist* 17 (1947), 1-35

---, *The Death and Rebirth of the Seneca*. 1969. Rpt. New York: Random House 1972

Wassenaer, Nicolaes van, *Historisch Verhael* (1624) in Jameson ed., *Narratives of New Netherlands*

Watson, Patricia A., "'The Hidden Ones': Women and Healing in Colonial New England." In Benes, ed., *Medicine and Healing*

Weiss, Roberto, *The Renaissance Discovery of Classical Antiquity*. Oxford: Basil Blackwell 1969

Welsford, Enid, *The Court Masque: A Study in the Relationship Between Poetry and the Revels*. New York: Russell and Russell 1962

Westbrook, Perry D., *William Bradford*. Boston: Twayne Publishers 1978

Whitaker, John O., Jr., ed., *National Audubon Society Field Guide to North American Mammals*. New York: Knopf 1980

White, Richard and William Cronon, "Ecological Change and Indian-White Relations" in H15, 417-429

White, Hayden, "The Noble Savage Theme as Fetish." In Chiappelli, ed., *First Images of America*

Whiting, B.J., ed., *Proverbs in the Early English Drama*. Cambridge: Harvard University Press 1938

---, ed., *Traditional British Ballads*. New York: Appleton-Century-Crafts 1955

Whitlock, Ralph, *The Folklore of Devon*. Totowa NJ: Rowman and Littlefield 1977

Wilbur, C. Keith, *The New England Indians*. Chester CT: Globe Pequot Press 1978

---, *Indian Handcrafts*. Chester, CT: Globe Pequot Press 1990

Williams, Jerry M. and Robert E. Lewis, eds., *Early Images of the Americas: Transfer and Invention*. Tucson: University of Arizona Press 1993

Williams, Roger, *A Key Into the Language of America*. London 1643. John J. Teunissen and Evelyn J. Hinz, eds. Detroit: Wayne State University Press 1973

---, *Letters of Roger Williams*. John Bartlett, ed., Narragansett Society Publication. North Providence RI

---, *Complete Writings*. 7 vols. New York: Russell and Russell 1963

Williams, William Carlos, *In the American Grain*. 1933. Rpt. New York: New Directions 1956

Williamson, George, *The Senecan Amble: A Study in Prose From from Bacon to Collier*. Chicago: University of Chicago Press 1951

Willison, George F., *Saints and Strangers: The Story of the Mayflower and the Plymouth Colony*. New York: Reynal and Hitchcock 1945

Willoughby, Charles C., *Antiquities of the New England Indians*. Peabody Museum of American Archaeology and Ethnology. Cambridge: Harvard University Press 1935

Wilson, Edmund, "Morose Ben Jonson." In *The Triple Thunders* (1938). Rpt. New York: Scribner's 1948

Wilson, K.J., *Incomplete Fictions: The Formation of English Renaissance Dialogue*. Washington D.C.: Catholic University of America Publications. 1985

Wind, Edgar, *Pagan Mysteries in the Renaissance*. New York: W.W. Norton 1958

Winslow, Edward, *Good News from New-England*. London 1624. Rpt. in Arber, ed. *The Story of the Pilgrim Fathers*

---, *Hypocrisie Unmasked: A True Relation of the Proceedings of the Governor and Company of the Massachusetts vs. Samuel Gorton*....London 1646. Rpt. Providence Club for Colonial Reprints #6 (1916)

Winthrop, John, *Journal* in *The Winthrop Papers*. Worthington C. Ford *et als*, eds. 3 Vols. Boston: Massachusetts Historical Society, Plimpton Press 1931

---, *The Winthrop Papers*. Allyn B. Forbes, ed. Massachusetts Historical Society. Boston: Merrymount Press 1943

---, *Winthrop's Journal*. "History of New England" 1630-1649. James K. Hosmer, ed. 2 Vols. New York: Scribner's 1908

---. "Christian Experience" [1607] in Vol 1: 154-68 of Ford, ed.

---, "A Model of Christian Charity" [1630] in Forbes, ed., Vol. II

Witherspoon, Alexander M., and Frank J. Warnke, eds., *Seventeenth Century Prose and Poetry*. (1929) Rpt. New York: Harcourt Brace Jovanovich 1982 (2nd enlarged edition)

Wood, Neal, *Cicero's Social and Political Thought*. Berkeley: University of California Press 1988

Wood, William, *New England's Prospect*. London 1634. Alden T. Vaughan, ed., Amherst: University of Massachusetts Press 1977

Woolf, Eric, *Europe and the People Without History*. Berkeley: Univeristy of California Press 1982

Woolverton, John Frederick, *Colonial Anglicanism in North America*. Detroit: Wayne State University Press 1984

Wright, Louis B., *The Elizabethans' America: A Collection of Early Reports by Englishmen on the New World*. London: Edward Arnold Publishers 1965

Wrightson, Keith, *English Society 1580-1680*. Rutgers University Press 1982

---,"Alehouses, Order and Reformation in Rural England 1590-1660." In E. Yeo, ed., *Popular Culture and Class Conflict*. Hassocks, England: Harvester Press 1981

Wyatt, Jean, "Giving Body to the Word: The Maternal Symbolic in Toni Morrison's *Beloved.*" *Publications of the Modern Language Association*, May 1993, 474-88

Yates, Frances A., *The Theatre of the World*. London: Routledge & Keegan Paul 1969

Young, *Chronicles of the Pilgrim Fathers of the Colony of Plymouth 1602-1625*. New York: DeCapo 1971

Young, Stanley P., *The Wolves of North America*. New York: Dover 1944

Youngken, Heber H., "The Drugs of the North American Indians." *American Journal of Pharmacy* 97 #3 (1925)

Zolla, Elemire, *The Writer and the Shaman: A Morphology of the American Indian*. R. Rosenthal, trans., New York: Harcourt Brace Jovanovich 1969

Zuckerman, Michael, "Pilgrims in the Wilderness: Community, Modernity and the Maypole of Merry Mount." *New England Quarterly* 50 (1977), 255-77

---, "The Fabrication of Identity in Early America." *William and Mary Quarterly*, 3rd series, Vol. 34: April 1977, 183-214

A Brief & True Relation
of European Writings
(Spanish, French, English, Dutch)
on "The New World"
that might have conditioned
the First-Hand American Observations
of a well-read, Early Modern
English Person
1493-1637

from SPAIN

1493 Cristobal Colon (Christopher Columbus), *Epistula de insulis nuper inventis* (pamphlet, printed at Basil: a Latin translation of his letter to King Ferdinand on his first-voyage discoveries). Colon's *Journals* and *Logs* published in **Oviedo** and **Martyr** (below). See also *Christopher Columbus: The Four Voyages*, J.M. Cohen, ed. New York: Penguin 1969

1507 Amerigo Vespucci, *Mundus Novus* (Waldseemuller trans.) on his 1503-5 voyages. Also published in French, *Le Nouveau Monde et navigacions faites par Emeric de Vespuce*, Paris 1516

1511 Peter Martyr (Martir de Angleria), *De Orbe Novo* (first volume)---further vols. in 1516, 1520, 1521, 1530; hence the eventual 1555 new title, *The Decades of the New World or West India*. English translation 1555 (vols. 1-3); an "abridged complete" 1577; the full text in English 1607

1522 Hernando Cortes, *Five Letters*, F. Bayard Morris, trans.; these letters on his 1519-1526 "campaigns" first widely published (at Antwerp) in French as *Des marches, iles et pays trouves*

1525 Giovanni da Verrazzano, accounts of his 1524-1528 voyages collected in Lawrence C. Wroth, ed. *The Voyages of Giovanni da Verrazzano* (New Haven: Yale University Press 1970)

1535 Gonzalo de Oviedo, Vol. 1 of *Historia general y natural de las Indias* (Vol. 2 1547: translated via Hakluyt 1552-1616, below)

1539 DeSoto in "Florida" **1540s** Coronado, DeVaca in Southwest (accounts below)

1552 Bartolome de Las Casas, *Brevissima relacion de la destruycion de las Indias*; at Seville

1553 Richard Eden, *A Treatise of the newe India*; at London

1555 Alvar Nunez Cabeza de Vaca, *La Relacion* (on Gulf of Mexico regions)

1560 Pedro de Castaneda y Nacera (with Coronado c. 1540s), *Relacion de la jornada de Cibola*

1576 Jose de Acosta, *How to Procure the Salvation of the Indians* (1589 English translation)

1577 R. Willes, *The History of Travayle in the West & East Indies*

1578 John Frampton, *A briefe description of the portes, creekes, bayes, and havens, of the Weast India*

1581 Thomas Nicholas, *The Discoverie and Conquest of the Provinces of Peru*

1583 Bartolome de Las Casas, *The Spanish Colonie*; at London

1589 Jose de Acosta, *The Natural and Moral History of the Indies* (English trans. 1604 by Edward Grimston)---often called the dominant model for cultural comparison till the late 1630s

1605 Francisco Lopez de Gomara (published in French at Paris, trans. Martin Fumee), *Histoire Generalle des Indes Occidentales*

1607 Gregorio Garcia, *Origen de los indios de el nuevo mundo*

1613-1625 The English compendium *Purchas His Pilgrimes* included multiple Spanish tracts by **Herrera, Acosta, Oviedo, de Gomara, Schmidel, de la Vega, el Inca, Xerez, Sancho, DeVaca, DeSoto** and **Las Casas**

from FRANCE

1483 Sir John Mandeville, *Travels of Sir John Mandeville*---a popular novel" based in pre-Columbus "world travel literature." Also published Lyon 1508: a 1968 translation by M.C. Seymour

1534 Jacques Cartier, *Relation originale du voyage de Jacques cartier au Canada en 1534*. Henry P. Biggar, ed., 1924

1557 Jean de Lery, *Histoire d'un voyage fait en la tere du Bresil* (reprinted 1580, 1586)

1558 Andre Thevet, *Les singularitez de la France antarctique*; at Paris

1563 J. Ribault, *The whole and true discoverye of Terra Florida*; at London

1566 T. Hackett, *A true and perfect description of the last voyage or navigation atempted by Captaine John Rybaut*

1566 Jean Bodin, *Method for the Easy Comprehension of History* (translation by B. Reynolds 1945)

1568 T. Hackett, *The new found worlde, or Antarctike*

1575 Louis Le Roy, *De la vicissitude ou variete des choses en l'univers*

1575 Sebastian Munster, *La cosmographie universelle de tout le monde*; at Paris; translated from Latin via Francois de Belleforest

1578   Jean de Lery, *Histoire...de Bresil*; at La Rochelle

1580   John Florio, *A shorte and briefe narration of the two navigations discoveries to the northweate partes called Newe Fraunce*

1580   Michel de Montaigne, "On Cannibals" and "On Coaches" (influential essays on New World-related themes); 5 editions by 1588---in English via John Florio translation 1603

1586   Jean de Lery, *Historia navigationis in Brasiliam, quae et America dicitur* and *Le Voyage au Brasil*; at Geneva

1586   Jean Bodin, *Six Books of a Commonwealth*

1587   Richard Hakluyt, ed., *A notable historie containing foure voyages made by certayne French captaynes unto Florida*; at London (French accounts included in this newer edition of Englishman Hakluyt's 1582 *Navigations*

1598   Jacques Cartier, *Discours du voyage*; at Rouen

1603   Samuel de Champlain, *Des Sauvages, ou, voyage*; at Paris

1609   Marc Lescarbot, *Nova Francia, or the description of that part of New France which is one continent with Virginia* (English translation by Pierre Erondelle, in Hakluyt)---See further entries on Lescarbot in first **Bibliography**

1616   Pierre Biard, *Relation de la Nouvelle France*; at Lyon

1610s-1640s   *The Jesuit Relations and Allied Documents* (Reuben Gold Thwaites, ed., 73 volumes

1630   Jacques de Miggrade, translation of **Las Casas**' *Tyrannies et cruautez de Espagnols*; at Rouen

1632   **Samuel de Champlain**, *Les voyages de la Nouvelle France occidentale, dicte Canada*; at Paris

1632   Gabriel Sagard, *Le grande voyage du pays des Hurons*; at Paris

1632   Paul Le Jeune, *Brieve Relation du Voyage de la Nouvelle France*---perhaps the earliest of Le Jeune's many writings (see *Jesuit Relations*)

1634   Paul Le Jeune, *Relation de ce qui s'est passe en la Nouvelle France en l'annee 1633*; at Paris

from ENGLAND

1497-98   John Cabot's voyage accounts published (collected in D.B. Quinn, ed., *The Newfoundland*)

1516   Sir Thomas More, *Utopia* (based partly in Vespucci's accounts)

1520-1555   Johannes Boemus, *Omnium gentium mores* and *Fardle of Facions*---influential collections of texts on "the ways of all peoples." English translation 1611 below

1565   John Hawkins' Florida voyages (published in Hakluyt 1589 below)

1567-1579   Sir Francis Drake's/Hawkins' voyages in California etc.; in Hakluyt 1589 as "The Third Troublesome Voyage..." and in Drake's 1628 *The World Encompassed*

1578   Richard Hakluyt, "Purposes and Policies To Be Observed in Colonization": published in Hakluyt 1582

1582   Richard Hakluyt, multi-volume compendium *Divers[e] Voyages to America*

1583   Edward Hayes, "A Report of the Voyage" of Sir Humphrey Gilbert to Newfoundland

1583   Sir George Peckham, *A True Report of the Late Discoveries, and possession, taken in the right of the Crown of England*

1584   Hakluyt, ed., "The Voyage of Captains **Amadas and Barlow**" (to Virginia); and his own *Discourse on Western Planting*

1585   Captain John Davis, accounts of *First Voyage* (rpt. in David, ed.)

1588   Thomas Harriot and John White, *A Brief and True Report of the New Found Land of Virginia*; at London (rpt. New York: Dover 1972)

1589   Richard Hakluyt, ed., *The Principall Navigations, Voyages and Discoveries of the English Nation....* (reprinted at London 1600)

1591-2   *The Last Voyage of* **Thomas Cavendish** (D.B. Quinn, ed.)

1596   Sir Walter Ralegh, *The Discoverie of...Empire of Guiana*

1602   Voyages of **Bartholomew Gosnold** (in Quinn, ed., *The English New England Voyages*)

1602   John Brereton, *A Brief and True Relation of the Discovery of the North Part of Virginia* (also in Quinn English New England Voyages)

1604   Sir Walter Ralegh, *History of the World*

1605   James Rosier, *A True Relation of the Most Prosperous Voyage Made This Present Year 1605 by Captain George Waymouth* (rpt. in H.S. Burrage, ed., *Early English and French Voyages*)

1607   Robert Gorges, *Relation of a Voyage into New England*

1608   John Smith, *True Relation of Occurences & Accidents in Virginia*

1609   Hakluyt publishes Spaniard **Hernando DeSoto**'s "Virginia Richly Valued...by Description of the mainland of Florida, her next neighbor"

1609 G. Percy, *Observations on...Virginia*---see also his 1611 *Advice for Investors in Virginia, Bermuda and Newfoundland* (Quinn ed.)

1611 Johannes Boemus, English translation (E. Aston) of *The Manners, Lawes, and customes of all nations*

1612 Robert Johnson (attributed; for the Virginia Company), *Nova Britannia* and *The New Life of Virginia* (Pt. 2), rpt. in Force *Tracts* 1

1613 Samuel Purchas, *Purchas His Pilgrimage, or Relations of the World* (rpt. 1617)

1614 Edward Brerewood, *Enquiries touching the Diversity of Languages and Religions Through the Cheif Parts of the World*---also in Purchas 1625

1615 Ralph Hamor, *A True discourse of the Present Estate of Virginia*

1616 John Smith, *Description of New England* (see also his *New England's Trials* 1620, and *Prospectus* 1624

1618 Sir Walter Ralegh, *Newes of Sir Walter Ralegh. With a true description of Guiana*

1622 Mourt's Relation, possibly written by Plimoth's Edward Winslow

1624 Edward Winslow, *Good Newes from New-England*

1625 William Morrell, *Nova Anglia, or Newe England: A Brief Enarration*

1625 Samuel Purchas, *Hakluytus Posthumus, or Purchas his Pilgrimes* (including Spanish accounts such as Acosta's)

1626 Sir William Vaughan, *The Golden Fleece*

1626 Philip Nichols, *Sir Francis Drake Revived: Calling Upon this dull or Effeminate Age to folowe his Noble Steps for Golde and Silver*

1628   Christopher Levett, *Voyage Into New England*

1630   Sir William Alexander, *Map and Description of New England*

1630   Francis Higginson, *New England's Plantation* (rpt. in Force Tracts)

1630   John White, *Planters Plea*

1634   William Wood, *New England's Prospect*

   NOTE: William **Bradford**'s *Of Plimoth Plantation* was not published till the 1850s; John **Winthrop**'s *History, Journals, Papers* etc. first circulating c.1825; Roger **Williams**' *Key Into the Language of America* 1643; "Pequot War" tracts (Underhill, Mason, Gardiner *et als*) post-1638; and John **Josselyn** (voyages 1638 and 1663) published 1674.

from the DUTCH

1610   Emanuel van Meteren, *On Hudson' Voyage*---English edition (1859) in Henry C. Murphy, ed., *Henry Hudson in Holland*

1610   Robert Juet, "The Third Voyage of Master Henry Hudson"---English translation in Purchas 1625

1612-1614   Voyages of **Adriaen Block** *et als* (published in **de Laet** 1625 below)

1624   Nicolaes van Wassenaer, *Historical Account of all the Most Remarkable Events which have happened in Europe, etc*....Published in separate volumes through 1630, this includes sections such as "Indians," "Encounter with the Mohawks," and "New Plymouth"

1625   Johannes de Laet, *New world, or Description of West-India* (1633 Latin translation *Novus Orbis*)

1633 David Pietersz De Vries, *Short Historical and Journal Notes of various voyages perfomed in the Four Quartewrs of the Globe...by...deVries*....Translation by Henry C. Murphy (1850s) in *Collections of the New York Historical Society*, second series III, 1-129

INDEX to *THOMAS MORTON*

Abenaki, 130, 136, 140-43, 145, 161, 191, 194, 197, 301; *see Kennebec, Native American, Beaver*
Acosta, Fr. Jose de, 93
Adiaphorism ("things indifferent"), 27, 59
Aesculapius (Asklepios), 56, 239
Aesop ("Ant and Bee"), 11, 36
Agamenticus (York, Maine), 301-4, 310, 316-18
Alehouse intellectuals, 188
Alexander, Sir. Wm. (Scot), 277
Allerton, Isaac (Plimoth), 175, 211
America, in legend/literature/lecture, 16, 33, 35-6, 39, 58-9; Chs. 5, 7; 283-5
"American Dream," 178, 186-7
"American" poetry, 86-9
Anglican Church, 11, 13, 15, 20, 25, 27, 32-4, 58, 241; *see King Charles I, Morton, Laud*
Anthropology, 89
"Antimasque," 83; *see Masque*
Ascham, Roger, 33, 37, 86

Ashley, Edward, 177; *see Bristol, Gun-trade, Intermarriage, Plimoth*
Ataraxia ("peace of mind"), 59, 122n50
Atheism, 59, 81n36, 87, 122
"Author's Prologue" (poem), 110, 234

"**B**acchanall Triumph" (poem), 108
Bagnall, Walter ("Great Wat," Ma-re Mount servant), 156, life 196-8, 213, 237; *see Gibbons, Morton /indentured men, Richmond Island*
"Barren Doe of Virginia," 14, 195
Beaver, Chs. 6, 7, 8
Bellamie, Jerome, 118
Beothuk, 296; *see Native American*
Bible (and New England), 183-88
Blackstone, Rev. Wm., 101, 128, 194, 215, 250
Boccaccio, Giovanni, 27n104
Book of Common Prayer, 11, 15, 32, 57, 64, 269; *see Anglican, Laud*
Boston (Shawmut), Illustrations 14-16; charter, 268-70; founding, 217, 249; laws vs. "Indian" trade, 188, 257; wage/price controls, 255; and Connecticutt, 293-4; inner politics, 294, 297; vs. Morton suit, 282, Ch. 9; *see Puritans, Dudley, Winthrop*
Bradford, Wm. (Plimoth), poetry of, 116; 163, Ch. 7 *passim*; youth,

163-5; charges vs. Morton, 194, 163-5, 263, 282; conflict w/Morton's history, 201-10; *see Plimoth, Reform*
Bradstreet, Anne, 119-22, 239
Brereton, John, 135
Breton, Nicholas, 28
Brewster, Wm. (Plimoth), 164-5, 206
Bristol (England), 68, 177, 184-5, Ch. 7 *passim*
Brutus (Brut the Trojan), 80
"[Master] Bubble," 28, 154
Bull, Dixie, 265

Cabot, John/Sebastian, 41; *see Bristol*
Canaan (New England as "parallel" to ancient Palestine), 184n76, 217, 283-4; *see Boston/founding, Evangelism, Mount Dagon, New English Canaan, Philistines, Renaissance. Samson*
Canaries (Islands), 262
Cape Anne, 26, 196
Cape Cod, 41, 173; *see Wampanoag, Nauset*
Capitalism, 21-3, 69, 73, 119, 127, 149-51, Chs. 6-7, 155-7, 166, 179, 180, 187, 192, 217, 252-5; and Native Americans, 277, 283-5
"Centaurs" (hunting teachers), 19
Champlain, Samuel de, 132n56, 145, 198; *see Lescarbot, New France*

Charity, 21n8, 61, 176; *see Neighborliness, West Country, Quietness*
Charles I, King, 63, 191, 265; and Morton law suit, 268-9, 277, 300; jdgmt. for Gorges/Morton, 270-4; *see Anglican, Laud*
Charles River, 145, 149, 211
Charles Town, *see Endicott, Salem, Boston/founding*
Chikatawbak (Neponset Massachusett Sachem), 14, 144-5, 283; llustrations 13-14, 20-1; *see Native American*
Cicero, Marcus Tullius, Ch. 2; *De Oratore*, 85, 91, 240
Cleeves, George, 299
Clifford's Inn (Morton's London "law school"), Illustrations 9-10; 6, 59-61, Ch. 3 *passim; see Inns of Court, Law, Morton*
Columbus, Christopher, 39
Connecticutt River Valley, 270, 293-6, 306; *see Hooker, Pequots*
Corbitant (Narragansett Sachem), 168, Ch. 7
Corn, 139, 141, 179, 182; *see Capitalism*
Council for New England, 191, 211, 263-7; *see Ashley, Bristol, Fishing, Gorges, Gun-trade, Laud, Morton*
Cradock, Mathew (Mass. Bay agent), 273, 298; *see Cleeves, Endicott, Ratcliffe*

Davis, Capt. John, 39, 97
de Rasieres, Isaac (New Netherland), 176
Dermer, Capt. Thos., 127, 147
Devonshire, 6, 14, 33-4, 157; see Clifford's, Morton, West Country
"Difference," 35
Diogenes, 40
Donne, John, 43, 50-1, 58
Drake, Sir Francis, 16, 39
Dudley, Thomas (Mass. Bay), 216, 258, 282, 297, 315; see Boston, Winthrop
Dutch, see Netherlands

Elizabeth I, Queen, 20, 33, 41-3, 58, 63, 225
Endicott, Capt. John (Salem), 188, 211, 310
England (social conditions), 2, 41-3, 157; see Reform, West Country
Epenow (Native New England man), 68
Epicurus, 158
Epidemic ("plague"), in Old World/England, 63; in New England, 137; 2nd wave 1630s, 277; see Native American
Eskimo (Native peoples), 139, 145
Ethnography, 89

Evangelism, 22-8, 60, 93-4, 108-110, Ch. 7, 189, 301; parody in Morton's 1634 letter, 272

Falcons (Hawks), 14, 19, 64, 195
Falstaff, 65
Fates, 20n8, 237, 240
Fishing (early transatlantic), 130-5, 201n86, Illustrations 1, 24-7; see Gun-trade, Gorges, Intermarriage, Native American, Revels
Fur trade, 145-7, 154, 158-9, 220-1; see Gorges, Gun-trade
Frobisher, Martin, 39

"Ganimedes and Jupiter," see Morton/sexuality/indentured men
Gardiner, Sir Christopher, 209, life 264-5, 312; see Morton/lawsuit
Gascoigne, George, 92-3
Gesta Grayorum (masque), 52, Ch. 3; 222-5
Gibbons, Edward (Ma-re Mount servant), 156, early life 196-8; helps Morton in 1st arrest, 208-9; church conversion, 213; letter to Winthrop Jr., 293; "General," 308; helps Morton at last trial, 316; see Bagnall, Plimoth, Salem, Isles of Shoals

Gilbert, Sir Humphrey, 39, 95-6, 131, 188
Golden Fleece, see Wm. Vaughan
"Golden Mean," 19, Illustration 5
Gorges, Sir Ferdinando, Chronology, Illustration 12; 3; on colonies/profits/self-government, 68; 127-9; and Council for New England 1630s, 263-4, 270-1; "cashiers" Morton, 300-302; *see Fishing, Gun-trade, Morton, Native American, Plimoth*
Gorges, Robert, 101, 128
Gorges, Thomas, 301-3
Gorton, Samuel, 297
Gosnold, Bartholomew, 97, 158
Greene, Charles (putative *Canaan* printer), 287-91
Guazzo, Sir Stefano, 30-1
Gun-trade, 145, 147, 155, 177, 191, 199, 209; Plimoth vs., 155, 177-8. 186, 202, 221; *see Ashley, Boston, Bristol, Council, Fishing, Fur trade, Intermarriage, Morton, Native American, Reform, Revels*

Hakluyt, Richard, 33, 39, 42, 49, 96, 130-2
Hariot, Thos., 245
Harvard University, 296
Hawthorne, Nathaniel, 5, 157

Hayman, Robt. (Quodlibets), 112, 287
Hawks, see Falcons
Healing, 11, 246; *see Aesculapius, "Masque," Native American, Revels*
Henry VIII, King, 9, 43
Hobbamok, 174
Hobbyhorse, 201
Homer, Ch. 2, 200
Hooker, Rev. Thos., Inns Master, 44; Connecticutt colonist, 294, 297
Horace, 80, 239
Hospitality, 20; *see Neighborliness*
Humanism, Ch. 2, 59, 93, 189; *see Cicero, Montaigne, Morton, Renaissance, Ronsard*
"Humors," 131-2, 221
Hutchinson, Anne (Mass. Bay), 297

"Indifferent, things," 27, 59, 202
Inns of Court (London "law schools"), 8, 10, 41-62, Illustrations 8-11; *see Donne, Elizabeth, Jonson, Morton, Shakespeare, "Masque"*
Intermarriage (early transatlantic), 128-32, 160, 184-5, 200, 217, 226
Ireland, 8, Ch. 1, 160; *see Gilbert, Morton/father*
Isles of Shoals, 208

James I, King 43, 45, 57, 63, 191

Jeffreys, Wm. (Weymouth), 194;
    letter from Morton to, 271; 312
Job, 11, 236
Jonson, Ben, 9, 43, 50-1, 52, 60, 62,
    107, 281; see Gesta, Inns,
    Masque

Kennebec River, 161, 193
Kiehtan (Cautontowitt), 143; see
    Native American

Laud, Wm. (Archbishop of
    Canterbury), 270, 272, 276,
    287, 300; see Anglican,
    Council, Morton lawsuit
Law (Morton and), 73, 79, 203, 256-
    61; study of at Inns, Ch. 3;
    and Star Chamber, 45; and
    common law, 45, 58; see
    Morton/lawsuit/"murther
    warrant"; Plimoth/gun-trade
Lescarbot, Marc (New France), 66,
    97, 159, 198, 219, 254, 280; see
    Champlain
Leland, Charles G., 111n46, 142-3
Levellers, 188
Levett, Capt. Christopher, 97, 142,
    147-8
"light of nature," 188-9
Lodge, Thos., and his *Scilla*, 51-2, 60;
    Illustration 6; see Inns, Ovid
London, Illustration 8, 46-8

Maine, 161, 201, 300; see Kennebec

Manit ("Manitou"), 142
Ma-re Mount, Chs. 5-8; remains
    today, 195n82; lists of goods
    taken from, 206-10, 258-9
Markham, Gervase, 17-18
"Martialists," 42-3, 153, 188-9; see
    "Pequot War"
Mason, Capt. John, 60, 105; see
    Gorges
Masque, development of, Ch. 3, see
    Gesta; and racist imagery, 55,
    58-9; use of in New England,
    130, 191-3, 220-1; as political
    manipulation, 245n118
Massachusett (collective name for
    Neponset, Pawtucket and
    other Native peoples), 143,
    148, 153-5; see Chikatawbak,
    Native American
"Massasoit" ("High Sachem")---
    Nanepashemet of Mystic,
    144; Ousamequin/Yellow
    Feather of Wampanoags,
    168, 174
Mass. Bay Colony, see Boston,
    Charles, Dudley, Endicott,
    Gorges, Laud, Morton/ law-
    suit, Puritans, Salem,
    Winthrop
Maverick, Samuel, 71, 194, 207, 215,
    250, 315, 317
Maypole(s), 6, 22, 24, 32, 55, 106;
    early fishermen's, 130, 195;
    Morton's cut down, 211;
    Illustrations 24-5; see Gun-
    trade, Ma-re Mount, Morton

Merry Mount (1930s MET Opera), 123, Illustrations 33-6
Miantonomi (Narragansett Sachem), 316
Micmac (Native people), 145; *see* Native American
Miller, Alice (Mrs. Thos. Morton), 5, 70-77, 80; *see* Morton/widows
Miller, George (Morton stepson), 74-5, 77n33, 80, 268
Milton, John, 281
"Mine Host," 64
"Moderation," 29, 59-61, 66-7, 285; *see Adiaphorism, Ataraxia, Atheism, Quietness, West Country*
Mohawk (Native people), 307; *see* Native American
Montaigne, Michel de, 29, 61, 65
More, Sir Thos., 21
Morrell, Rev. Wm (*New-England*, poem), 101

MORTON, THOMAS---basic biography *iii*, Chronology; birth, 5, 7; Catholic sympathies, 15, 25-6, 56, 64; and Christianity, 2, 25-7; Devonshire origins, 6; education, Ch. 1, 29, 36-8, 44, 48, 51, 57; falconry, 19, 64; father, 7, 72; "genial" upbringing, 7, 20; as hunter "nursed by Centaurs," 16-19, 64, 81; and indentured men, 155-6, 237; at Inns of Court, 41-62; mother, 10-14; "neece" Sara, 9, 306; racial hierarchies, 24, 28; sexuality, 16, 52, 81, 199; "widows," 14;

---, arrives America, ch. 4, 81, 127-35, 151; American tenure, 191; land-patent (?), 71; Gun-trading, Chs. 5-7; 1627 Revels, Illustrations 24-7, 199-200; 1st arrest, 203-210;

---, 2nd arrest, 214-17, 255-61; alleged crimes, 256; "murther warrant," 78-9, 203-4, 256, 263; house-burning, 258-9; lawsuit vs. Salem/Mass. Bay/Plimoth, 262-7, 272-4, 278, 309; victory letter 1634, 271-4; will 305;

---, last arrival in America, 299-301, 304, 307; imprisoned, 311-12, release petition, 314; remains, 318;

---, "missing" records about, 260; attempts on his life, 314; and "book learning," 11, 29, 132; and ethnocentrism/racism, 55, 58-9, 105, 181-4, 187-8; and oratory, 283; seal/signature, Illustration 3; status as first American poet in English, 125

Moswetusett Hummock, 146
"Mount Dagon," 212; *see Philistines*
Mount Wollaston, 146, break-up of, 154

Narragansetts (Native people), 144, 168, 170, 307, 316; *see* Native American

Native American(s)---Chronology, Illustrations 13, 14, 20-27; **general portrait of in New England**, 137-44; and "American" poetry, 86-9, 116, 125, 220; early transatlantic contacts, 35-6, 68, 127-36, 144-8; "fertility," 229; healing, 200, 246, "Masque"; history, from "Paleo" (138) to "Archaic" (139) to "Woodland" (140); and land, 152-3, 228, 284; oratory, 229, 246; shaman/powah, 245-6; social structure(s), gender relations, 141-3; at Morton's Revels, 195-99, 231-4; praying towns, 180; stereotypes of "dangerous" created, Ch. 7; warfare, 147

Nausets, 173; *see* Native American

"Nectar," 54, 107-8

Neighborliness, 15, 193, 203, 208, 216; *see* Quietness, West Country

Neoplatonism, 107-8

Neponset (Massachusett Native people), Illustration 14, 135, 144-8; *see Chikatawbak, "Masque," Native American*

Netherlands, Illustration 17; 41-2, 127, 165, 176, 248, 275

New English Canaan (Amsterdam? London? 1637), Facsimile pages, w/ Illustrations 28-30; composition of, 152, 262-4, 281-7; copies confiscated, 291; critique of, 284-5; influences, 298, Chs. 3, 9 *passim*; origins in lawsuit vs. New England Puritans, 221, 281-91; poetry of, "Antimasque" and "Masque"; publication, 287-91; reception---*Sampler*, reviews 1630s, 297-8, 311; related Morton texts, *see Quo Warranto*, 278, *1634 letter*, 271

"New creed" of Canaan, 181

New France, 130-2, 198; *see Champlain, Lescarbot*

New Netherland, 130-2; *see de Rasieres*

Niobe, 227, 230, 240; *see Epidemic, Native American, Ovid, Scilla, Squa Rock*

Nipmuc (Native people), 137, 194; *see Native American, "Bubble"*

Oedipus, 107, 230, "Masque"; *see Epidemic*

Oldham, John, 210, 271, death 295

Ovid, 36, 91, 110, 230; *see Lodge, Scilla, Illustrations 6, 21*

"Paradise" (writings on New England), 67, 118n47, 152
Parmenius, Stephen, 33, 95-6
Passonagessit, 135, 146, 213
Pennacook (Native people), 137; see Native American
Pequot (Native people), 137, 194, Illustration 20; "Pequot War," 285, 293-6; see Native American
Perkins, Wm., 26, 165, 188
Philistines, 58, 184, 212
"Pilgrims," Ch. 7; see Plimoth
Piscataqua, 194, 316
"Plague," see Epidemic
Plato, vs. poets, 83-5; on poetry, 100, 119; in the Renaissance, 116n45
Pleiade, la, 86n39, 116n45; see Renaissance, Ronsard
Plimoth Plantation, 70, 108, 153, 161, 163; early history, 164-76; failed communism, 179, 282; and Connecticutt, 294; Morton's recognition of, 187, 281; Morton's last stay there, 307-9; see Allerton, Ashley, "Barren Doe," Boston, Bradford, Brewster, Capitalism, Gun-trade, Kennebec, Puritans, Reform, Salem, Standish, Weymouth, Winslow
Poe, Edgar Allan, 123, 125

"Poem, The" (May Day 1627), 60, 106, 136, 200, "Masque"; see Scilla, "The Song"
Poetry, Renaissance theories of, 85-95
Popham (early "Maine"), 68
Poststructuralism, 87, 120, 220
Powahs, 143n61; see Native American, Healing
Powhatan (Native peoples of "Virginia"), 67, 100
Pratt, Phineas (Weymouth), 170, 174
Pring, Martin, 68
Protestantism, 21, 58; see Reform
Proteus, 55, 121-3; "Masque of," in Gesta, 55, 159, 222-4; see Humanism, Renaissance
Purchas, Samuel, 67
Puritans, Ch. 1, 21, 93 (poetry); 122n50; colonial methods, Ch. 7, 188, 214-15, 255-7; suppressions of, 270; ; Illustrations 16, 25; see Boston, Bradford, Bradstreet, Dudley, Endicott, Gibbons, Plimoth, Reform, Salem, Winthrop, Winslow
Puttenham, George, 95
Pygmalion, 125

"Quietness," 24; and racial hierarchies, 24, 28; philosophical, 59-61; see Neighborliness
Quo Warranto (Gorges/Morton

document of legal process), 278

Ralegh, Sir Walter, 21, 28, 39, 50, 97, 149, 150-1; *see Capitalism*
Ratcliff(e), Philip (Mass. Bay servant, Morton lawsuit witness), 265-6
Reform, 21-24, 42, 93-4, 119-24, Ch. 7, 188-9, and American "pollution," 191, 251-3, 282-3; *see Evangelism, Stubbes*
Renaissance, 29-32, 34-5, 58-60, 107-8, 121-2, 128, 285; *see "Antimasque," "Masque"*
Revels, Ch. 1, 130-1, 192-3, 195; Native view of, 245; Illustrations 24-5; *see Fishing, Gun-trade*
Richmond Island, 197; *see Bagnall*
Rigby, Sir Alexander, 303, 305, 317
Ronsard, Pierre de, 65, 107-8; *see La Pleiade, Renaissance, Scilla*
Rosier, James, 136, 139

Salem, 187-8, 213; early famine, 215
Samoset, 153
Samson, 236
Sandys, George, 110
Scepticism, 27, 61, 122
Scilla, 232-4, 242; *see Lodge, Ovid, "The Poem," Revels, Illustrations 6, 21*
Scogan/Scogan's Choice, 11, 238

Shakespeare, Wm., 52, 65-6, 94, 223; *see Gesta, Inns*
Sidney, Sir Philip, 33-4, 52, 86, 90, 92, 241
Slavery in New England, 296
Smith, Capt. John, 68, 98-101, 114, 157, 296
Socrates, 189
"Song, The" (poem), 60, 81, 107-8; *see Jonson, Revels*
Spain, 7, 41-2, 63; and English colonies, 16, 66, 128, 160; peace with, 63, 66; *see Acosta, Chronology, Bibliography 2; Spaniard de Molina on Virginia, 156*
Spenser, Edmund, 106, 227
Squa Rock/Squantum peninsula, 151, 234; Illustration 21
Squanto, *see Tisquantum*
Stam, J.F., (putative printer of *Canaan*), 288-90
Standish, Capt. Myles (Plimoth), 41, 167, 174, 205, 308
Star Chamber, 47; and confiscation of *Canaan*, 291
Stationers Register, 287-90
Stubbes, Philip, 24, 51, 229; *see Reform*

Tacitus, 35
Tillam, Thomas, 116-18
Tisquantum (New England Native), 153, 168, 175; *see Gorges*

Triton, 235; tritons on *Canaan* front page, 290
Tompson, David (Scot), 194
Tyler, Moses Coit, 109-12, 219

Unity (Morton's 1st arrival ship), 130-35

Vaughan, Sir Wm. (*Golden Fleece*), 103-5
Verrazzano, Giovanni de, 136, 284
Virgil, 36, 84, "Masque" *passim*
Virginia, 67, 98-9, 110, 156, 172-3, 245, 296

Wollaston, Captain, 72, 134, 154; see Mount Wollaston, Ma-re Mount
Wampanoag (Native people), 168, 170; Illustrations 13, 14, 20; see Native American
Wessaguscus/usset, "the narrow place": 101, 128; see Weymouth
West Country, 6, 11-15; neighborliness, 17, 19-20, 39, 193; and reform, 21-24, 27, 235; in Civil War, 302; see Devonshire, Morton
Weston, Andrew, 101, 132
Weymouth, Ch. 7; 271; Massacre, 170-75; see Jeffreys, Weston
"Wild" people/"wilderness," 132, 196
Williams, Roger, 118, 131, 295

Winslow, Edward (Plimoth), 161, Ch. 7; vs. Morton in court, 275; letter on Morton's final return to America, 307
Winstanley, Gerrard (Diggers), 188
Winthrop, John, editors of works 204-5; and "murther warrant" vs. Morton, 203-4; meets Native woman, 255; early life, 250-55; American colony "Reasons," 253; 268; Morton's threat to his ears, 274, 312; Native "boy" servant, 296; and "Pequot War," 285, 296; and Morton's final American days, 317-18; see Boston, Puritans, Reform
Winthrop, John Jr., letter from Gibbons to, 293
Women, English, 10-14, 186-7, see Alice Miller, "Barren Doe," Elizabeth I, Morton/mother/widows, Reform
---, Native American, 141-3; see Intermarriage, Morrell, "The Poem," "The Song," Revels, Scilla
Wood, Wm. (*New England's Prospect*), 115, 170, 297
"Worthies, The Nine," 33

***
****

1) Atlantic Sea-Routes between Europe, West Indies and the Americas
[adapted from K.R. Andrews ed., *The Westward Enterprise*]

2) England and the borders of its Counties

Thomas Morton

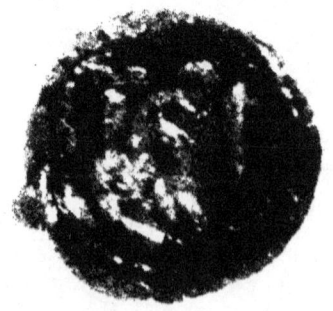

3) Photo of (goat's head) Seal-impression, and Signature, of Thomas Morton [in Banks, "Morton"]

4) "The Wrong" Thomas Morton-portrait in *The Dictionary of Literary Biography* [shown therein from chest-height up; original portrait in British Museum: DLB (1984) Vol. 24: 231]

Th'Ancients used Water not the Sand
Which in like glasses did the Hours command
Yo haue renew'd to vs Times beaten Track
Doe cast our Water by your Almanack
Physick inventions haue giv'n many Name
But this of Urine giues our Morton Fame.

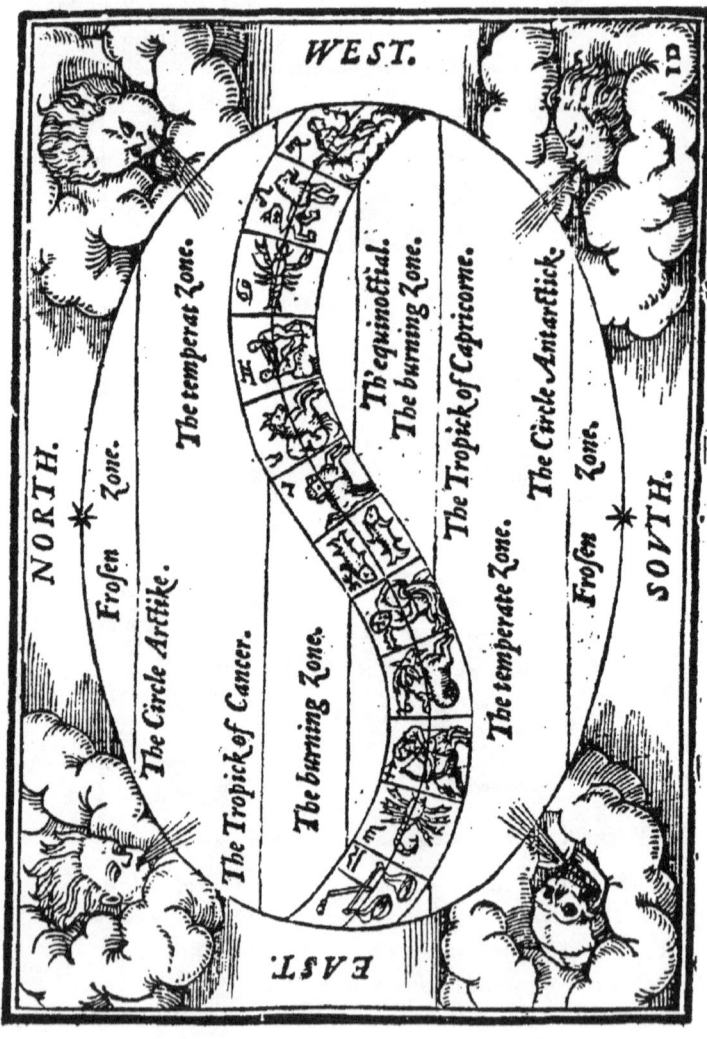

5) Renaissance world-map showing "the Golden Mean" or Temperate Zones, with Zodiac [rpt. in Heninger, *The Cosmographical Glass*]

6) Frankfort 1580 woodcut, "De Glauco" (Glaucus and Scilla by the Shore) from *Picta Poesis Ovidiana* [British Museum: rpt. in Keach]

7) Conception of Lescarbot's *The Theatre of Neptune* in New France [from Richardson ed. 1927]

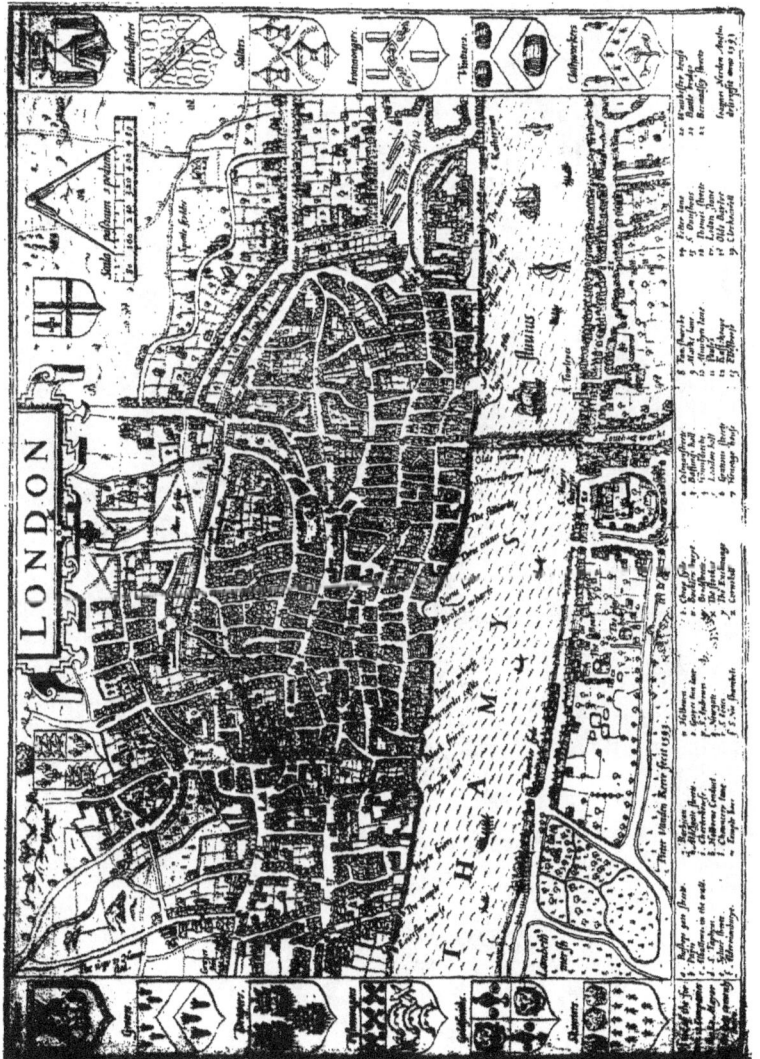

8) Map of London c. 1593 by John Norden, engraver
[in Ivor Brown, *London: An Illustrated History*. London: Studio 1965]

9) The Inns of Court: "Corner in Clifford's Inn," [from Loftie's *The Inns of Court*]

10) The small garden behind Clifford's Inn
[from Loftie]

11) The Inns of Court: Middle Temple Hall
[from Loftie]

12) Sketch of Sir Ferdinando Gorges' home, "Ashton Phillips," in Somerset, [from Frost, *Immortal Voyage*]

13) Native American "New England" at the beginning of European contact
[adapted from Trigger, ed. *Handbook* vol 15 *The Northeast*, 161]

14) Massachusetts Bay c. 1620-1630
[adapted from Carl Seaburg, *Boston Observed*. Boston: Beacon 1971]

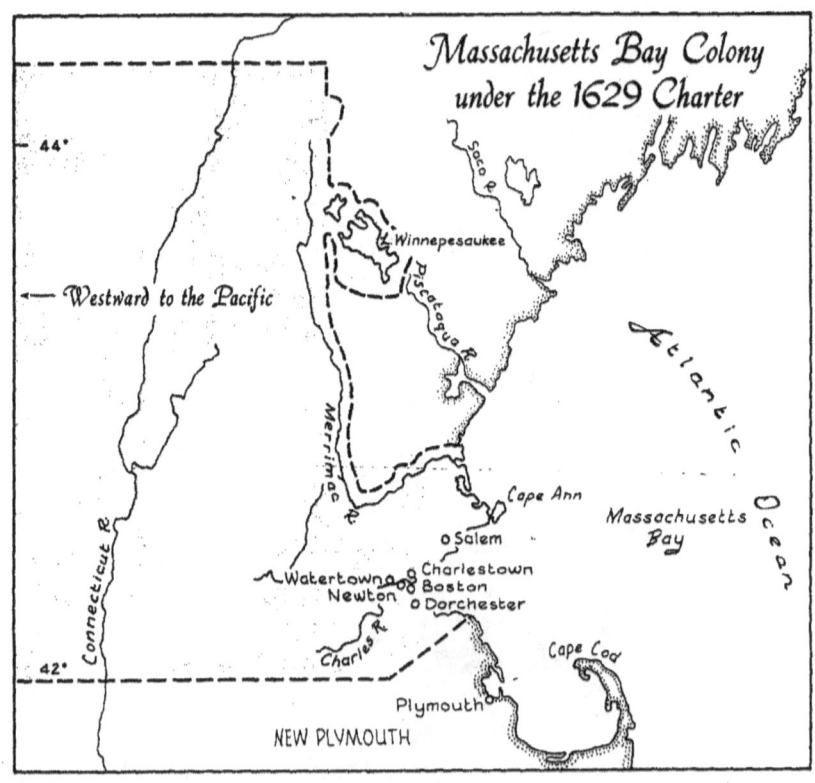

15) Map showing Massachusetts Bay Colony's 1629 chartered lands
[from Barch/Lefler, eds., *Colonial America*]

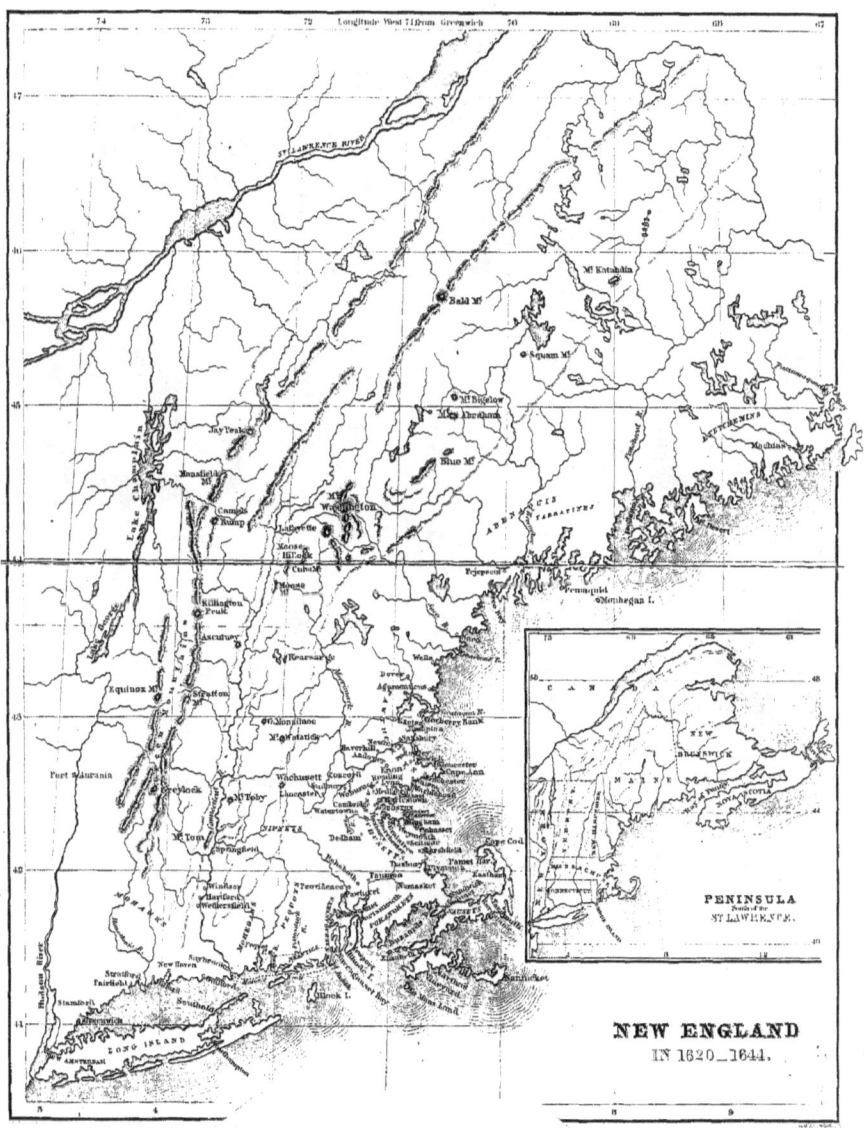

16) Colonial New England by the 1640s
[adapted from Palfrey *History of New England*]

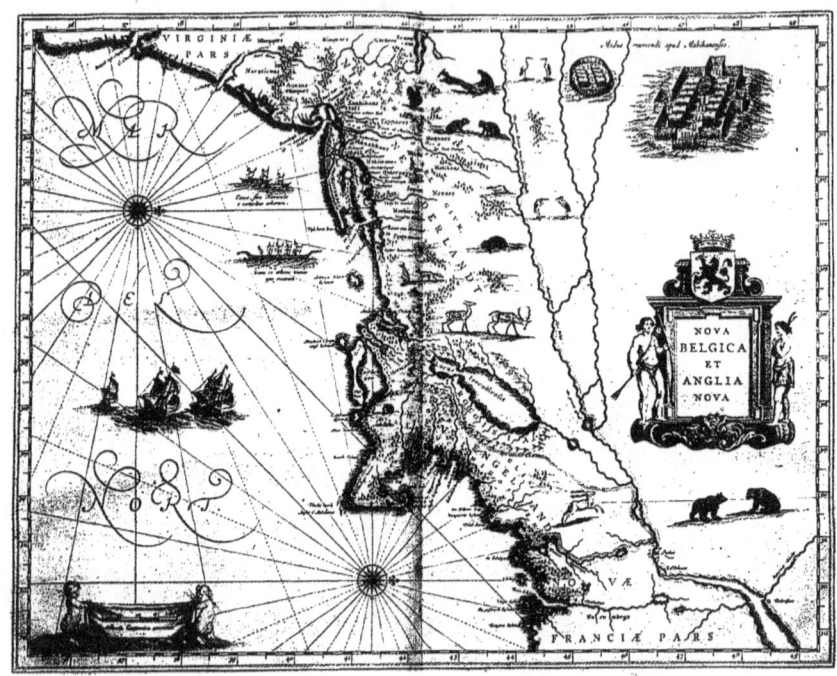

17) Adriaen Block's 1635 map of [New England] showing "Lake of the Erocoise" [adapted from *New England Begins* 22]

18) 1800s view "Seaward from Mount Wollaston" [from the library of William Bowman, Weymouth MA; and in *Colonel John Quincy of Mount Wollaston*, Boston: Ellis Co. 1909]

19) 1840s sketch, "Mt. Wollaston" from Frost's *Immortal Voyage*

20) a Native New England village in the 1600s
[from the Mashantucket Pequot library]

21) Squa Rock, in Squantum, Mass.

22) Hopewell carving of "Mother & Child" [from Milwaukee Public Museum, est. c. 500 BC-500AD]; and "Mother and Child" limestone effigy, from Annisquam, Mass. [est. 500 AD] — sketch in Bragdon *People* 177]

23) Native American calendar-site in Connecticutt

[diagram ©1998 by artist/archaeologist David Wagner: see bibliography]

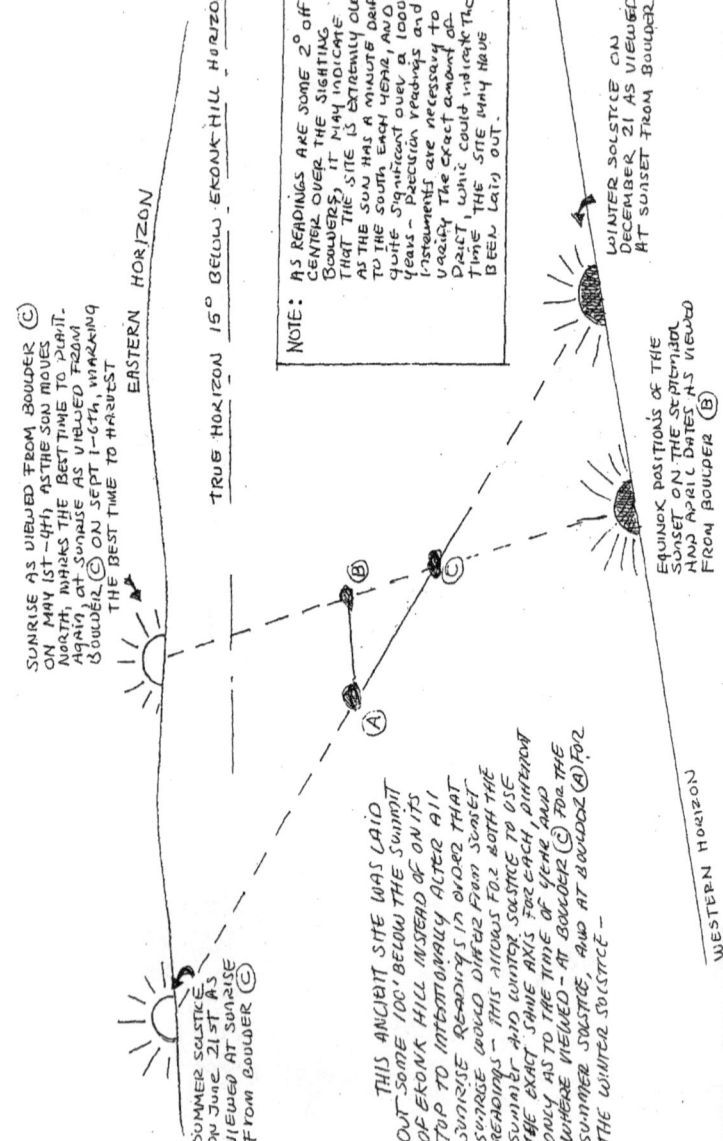

24) "Festivities at Merry Mount," May 1627 [this unsourced reprint in Frost]

25) "Myles Standish Breaks Up...Effort to Fraternize"
[from Pilgrim Society illustration rpt. in *Yankee*]

26) Historian G. Stinson Lord c. 1950s with archaeological artifacts he recovered from Ma-re Mount: now at Quincy Historical Society [photo courtesy of William Bowman, Weymouth MA]

325 YEAR-OLD AX-HEAD, used for trading with the Indians, is one of the few surviving relics from the site of Thomas Morton's trading post at Mount Wollaston. Beside it are two whetstones. The one in the center was unearthed with the ax-head, and the other is cut from the rock on Richmond Island, known to be the source of Morton's whetstones.

Quincy May Obtain Relics From Morton Trading Post

By IAN McINTYRE

Relics from Thomas Morton's Indian trading post in Merrymount may be presented to the Quincy City

27) [from "Quincy Patriot Ledger" 1955]

NEW ENGLISH CANAAN
OR
NEW CANAAN.

Containing an Abstract of New England,

Composed in three Bookes.

The first Booke setting forth the originall of the Natives, their Manners and Customes, together with their tractable Nature and Love towards the English.

The second Booke setting forth the naturall Indowments of the Country, and what staple Commodities it yealdeth.

The third Booke setting forth, what people are planted there, their prosperity, what remarkable accidents have happened since the first planting of it, together with their Tenents and practise of their Church.

Written by Thomas Morton of Cliffords Inne gent, *upon tenne yeares knowledge and experiment of the Country.*

Printed at AMSTERDAM,
By JACOB FREDERICK STAM.
In the Yeare 1 6 3 7.

28) Original first page of *New English Canaan,* 1637
[five original folios of pages follow]

NEW ENGLISH CANAAN,
OR
NEW CANAAN.

Containing an Abstract of New England.

Composed in three Bookes.

The first Booke setting forth the originall of the Natives, their Manners and Customes, together with their tractable Nature and Love towards the English.

The second Booke setting forth the naturall Indowments of the Countrie, and what staple Commodities it yeeldeth.

The third Booke setting forth what people are planted there, their prosperity, what remarkable accidents have happened since the first planting of it; together with their Tenents, and practise of their Church.

Written by THOMAS MORTON *of Cliffords Inne, Gent. upon ten yeeres knowledge and experiment of the Countrie.*

Printed for *Charles Greene*, and are sold in Pauls Church-yard. 1632

29) Facsimile of the only "1632" front page of *Canaan*
[British LibraryPBMIC 39042]

NEW ENGLISH CANAAN;

OR,

New Canaan,

CONTAINING

AN ABSTRACT OF NEW ENGLAND.

COMPOSED IN THREE BOOKES.

The first setting forth the Originall of the Natives, their Manners and Customs. Together with their tractable Nature and Love towards the English.

II. *The Natural Indowments of the Countrie, and what Staple Commodities it yeeldeth.*

III. *What People are planted there, their Prosperity, what remarkable Accidents have happened since the first planting of it; together with their Tenents and Practise of their Church.*

WRITTEN BY

THOMAS MORTON, OF CLIFFORDS INN, GENT.

Upon ten Yeers Knowledge and Experiment of the Country.

Printed by *Charles Green.* 1632.

30) Front page of *Canaan* from Force's 1832 *Tracts* reprint edition [Vol. 2]

NEW ENGLISH CANAAN,
OR
NEW CANAAN.

The Authors Prologue.

I F art & industry should doe as much
As Nature hath for Canaan, not such
Another place, for benefit and rest,
In all the universe can be possest.
The more we prooue it by discovery,
The more delight each object to the eye
Procures, as if the elements had here
Bin reconcil'd, and pleas'd it should appeare,
Like a faire virgin, longing to be sped,
And meete her lover in a Nuptiall bed,
Deck'd in rich ornaments t' advaunce her state
And excellence, being most fortunate,
When most enjoy'd, so would our Canaan be
If well imploy'd by art & industry (wombe
Whose offspring, now shewes that her fruitfull
Not being enjoy'd, is like a glorious tombe,
Admired things producing which there dye,
And ly fast bound in darck obscurity,
The worth of which in each particuler,
Who list to know, this abstract will declare.

NEW

NEW ENGLISH CANAAN,
OR NEW CANAAN.

The first Booke.

Containing the originall of the Natives, their manners, & Customes,
with their tractable nature and
love towards the English.

CHAP. I.

*Prooving New England the principall part of all
America, and most commodious and fitt for
habitation.*

HE wise Creator of the universall
Globe, hath placed a golden meane
betwixt two extreames: I meane the
temperate Zones, betwixt the hote
and cold; and every Creature, that
participates of Heavens blessings, with
in the Compasse of that golden meane, is made most
apt

B 2

I have observed that they will not be troubled with superfluous commodities. Such things as they finde, they are taught by necessity to make use of. they will make choise of; and seeke to purchase with industry so that in respect, that their life is so voyd of care, and they are so loving also that they make use of those things they enjoy (the wife onely excepted) as common goods, and are therein, so compassionate that rather than one should starve through want, they would starve all, thus doe they passe away the time merrily, not regarding our pompe (which they see daylly before their faces) but are better content with their owne, which some men esteeme so meanely of.

They may be rather accompted to live richly, wanting nothing that is needefull; and to be commended for leading a contented life, the younger being ruled by the Elder, and the Elder ruled by the Powahs, and the Powahs are ruled by the Devill, and then you may imagin what good rule is like to be amongst them.

They make use of ordinary things, one of anothers as common.

F I N I S.

NEW ENGLISH CANAAN,
OR NEW CANAAN.

The second Booke.

Containing a description of the bewty of the Country with her naturall indowements, both in the Land and Sea, with the great Lake of Erocoise.

CHAP. I.

The generall Survey of the Country.

IN the Moneth of Iune, Anno Salutis: 1622. It was my chaunce to arrive in the parts of New England with 30. Servants, and provision of all sorts fit for a plantation: And whiles our howses were building, I did indeavour to take a survey of the Coun-

Country: The more I looked, the more I liked it. And when I had more seriously considered, of the bewty of the place, with all her faire indowments, I did not thinke that in all the knowne world it could be paralell'd. For so many goodly groues of trees, dainty fine round rising hillucks: delicate faire large plaines; sweete cristall fountaines, and cleare running streames, that twine in fine meanders through the meads, making so sweete a murmering noise to heare, as would even lull the sences with delight a sleepe, so pleasantly doe they glide upon the pebble stones, jetting most jocundly where they doe meete; and hand in hand runne downe to Neptunes Court, to pay the yearely tribute, which they owe to him as soveraigne Lord of all the springs. Contained within the volume of the Land, Fowles in abundance, Fish in multitude, and discovered besides; Millions of Turtledoves one the greene boughes: which sate pecking, of the full ripe pleasant grapes, that were supported by the lusty trees, whose fruitfull loade did cause the armes to bend, which here and there disperssd (you might see) Lillies and of the Daphnean-tree, which made the Land to mee seeme paradice, for in mine eie, t'was Natures Masterpeece: Her cheifest Magazine of all, where lyves her store: if this Land be not rich, then is the whole world poore.

What I had resolved on, I have really performed, and I have endeavoured, to use this abstract as an instrument, to bee the meanes, to communicate the knowledge which I have gathered, by my many yeares residence in those parts, unto my Countrymen,

A famous Country.

Their fountaines are as cleere as Cristall.

Greate store of fowles, fish and venison, &c.

to the end, that they may the better perceive their error, who cannot imagine, that there is any Country in the universall world, which may be compared unto our native soyle. I will now discover unto them a Country whose indowments are by learned men allowed to stand in a parralell with the Israelites Canaan, which none will deny, to be a land farre more excellent then Old England in her proper nature.

This I confider I am bound in duety (as becommeth a Christian man) to performe, for the glory of God, in the first place; next (according to Cicero,) to acknowledge that, *Non nobis solum nati sumus, sed partim patria, partim parentes, partim amiti vindicant.*

For which cause I must approove of the indeavours of my Country men, that have bin studious to inlarge the territories of his Majesties empire by planting Colonies in America.

And of all other I must applaude the judgement of those that have made choise of this part (whereof I now treat) being of all other most absolute, as I will make it appeare, hereafter by way of paralell, among those that have setled themselvs in new England, some have gone for their conscience sake, (as they professe) & I wish that they may plant the Gospel of Iesus Christ: as becommeth them, sincerely and without faction, whatsoever their former or present practises are (which I intend not to justifie, howsoever they have deserved (in mine opinion) some commendatoires, in that they have furnished the Country, so commodiously in so short a time, although it hath bin but for their owne profit, yet posterity will taste the sweetnes of it, and that very sodainly.

And

CHAP. XIV.

Of the Revells of New Canaan.

THe Inhabitants of Pasonagessit (having translated the name of their habitation from that ancient Salvage name to Ma-re Mount, and being resolved to have the new name confirmed for a memorial to after ages) did devise amongst themselves to have it performed in a solemne manner with Revels, & merriment after the old English custome: prepared to sett up a Maypole upon the festivall day of Philip and Iacob, & therefore brewed a barrell of excellent beare, & provided a case of bottles to be spent, with other good cheare, for all commers of that day. And because they would have it in a compleat forme, they had prepared a song fitting to the time and present occasion. And upon Mayday they brought the Maypole to the place appointed, with drumes, gunnes, pistols, and other fitting instruments, for that purpose; and there erected it with the help of Salvages, that came thether of purpose to see the manner of our Revels. A goodly pine tree of 80. foote longe, was reared up, with a peare of buckshorns nayled one, somewhat neare unto the top of it: where it stood as a faire sea marke for directions; how to finde out the way to mine Hoste of Ma-re Mount.

A Maypole.

And because it should more fully appeare to what end it was placed there, they had a poem in readines made, which was fixed to the Maypole, to shew the new name confirmed upon that plantation; which although it were made according to the occurrents

of the time, it being Enigmatically composed) pusselled the Seperatists most pittifully to expound it, which (for the better information of the reader) I have here inserted.

THE POEM.

RIse Oedipeus, and if thou canst unfould,
What meanes Caribdis underneath the mould,
When Scilla sollitary on the ground,
(Sitting in forme of Niobe) was found;
Till Amphitrites Darling did acquaint,
Grim Neptune with the Tenor of her plaint,
And caused him send forth Triton with the sound,
Of Trumpet lowd, at which the Seas were found,
So full of Protean formes, that the bold shore,
Presented Scilla a new paramore,
So stronge as Sampson and so patient,
As Job himselfe, directed thus, by fate,
To comfort Scilla so unfortunate.
I doe professe by Cupids beautious mother;
Heres Scogans choise for Scilla, and none other;
Though Scilla's sick with greefe because no signe,
Can there be found of vertue masculine.
Esculapius come, I know right well,
His labour's lost when you may ring her Knell,
The fatall sisters doome none can withstand,
Nor Cithareas powre, who poynts to land,
With proclamation that the first of May,
At Ma-re Mount shall be kept hollyday.

The man who brought her ever was named Samson Iob.

The

To take in hand, what Eacus this taske,
Is such as harebrain'd Phaeton did aske,
Of Phebus to begird the world about,
Which graunted put the Netherlands to rout.
Presumptious fooles learne wit at too much cost,
For life and labour both at once bee lost.
Sterne Radamantus being last to speake,
Made a great hum and thus did silence breake,
What if with ratling chaines or Iron bands,
Hidra be bound either by feete or hands,
And after being lash'd with smarting rodds,
Hee be convey'd by Stix unto the godds,
To be accused on the upper ground,
Of Lese Majestatis this crime found,
T'will be unpossible from thence I trowe,
Hidra shall come to trouble us belowe,
This sentence pleasd the friends exceedingly,
That up they tost their bonnets and did cry,
Long live our Court in great prosperity.
The Sessions ended some did straight devise,
Court Revells antiques and a World of joyes,
Brave Christmas gamballs, there was open hall,
Kept to the full; and sport the Divell and all,
Labourisde;sfied the loomes are laid away,
And this proclaim'd the Stigean Holli day,
In came grim Minos with his mosty beard,
And brought a distillation well prepar'd,
And Eacus who is as suer as text,
Came in with his preparatives the next,
Then Radamantus last and principall,
Feasted the Worthies in his sumptuous hall.

There Caron Cerberous and the rout of feinds,
Had lap enough and so their pastims ende.

THE ILLVSTRATIONS.

NOw to illustrate this Poem, and make the fence more plaine, it is to be confidered that the Persons at Ma-re-Mount were seaven, and they had seaven heads and 14. feete, these were accounted Hidra with the seaven heads; and the Maypole with the Hornes nailed neere the topp, was the forked tayle of this suppofed Monster, which they (for want of skill) imposed: yet feared in time (if they hindred not mine Host) heewould hinder the benefit of their Beaver trade, as hee had done (by meanes of this helpe) in Kyuy back river finely, ere they were a wares, who comming too late, were much dismaide to finde that mine Host his boate had gleaned away all before they came; which Beaver is a fitt companion for Scarlett: and I beleeve that Iafons golden Fleece was either the same, or some other Fleece not of so much value.

This action bred a kinde of hart burning in the Plimmouth Planters who after, fought occasion against mine Host to overthrowe his undertakings, and to destroy his Plantation, whome they accoumpted a maine enemy to theire Church and State.

Now

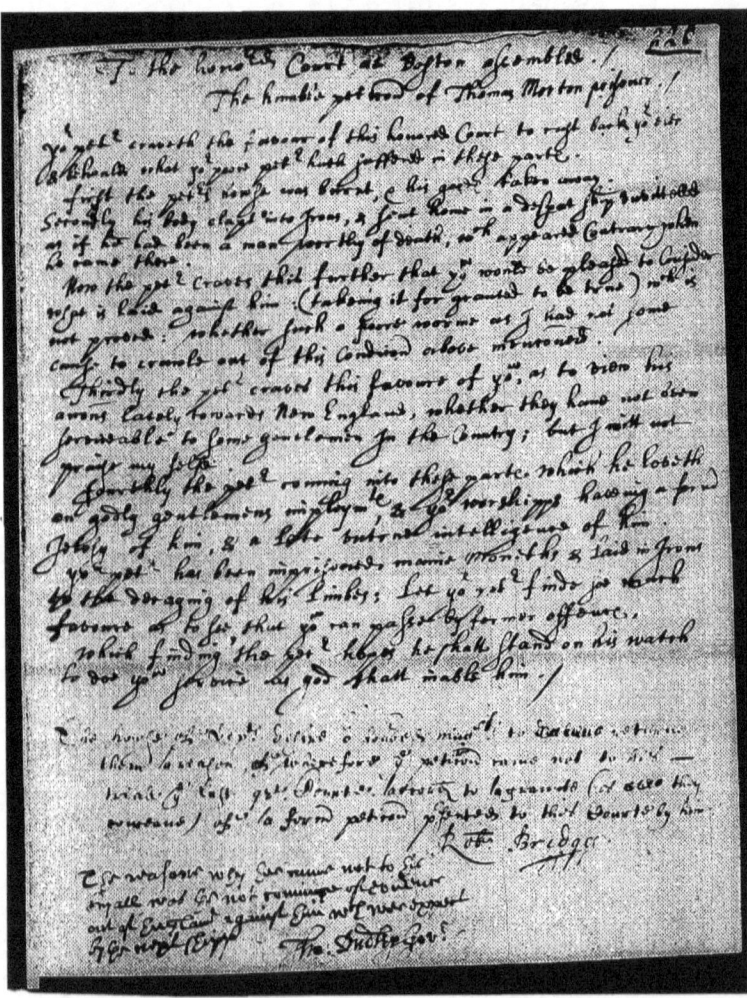

32) Facsimile of Thomas Morton's 1645 "Petition to the Honourable Court at Boston"
[Mass. Historical Society Collections]

MERRY MOUNT

OPERA

In Four Acts of Five Scenes

LIBRETTO BY
RICHARD L. STOKES

MUSIC BY
HOWARD HANSON

Copyright MCMXXXIII by HARMS, INC., NEW YORK

International Copyright Secured   Made in U. S. A.
ALL RIGHTS RESERVED

33) Libretto front page of New York Metropolitan Opera's 1933 *Merry Mount*

Met. Opera's *Merry Mount* set for Act 1

Merry Mount Act 2

Merry Mount Act 3

www.ingramcontent.com/pod-product-compliance
Lightning Source LLC
Chambersburg PA
CBHW020345170426
43200CB00005B/53